Juran on Quality by Design

The New Steps for Planning Quality into Goods and Services

J. M. Juran

THE FREE PRESS
A Division of Macmillan, Inc.
NEW YORK

Maxwell Macmillan Canada
TORONTO

Maxwell Macmillan International
NEW YORK OXFORD SINGAPORE SYDNEY

The Free Press
A Division of Macmillan, Inc.
866 Third Avenue, New York, N.Y. 10022

Maxwell Macmillan Canada, Inc.
1200 Eglinton Avenue East
Suite 200
Don Mills, Ontario M3C 3N1

Macmillan, Inc. is part of the Maxwell Communication Group of Companies.

Printed in the United States of America

printing number

2 3 4 5 6 7 8 9 10

Library of Congress Cataloging-in-Publication Data

Juran, J. M. (Joseph M.)
Juran on quality by design: the new steps for planning quality into goods and services / J. M. Juran.
p. cm.
Includes bibliographical references and index.
ISBN 0-02-916683-7
1. Quality control. 2. Production management—Quality control. I. Quality by design. II. Title.
TS156.J854 1992
658.5'62—dc20 91-29206
CIP

Contents

Preface and Acknowledgments

This book had been in incubation for some years, but the first draft was published in April 1985. Copies were sent to about fifty organizations in the United States and abroad for critique. The response was gratifying; the critiques were forthright and constructive.

Those critiques were summarized to serve as the main agenda for a two-day conference which was held in Stamford, Connecticut, during August 1985. That conference was attended by forty persons, representing twenty-five different organizations. It was a memorable event due to the presence of so many leading authorities and incisive thinkers in the field of managing for quality.

One consensus of the Stamford conference was that the book should be designed to be generic, i.e., applicable universally. As a consequence, the concepts, the associated case examples, the tools, and the techniques are all structured to be applicable universally:

To products in general—both goods and services

To all levels in the hierarchy, from the chief executive to the work force

To all functions: general mangement; product development; operations (office, factory, service); human relations; and the like.

To all industries: service as well as manufacture and public sector as well as private sector

A further step in the evolution of *Juran on Quality by Design* was field testing of the structured approach. This testing was made possible through the continuing cooperation of the organizations which had participated in critiques and in the Stamford conference. Field tests were set up at organizations as follows:

Automotive Division, American Society for Quality Control

Bureau of Labor Statistics, U.S. Department of Labor (two projects)

Caterpillar, Inc. (three projects)

General Motors Advanced Engineering Center

Juran Institute, Inc.

Packaging Corporation of America (a Tenneco Company)

Instrument Group, Perkin-Elmer Corporation (two projects)

Collectively, the critiques, the Stamford conference, and the field tests constituted an unprecedented collaboration between a consulting organization and the managers who face realities. That collaboration provided many insights into the applicability of a universal approach to quality planning. That same collaboration also served to clarify the functions to be served by *Juran on Quality by Design.*

The following is our explanation of the key and triangle symbols used in the margin of the book:

A *key* is used to designate a concept of uncommon importance—a key concept.

A *triangle* is used to designate tasks for upper managers.

We are grateful to the staff members of Juran Institute who participated in preparing and editing the text, conducting the supporting researches, preparing the visual aids, and otherwise removing a prickly burden from our backs. Our thanks go to:

Marilyn M. Schmid, who smoothly integrated the several word processing systems used in producing the text.

Caroline M. DeFilippis, who prepared many of the tables and charts

Laura E. Halloran, who organized and arranged publication of the completed book

Michael J. W. Gibson and Randolph Warren for their editorial contributions

Gabriel A. Pall and James F. Riley for their contributions to Chapter 11 on the subject of business process management

Special thanks to Laura A. Sutherland, Dr. Juran's assistant, who patiently and skillfully handled the typing, page layout, and the many other details involved in organizing and preparing the text for publication

] 1 [

How to Think About Quality Planning

Purpose of This Chapter

This chapter explains why a book on quality planning is needed. It describes quality planning as a basic managerial process. It also shows the relationship of quality planning to the overall way in which companies manage for quality.

Why a Book on Quality Planning?

There are persuasive reasons for a book on quality planning. During the 1960s and 1970s many domestic U.S. companies lost their quality leadership to new, aggressive competition. The most obvious consequence was loss of market share. For example, here is a partial list of goods for which imports had gained a significant share of the North American market by 1980.*

Stereo components	Athletic equipment
Medical equipment	Computer chips
Color television sets	Industrial robots
Hand tools	Electron microscopes
Radial tires	Machine tools
Electric motors	Optical equipment

The reasons for the loss in share of market were related mainly to quality, in two respects:

*Adapted from Stephen Wheelwright, Stanford University, March 20, 1984.

The imports had quality features that were perceived as better meeting customer needs.

The imports did not fail in service as often as the domestic products.

All this is pertinent to "Why a book on Quality Planning." *Product features and failure rates are largely determined during planning for quality.*

Loss of market share is not the only reason behind a book on planning for quality. A second major force has been the phenomenon of "life behind the quality dikes." We have learned that living in a technological society puts us at the mercy of the continuing operation of the goods and services that make such a society possible. In turn, such continuing operation depends absolutely on the quality built into those goods and services. Without such quality we have failures of all sorts: power outages, interruptions in communication and transportation, inoperative appliances. At the least these failures involve annoyances and minor costs. At their worst they are terrifying—Chernobyl, Bhopal.

A third major force has been the gathering awareness by companies that they have been enduring excessive costs due to chronic quality-related wastes. In the U.S.A. about a third of what we do consists of redoing work previously "done." This redoing consists of correcting errors, rewriting documents, scrapping or reprocessing factory goods, responding to customer complaints, and so on.

Some managers question that figure of one-third redoing as applied to their own companies. Of course, the figure varies widely among industries, companies, and processes. However, it is easy to be led astray.

In one company, 2.4 percent of the invoices were protested by customers. To placate those customers was taking about half the time of the sales force.

In some banks only about 1.0 percent of the checks (printed with magnetic ink) fail to be processed successfully by the automated equipment. Yet it takes as much human time to process that 1 percent by hand as to process the other 99 percent by machine.

Our Quality Problems Have Been Planned That Way

Numerous specific quality crises and problems have been traced to the way in which quality was planned in the first place. In a sense, *we planned it that way.* There is no implication that the planners were incompetent, malicious, or otherwise deficient. On the contrary, the planners have generally been quite experienced and dedicated. Instead they faced multiple obstacles: unrealistic schedules, tight budgets, inadequate data bases. However, none of these realities diminishes the validity of the assertion that "we planned it that way." Moreover, so long as the conditions of the past remain in effect, we will continue to plan it that way.

> In the factories, many product designers developed new products, and then delivered the product specifications to the Manufacturing Department. This was known as "throwing the designs over the wall," since there had been no participation by the manufacturing managers. This practice unilaterally created severe crises for the manufacturing managers.

> In the offices electronic data processing opened up opportunities for processing information more promptly, and with fewer errors. However, many companies proceeded to convert their manual systems directly into electronic systems without first getting rid of the deficiencies in the manual systems. As a result, their manual mess became an automated mess.

Quality Planning Has Been Done by Amateurs

Some of those obstacles faced by the planners are beyond their control. One major obstacle, however, stems from a deficiency which the planners can remedy. That obstacle is "quality planning by amateurs," which is also a major reason for writing this book.

The question "Who does the quality planning?" has relevance to every step on the quality planning road map. What is critical is that *most quality planning has been done by amateurs*—by people who have not been trained in the use of the "quality disciplines."

All planners are faced with meeting multiple goals: a budget, a schedule, a quality specification, a mandated procedure, a government regulation, and so on. The functional planners (such as product developers) are generally experts in their function, but they lack expertise in the "quality disciplines"—the methodology, skills, and tools required to plan for quality. Yet the planners do engage in quality planning since their goals include quality goals. Lacking expertise in the quality disciplines, they are amateurs in the best sense of that word.

Many companies have tried to deal with this problem by making quality specialists (quality engineers, reliability engineers) available to the planners as consultants. It hasn't worked very well. What has worked much better has been to train the planners themselves in use of the quality disciplines—to train the amateurs to become professionals at quality planning.

A major decision to be made by upper managers relates to this matter of "quality planning by amateurs." The principal options are

(a) Provide the amateurs with consulting service, or

(b) Train the amateurs to become professionals.

In the experience of the authors, companies which have adopted option (b) have outperformed those who have followed option (a). The decision faced by upper managers is whether to mandate training the amateurs to become professionals.

The Mission of This Book

The mission of this book is to assist companies to achieve quality leadership through mastery of how to plan for quality. To carry out this mission, the book is organized as follows:

Chapter 1 (this chapter) defines quality planning as a universal series of steps and shows the relationship of that series to the overall way in which we manage for quality.

Chapters 2 through 8 examine that universal series in detail, step by step.

Chapters 9 through 11 show how to implement that universal series into the various levels of the company hierarchy.

The remaining chapters present supporting methodologies and case examples of planning for quality.

The Epilogue includes a discussion on "What should I do on my return?"

Figure 1-1 shows graphically how the book is organized.

The Need for Unity of Language

Managing for quality has, over the years, undergone some profound changes, especially during the 20th century. Figure 1-2 lists many of

Chapter	
1	How to think about quality planning; relation of quality planning to how we manage for quality
2	Establish quality goals
3	Identify the customers
4	Determine customer needs
5	Provide measurement
6	Develop product features
7	Develop process features
8	Develop process controls; transfer to operations
	Application of Quality Planning
9	Strategic quality planning
10	Multifunctional quality planning
11	Departmental quality planning
12–16	Methodologies and case examples
Epilogue: Includes "What should I do on my return?"	

FIGURE 1–1 Organization of Planning for Quality, Second Edition

the major forces that have emerged over the years, along with the responsive strategies adopted by the impacted organizations. Inevitably such forces and responses have required revisions in language as well. For this reason we shall define key words and phrases as we go along. A good starting place is with the word "product."

Product

A product is the output of any process. The economist defines "products" as goods and services. That is also the definition adopted by this book. The term "product" includes various subclassifications:

Goods are physical things—pencils, color television sets.

Service is work performed for someone else. Entire industries are established to provide services in such forms as central energy, transportation, communication, entertainment, and so on. Service also includes work performed for someone else *within* companies, e.g., payroll preparation, recruitment of new employees, plant maintenance. Such services are often called support services.

Software has more than one meaning. A major meaning is instruction programs for computers. Another major meaning is information generally: reports, plans, instructions, advice, commands.

Conditions and Forces	*Strategies Adopted in Managing for Quality*
Hunger, food gathering	"Incoming" inspection by consumers
Division of labor—food suppliers	Inspection by consumers in village marketplaces
Early manufacturers; rise of village craftsmen	Reliance on skill and reputation of craftsmen
Expansion of commerce beyond village boundaries	Specification by sample; export controls by inspection; warranties
The guilds	Specifications: materials, processes, products; export controls, audits
The Industrial Revolution	Written specifications; measurement, instruments, test laboratories; extension of inspection; standardization
The Taylor System	Central inspection departments
Growth of volume and complexity	Quality assurance departments; quality engineering; reliability engineering
World War II	Training in statistical quality control
Life behind the quality dikes	Special organization and processes to protect society; audits
The Japanese revolution in quality (Japanese strategies)	Upper managers personally in charge Training in managing for quality extended to all functions Quality improvement at a continuing revolutionary pace QC Circles
The Japanese revolution in quality (U.S. response)	Efforts to restrict imports Numerous strategies undergoing test

FIGURE 1–2 Changing Forces and Responsive Strategies
SOURCE: J. M. Juran, *Juran on Leadership for Quality.* New York, Free Press, 1989, p. 11.

Product Features

A product feature is a property possessed by a product that is intended to meet certain customer needs and thereby provide customer satisfaction. Product features may be technological in nature: fuel consumption of a vehicle, dimension of a mechanical component, uniformity of voltage of an electric power supply, a spelling check dictionary on an electronic typewriter. Product features may also take other forms: promptness of delivery, ease of maintenance, courtesy of service. A more technical definition of product feature is "quality characteristic."

Customer Satisfaction; Product Satisfaction

Customer satisfaction is a result achieved when product features respond to customer needs. It is generally synonymous with product satisfaction. Product satisfaction is a stimulus to product salability. *The major impact is on share of market, and thereby on sales income.*

Product Deficiency

A product deficiency is a product failure that results in *product dissatisfaction.* Product deficiencies take such forms as power outages, failures to meet delivery dates, inoperable goods, blemished appearance, or nonconformance to specification. *The major impact is on the costs* incurred to redo prior work, to respond to customer complaints, and so on.

Customer Dissatisfaction; Product Dissatisfaction

Product deficiencies are in all cases sources of customer *dissatisfaction.* This may in turn lead to specific customer reactions: complaints, returns, unfavorable publicity, lawsuits, and so on.

Product deficiencies may also cause the customer to avoid buying the product in the future despite its superior features. In this way, product salability is influenced in two ways:

The first sale to a customer is heavily influenced by the product features. At the time, the customer does not know what the product deficiencies will be.

Subsequent sales to that customer are heavily influenced by the extent of deficiencies encountered during use of the product, and by the service rendered with respect to those deficiencies.

Product Satisfaction and Product Dissatisfaction Are Not Opposites

Product satisfaction has its origin in product features and is why clients buy the product. Product dissatisfaction has its origin in nonconformances and is why customers complain. There are many products that give little or no dissatisfaction; they do what the supplier said they would do. Yet the products are not salable if some competing product provides greater product satisfaction.

For many years the copying of documents was done by use of carbon paper, "ditto" ink, "mimeograph" stencils, and so forth. The xerographic copier made all those methods obsolete because of its feature of copying documents direct from an original. Today, if someone produced a mimeograph process that was absolutely free from field failures, it would be unsalable because of its inability to copy direct from an original document.

Customer

A customer is anyone who is impacted by the product or process. Customers may be external or internal.

EXTERNAL CUSTOMERS. These are impacted by the product but are not members of the company that produces the product. External customers include clients who buy the product, government regulatory bodies, and the public (which may be impacted due to unsafe products or damage to the environment).

INTERNAL CUSTOMERS. They are impacted by the product, and are also members of the company that produces the product. They are often called "customers" despite the fact that they are not customers in the dictionary sense, that is, they are not clients.

The Meanings of Quality

The dictionary offers about a dozen definitions of the word "quality." Two of them are of major importance to managers.

Product features is one of these definitions. In the eyes of customers, the better the product features, the higher the quality.

Freedom from deficiencies is the other major definition of quality. In the eyes of customers, the fewer the deficiencies the better the quality.

Some customers, especially consumers, do not necessarily recognize that there are two rather different kinds of quality. Their vagueness may give rise to such comments as "I know it when I see it." Managers must recognize this distinction, however, since the respective impacts are on matters as diverse as salability and costs.

Figure 1-3 sets out the two definitions in more detailed form. The main lessons for the manager are:

> Product features impact sales. As to this kind of quality, higher quality usually costs more.
>
> Product deficiencies impact costs. As to this kind of quality, higher quality usually costs less.

Despite the differences in these two kinds of quality, it would be convenient to have a short, simple phrase to describe them together. To date there has been no consensus on adoption of such a phrase. The phrase "fitness for use" has gained some followers, as have some other phrases. It is unlikely that two concepts so different can be encompassed in one terse phrase.

Product Features Which Meet Customer Needs	*Freedom from Deficiencies*
Higher quality enables companies to:	*Higher quality enables companies to:*
Increase customer satisfaction Make products salable Meet competition Increase market share Provide sales income Secure premium prices Major effect is on sales Usually, higher quality costs more	Reduce error rates Reduce rework, waste Reduce field failures, warranty charges Reduce customer dissatisfaction Reduce inspection, tests Shorten time to put new products on the market Increase yields, capacity Improve delivery performance Major effect is on costs Usually, higher quality costs less

FIGURE 1-3 The Principal Meanings of Quality
SOURCE: from J. M. Juran, *Juran on Leadership for Quality*. New York, Free Press, 1989, p. 16.

The above definitions of quality do not meet with universal acceptance. Many companies have arrived at other definitions which they feel are consistent with the needs of their industry and with their own dialect. Their definitions often extend to the "subsets"—the detailed ingredients contained in the broad definitions. As to these subsets there are divergent views. Figure 1–4 classifies the more usual ingredients to show how widely they are included or excluded in company definitions of quality.

There is no possibility of adoption of universal definitions until a

Widely Included in Definition of Quality	*Widely Debated*	*Widely Excluded*
Quality of Services: Features Performance Competitiveness Promptness Courtesy Process capability Freedom from errors Conformance to standards, procedures	Internal processes (e.g., recruitment; payroll preparation) Cycle time Promptness Freedom from error Competitiveness Workplace safety	Price Costs (other than due to deficiencies) Employee absenteeism Social responsibilities: to employees, to public (e.g., the environment)
Quality of Goods: Features Performance Competitiveness "User friendly" Product safety Freedom from field failures Reliability Maintainability Availability of spares Durability Esthetic appeal Process capability Process yields Cost of poor quality Conformance to specifications, standards, procedures		

FIGURE 1–4 Definitions of Quality—Usual Ingredients

glossary, sponsored by a recognized standardization body, has been evolved.

Big Q and Little Q

The main reason for all that inconsistency in terminology is the fact that the *terminology has been changing*. The change has its origin in the quality crisis, and has been so profound as to give rise to the concept of "Big Q and little Q." Figure 1–5 shows this concept in tabular form.

Until the 1980s managers generally associated quality with factories, manufactured goods, and production processes. During the 1980s there emerged a wide trend to broaden the definition of quality to include the contents shown in Figure 1–5. The willingness to accept this trend has varied. Those most willing have been the quality managers and the upper managers. Those most reluctant have been managers in the technological areas and in certain staff functions, such as finance and human relations.

The Conformance Definition: Limitations and Merits

Some companies have defined quality in terms such as conformance to specification, or conformance to standards. These are dangerous definitions when applied at managerial levels. At those levels what is essential is that the products respond to customer needs. Conformance to standards is only one of many means to that end.

Conformance by its nature relates to static standards and specifications, whereas quality is a moving target. Many standards include provision for chronic wastes. Defining quality as conformance helps to perpetuate those wastes. For some qualities, 100 percent conformance means defect-free product. That is a useful goal, but what produces salability is product features that respond to customer needs.

> In New York City a builder erected a building which ended up about 814 feet high. The height authorized by the permit was 803 feet. The builder asserted that the extra height was mainly the result of thickening each floor slab in order to increase the stability of the building. No additional floors or floor space were gained. However, the New York City Planning Commission refused to approve the structure on the grounds that the extra height would not "relate harmoniously to all

Topic	*Content of Little Q*	*Content of Big Q*
Products	Manufactured goods	All products, goods and services, whether for sale or not
Processes	Processes directly related to manufacture of goods	All processes; manufacturing support; business, etc.
Industries	Manufacturing	All industries; manufacturing; service; government, etc., whether for profit or not
Quality is viewed as:	A technological problem	A business problem
Customer	Clients who buy the products	All who are impacted, external and internal
How to think about quality	Based on culture of functional departments	Based on the universal Trilogy
Quality goals are included:	Among factory goals	In company business plan
Cost of poor quality	Costs associated with deficient manufactured goods	All costs which would disappear if everything were perfect
Improvement is directed at:	Departmental performance	Company performance
Evaluation of quality is based mainly on:	Conformance to factory specifications, procedures, standards	Responsiveness to customer needs
Training in managing for quality is:	Concentrated in the Quality Department	Companywide
Coordination is by:	The quality manager	A quality council of upper managers

FIGURE 1–5 Contrast, Big Q and Little Q

structures or open space in the vicinity in terms of scale, location and access to light and air.''

The conformance definition does have a place—in the lower levels of the company. In those levels the personnel are often unaware of what customer needs are. (Some are unaware that they have customers). Nevertheless these same people require clear definitions of their responsibility with respect to quality. One way of defining those responsibilities is to provide them with specifications and procedures. The responsibilities then become to follow the procedures and to meet the specifications.

As is evident, the conformance definition is the traditional form—straight out of little Q.

Planning and Quality Planning

As used in this book, planning is the activity of (a) establishing goals, and (b) establishing the means required to meet those goals. When this definition is applied to quality, the result is:

> Quality planning is the activity of (a) establishing quality goals and (b) developing the products and processes required to meet those goals.

In using this definition, note that quality planning is required for numerous products, not only the goods and services sold to clients, but also many internal products: purchase orders, invoices, reports. Quality planning is also required for numerous processes, many of which are internal business processes, e.g., recruitment of new employees, preparing sales forecasts, producing the invoices.

Explaining Quality Planning to Upper Management

Earlier in this chapter we saw that most quality planning has been done by amateurs. These amateurs have included the upper managers. To convert those amateurs into professionals is a cultural change which requires the active participation of the upper managers. As a prerequisite it is necessary to explain to upper managers how to think about quality and quality planning. We have learned from experience that making such an explanation becomes simplified if we make use of a financial analogy. The explanation starts by first looking at how upper managers manage for finance. That answer is obvious—financial management is carried out by the use of three managerial processes:

FINANCIAL PLANNING. This planning is centered on preparation of the annual financial budget. In turn, this preparation involves a companywide process that starts by proposing the financial goals to be reached in the year ahead. These goals are then "deployed" in order to identify the deeds that must be done to reach the goals. The deeds are then translated into money equivalents. Such translation permits summary and analysis to determine the financial consequences of doing all those deeds. The resulting budget is a publication of the financial goals for the company and its various divisions and departments.

FINANCIAL CONTROL. This well-known process is used to aid managers in reaching the established financial goals. The process consists of evaluating actual financial performance; comparing this with financial goals; and taking action on the difference—the accountant's "variance." There are numerous subprocesses for financial control: cost control, expense control, inventory control, and so on.

FINANCIAL IMPROVEMENT. This process takes many forms: cost reduction projects, purchase of new facilities to improve productivity, speeding up the invoicing process, development of new products to increase sales, acquisition of other companies, and others.

The Juran Trilogy®

Managing for quality is done by use of the same three managerial processes of planning, control and improvement. Now the names change to:

Quality planning

Quality control

Quality improvement

We shall refer to these three processes as The Juran Trilogy (for elaboration, see Juran, 1986). Conceptually these processes are identical with those used to manage for finance. However, the procedural steps are special, and the tools used are also special.

QUALITY PLANNING. This is the activity of developing the products and processes required to meet customers' needs. It involves a series of universal steps which can be abbreviated as follows:

NOTE: The Juran Trilogy® is a registered trademark of Juran Institute, Inc.

Establish quality goals

Identify the customers—those who will be impacted by the efforts to meet the goals

Determine the customers' needs

Develop product features that respond to customers' needs

Develop processes that are able to produce those product features

Establish process controls, and transfer the resulting plans to the operating forces

We shall look at this process in detail during the remainder of this book.

QUALITY CONTROL. This process consists of the following steps:

Evaluate actual quality performance

Compare actual performance to quality goals

Act on the difference

QUALITY IMPROVEMENT. This process is the means of raising quality performance to unprecedented levels ("breakthrough") The methodology consists of a series of universal steps:

Establish the infrastructure needed to secure annual quality improvement

Identify the specific needs for improvement—the improvement *projects*

For each project establish a project team with clear responsibility for bringing the project to a successful conclusion

Provide the resources, motivation, and training needed by the teams to:

Diagnose the causes

Stimulate establishment of remedies

Establish controls to hold the gains

Three Universal Sequences

Notice that each of those three processes has been generalized into a universal sequence of steps. Those same three universal sequences have been discovered and rediscovered, over and over again, by prac-

Managing for Quality		
Quality Planning	*Quality Control*	*Quality Improvement*
Establish quality goals Identify who are the customers Determine the needs of the customers Develop product features which respond to customers' needs Develop processes able to produce the product features Establish process controls; transfer the plans to the operating forces	Evaluate actual performance Compare actual performance to quality goals Act on the difference	Prove the need Establish the infrastructure Identify the improvement projects Establish project teams Provide the teams with resources, training, and motivation to: Diagnose the causes Stimulate remedies Establish controls to hold the gains

FIGURE 1–6 The Three Universal Processes of Managing for Quality

ticing managers. Figure 1–6 shows these sequences in abbreviated form.

The Juran Trilogy Diagram

The Trilogy concept is not merely a way to explain managing for quality to upper management. It is also a *unifying concept which extends companywide.* Every function has unique features, as does every product or process. Yet for every one of them, we manage for quality using the same three generic processes of the Trilogy: planning, control, and improvement.

The three processes of the Trilogy are interrelated. Figure 1–7, The Juran Trilogy Diagram, shows this interrelationship.

Figure 1–7 is a graph with time on the horizontal axis and cost of poor quality (quality deficiencies) on the vertical axis. The initial activity is quality planning. The planners determine who are the customers and what are their needs. The planners then develop product and process designs that are able to respond to those needs. Finally, the planners turn the plans over to the operating forces.

The job of the operating forces is to run the processes and produce

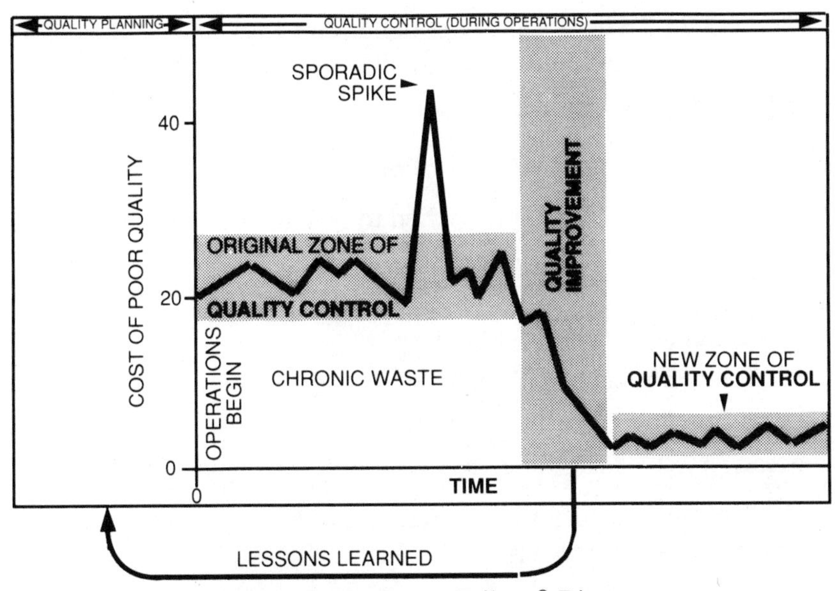

FIGURE 1–7 The Juran Trilogy® Diagram

the products. As operations proceed it soon emerges that the process is unable to produce 100 percent good work. Figure 1–7 shows that 20 percent of the work must be redone because of quality deficiencies. This waste then becomes chronic, because *it was planned that way.*

Under conventional responsibility patterns the operating forces are unable to get rid of that planned chronic waste. What they do instead is to carry out *quality control*—to prevent things from getting worse. Control includes putting out the fires, such as that sporadic spike.

Figure 1–7 also shows that in due course the chronic waste was driven down to a level far below the level that had been planned originally. That gain was achieved by the third process in the Trilogy, "quality improvement." In effect, it was realized that the chronic waste was also an opportunity for improvement. So steps were taken to seize that opportunity.

The Juran Trilogy Diagram and Product Deficiencies

The Trilogy diagram (Figure 1–7) relates to *product deficiencies.* The vertical scale therefore exhibits such units of measure as cost of poor quality, error rate, percent defective, and service call rate. On this same scale, perfection is at zero. *What goes up is bad.*

The result of reducing product deficiencies has been to reduce the cost of poor quality, meet more delivery promises, and reduce customer dissatisfaction.

The Trilogy Diagram and Product Features

When the Trilogy diagram is applied to product features, the vertical scale changes. Now the scale exhibits units of measure for such features as:

Rated hours of life

Millions of instructions per second

Load-carrying capacity

Mean time between failures

For the above features, *what goes up is good.* For certain other product features, what goes up is bad. For example:

Waiting time in queues

Power consumption

Maintenance hours per 1,000 operating hours

Time to restore service

For ease in interpreting the diagrams, we shall label the vertical scales as follows:

For *quality deficiencies* we shall label the vertical scale "Cost of Poor Quality." In such diagrams *what goes up is bad.* An example is Figure 1-7.

For *quality features* we shall label the vertical scale "*Product Salability.*" In such diagrams *what goes up is good.*

An example of using product salability as the vertical scale is the well-known model of the trends of Japanese versus Western quality (Figure 1-8). This diagram has been helpful in demonstrating to managers the importance of maintaining a high rate of improvement, year after year (Juran, 1981; 1985).

Quality Planning Distinguished from Quality Control

This distinction is fairly obvious. Quality *planning* deals with setting goals and with establishing the means required to reach those goals. Quality *control* deals with execution of plans—conducting opera-

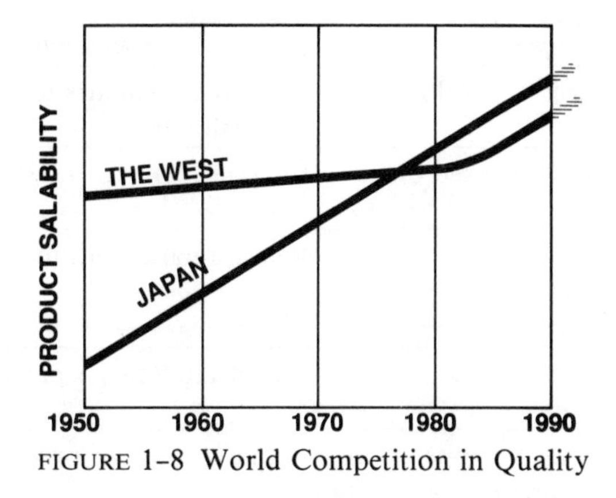

FIGURE 1–8 World Competition in Quality

tions so as to meet the goals. Quality control includes monitoring operations so as to detect differences between actual performance and goals. (The accountant's term for such differences is "variances".) In addition, quality control includes taking action (firefighting) to restore the status quo in the event that variances do appear.

Quality Planning Distinguished from Quality Improvement

This distinction is best brought out by the alligator analogy—the plight of the fabled manager who was up to his waist in alligators. Under that analogy each live alligator is a chronic waste, a potential quality improvement project. Each completed improvement project results in a dead alligator.

If our fabled manager succeeded in exterminating all alligators, then quality improvement would be complete—for the moment. However the manager would not be finished with alligators. The reason is that *the planning process has not changed.*

In effect, the quality planning process is a dual hatchery. A benign hatchery produces new, useful quality plans. A malignant hatchery produces new alligators. Quality improvement can take care of the existing alligators, one by one. To stop the production of new alligators, however, requires shutting down that malignant hatchery.

How to Shut Down the Hatchery

Shutting down that hatchery requires an array of remedies, all of which involve changes in the quality planning process:

Cause	*Remedy*
Quality planning is being done by amateurs	Train the amateurs to be professionals
Quality planning is focused on little Q	Enlarge focus to Big Q
Planning is done without participation by those who are impacted	Require participation
Planning is done by use of empirical methods	Adopt modern systematic methods
Plans are transferred to operations without proof of process capability	Require proof of process capability

There are also differences in the basics. Quality improvement is directed at chronic problems, requiring diagnosis to discover the causes and providing remedies to get rid of the causes. Quality planning is directed at meeting customer-oriented goals, requiring application of the quality planning road map (Figure 1–9).

(There are also some commonalities. For many quality improve-

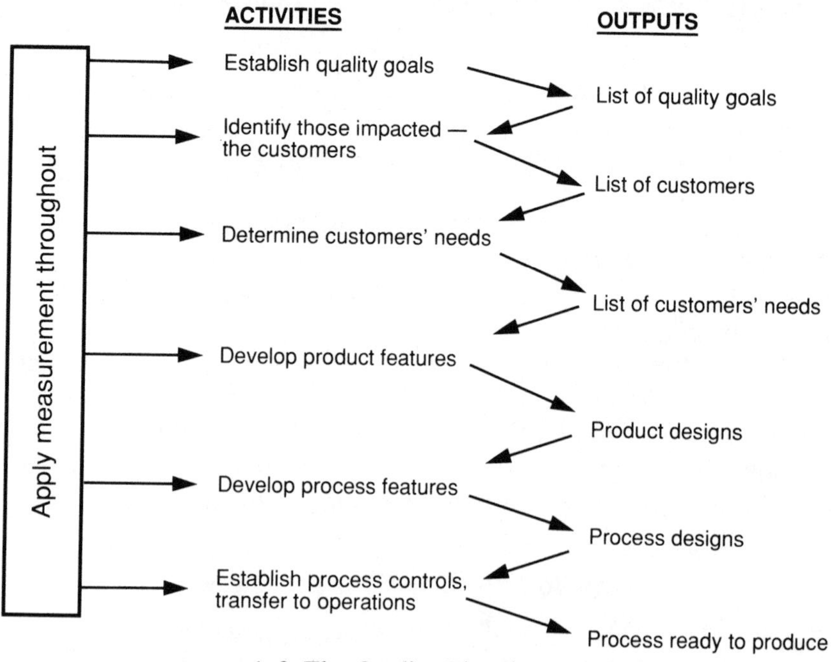

FIGURE 1–9 The Quality Planning Road Map

ment projects the remedy consists of replanning. In addition, certain skills and tools are common to both processes).

The Quality Planning Road Map

We saw in Figure 1-6 that quality planning is done by a universal series of steps. If we expand Figure 1-6 into a series of input-output diagrams, and also include the activity of measurement, the result is Figure 1-9.

We shall refer to Figure 1-9 as *the quality planning road map.* The next few chapters will follow that road map, step by step.

In Figure 1-9 the steps are shown in their usual chronological sequence. However, the measurement step is off to the side in order to show that it applies to all the planning steps. The steps of the quality road map are stitched together by several commonalities:

1. The interlocking input-output chain, in which the output for any step becomes the input for the next step
2. A series of spreadsheets (see Figure 1-10), which make the

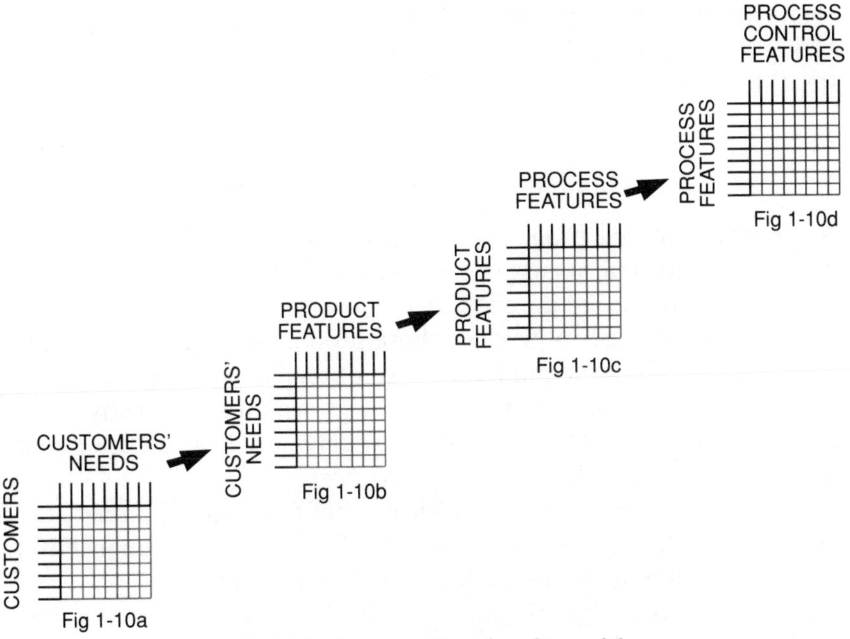

FIGURE 1-10 Generic Planning Spreadsheets

details of the interrelationships readily understandable and accessible

3. A common, coherent system of measurement—units of measure and sensors—which applies to each step as well as to the entire sequence
4. A triple role concept, under which every activity involves the triple role of customer, processor, and supplier (see below).

It may seem surprising that one such road map is so universal—that it can provide directions for planning a very wide range of products and processes. Yet such is the case. Many practicing managers have invented and reinvented similar road maps. Many company procedures include similar road maps for specific products or processes. That road map has been field tested, extensively. That same road map becomes our guide for the rest of this book.

Not Always Consecutive

The road map shows the planning steps taking place in a consecutive manner, each step following the previous one chronologically. Such an approach can do a lot of damage unless provision is made for participation, early warning, joint planning, and so on. The most complete of such provisions is often called concurrent planning. It makes use of a broad-based planning team that is working on all the steps, but concurrently instead of consecutively.

Quality Planning Spreadsheets

As quality planning progresses, it collects a great deal of information. There are many customers, each with multiple needs. Many product features are required to meet those needs, and many process features are required to produce those product features. The resulting combinations are so numerous that it becomes necessary to establish a structured means of organizing the information for ready interpretation and access. The most widely used structure is a multidimensional table called a *spreadsheet.*

There are many types of spreadsheets, but four types dominate the use of spreadsheets in quality planning. Figures 1–10a through 1-10d shows these dominant spreadsheets in their generic form.

In Figure 1–10a the horizontal rows list the various *customers.* The vertical columns show the *needs* of those customers. The intersections are codemarked to show the degrees of relationship between customers and needs.

In Figure 1–10b the customer needs have been moved to the horizontal rows. The vertical columns are then used to show the *product features* required to meet those customer needs.

In Figure 1–10c the product features have been moved to the horizontal rows. The vertical columns are then used to show the *process features* required to produce those product features.

Finally in Figure 1–10d the process features have been moved to the horizontal rows. The vertical columns are then used to show the *process control features* required to keep the processes in a steady state.

The Triple Role Concept

Every unit of the organization—the entire company, each division, each department, each person—carries out a process and produces a product. We shall call any such unit a *processor team*. Each processor team carries out three quality-related roles, which are depicted in Figure 1–11—the TRIPROL® diagram.

The TRIPROL diagram shows the interrelationship among three roles:

Customer. The processor team acquires various kinds of inputs which are used in carrying out the process. The processor team is a customer of the suppliers who provide the inputs.

Processor. The processor team carries out various managerial and technological activities in order to produce its products.

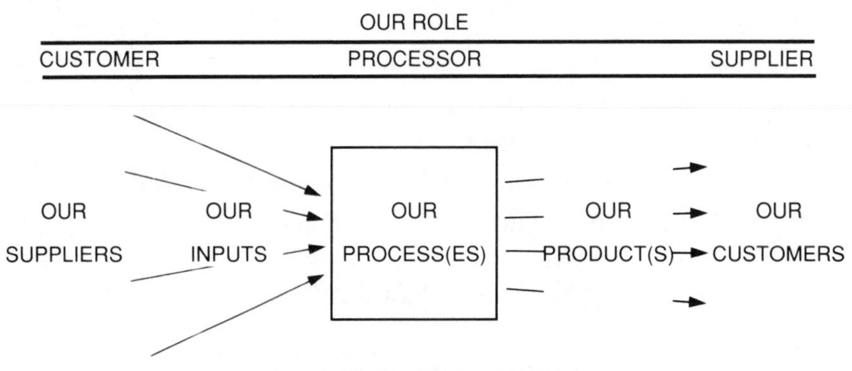

FIGURE 1–11 The Triprol® Diagram

Supplier. The processor team supplies its products to its customers.

The concept of the triple role is simple enough. However, the application can become quite complex because of the presence of large numbers of suppliers, inputs, processes, products, and customers. The greater the complexity, the greater the need for an orderly, structured approach to quality planning. The backbone of this structure is the quality planning road map. The memory system is the spreadsheets.

The Roles of Upper Managers

As we work our way down the quality planning road map, we shall encounter various stages at which specific decisions and actions are faced by upper managers. We will identify these by an action symbol consisting of a stylized triangle representing an organization pyramid. Each chapter will identify the managerial action items appropriate to that chapter. These same action items will then be summarized at the end of the respective chapters. In addition, the Epilogue will include an edited version of the action items collectively.

It is now clear that upper managers have a vital role to play in the quality planning process. This role requires extensive personal participation. It cannot be delegated, since a major change in company culture is needed. During the 1980s many upper managers adopted strategies that involved setting vague goals and then delegating to the rest of the organization the responsibility for meeting those vague goals. The most usual results were a loss of several years, a residue of divisiveness, and a loss of credibility.

Relative to the subject matter of this chapter, a role for upper managers is that of reducing confusion in the company by standardizing the meanings of the key terms that pertain to managing for quality. An effective way to do this is to assign a team to:

Identify the key terms for which standardized definitions could significantly improve communication

Develop agreed definitions for these key terms

Publish the agreed definitions in an official glossary

On to the Quality Planning Road Map

This chapter has explained why a book on quality planning is needed. It has also explained how to think about quality and has generalized the quality planning process—the quality planning road map.

During the next few chapters, we shall follow that road map, step by step. The first of those steps is Establish Quality Goals. That is the subject of the next chapter.

High Points in Chapters

Each chapter of this book will conclude with a summary of the high points of that chapter. Those high points should be among the focal points for in-house training. A second summary will list the nominations of specific actions to be taken by managers.

List of High Points

Product features and failure rates are largely determined during planning for quality.

In the United States about a third of what we do consists of redoing work previously "done."

Our quality problems have been planned that way.

Most quality planning has been done by amateurs.

What has worked well has been to train the amateurs to become professionals at quality planning.

Product satisfaction and product dissatisfaction are not opposites.

Product features impact sales. As to this kind of quality, higher quality usually costs more.

Product deficiencies impact costs. As to this kind of quality, higher quality usually costs less.

The concept of "Big Q" is replacing that of "little Q."

Managing for quality is done by use of three managerial processes: quality planning, quality control, and quality improvement.

Quality planning is the activity of (a) establishing quality goals and (b) developing the products and processes required to meet those goals.

To stop the production of new alligators requires shutting down the alligator hatchery.

Quality planning is done by a universal series of steps—the quality planning road map.

Upper managers have a vital role to play in the quality planning process.

Tasks for Upper Managers

Assign a team to prepare and publish agreed definitions for the key terms relating to managing for quality.

Decide whether to mandate training the planners, who are typically amateurs in matters of quality, to become professionals.

] 2 [

Establish Quality Goals

Purpose of This Chapter

The purpose of this chapter is to explain:

The nature and origin of quality goals

The relation of quality goals to the strategic business plan

How quality goals initiate the journey down the quality planning road map

The Nature of Quality Goals

We define a goal as an aimed-at target—an achievement toward which effort is expended. Applied to quality,

A quality goal is an aimed-at quality target.

A goal typically includes a number and a time table.

Does Quality Planning Include Establishing Quality Goals?

We have defined quality planning as (a) the activity of establishing quality goals, and (b) developing the products and processes required to meet those goals. This definition is based on the reality that it is not possible to plan in the abstract. One can plan only after the goal has been established.

The prevailing dialects differ on whether the term ''planning'' includes establishing the goals. The widely used term ''Strategic Planning'' is almost always interpreted to include the setting of strategic goals. In contrast, some parts of industry (and academia) interpret the word ''planning'' as being limited in scope to the activity of establishing the means to be used to attain goals.

> For example, it is common in manufacturing companies to organize functional departments whose mission is to "plan for manufacture." These departments seldom establish the product quality goals—that responsibility rests with a product design department.

For this Second Edition of *Planning for Quality,* we have included goal setting as a part of the quality planning road map. In our judgment such inclusion is in line with the majority of the prevailing practice and with the prevailing trends.

Tactical Quality Goals

Quality goals abound in developed countries. This is a consequence of the convergence of (a) unbounded human needs, and (b) the ability of an industrial society to satisfy human needs. These needs then become quality goals and generate subgoals in such forms as product features, process features, and process control features.

We shall refer to these numerous quality goals as *tactical* quality goals, to distinguish them from *strategic* quality goals. Under the traditional little Q concept, quality goals were almost exclusively tactical in nature. They were established by functional departments at the middle and lower levels of companies, e.g., at factory levels.

Strategic Quality Goals

Strategic quality goals are established at the highest company levels and are a part of the companies' business plans. This concept of strategic quality goals is a logical result of the movement to give quality the top priority among the companies' goals. This same concept has been reinforced by the movement to adopt the concept of Big Q.

Strategic quality goals are in addition to, not instead of, tactical quality goals. Meeting the tactical goals remains the problem it has always been. However, as we shall see, the addition of strategic quality goals has a profound effect on the entire approach to setting quality goals and on planning to meet them. This profound effect extends to the roles of all who are involved in setting and meeting quality goals.

Which Comes First, Goals or Needs?

The authors of this book had a lively debate among themselves as to what is the first step on the quality planning road map. Is the first step establishment of quality goals, or is the first step identification of customers and their needs? It turned out that the question has some parallels to the question, Which came first, the chicken or the egg?

From one viewpoint, establishment of goals comes first. The major goal of suppliers is to establish sources of income. A major step toward reaching that goal is to identify customers and their needs. Looked at in this way, the sequence consists of setting a goal, followed by identifying customers. The needs of those customers then become subgoals for the suppliers. Those subgoals then require identifying additional customers whose needs then become sub-subgoals, and so on.

From another viewpoint, establishment of needs comes first. Some customer recognizes an unsatisfied need. The unsatisfied need then tends to motivate the customer's behavior. The motivation may extend to the point where the customer actively sets out to satisfy that need. In that event, the customer converts the need into a goal—an aimed-at target—of meeting that unsatisfied need. The sequence has been recognition of a need, followed by setting a goal of meeting that need.

Customers' Needs Become Suppliers' Goals

It becomes evident that there is an intimate relationship between needs and goals. One person's needs can become that person's goals. Also, one person's needs can become another person's goals. It follows that in addressing the question Which comes first? we must keep in mind that when two parties are involved—customer and supplier—each views the sequence of needs and goals differently. The needs of customers become the goals of suppliers. (Then, as goals are subdivided, the sequence continues—more customers, more customer needs, becoming more subgoals, and so on.) So the question Which comes first? is incomplete until we clarify "from whose viewpoint?"

When the authors were discussing this problem, it became evident that either sequence could logically be adopted. It was also evident that irrespective of which sequence was adopted, the subsequent quality planning road map would be the same.

The authors concluded, *not* unanimously, to regard "Establish Quality Goals" as the first step on the quality planning road map. A persuasive argument in this choice was the seeming reality that it is not possible to plan in the abstract. One can plan only after the goal has been established. Viewed in this way, the establishment of a goal is what starts the journey down the remaining steps of the quality road map.

The Origin of Quality Goals

Quality goals have multiple origins. In the case of business enterprises, many of the quality goals originate from customer needs. Each customer need becomes a goal to be met. Such goals can be said to be *market driven.*

Other quality goals can be regarded as *technology driven.* They usually arise when a company develops a new technological concept that has never before been marketed. It is then necessary to create a market by convincing customers that they need the service provided by the new concept.

An example was the "Walkman" type of audio cassette player. The company that developed this product did not do so in response to known customer needs. It gambled that the product could create a market.

A further source of quality goals is the inner drives of human beings. The meticulous housekeeper devotes much energy to maintaining a spotless home. Some managers similarly strive for perfection in the management of their companies.

Yet another source of quality goals is the mandates imposed by social forces: the laws, regulations, peer pressures, and behavior patterns imposed by the culture.

It is evident that there are multiple sources of quality goals. However, most quality goals can be said to originate with customer needs, provided we broaden the definition of "customer" to include anyone who is impacted by our activities.

The Origin of Strategic Quality Goals

Strategic quality goals is a special category that has only recently entered the business plans of companies. Because the concept has a profound effect on operations as well as on quality planning, we shall examine the events leading up to establishing strategic quality goals. This examination takes us into a semantic jungle, since the terminology has not been well standardized, so we shall define the key terms as we go along. (These same definitions are listed in the Glossary at the end of this book.)

The Vision

Some companies have adopted the word "*vision*" as an expression of what they would like to accomplish, or where they would like to be, sometime in the future. Statements of the vision take such forms as:

To be the low cost producer

To be the market leader

To be the leader in innovation

To be the quality leader

Such statements by themselves are not much more than a wish list. Publication of such statements, no matter how eloquently done, does not tell the people in the organization what they should do that is different from what they have done in the past. The vision statement must somehow be converted into a list of specific goals to be reached, along with the road to be followed in order to meet those goals. That conversion is accomplished by the planning process.

(*Note* that the word "vision" is not in universal use. Other terms also in use are: objective, goal, mission, aim, target, intention, etc.)

Policies

Many companies publish guides to managerial action, known as management "*policies*." These take such forms as:

We will promote from within

We will not be undersold

Our products should meet customers' perceptions of good quality

Our products should equal or exceed competitive quality

Such policies are typically approved at the highest organization levels, and do influence managerial action, especially if they are enforced through audits and the reward system.

From Visions to Strategic Quality Goals

Visions resemble wishes. They have little relation to reality until they are converted into specifics—into quantitative goals which are to be met within a specific time span.

When the Ford Motor Company embarked on the Taurus model

of automobile (in the early 1980s), one of the visions was to restore profitability. The quality-related goal became "best in class."

The new, high priority assigned to quality, along with the adoption of Big Q, has created a trend to expand strategic business planning to include strategic quality goals. Here are some actual examples of strategic quality goals established as part of companies' business plans:

Make the Taurus/Sable models at a level of quality that is best in class. (Ford Motor Company)

Improve product and services quality ten times by 1989. (Motorola's goal in January 1987)

Reduce the cost of (poor) quality by 50 percent in five years. (3M Corporation in July 1982)

Reduce billing errors by 90 percent (Florida Power & Light Company)

(Note that all of the above goals relate to major processes, namely: new product launching, customer service, reduction in chronic waste, billing.)

Subject Matter of Strategic Quality Goals

Despite the uniqueness of specific industries and companies, certain subjects for strategic quality goals are widely applicable:

Product performance. This goal relates to major performance features which determine response to customer needs: promptness of service, fuel consumption, mean time between failures, courtesy. These features directly influence product salability.

Competitive performance. This has always been a goal in market-based economies, but seldom a part of the business plan. The trend to make competitive quality performance a part of the business plan is recent but irreversible.

Quality improvement. This goal may be aimed at improving product salability and/or reducing the cost of poor quality. Either way, the end result after deployment is a formal list of quality improvement projects with associated assignment of responsibilities.

Cost of poor quality. The goal of quality improvement usually includes a goal of reducing the costs due to poor quality. While these costs are not known with precision, they are known to be very high. Despite the lack of precise figures, it is feasible, through estimates, to bring this goal into the business plan and to deploy it successfully to lower levels.

Performance of major processes. This goal has only recently entered the strategic business plan. The goal relates to the performance of major processes that are multifunctional in nature, e.g., new product launching, billing, bidding for business, purchasing. For such "macroprocesses," a special problem is: Who should have the responsibility for meeting the goal? We shall discuss this shortly, under the heading "Deployment to Whom?"

Benefits of Strategic Quality Goals

Establishment of strategic quality goals is a vital first step toward translating the vague vision into reality. Taking this first step also yields some major benefits relative to quality:

The process of selecting the goals stimulates unity of purpose among the upper managers.

Since the goals must be approved at high levels, the upper managers become personally participative.

Goals that are a part of the business plan are much more likely to secure the needed resources.

The reward system associated with the business plan makes it more likely that the goals will be met.

Nominations of Strategic Quality Goals

The goals selected to enter next year's business plan ideally are chosen from a list of *nominations made by all levels* of the hierarchy. Only a few of these nominations will survive the screening process and end up as part of the strategic goals. Other nominations may instead become goals for lower levels in the hierarchy. Many nominations will be deferred—they were unable to secure the necessary priority.

Upper managers should become a source of nominations for strategic quality goals, since they receive important inputs from sources such as:

Membership on the quality council

Contacts with customers

Periodic reviews of performance against quality goals

Quality audits conducted by upper managers

Contacts with upper managers in other companies

Quality Goals at Tactical Levels

Historically the great majority of quality goals have been established at middle and lower levels of the hierarchy. These goals are mandated by the large numbers of customer needs, plus the associated product features and process features. This pattern will continue for years to come.

In companies that have gone over to use of strategic quality goals, the deployment process (see below) will create additional quality goals to be met at the tactical level.

The upper managers cannot become involved with individual tactical quality goals—the numbers of these goals are overwhelming. However, the upper managers can and should become involved with the approach used to deal with the tactical quality goals *collectively.* That approach includes such matters as participative planning, a structured approach to replace empiricism, and training for the planning personnel. We shall examine these matters in later chapters.

Bases for Setting Quality Goals

An important consideration in setting quality goals is the choice of the proper basis.

Technology as a Basis

At the lower level of the hierarchy, the quality goals are established largely on a *technological* basis. Most of these goals are published in specifications and procedures which define the quality targets for the supervisory level and the nonsupervisory workers.

The Market as a Basis

Quality goals that affect product salability should be based primarily on *the market*—meeting or exceeding market quality. Some of these goals relate to projects with a long lead time, e.g., a new product development involving a cycle time of several years; computerizing a major business process; a large construction project that will not come on stream for several years. In such cases the goal should be set so as to meet the competition estimated to be prevailing *when the project is completed.*

In industries that are natural monopolies (e.g., certain utilities), the companies often are able to make comparisons through use of industry data banks. In some companies there is internal competition as well—the performances of regional divisions are compared with each other.

Some internal suppliers are also internal monopolies. Common examples include payroll preparation, facilities maintenance, cafeteria service, and internal transportation. However, most internal monopolies have potential competitors: outside suppliers who offer to sell the same service. So the performance of the internal supplier can be compared with the proposals offered by an outside supplier.

Benchmarking

"Benchmarking" is a recent label for the concept of setting goals based on knowing what has been achieved by others. The concept includes setting goals based on the market—what has been achieved by external competitors. It also considers what has been achieved by internal competitors: subsidiaries, other divisions, other models. It avoids the risks of using historical performance as the sole basis for setting goals. The term benchmarking has been applied to cases such as:

The best in class concept adopted for the Ford Taurus model of automobile

A requirement that the time required to render service to customers be no greater than that provided by the most effective competitor

A requirement that the reliability of a new product be at least equal to that of the product it replaces, and at least equal to that of the most reliable competing product

Implicit in the use of benchmarking is the concept that the resulting goal is attainable, since it has already been attained by others. (For elaboration, see Camp, 1989.)

History as a Basis

A third and widely used basis for setting quality goals has been *historical* performance, that is, the goals parallel past performance.

(Sometimes this is tightened up in order to stimulate improvement.) For some products and processes, the historical basis is an aid to needed stability. For other cases, notably those involving high chronic costs of poor quality, the historical basis has done a lot of damage by helping to perpetuate a chronically wasteful performance.

During the goal-setting process, upper managers should be on the alert for such misuse of the historical basis. Goals for cases of chronically high cost of poor quality should be based on planned breakthroughs using the quality improvement process.

Quality Goals Are a Moving Target

It is widely recognized that quality goals must keep changing in order to respond to the changes that keep coming over the horizon: new technology, new competition, social upheavals, threats, opportunities. What is not so widely done is to provide the means needed to evaluate the impact of those changes and to revise the goals accordingly.

Companies that provide these means do so by requiring annual reviews of competitive performance and of other information, which may show what the trends in progress are. In some companies there is an annual quality audit conducted by the upper managers. Preparation for this audit includes review of changes that have taken place since the previous audit.

Companies that employ the concept of benchmarking usually emphasize that they are on the alert to evaluate the changes taking place, and to take account of these changes during the benchmarking process.

Hierarchies of Quality Goals

Quality goals exist in hierarchies—in multiple levels or layers. These hierarchies tend to assume the shape of pyramids. At the peak are a few goals, each of primary importance. These goals then break down into secondary goals, tertiary goals, and so on. The numbers of goals multiply as this breakdown progresses into the lower levels of the hierarchy. To illustrate:

> A primary human goal is good health. Health is also a very broad goal. Planning to meet that goal requires breaking the

> term "health" down into its components, such as alertness, not getting tired, enjoying meals, sleeping well, prompt recovery from ailments, looking good. In turn, each of these secondary goals breaks down into tertiary goals. For example, the secondary goal of alertness breaks down into such goals as good vision, good hearing, and quick reflexes. These breakdowns continue until a point is reached where it is possible to provide the specific means that enable the goal to be met, such as glasses for good vision.

A similar hierarchy of goals is found in goods. The automobile is a widely understood example.

> The primary goal is effective transportation. The secondary goals are safety, comfort, economy, spaciousness, durability, appearance, etc. (not necessarily in that order). One of these secondary goals—economy—gives rise to such tertiary goals as low purchase price, low financing cost, low operating and maintenance cost, and high resale value. In turn, the tertiary goal of low operating and maintenance cost breaks down into such further goals as warranty coverage, fuel efficiency, dependability, and adequate service. These breakdowns continue until each goal becomes definable in technological terms.

This breakdown of goals is a part of the quality planning process. The hierarchy of goals is derived from a corresponding hierarchy of customer needs. In turn, the hierarchy of goals results in hierarchies of product features and process features, which we shall examine in later chapters.

In effect, the quality planning process consists of a series of alternating (a) goal setting with (b) planning how to meet the goals:

> Primary goals are established, requiring breakdown into secondary goals as well as taking some steps down the quality road map.
>
> Planning is then done for the secondary goals, including breakdown into tertiary goals.
>
> This alternation continues until the goals become so specific that specific means can be provided to meet them without the need for further breakdown.

Deployment of Quality Goals

"Deployment" as used here means subdividing the goals and allocating the subgoals to lower levels.* Such deployment accomplishes some essential purposes:

The subdivisions and allocations continue until they identify the actions to be taken—the specific deeds to be done in order to meet the goals.

The allocation of responsibility becomes more and more narrowly focused until it assigns specific responsibility for doing the specific deeds.

Those who are assigned to be responsible respond by determining the resources needed and communicating this to higher levels.

Such deployment provides for communication both up and down the hierarchy. It also provides the lower levels with the opportunity to participate in the planning process. Strategic quality goals may be proposed at the top. The lower levels then identify the deeds that, if done, will collectively meet the goals. The lower levels also submit the bill: To do these deeds, we need the following resources. The subsequent negotiations then arrive at an equilibrium which balances the value of meeting the goals against the cost of doing so.

The two-way communication feature of the deployment process (a Japanese term is "catch ball") has turned out to be an important aid to getting results. Feedbacks from companies using this process suggest that it outperforms the process of unilateral goal setting by upper managers. Florida Power & Light Company calls this approach "policy deployment" (Brunetti, 1987).

This same two-way communication feature requires that the recipients be trained in how to respond. The most useful training is prior experience in quality improvement projects.

Many quality goals are in the nature of comprehensive "elephant-size" quality improvement projects, which ultimately must be cut up into "bite-size" projects. For example:

1. A strategic quality goal is established: Reduce the cost of poor quality by X million dollars. This goal is then deployed to the various divisions by setting a quota for each. These quotas

*A note on terminology: Some companies use the term "policy deployment" to designate deployment of quality goals. This usage seems to be the result of difficulties in translation from the corresponding Japanese term.

must in due course be broken down into "bite-size" projects, however, using the Pareto principle and other tools of the quality improvement process.

2. An airline goal of attaining Y percent on-time arrivals may require projects to deal with such matters as:

   The *policy* of delaying departures in order to accommodate delayed connecting flights

   The *organization* for decision making at departure gates

   The need for revisions in *departmental procedures*

   The state of *employee behavior* and awareness.

3. Any goal of improving timeliness of service requires a breakdown of the broad service process into its components, identifying the vital few, and then considering each as a project, along with the broad "macroprocess" itself.

Deployment to Whom?

To some degree, deployment of strategic quality goals can follow hierarchical lines: corporate to division; division to functional department; etc. However, this arrangement fails when goals relate to "macroprocesses."

Major activities of companies are carried out by use of interconnecting networks of macroprocesses. Each macroprocess is a multifunctional system consisting of a series of sequential operations. Being multifunctional in nature, there is no single "owner," and hence no obvious answer to the question: Deployment to Whom?

We shall have a detailed look at ownership of macroprocesses in Chapter 10, "Multifunctional Quality Planning." At this point what is pertinent is that there should be no vagueness on the question of "Deployment to Whom?" In deploying goals that involve multifunctional processes, the upper managers should face squarely the question of "Deployment to Whom?"

A trend toward deployment of goals to teams is exemplified in the automotive industry by the Ford Taurus case, in which the goal of attaining "best in class" was deployed to "Team Taurus" (Veraldi, 1985), and by the adoption of the team approach to designs at GM and Chrysler as well.

There are also reported cases in which the team included the impacted supplier(s) or other external agencies. For an example of a joint supplier–customer project, see Kegarise and Miller (1986).

The Effect of "Big Q"

The growing adoption of the concept of "Big Q" has broadened the scope of strategic quality goals. Traditionally these goals have related to performance of such major functions as:

Prices paid for purchased goods and services

Promptness of customer service

Extent of scrap and rework in manufacture

The new goals reflect the growing awareness of the importance of such business processes as billing, recruitment, payroll, and bidding for contracts. This growing awareness is evident in emerging strategic quality goals, such as:

Shortening the time for the new product launch cycle (Pisano, 1986)

Improving the accuracy of the sales forecast (Wolf, 1985)

Establishing supplier relations on a teamwork basis (Branco and Willoughby, 1987)

This same concept of "Big O" has promise of becoming a unifying force for dealing with the contention that "my industry (or company, function, etc.) is different." The technologies and markets certainly differ. However, the business processes and macroprocesses are quite similar for all industries. In addition, the areas of similarity are much greater than the areas of difference.

Provision of Resources

Resources are the price to be paid for the benefits of meeting goals. These resources parallel those required to establish and maintain the traditional goals of companywide financial management. More specifically, the resources include:

The effort needed to establish the basic strategic goals system, including processes for goal setting and deployment, evaluation of results, and recognition and rewards

Training in operation of the system

The effort required, at all levels, to administer the system on a continuing basis.

In the absence of some form of strategic quality goals, a major obstacle to making progress in quality has been lack of resources. This has been widely demonstrated in efforts to go into quality improvement projects. To bring such projects to completion requires various resources: time for project team members to guide the projects; support from technicians and specialists; training in various skills and tools. With the exception of some aspects of training, these resources have not been provided adequately. In turn, lack of the resources has starved out many efforts to improve quality on a scale that offered major benefits.

The strategic goals approach, being tied into strategic business planning, offers a way to provide the needed resources. Strategic business planning has long included a positive approach to bringing out into the open the resources required to meet the strategic business goals. For example, a common business goal is to increase sales by X percent. The budgetary process typically includes identification of the resources needed: additional manufacturing capacity, more inventory, additional sales personnel, etc. The associated discussions focus on the extent to which the added resources will provide acceptable returns on the investment.

Those who are apprehensive about "corporate interference" (see below) should note that the use of strategic quality goals provides a recognized channel for dealing with the problem of securing resources.

Corporate Interference

In some companies the setting of strategic quality goals faces resistance from the autonomous divisions (or from the functional departments) on the grounds of "corporate interference." It is a fact that establishment of strategic quality goals reduces some of the autonomy previously enjoyed by these divisions and departments. Such reduction in autonomy is never welcomed, even if the associated human relations are harmonious. Where they are less than harmonious, the problem can become severe.

The nature of this reduction in autonomy becomes evident if we look sideways at the finance function. In virtually all large companies, the corporate headquarters office "interferes" in divisional financial affairs in three major ways:

Approval of the divisional financial budgets

Approval of the divisional financial plans for meeting their budgets

Review of divisional financial performances against budgets

The parallel "interference" with respect to quality consists of actions taken by the corporate headquarters office to:

Approve divisional quality goals

Approve divisional plans for reaching the quality goals

Review of divisional quality performance

The major difference is that in the case of finance the practice is of long standing, whereas in the case of quality, the practice is just beginning. However, introduction of strategic quality goals does in fact interfere with some prior monopolies, and this is one of the prices to be paid.

Quality Goals at Lower Levels

Strategic quality goals are few in number. However, each is very important, so each commands the attention of the upper managers. In contrast, the tactical goals are extremely numerous. They are the useful many, so they command the attention of the lower levels in the hierarchy.

During this chapter the emphasis has been on strategic quality goals and their deployment. This emphasis is necessary in view of the powerful trend to bring quality goals into strategic business planning. These strategic quality goals are in addition to, not instead of, the long standing tactical quality goals. However, the strategic goals will necessarily influence the pattern of the tactical quality goals as well.

Other chapters to come will deal extensively with the tactical quality goals:

Customer needs give rise to quality goals, and will be discussed in Chapter 4, "Determine Customer Needs."

Product features give rise to quality goals, and will be discussed in Chapter 6, "Develop Product Features."

Process features give rise to quality goals, and will be discussed in Chapter 7, "Develop Process Features."

Process control features give rise to quality goals, and will be discussed in Chapter 8, "Develop Process Controls."

Still other quality goals are generated from other sources, such as efforts to improve quality, training for quality, and motivation for quality. It will be seen that the strategic quality goals are numerically only the tip of a very large pyramid. The bulk of that pyramid consists of the tactical quality goals.

Next Step: Identify the Customers

Once established, the quality goals become inputs to the next step on the quality planning road map: Identify the Customers. The next chapter is devoted to that step.

List of High Points

A quality goal is an aimed-at quality target.

It is not possible to plan in the abstract. One can plan only after the goal has been established.

Visions have little relation to reality until they are converted into quantitative goals, which are to be met within a specific time span.

Quality goals that affect product salability should be based primarily on the market.

In cases involving high chronic costs of poor quality, the historical basis for setting strategic quality goals has done a lot of damage by helping to perpetuate a chronically wasteful performance.

Goals for cases of chronically high cost of poor quality should be based on planned breakthroughs using the quality improvement process.

Quality goals are a moving target.

In deploying strategic quality goals, there should be no vagueness on the question "Deployment to whom?"

Establishment of strategic quality goals reduces some of the autonomy previously enjoyed by the autonomous divisions and functional departments.

Tasks for Upper Managers

Upper managers should become a source of nominations for strategic quality goals.

During the goal-setting process, upper managers should be on the alert for misuse of historical performance as a basis.

In deploying goals that involve multifunctional processes, upper managers should face squarely the question "Deployment to whom?"

] 3 [

Identify the Customers

Purpose of This Chapter

The purpose of this chapter is to show how to identify who are the customers—those who will be impacted or affected by the products and processes required to attain the quality goals. Customers include both those who are impacted if the goals are attained and those who are impacted if the goals are not attained. (The word customer is used here in the Big Q sense: anyone who is impacted).

For this chapter the input–output diagram is shown in Figure 3–1.

The *input* consists of the established quality goals.

The *process* consists of the activities conducted to discover who will be impacted by the means used to attain the goals.

The *output* is a list of those impacted: the customers.

Putting the Question on the Agenda

To discover who is impacted, we must put the question on the agenda. Many managers simply *assume* that they already know who the customers are. That assumption is usually quite valid as to the clients, those who buy the products. These clients are certainly the most important single category of customers, but they are only a small per-

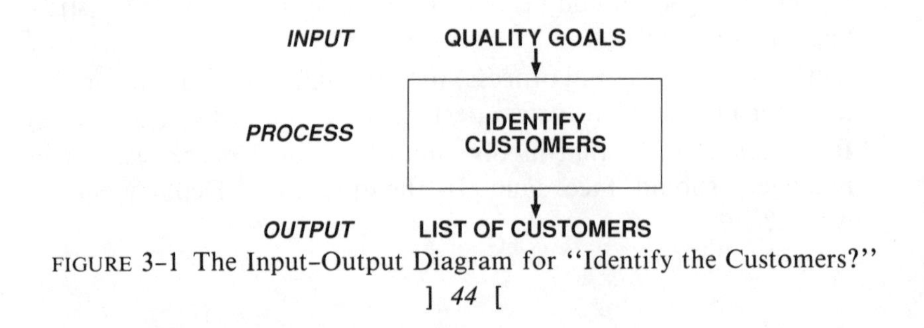

FIGURE 3–1 The Input–Output Diagram for "Identify the Customers?"

centage of the persons impacted. Most products are not "sold" in the literal sense of that word. Some of these "unsold" products are letters, price quotations, purchase orders, and invoices, which are sent out to external customers. Others consist of the vast array of *internal* products that go to internal customers: information, data, physical components, commands, advice, requests, and so on.

> In one large company an "advanced engineering" team spent a good deal of effort to determine the ingredients of "the factory of the future." The team findings were then compiled into a book, which provided detailed information about these ingredients. Because of the effort involved, the book was classified as "secret," and the distribution was strictly limited to very high-level officials.
>
> For some months after the publication of the book, there was no feedback from the recipients. (Such silence is usually an indication that the book is not being used.) Then an occasion arose which raised the question, "Who are the customers for this book"? It was suddenly realized that those high-level officials were not potential users of the books. Those who could make real use of the books were the various engineering and factory managers, yet they were not on the distribution list. Even worse, they had not been consulted as to their needs.
>
> Surprises can also arise at the lower levels of organization.
>
> An electric utility conducted a survey to discover employee perceptions relative to quality. One finding was that at the lower levels only 25 percent of the employees considered themselves as having customers.

The need to "put the question on the agenda" becomes even more obvious when we look closely at that proliferation of "unsold products."

> A process produces invoices in six copies. These invoices are products, and they end up in six different final destinations. Along the way the invoices impact various intermediate process steps. Each of the six final destinations, as well as each intermediate step, is a customer.
>
> Another process carries out the activity of cutting gear teeth. It receives "blanks" from a supplier and operates machines

that cut gear teeth into the blanks. It then sends the cut gears on their way to subsequent processes, which cut keyways, heat treat, grind and lap, store, ship, assemble into gear boxes, assemble gear boxes into vehicles, sell the vehicles, operate the vehicles, maintain the vehicles, etc. Each of those subsequent impacted activities is a customer.

The Flow Diagram

Proliferation of products and processes creates a corresponding proliferation of customers. To discover who is impacted, not only must we put the question on the agenda; we must also provide tools for answering the question. A major tool for this purpose is the flow diagram.

The flow diagram is a graphic means for depicting the steps in a process. Figure 3–2 (p. 47) is a simple example.

Basic Symbols

Most flow diagrams are constructed from a few basic symbols:

The *activity symbol* is a rectangle which designates an activity. Within the rectangle is a brief description of that activity.

The *decision symbol* is a diamond which designates a decision point from which the process branches into two or more paths. The path taken depends on the answer to the question that appears within the diamond. Each path is labeled to correspond to an answer to the question.

The *terminal symbol* is a rounded rectangle which unambiguously identifies the beginning or end of a process, according to the word within the terminal. "Start" or "begin" is used to designate the starting point of process flow; "stop" or "end" is used to designate the end of process flow.

The *document symbol* represents a document pertinent to the process.

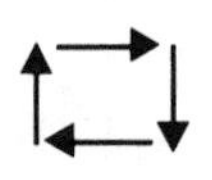

The *flow line* represents a process path that connects process elements, e.g., activities, decisions; the arrowhead on a flow line indicates direction of process flow.

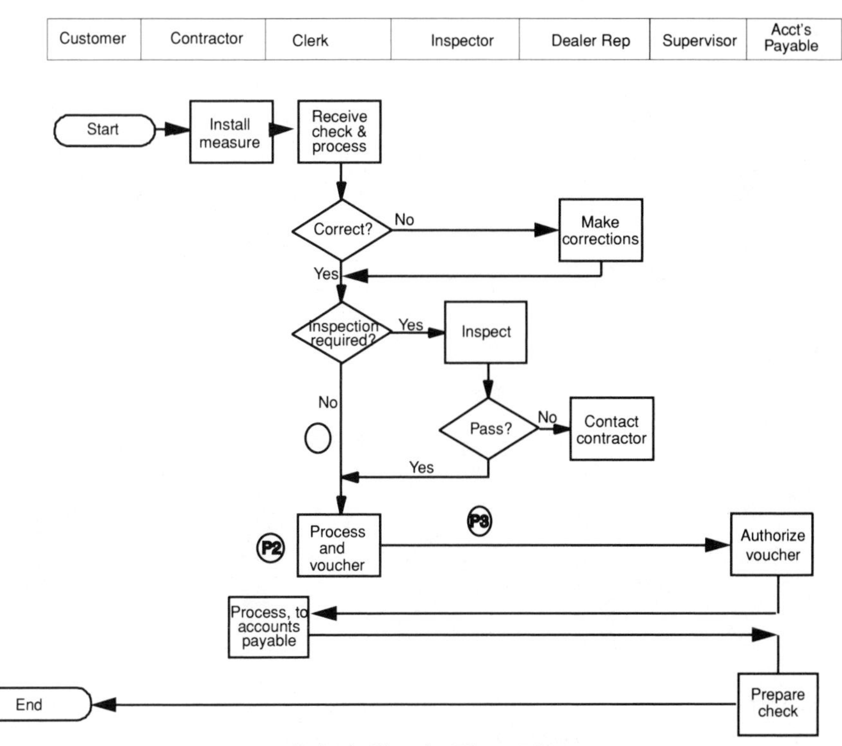

FIGURE 3–2 A Simple Flow Diagram
SOURCE: Florida Power & Light.

The *connector* is a circle which is used to indicate a continuation of the flow diagram.

Dealing with Complexity

When flow diagrams become complex, it is helpful to prepare a schematic to show the broad flow. Figure 3–3 shows such a schematic for the process of preparing invoices in a large power company.

Such a schematic helps the readers to visualize the interrelationships among the more detailed subdiagrams.

Another way of dealing with complexity is to show the "macro-process" in a broad schematic and an associated "microprocess" in a satellite diagram, as in Figure 3–4.

Benefits of Flow Diagrams

When flow diagrams are prepared by multifunctional teams, the team members usually derive multiple benefits. They report that the flow diagram:

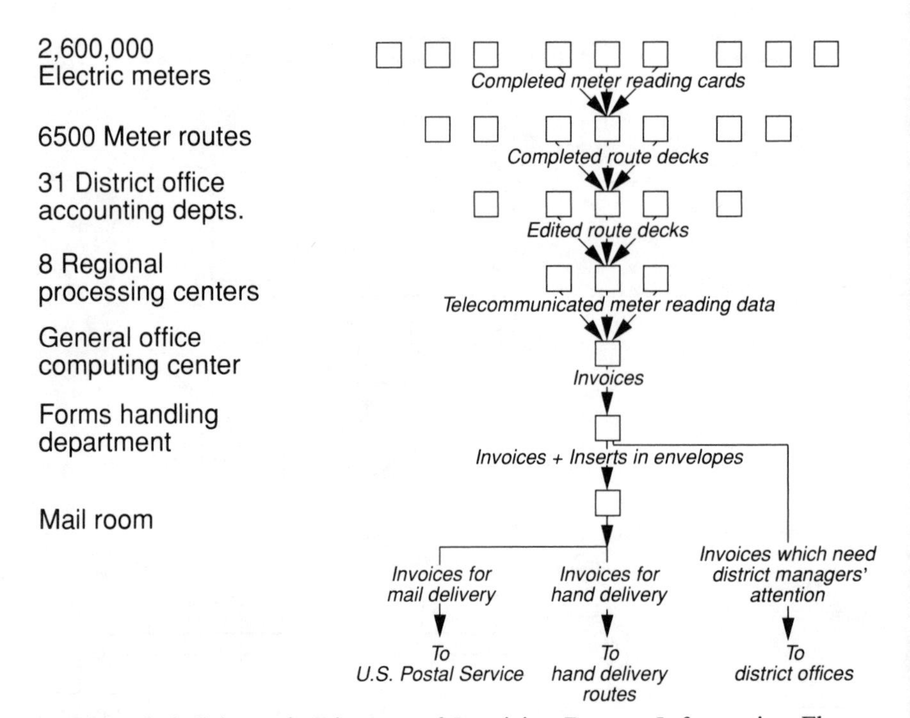

FIGURE 3–3 Schematic Diagram of Invoicing Process Information Flow
Courtesy Florida Power & Light.

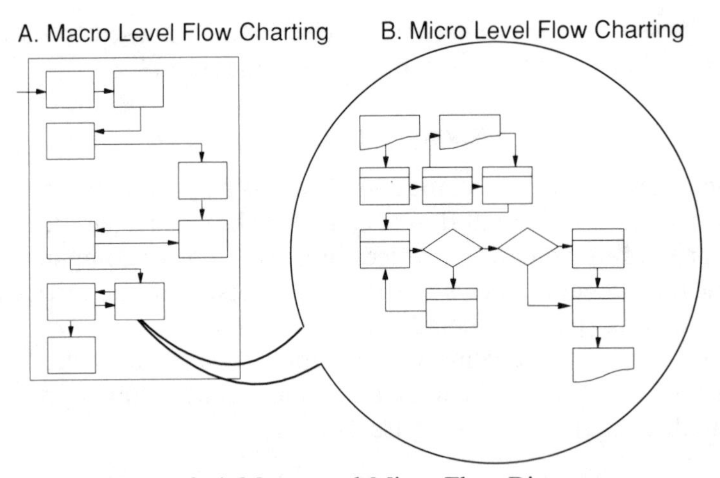

FIGURE 3–4 Macro and Micro Flow Diagrams
SOURCE: AT&T Network Operations Group.

Provides understanding of the whole. Each team member is fully knowledgeable about his or her segment of the process but not fully knowledgeable about the complete process. The flow diagram supplies the missing knowledge to an unprecedented degree.

Identifies customers previously neglected. A surprising finding by some teams is that in the past much planning had been done without first identifying all the important customers. It had been widely assumed that "everyone knows" who the customers are. But it turned out that without the discipline of preparing the flow diagram, some essential customers had been neglected or even overlooked. The most widespread areas of neglect have consisted of internal customers. However, when teams specifically address the question "Who are the customers?" they identify more clearly the external customers as well.

Identifies opportunities for improvement. Most flow diagrams exhibit subprocesses or "loops," which are a form of redoing what was done previously. Figure 3–5 is an example of a flow diagram

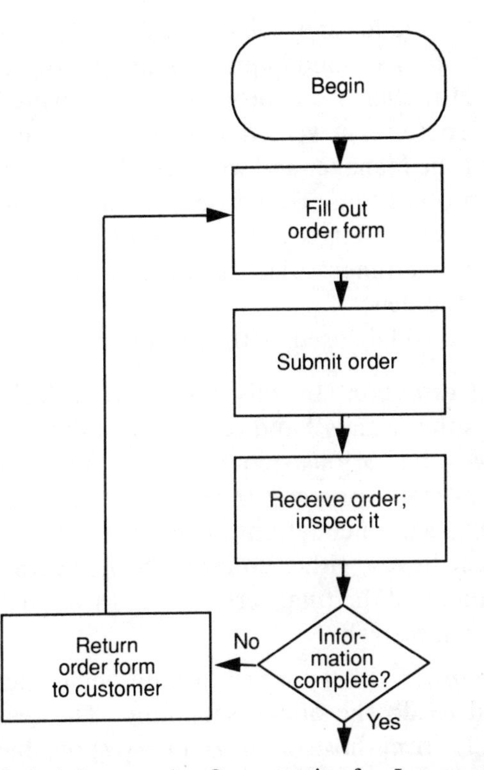

FIGURE 3–5 A Loop—An Opportunity for Improvement

which exhibits such a loop. Each such loop can be regarded as an opportunity for improvement—a chronic deficiency which should not be carried over into the new or revised plan.

Makes it easier to set boundaries. Every process interacts with some of the other processes within and outside of the company. These others interact with still other processes, and ultimately every company process is affected. It is out of the question to pursue these interactions to the bitter end—we would wind up replanning the work of the entire company. So we establish a boundary based on our judgment. The flow diagram provides a graphic aid for setting the boundary.

Note that at the outset the flow diagram serves to provide an understanding of the status quo—what has been going on in the past. Then, as planning proceeds, the flow diagram becomes an aid to revision. It provides an understanding of who will be impacted.

Sources of Flow Diagrams

Companies have made extensive use of flow diagrams to depict process flow. Examples abound in prior planning projects and in reports of all kinds. However, most process flow information either exists in narrative form (e.g., in written procedures) or is unwritten, existing in the heads of the manager and workers. When we undertake a quality planning project, the prior process flow studies can be helpful, especially if they reflect the discipline of flow diagram analysis. However, each planning project requires updating the old as well as providing for the new.

There are two widely used methods for creating the flow diagram:

1. *The investigator.* In this approach a trained investigator "makes the rounds" and confers with the personnel who preside over the various steps in the process. From these inputs the investigator prepares the flow diagram along with an analysis and recommendations. These are then discussed with the pertinent heads, either collectively or individually. Revisions are made, and the final version goes through recognized channels for approval.
2. *The team.* In this approach a multidepartmental team is appointed to do the quality planning. The team members are generally from those organizations responsible for the various steps in the process. The team then proceeds to develop the

flow diagram and the associated analysis (for an example, see Engle and Ball, 1986).

Both of these methods have been widely tested. Those who have used the team approach generally feel that the resulting *participation* is the key to good quality planning. Team members welcome participation in planning projects that affect their responsibility. Many of these same team members relate prior experiences in which their participation had been too late—the major decisions had already been made and had become irreversible. It was refreshing to them to be brought in at the outset so that their contribution would be influential.

Who Are the External Customers?

To identify the customers it is helpful at the outset to anticipate that there will be two lists: external and internal customers.

The term "external customers" is used here in the sense of persons or organizations who are not a part of our company but who are impacted by our activities.

The term "internal customers" is used in the sense of those who are a part of our company and who are also impacted by our activities.

These definitions are not 100 percent accurate, but they are valid to a high degree.

Next, it is helpful to make use of "brainstorming" by a multifunctional team to address the question of who the external customers are.

When a team in the Internal Revenue Service (IRS) addressed the question of who were the external customers of the IRS, it promptly identified the following:

The taxpayers

The Treasury Department (the official "boss" of the IRS)

The Administration (The Office of the President)

The Congress

The practitioners (the accountants and lawyers who help the taxpayers prepare their tax returns)

The media

The tax courts

During such brainstorming the obvious customers will be listed promptly. Then additional customers will emerge. Some of these will come as surprises—"That was never brought up before."

Some organizations take special care to identify external customers and to anticipate their needs.

> A builder of swimming pools sends a letter to the *neighbors of clients* to assure them that during the period of construction the workmen will take care to keep noise and dirt to a minimum, and to maintain safe conditions.

> The Federal Consumer Price Index influences the incomes and expenses of tens of millions of external customers: Social Security beneficiaries, food stamp recipients, workers under escalator clauses, federal retirees, and so on. (It has many other influences as well.)

In contrast, failure to identify external customers (or even *potential* external customers) can create severe problems or magnify minor problems.

> The outpouring of legislation relative to environmental protection had its origin in the realization that the cumulative effects of disposal of many toxic wastes were a threat to human safety. As a corollary it has become difficult to find sites for disposal of wastes because of opposition by the local public and even by those who live along the potential travel routes.

A prickly type of external customer is the media. Their mission is to inform their clientele as to ongoing events, but they do so with an eye on how to increase their own revenue. Their influence can be enormous. They can enlarge or destroy reputations.

> In one federal bureau a few forms filed by the public were singed in an optical character reader because of operation by an improperly trained worker. The incident was leaked to the press. What emerged was a story to the effect that the bureau had destroyed many forms by burning them.

Suppliers as External Customers

There is general awareness that suppliers need feedback from their customers. In most cases this has been limited to feedback in the form of *dissatisfactions:* complaints, claims, returns, lawsuits, etc. Much less attention has been paid to feedback in the form of prior experience and aids to planning.

> Two automobile makers both bought products from the same supplier of automobile seats. One company considered the supplier troublesome: poor quality, late delivery. The other company regarded the supplier as delivering superior quality. Both companies provided the supplier with the basics: a contract, a schedule, specifications, and drawings. The second company went further. It identified the key features to be controlled by the supplier. It also provided the supplier with information on how the product is assembled, how the product is used and misused, the environments of use, and prior problems encountered.

One company has included this concept (the supplier as an external customer) in its model of the triple role diagram. The model is shown in Figure 3-6.

Who Are the Internal Customers?

Most products and processes exist to serve internal customers. The internal relationships tend to be informal, resulting in a hazy perception of who the customers are and how they are impacted. The problem is at its worst in the case of "macroprocesses," which are multifunctional in scope and therefore tend to conflict with the jurisdictional boundaries of the functional departments.

Identifying who is impacted can be done in large part by "follow-

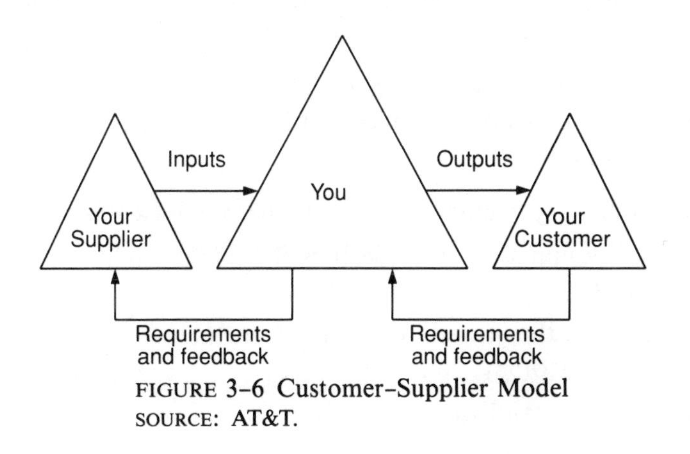

FIGURE 3-6 Customer-Supplier Model
SOURCE: AT&T.

ing the product," using multifunctional teams aided by flow diagrams. Some companies encourage the use of internal "contracts" that spell out various essential features of the internal relationships. The effort to put an agreement on paper certainly increases the likelihood of identifying who the internal customers are.

Some internal customers remain hidden from view until the proper event brings them out into the open.

> The salary increase given to the city police force is closely studied by the other categories of city employees to assure that traditional parity is maintained. They contend, vigorously, that they are indeed impacted.

It is quite likely that improvement of the quality planning process can gain as much by better identifying who the internal customers are as by better identifying who the external customers are.

In some situations the same person is both an internal and an external customer.

> Every reorganization has an effect on the career pattern of some company employees. Each of such employees is of course an internal customer. However, every employee is present in the company in two capacities: (1) as a subordinate within the company, and (2) as a free citizen. In this second capacity he or she is an external customer.

A Customer Is a Cast of Characters

The term customer is often used loosely, so it is not clear whether the reference is to an organization unit or to a person. Such looseness contributes to vagueness as to who is the customer.

> A salesperson selling supplies to a hospital soon learns that the decision of whose supplies will be bought is influenced by numerous persons:
>
> The purchasing manager who signs the purchase contract
>
> The quality manager who specifies the quality assurance procedures
>
> The heads of the various specialist departments: X-ray, obstetrics, histology, etc.
>
> The physicians and surgeons

The nurse corps

Various administrative heads

And so on

One practical hospital administrator used the cast of characters principle when faced with the need to build a new wing for the hospital. He first carefully planned one room. Then he collected inputs from a cast of characters:

The patients

Family members who visited the patients

The physicians

The nurses

Technicians who brought in test equipment which they then used in the room

The paraprofessionals

The maintenance personnel

The cleaning personnel

Not until the administrator had accumulated the needed feedback from these and other customers did he build the rest of the hospital wing.

Identifying the complete cast of characters improves decision making while reducing the risk of unpleasant surprises.

An important element of Ford Motor Company's development of the Taurus model was the participation of those impacted. As a prerequisite this required identifying the cast of characters within each major internal functional organization.

Owners of valuable works of art are periodically faced with the need for restoration. Such restorations are entrusted to recognized experts. It has turned out that the cast of characters includes the public, the scholars, and even the dead artist! (The dead artist is represented by the estate or the family.) All of these, especially the scholars, may have definite views on what should or should not be done relative to restoration (Tomkins, 1987).

A familiar form of the cast of characters is the merchant chain. Sales from the original supplier may go through several intermediaries before reaching the ultimate user.

> An American maker of soups had been trying to market its products in Japan through intermediaries such as importers and distributors. When the company established a contract directly with a large Japanese chain of food retailers, its sales rose sharply (*Business Week,* 1988).

A similar situation exists in the form of chains of processors. For many companies the client is a processor (converter, etc.) who sells to the next processor. Now the need is to discover who those subsequent processors are, since each is potentially a customer.

(A parallel cast of characters can exist with respect to suppliers. The immediate supplier may have little to do with the key qualities needed by the customer; some earlier producer in the supplier chain may have been decisive as to the presence of those key qualities).

The cast of characters always includes those whose vested interests are threatened. Human history records many instances of violent confrontation when new technology threatened the livelihood of those engaged in traditional ways.

> The eighteenth-century English hand sawyers who repeatedly destroyed water-powered sawmills had their counterparts in the nineteenth-century Luddites who broke up textile machinery. In a similar vein, American teamsters smashed the first pipelines emerging from the Pennsylvania oil fields. Their factory counterparts bitterly resisted the introduction of the Taylor system into the shops.

> In the 1980s the airlines introduced self-ticketing machines in some airports. Some travel agency organizations promptly threatened to boycott any airline that used such machines.

Managers should also be on the alert for the influence of those who may seem too remote to be called customers but who nevertheless have great influence over decision making.

> Various critics (in art, literature, the theater, etc.) can be influential and even decisive as to the success of an art form, a book, a play, etc.
>
> The findings of certain independent testing laboratories can

greatly aid or damage the market for specific products and even classes of products.

A further concept related to the cast of characters is that of "leading users," who may be influential outsiders such as chairpersons of key committees or respected journalists. Figure 3-7 lists a number of types of such leading users, derived from Mintzberg but applied to the field of medical/veterinary electronics (Olsson and Rommer, 1986).

Classification of Customers: Vital Few

As projects grow in size, the number of customers proliferates. These customers are not equally impacted. Neither are they of equal importance to the planners. It becomes necessary to classify the customers in ways that enable the planners to allocate priorities and resources based on the relative importance of the customers and the impacts.

For example, hotel rooms are booked by two types of clients: (1) travelers who arrive one by one at random and (2) organizers of meetings and conventions who book blocks of rooms far in advance. The organizers of meetings and conventions constitute the vital few customers. They receive special attention from the hotel. The travelers are the useful many, and they receive standardized attention.

There are several overlapping ways of classifying the customers. The first of these ways is the familiar Pareto analysis to separate the vital few from the useful many.

Pareto Analysis

In any population that contributes to a common effect, a relative few of the contributors account for the bulk of the effect. This phenomenon is widely known as the Pareto principle (see the Appendix to this chapter; also Juran, 1964). For example, marketers have found that about 80 percent of the total sales volume comes from about 20 percent of the clients. These "vital few" clients are often called key customers. This relationship can be shown graphically, as in Figure 3-8.

The Pareto principle has been found to apply to a wide range of human activities (listed on p. 59):

Mintzberg's 10 Leader-types		
Type	*Definition*	*Characteristics (in our situation)*
1. The figurehead	A symbolic leader; it is his job to carry out various socially determined tasks.	Chairman at meetings. Participates when the medical students graduate or as judge at the cattle show.
2. Leader	Responsible for motivation and activating the employees. In charge of recruitment, education, and the like.	Advocates new methods. In charge of projects run by the scientifical association or the trade association.
3. Connector	Maintains a self-made network of contacts within and outside the organization	Director in other companies; has international contacts.
4. Monitor	Seeks and receives several pieces of qualified information (topical) in order to reach total knowledge of the organization and its context.	Familiar with what goes on in his field of interest. Receives information from international contacts.
5. Disseminator	Intermediary of information to employees received either from third party or from members of the organization itself. Some of this information is objective, some is interpreted.	Passes on mail in the organization with information as the purpose. Verbal contacts causing flow of information to and from colleagues and employees.
6. Spokesman	Intermediary of information about the plans, policies, actions, results, etc. of the organization to third party. Serves as an expert concerning the trade of the organization	Writes articles in trade papers and gives lectures.

FIGURE 3–7 Examples of "Leading Users"

Mintzberg's 10 Leader-types		
Type	*Definition*	*Characteristics (in our situation)*
7. Operation manager	Seeks new possibilities in the organization and in its context. Initiates "improvement projects" which should cause changes.	Plans the future strategy and decides investments.
9. Resource distributor	Responsible for the distribution of the organization's various resources—actually making and/or approving all the important decisions in the organization.	Has influence on budgets and operating personnel.
10. Negotiator	Responsible representative of the organizations in important negotiations.	Can bind the company. Representative in trade association.

FIGURE 3–7 *Continued*

A relative few suppliers are associated with most of the quality problems and late deliveries.

A relative few employees account for most of the accidents, absences, drug use.

A relative few criminals account for most of the crimes committed.

A relative few authors account for most of the published books and papers.

The methodology of making the Pareto analysis is generally as follows:

Prepare a written list of the customers

Arrange this list in the order of importance

Identify the vital few—those for whom planning is to be done on an *individual* basis

Identify the useful many—those for whom planning is to be done on a *group* basis

Once the analysis has been made, the planning process moves on to the next steps on the quality planning road map.

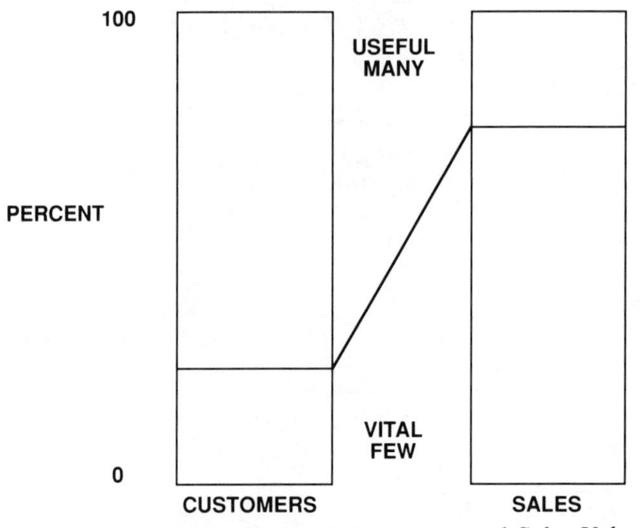

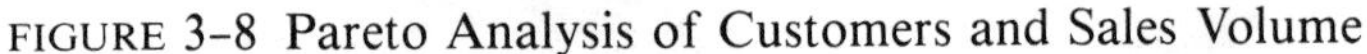
FIGURE 3–8 Pareto Analysis of Customers and Sales Volume

Key Interfaces

Companies and their clients interface in multiple ways. The most familiar examples are seen in service companies. A hotel guest may have occasion to interface with multiple hotel employees: doorman, reception clerk, bellman, telephone operator, housekeeper, dining room waiter, cashier, etc. Among such multiple contacts some may be *key interfaces*. To illustrate:

Business	*Example of Key Interface*
Banking	Bank teller and depositor
Restaurant	Waiter and diner
Hotel	Reception clerk and guest
Retailing	Salesperson and shopper
Telephone	Operator and subscriber

Part of the answer to the question "Who are the customers?" consists of identifying the key interfaces.

The concept of key interfaces spreads across the entire hierarchy and sometimes affects grand strategy.

> A leading company in sale of travelers' checks has more than 100,000 sales outlets (banks, etc.). The number of transactions is huge, so that even a low error rate generates

many errors. The resulting customer complaints require prompt remedial action. To this end the company made a substantial investment in an electronic capability which provides the customer service people with ready access to the history of the pertinent transactions.

A leading newspaper concluded that their major category of customers was the advertisers. This conclusion required a revision of priorities among the internal processes of the newspaper. A major problem faced by advertisers is to keep their copy up to date in response to last-minute developments. As a result, advertising copy is late when delivered to the newspaper, and leaves little time to meet the newspaper's deadline for going to press. It became necessary for the newspaper to revise its internal processes in ways which would give top priority to dealing with late advertising copy.

Significant Impacts

A related concept for identifying the vital few customers is that of significant impacts. This concept is based on the fact that while our actions impact many customers, those impacts are not equally important—they follow the Pareto principle. We can make use of this fact by looking for the vital few—the significant impacts. To amplify the concept it is helpful to define the term "processor team" previously referred to in Chapter 1, under "The Triple Role Concept."

A *processor team* is any person or organization unit that carries out a prescribed process in order to produce a product. A processor team can be *any* organization unit: the company; a division; a department; a crew; an individual. (We sometimes refer to a versatile individual as a one-man gang).

The accompanying boxed tabulation shows some categories of processor teams and the associated significant customer impacts.

Organizing the Information: The Spreadsheet

For large projects the proliferation of customers, along with multiple customer needs and the various degrees of impact, results in very large numbers of combinations. To keep track of all these combinations requires some sort of organized memory system. A popular such system is the spreadsheet (table, matrix, etc.). Figure 3-9 is a spreadsheet of the sort known in the United States as the "House of Quality," part of the planning tool known as quality function deployment (QFD).

In this figure the various customers are listed in the horizontal rows. The vertical columns are used to accumulate the needs of the customers as those needs are identified (see Chapter 4). The intersections are coded to show (in this case) the intensity of the relationships between customers and their needs. Such spreadsheets display a great deal of information in a format that "reads at a glance." As a result, these spreadsheets are increasingly being used by quality planners.

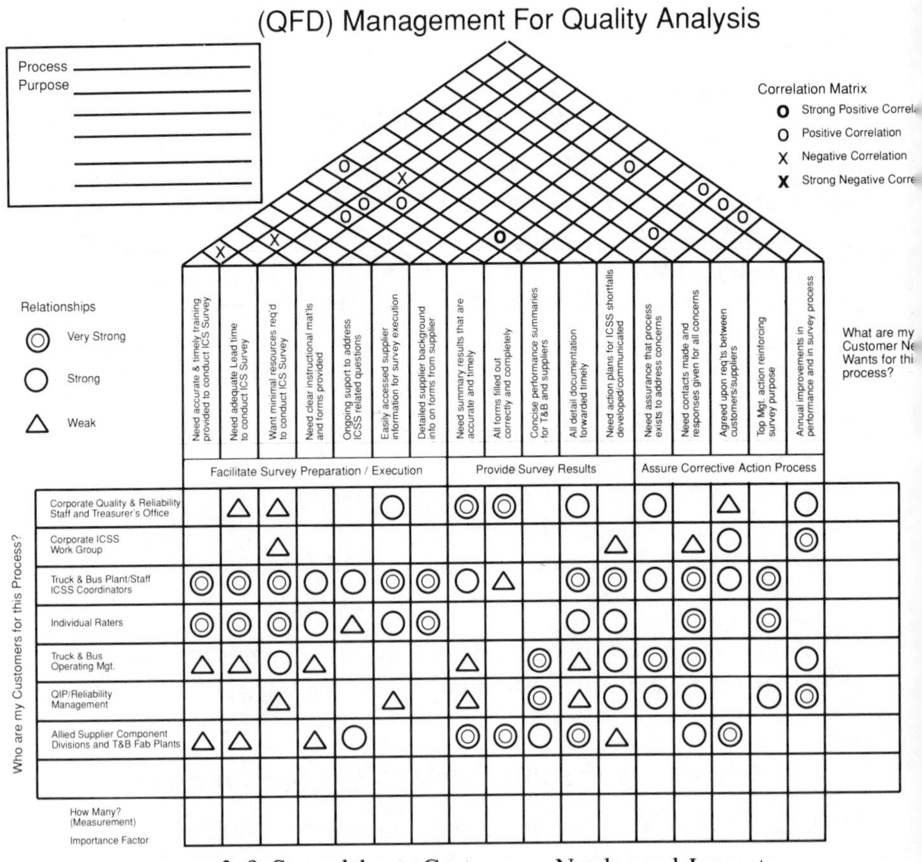

FIGURE 3-9 Spreadsheet: Customers, Needs, and Impacts
SOURCE: General Motors Truck & Bus

Processor Team	*Examples of Customers Who Are Significantly Impacted*
Our Company	***Clients*** They buy from us and are the source of our income. ***Ultimate users*** Even though they may not make the buying decision, their feedback on use of the product strongly influences those who do the buying. ***Regulators*** Their rules are a form of mandated needs to be met. ***The public*** They influence the climate in which we operate.
Market Research	Marketers; Product Developers
Product Development	Process Developers
Process Development	Operations Personnel
Order Editing	Operations Personnel
Accounts Receivable	Clients
Any Person	The Supervisor
Any Supervisor	The Subordinates

Classification of Customers: Useful Many

Each of the useful many* customers is of limited importance to the supplier. However, *collectively* the useful many should be regarded as a member of the vital few. There are several categories of the useful many customers. Those most frequently met are consumers, the workers, and the public.

Consumers

As used here a consumer is a small-volume buyer for personal use. Consumers supply the purchasing power that supports many industries, including some of the giants, (e.g., public utilities, government bodies, merchant chains). Through their use of the product these

**A note on marketers' terminology.* Any marketer knows that a relatively few "key" customers account for most of the sales volume. Each such customer may be designated as "primary," "vital," "major," etc. However, marketers avoid openly designating any of the remaining (non-key) customers as "minor," "secondary," etc. The stated position of the marketers is that every customer is important and should be treated as such.

consumers become well-informed as to quality of product. No one knows more about the conditions under which the product is used, neglected, or misused. No one is more qualified, by experience, to make judgments as to likes and dislikes.

Of course, consumers also reach conclusions (perceptions) from all this experience. They then make use of these perceptions in various ways:

They reach decisions on what to buy or not to buy in the future

They communicate their perceptions to others

They generate ideas which might help suppliers to meet customer needs more completely

Such perceptions can be of great value to quality planners. The approach to acquiring those perceptions will be discussed in Chapter 4, "Determine Customer Needs."

The Workers

The term "workers" (also "work force") usually refers to nonsupervisory employees in nonprofessional work categories. In manufacturing companies many of these employees are production workers on the factory floor. In service companies the workers include "front line" employees who deal directly with paying customers. In both kinds of companies the workers include various categories of maintenance, clerical, and administrative employees who provide support to the operating personnel.

As in the case of consumers, the workers have knowledge in depth with respect to needs for quality. This knowledge is derived from extensive "residence" in the workplace and from the repetitive performance of numerous cycles of processing in that workplace. As a consequence of all that residence and processing, the workers develop expertise in such matters as condition of the facilities, environmental variations in the workplace, support provided (or denied) by service departments, variations in inputs to the process, and consistency of management actions.

Such expertise is a useful input to many planning projects. For some projects, the input is indispensable. All of which means that the workers should be regarded as internal customers who can tell the planners a great deal about quality needs.

The Public

Members of the public may be impacted by us even though they do not buy our products. The most obvious impacts relate to product safety or to damage to the environment. There are other impacts as well. The public keeps an eye on our company and judges our behavior as a citizen in the community. This judgment is based on such inputs as:

What our employees have to say about our personnel policy

What our suppliers say about our business practices

The appearance of our facility

Our responsiveness to community activities and problems

These judgments then contribute to a climate that can help or hinder our operations. In extreme cases this climate can become a major influence in our ability to meet our goals. Accordingly, the public is to be regarded as a customer despite the fact that its members may not be clients.

Structured Quality Planning: Mandated or Not?

Up to now our discussion of quality planning has brought in a number of elements of a structured approach to doing the planning. These elements have included:

Put on the agenda the question of who is the customer, to be discussed as a topic in its own right

Provide participation to customers and suppliers, internal as well as external

Prepare flow diagrams as an aid to identifying who is impacted

Record the emerging information on spreadsheets.

In succeeding chapters we shall see many more such elements of structure. Collectively these raise a question to be faced by upper managers: Should a structured approach to quality planning be mandated?

Whether to mandate such a structured approach is a question to be decided by the upper managers, on the merits. In making this decision, the managers should consider:

The previous track record relative to planning for quality. The less favorable the record, the greater is the need for a change in the approach to quality planning.

The size of the company and the complexity of its products. The larger and more complex the quality problems, the greater is the need for a structured approach to quality planning.

The Quality Planning Road Map Application to the Jobs of Upper Managers

Upper managers should become personally exposed to the key elements of the quality planning road map.

In one company the very top managers—about thirty in number—devoted a day to taking training in planning for quality. Those present were:

The office of the chairman: the chairman and CEO; the president; the executive vice president

The division general managers

The corporate staff vice presidents

During that day they organized three focus groups. One group focused on the office of the chairman; the second group focused on the job of general manager; the third group focused on the job of corporate staff vice president. Each focus group was asked to address the following questions:

Who are the customers of this job?

What are the needs of these customers?

To what extent are these needs being met?

What is to be done?

The managers devoted ninety minutes to the exercise, and they were able to cover a surprising amount of ground. They presented their findings on spreadsheets, and these led to an animated discussion. The exercise also gave them a brief insight into the methodology associated with a structured approach to quality planning.

The experience undergone by these managers suggests strongly that:

△ Upper managers should personally participate in applying the quality planning road map to their own jobs.

On to Customers' Needs

Identifying the customers opens the way to determining customers' needs. That is the subject of Chapter 4, "Determine Customer Needs."

List of High Points

To discover who are the customers, we must first put on the agenda the question: "Who are the customers?"

The flow diagram is a major tool for answering the question: "Who are the customers?"

When flow diagrams are prepared by multifunctional teams, the team members usually derive multiple benefits.

Each loop that requires redoing of work can be regarded as an opportunity for improvement.

Those who have used the team approach for preparing flow diagrams generally feel that the resulting *participation* is the key to good quality planning.

Most products and processes exist to serve internal customers.

A customer is a cast of characters.

The cast of characters always includes those whose vested interests are threatened.

Tasks for Upper Managers

Determine whether to mandate a structured approach to quality planning.

Upper managers should personally participate in applying the quality planning road map to their own jobs.

Appendix to Chapter 3

Then and Now in Quality Control

The Non-Pareto Principle; Mea Culpa

J.M. Juran, *Contributing Editor*

The "Pareto principle" has by this time become deeply rooted in our industrial literature. It is a shorthand name for the phenomenon that in any population which contributes to a common effect, a relative few of the contributors account for the bulk of the effect.

Years ago I gave the name "Pareto" to this principle of the "vital few and trivial many." On subsequent challenge, I was forced to confess that I had mistakenly applied the wrong name to the principle.[1] This confession changed nothing—the name "Pareto principle" has continued in force, and seems destined to become a permanent label for the phenomenon.

The matter has not stopped with my own error. On various occasions contemporary authors, when referring to the Pareto principle, have fabricated some embellishments and otherwise attributed to Vilfredo Pareto additional things which he did not do. My motive in offering the present paper is in part to minimize this tendency to embroider the work of a distinguished Italian economist. In addition, I have for some time felt an urge to narrate just how it came about that some early experiences in seemingly unrelated fields (quality control, cryptanalysis, industrial engineering, government administration, management research) nevertheless converged to misname the Pareto principle.

It began in the mid-1920s when as a young engineer I observed (as had many others before me) that quality defects are unequal in frequency, i.e., when a long list of defects was arranged in the order of frequency, a relative few of the defects accounted for the bulk of the defectiveness. As I moved into quality management posts in the late 1920s and the 1930s, I observed

Reproduced from *Quality Progress,* May 1975, pp. 8–9.

(as had many others before me) that a similar phenomenon existed with respect to employee absenteeism, causes of accidents, etc.

During the late 1930s I moved out of the field of quality control to become the corporate industrial engineer for Western Electric Company. In this capacity, one of my responsibilities was to visit other companies to exchange experiences in industrial engineering practices. One of the most exhilarating of these visits was to General Motors Corporation's headquarters. There I found an uncommonly competent team of managers facing up to the then new problems of collective bargaining. As an incidental tool, they had put together an assortment of data processing machinery to enable them to compute the cost of any new labor union proposal. This they did by programming the machines and then running the (punched) employee record cards through the program. It was an ingenious concept, and their system was quite advanced for those days. However, the electro-magnetic machinery then in use took hours and even days to process those hundreds of thousands of cards, so that the managers often found themselves waiting for the machines to grind out the results.

It is a part of our chronicle that these General Motors managers were a keen, inquisitive lot, and were ever on the alert for anything new. Thus, when it happened on one occasion that the card readers were producing gibberish, the managers not only found the cause to be a miswired plug board; they also realized that they had stumbled onto a means for creating messages in cipher. As a form of comic relief from the grueling hours to which they were often subjected, they used some of the waiting time to dig further into this enciphering system. The more they got into it, the more convinced they became that they had evolved a cipher system which could not be broken.

During the relaxation of a luncheon, they told me of this unbreakable cipher system, and I laughed at them. As it happened, I was no slouch in such matters, since my work in the Signal Corps Reserve was precisely on this subject. Naturally, one thing led to another, and before the day was done I had rashly accepted their tender of an enciphered message to break. Break it I did, though it took until three o'clock in the morning. (Thereafter my sleep was short but blissful.)

They were stunned by the news that the unbreakable had been broken, and for the rest of the visit the agreeable aura of a miracle man followed me about. As a by-product, some hitherto secret doors were opened up to me. It was one of these doors which led me, for the first time, to the work of Vilfredo Pareto. The man who opened that door was Mr. Merle Hale, who presided over the executive salary program of General Motors.

Hale showed me a research he had conducted by comparing the executive salary pattern prevailing in General Motors with one of the mathematical models which Pareto had once constructed. The fit was surprisingly close. I registered the incident in my memory along with the fact that Pareto had made extensive studies of the unequal distribution of wealth, and had in addition formulated mathematical models to quantify this maldistribution.

In December 1941, the month in which the United States entered World War II, I took a "temporary" assignment as a federal government administrator. The original six weeks stretched into four years and as a by-product gave me an insight into the problems of managing the federal government. Of course, the principle of the vital few and trivial many had wide application. At the end of the war (1945) I embarked on a career dedicated to the field of management: research, writing, teaching, consulting, etc. By the late 1940s, as a result of my courses at New York University and my seminars at American Management Association, I had recognized the principle of the "vital few and trivial many" as a true "universal," applicable not only in numerous managerial functions but in the physical and biological worlds generally. Other investigators may well have been aware of this universal principle, but to my knowledge no one had ever before reduced it to writing.

It was during the late 1940s, when I was preparing the manuscript for *Quality Control Handbook,* First Edition, that I was faced squarely with the need for giving a short name to the universal. In the resulting writeup,[2] under the heading "Maldistribution of Quality Losses," I listed numerous instances of such maldistribution as a basis for generalization. I also noted that Pareto had found wealth to be maldistributed. In addition, I showed examples of the now familiar cumulative curves, one for maldistribution of wealth and the other for maldistribution of quality losses. The caption under these curves reads "Pareto's principle of unequal distribution applied to distribution of wealth and to distribution of quality losses." Although the accompanying text makes clear that Pareto's contributions specialized in the study of wealth, the caption implies that he had generalized the principle of unequal distribution into a universal. This implication is erroneous. The Pareto principle as a universal was not original with Pareto.

Where then did the universal originate? To my knowledge, the first exposition was by myself. Had I been structured along different lines, assuredly I would have called it the Juran principle. However, I was not structured that way. Yet I did need a shorthand designation, and I had no qualms about Pareto's name. Hence the Pareto principle.

The matter might well have rested there had there been a less than enthusiastic response to the universal. Instead, the new universal became the subject of wide use and reference. I contributed to this dissemination by coining and popularizing the term "vital few and trivial many" in the widely read "universals" paper,[3] and in the moving picture film I prepared for American Management Association on the "breakthrough" process. The resulting wide usage also brought me some challenges (from Dorian Shainin and others) as to the attribution to Pareto. These challenges forced me to do what I should have done in the first place—to inform myself on just what was it that Pareto had done. It was this examination which made clear to me what I had seen only dimly—that Pareto's work had been in in the economic sphere and that his models were not intended to be applied to other fields. To make matters worse, the cumulative curves used in *Quality Control Handbook,* First Edition, should have been properly identified with Lorenz.[1,4]

To summarize, and to set the record straight:

"1. Numerous men, over the centuries, have observed the existence of the phenomenon of vital few and trivial many as it applied to their local sphere of activity.

"2. Pareto observed this phenomenon as applied to distribution of wealth, and advanced the theory of a logarithmic law of income distribution to fit the phenomenon.

"3. Lorenz developed a form of cumulative curve to depict the distribution of wealth graphically.

"4. Juran was (seemingly) the first to identify the phenomenon of the vital few and trivial many as a 'universal,' applicable to many fields.

"5. Juran applied the name 'The Pareto Principle' to this universal. Juran also coined the phrase 'vital few and trivial many' and applied the Lorenz curves to depict this universal in graphic form."

Notes

1. J. M. Juran, "Pareto, Lorenz, Cournot, Bernoulli, Juran and Others," *Industrial Quality Control,* October 1950, p. 25.
2. J. M. Juran, ed., *Quality Control Handbook,* First Edition New York. McGraw-Hill Book Company (1951), pp. 37–41.
3. The first published use of this term was likely in my paper, "Universals in Management Planning and Controlling," *The Management Review,* November 1954.
4. M. O. Lorenz, "Methods of Measuring the Concentration of Wealth," *American Statistical Association Publication,* 9 (1904–5): 200–219.

] 4 [

Determine Customer Needs

Purpose of This Chapter

The purpose of this chapter is to show how to determine the needs of customers.

The input-output diagram is shown in Figure 4–1.

The input is the list of customers as developed during Chapter Three.

The process consists of applying a broad variety of means for identifying the needs of customers, both external and internal.

The output is the list of customers' needs.

The Scope of Human Needs

Human needs seem to be unbounded, both in volume and in variety. Most human beings are acquisitive. Given the opportunity they will amass large domains of territory, large amounts of money, numerous servants, dictatorial political power, and so forth. Of course, most people never reach such states of dominance. The rest try, in more modest ways, to meet needs for survival, security, comfort, and so on. These needs keep expanding as affluence grows.

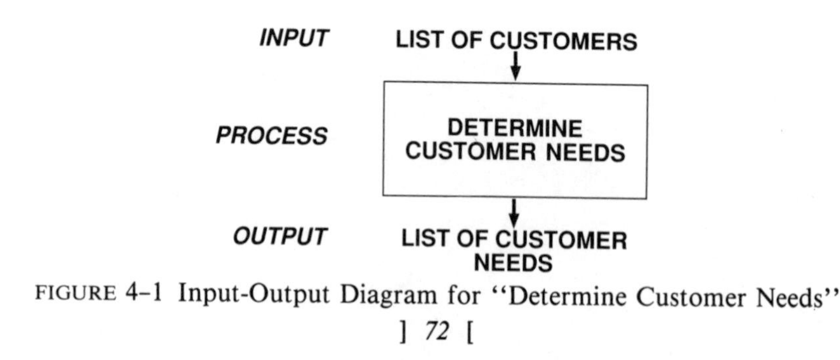

FIGURE 4–1 Input-Output Diagram for "Determine Customer Needs"

This complexity of human needs is further complicated by such variables as the prevailing culture of the society, the level of technology, and others. The resulting jungle of complications requires that before we talk of determining customer needs we first classify human needs in some logical way. Once we have such a classification it becomes easier to discuss how to identify customer needs and how to translate those needs into language that enables the suppliers to take responsive action.

There are various ways of classifying customer needs. In this book we have chosen a classification based on the following:

Stated needs
Real needs
Perceived needs
Cultural needs
Needs traceable to unintended use

Stated Needs and Real Needs

Customers commonly state their needs as seen from their viewpoint, and in their language. This is especially the case with those external customers who are also clients. A common example involves the purchase of goods.

Clients may state their needs in terms of the goods they wish to buy. However, their real needs are for the services those goods can provide. To illustrate:

Client Wishes to Buy	*Client Really Wants*
Food	Nourishment; pleasant taste
Automobile	Transportation
Color TV	Entertainment
House	Living space
House paint	Colorful appearance; freedom from maintenance

Failure to grasp the difference between stated needs and real needs can have serious consequences.

Two companies competed with each other for the market in sale of hair nets. (In those days such nets were used to hold women's hair in place following a visit to the hairdresser).

> The competitors focused their attention on the product progression—the kind and color of the fibers, the process for making the nets, the packaging, the sales channels, and so on. Both competitors became extinct when a chemist came up with a spray that could invisibly hold women's hair in place. Although the customers had said they wanted to buy hair nets, what they really needed was some adequate means for holding their hair in place.

The principle behind this difference (stated needs and real needs) was elaborated in a classic paper, "Marketing Myopia" (Levitt, 1975). Levitt stressed the distinction between product-orientation and customer-orientation. In his view, the railroads missed an opportunity for expansion because of their focus on railroading rather than on transportation. The moving picture studios similarly missed an opportunity to participate in the growing television industry as a result of their focus on movies rather than on entertainment.

It is evident that to understand the real needs of customers (clients in the above cases) requires answers to such questions as:

> Why are you buying this product?
>
> What service do you expect from it?

Perceived Needs

Customers understandably state their needs based on their perceptions. Some of those perceptions are product-related. Others may seem to have little to do with the product. Examination of such cases often suggests that there is a difference in perception, between customers and suppliers, as to what is included in the term "product." Each such difference between customers and suppliers is a potential troublemaker as well as an opportunity.

The service industries abound in instances in which customer perceptions differ from supplier perceptions of what constitutes product or quality.

> Two men are in need of haircuts. One goes to a barbershop inhabited by barbers. The other goes to a "salon" inhabited by "hair stylists." Each is shorn by a skilled artisan. Each emerges with essentially the same outward appearance. What differs is (a) the prices they have paid, and (b) their perceptions of what is included in "product."

The fast food industry has grown enormously based more on the speed of service than on the perceived quality of the food.

Public utilities and government tax collectors receive numerous complaints relative to the amount owed. They also receive numerous complaints relative to the complexity of the invoices and the forms.

Customers of gambling houses relate distorted perceptions about what happened to them during the encounter. Success stories are loudly proclaimed. Modest winnings are disclosed only with assurances that it was great fun. Nobody has suffered serious losses (Kahn, 1987).

To mail a letter requires buying a postage stamp costing (usually) less than a dollar. If the postage stamp has been printed imperfectly, it may have a perceived value running to thousands of dollars.

Such perceptions in the service industries have their counterparts in manufacture and in distribution. Again the cases abound.

There are factories in which chocolate-coated candies are carried by a belt to the packaging department. At the end of the belt are two teams of packagers. One team packs the chocolates into modest cardboard boxes destined for budget-priced merchant shops. The other team packs the chocolates into satin-lined wooden boxes destined to be sold in deluxe shops. The resulting price for a like amount of chocolate can differ by several fold. The respective purchasers encounter other differences as well: the decor, the extent of service, the box. However, the chocolates are identical. In fact, while a chocolate is still on the belt, it has no way of predicting whether it will end up in a budget shop or in a deluxe shop.

A steel mill lost some of its sales of stainless steel for reasons unrelated to the quality of the steel. The client in question was a machine shop that made stainless steel fittings to be sold to companies in the aerospace industry. These companies stressed cleanliness in the workshops. (Some of those fittings were on the moon.) The machine shop observed that the stainless steel as received was dirty, oily, and wrapped in a nondescript manner. In contrast, a competing steel mill delivered its steel in a clean, neatly wrapped condition. When the steel company's salesmen explained all this to its factory personnel, the reaction was: "The steel will make good fittings. The customer is crazy."

A merchant (Stew Leonard) who displayed his fish in transparent wrappings encountered consumer resistance. All clients wanted fresh fish, but some were suspicious—to them, wrapped fish were less than fresh. The merchant then created an additional display case in which unwrapped fish were displayed on ice. That satisfied the resistant customers. Other customers preferred the wrapped fish. But all the fish, wrapped and unwrapped, had been bought that same morning at the Fulton Fish Market. In this case the real need was fresh fish. Some customers had the perception that only unwrapped fish were fresh. Other customers accepted on faith that the wrapped fish were fresh. The merchant designed his affairs to satisfy all customers' perceptions.

Note in the cases of the haircuts and the chocolates that some customers pay handsomely for perceived differences. The suppliers accept this reality and organize matters to take advantage of it. Some suppliers may consider the customers' perceptions as "unreal," but in such cases it is the suppliers who may pay handsomely. In other cases the suppliers design a new approach so as to respond to the customers' perceived needs.

Cultural Needs

The needs of customers, especially internal customers, go beyond products and processes. They include needs for self-respect, respect of others, continuity of habit patterns, and still other elements of what is broadly called the cultural pattern. A great deal of failure to determine what customer needs are is traceable to failure to understand the nature and even the existence of this cultural pattern.

The concept of cultural patterns may be summarized about as follows:

Every organization is also a human society. Large organizations harbor many such societies.

Every human society evolves a pattern of beliefs, habits, practices, etc., based on its accumulated experience. This is known as the cultural pattern.

This pattern provides the society with certain elements of stability: a system of law and order, explanation of mysteries, rituals, taboos, status symbols, and so on. These elements are viewed by the society as possessing important values.

Any proposed change becomes a threat to these important values and hence will be resisted until the nature of the threat is understood.

The resistance is not limited to the organized societies. It extends to the individual members who may feel that their personal values are threatened.

Sometimes these cultural needs make headlines.

> In 1986 the Bank of Canada issued a series of paper money bills of five-dollar denomination. The design included a picture of the parliament buildings and a flag flying from the tower. Close examination (using a magnifying glass or superb eyesight) disclosed that the flag was not the Canadian Maple Leaf; it was a flag left over from the British era. There was a sharp protest from the French Canadian sector.

In other cases the cultural needs are not stated openly. Instead, they are stated in disguised form. A widespread example relates to "turf," that is, the "ownership" of some area of responsibility, expertise, or the like. Such ownership confers status; a threat to the ownership is a threat to that status.

> A proposed new process threatens to eliminate the need for some human expertise; the expertise will be built into the technology. The present human experts will resist introduction of the new process. Their stated reasons will be on plausible grounds—the effect on costs, on other customer needs, etc. The one reason they will not give is: "This change will reduce my status." Yet that may be the real reason.

Similarly, there may be resistance to the creation of teams to conduct analyses in areas formerly regarded as a monopoly of some expert analyst. The "Not Invented Here" syndrome is traceable to this same fierce protection of turf.

We should look for the real reasons behind the stated reasons. In the case of cultural resistance, the real reasons are seldom obvious; the disguises are usually subtle. We should also look beyond the stated reasons to understand what are the potential threats to the cultural patterns of the human beings involved. It is often possible to meet the objections while also meeting company needs (see Chapter 12, under "Dealing with Cultural Resistance: Rules of the Road"; see also Juran, 1964).

Needs Traceable to Unintended Use

Many quality failures arise because the customer uses the product in a manner different from that intended by the supplier. This practice takes many forms:

Untrained workers are assigned to processes requiring trained workers.

Equipment is overloaded or is allowed to run without adherence to maintenance schedules.

Documents are misfiled.

Automobile bodies rust because the designers are not aware that they will be exposed to use of salt on the roads.

The toll-free number intended for use as a "hot line" is used for making routine inquiries.

What is critical in all this is whether the quality planning should proceed based on *intended use or actual use.* The latter often requires adding a factor of safety during the planning:

Fuses and circuit breakers are designed into electrical circuits for protection against overloads.

Software is written to detect spelling errors.

Public utility invoicing may be designed to guard against errors in reading the meters, by providing a check against the prior history of usage.

Such factors of safety may add to the cost. Yet they may well result in an optimal overall cost by helping to avoid the higher cost arising from actual use or misuse. What is essential is to learn:

What will be the actual use (and misuse)

What are the associated costs

What are the consequences of adhering to intended use

Acquiring such information obviously requires close teamwork between supplier and customer.

Customer Needs Related to Product Satisfaction

A further classification of customer needs is the separation of those needs as between product satisfaction and product dissatisfaction. Both of these species must be considered during the journey on the quality planning road map. (For elaboration of the distinction between product satisfaction and product dissatisfaction, see Chapter 1, under "The Need for Unity of Language").

The Influence of Technology

During 1986 the Cooper-Hewitt Museum in New York City staged an exhibition of influential consumer products that had emerged in the years 1936 to 1986. The title was "I'll Buy That: 50 Years of Goods and Services." There were fifty products in the list. Most of them were goods that had originated in the laboratories of technology: antibiotics, color TV, frozen foods, personal computers. The list also included about a dozen services: air travel, credit cards, health insurance, Social Security. (The exhibition catalog *I'll Buy That* was published by Consumer Report Books, 1986.)

Those products (and a great many others) have provided remarkable benefits to human beings who live in developed countries. However, those same human beings have become dependent on the continuing performance of those same products. Any break in that continuity (of power supply, telephone service, transportation, etc.) results in crises, which range from the irritating many to the terrifying few.

That same dependence has in turn created new categories of customer needs as well as revising the relative importance of older categories. It is useful to look at several of the more important categories.

Human Safety

Technology places dangerous products into the hands of amateurs. It also creates dangerous by-products that threaten human health, safety, and the environment. The extent of all this is so great that much of the effort of product and process planning must be directed at reducing these risks to an acceptable level. Numerous laws, criminal and civil, mandate such efforts. Extensive training is carried out to enable the planners to make such efforts effective.

"User Friendly"

The "amateur" status of many users has given rise to the term "user friendly" to describe that product feature which enables amateurs to make ready use of technological products. For example:

> The language of published information should be simple, unambiguous and readily understood. Notorious offenders have included legal documents, owners' operating manuals, forms to be filled out, etc. Widely used forms (e.g., federal tax returns) should be field tested on a sample of the very people who will later be faced with filling out the forms.

> Products should be broadly compatible. Much of this has been done through standardization committees or through natural monopolies such as the telephone system. An example of lack of such compatibility during the 1980s was the personal computer. Many personal computers were able to "talk" to computers made by the same manufacturer but not to computers made by other manufacturers.

Promptness of Service

Services should be prompt. In some cultures a major element of competition is promptness of service. (The growth of the fast food industry is based mainly on such promptness). Interlocking schedules (as in mail delivery or in airline travel) are another source of a growing demand for promptness. Still another example is the growing use of "just in time" manufacture, which requires dependable deliveries of materials in order to minimize inventories.

All such examples demonstrate the need to include the time element in planning to meet customer needs.

Keeping Customers Informed

Customers are quite sensitive to being "victimized" by secret actions of a supplier. When such secrets are later discovered and publicized, the damage to the supplier's quality image can be considerable.

> In a highly publicized case, Oldsmobile cars were being delivered containing Chevrolet engines. In due course the manufacturer made restitution, but not before suffering much adverse publicity.

> It has long been common practice for auto makers, as part of their source of quality assurance data, to supply new vehicles to employees (managers and engineers) to be driven over the weekend for the purpose of logging performance data. During the mid-1980s it was discovered that Chrysler Corporation's practice included disconnecting the odometers during these tests. As a result, buyers of these cars were unknowingly getting a car somewhat less than new. To make matters worse, cars that suffered damage during the tests were assertedly repaired and nevertheless sold as new. In due course the company offered restitution, but it endured adverse publicity as well as a federal indictment (Holusha, 1987).

The above cases are examples of a whole host of instances in which nonconforming products are being shipped to unwary customers. In the great majority of cases, the products are fit for use despite the nonconformances. In other cases the matter may be debatable. In still other cases the act of shipment is at the least unethical and at the worst illegal.

What is common to all is that the customer is not informed. The most usual reason for this omission is a default, a failure to raise the question: What shall we tell the customers? It would be most helpful if every nonconformance document included a blank space headed "What is to be communicated to the customers?" The decision may well be to communicate nothing, but at least the question has been faced.

Customer Needs Related to Product Dissatisfaction

In the event of product failure, a new set of customer needs emerges: how to get service restored, and how to get compensated for the associated losses and inconvenience.

Clearly, the ideal solution to all this is to plan quality in ways such that there will be no failures. We shall have a look at that in Chapter 6, "Develop Product Features," and Chapter 7, "Develop Process Features." At this point we shall look at what customer needs are when failures do occur.

Warranties

The laws governing sales imply certain warranties given by the supplier. In simple societies these implied warranties were reasonably effective. In more complex societies it has become necessary to provide specific, written contracts to define just what is covered by the warranty, and for how long a time. In addition it should be clear who has what responsibilities.

For some years these matters were vaguely described in many written warranties. Often this vagueness was intentional. Then, during the 1970s, legislation was enacted to reduce this vagueness, and the result has been positive. However, the service actually provided on warranties varies remarkably. The media often have a field day reporting the horror stories, but thorough researches have made clear that in the aggregate the service on warranties has been less than satisfactory (Center for Policy Alternatives, 1974).

Meanwhile, the use of warranties as a tool for competition has intensified. Extension of warranty coverage increases costs unless action has been taken to design products and processes so as to reduce the incidence of field failures. Such action transfers the competition to the original planning, which is where it should be (see Juran, 1988, Section 19, under "Business Opportunities Through Warranties").

Improving Service on Customer Complaints

Response to customer complaints has been studied extensively. These studies have identified the key features of a good response system and have indicated how to design a service plan that meets customer needs (see Juran, 1988, Section 20, "Customer Service," and United States Office of Consumer Affairs, 1985–86).

Once such a service plan has been installed there remains the problem of assuring that the service departments follow the plan. Changing the procedures is not enough. There must also be changes in priorities, in reporting of service performance, in the reward system, and so on. In the absence of such changes, the likelihood is that the former priorities will remain in place.

> A major automobile manufacturer undertook to improve customer service on warranties (and on other matters). In that industry the service on warranties is typically provided by the dealers who sell the vehicles. However, the manufacturer oversees the performance of the dealers, including the performance of their service departments. In this case the manufacturer raised the weight given to quality during the rating of service department performance. The new weight

became 50 percent—the weight given to quality of service was now as great as the weight of all other parameters combined.

Effect of Complaint Handling on Sales

While complaints deal primarily with product dissatisfaction, there is a side effect on salability. This effect has been researched in studies commissioned by the Office of Consumer Affairs and carried out by Technical Assistance Research Programs Institute (TARP). The findings may be summarized as follows:

Of the customers who were dissatisfied with products, nearly 70 percent did not complain. The proportions who did complain varied depending on the type of product involved. The reasons for not complaining were principally the effort to complain was not worth it; the belief that complaining would do no good; lack of knowledge of how to complain.

Over 40 percent of the complaining customers were unhappy with the responsive action taken by the suppliers. Here again the percentage varied depending on the type of product involved.

Future salability is strongly influenced by the action taken on complaints.

Figure 4–2 shows broadly the nature of consumer behavior following product dissatisfaction.

This strong influence extends to brand loyalty. Figures 4–3a, 4–3b, and 4–3c show the extent of this influence as applied to "large ticket" durable goods, financial services, and automobile services respectively. A similar strong influence extends also to product line loyalty.

That same research concluded that an organized approach to complaint handling provides a high return on investment. The elements of such an organized approach may include:

A response center staffed to provide twenty-four-hour access by consumers

A toll-free telephone number

A computerized data base

Special training for the personnel who answer the telephones

Active solicitation of complaints to minimize loss of customers in the future

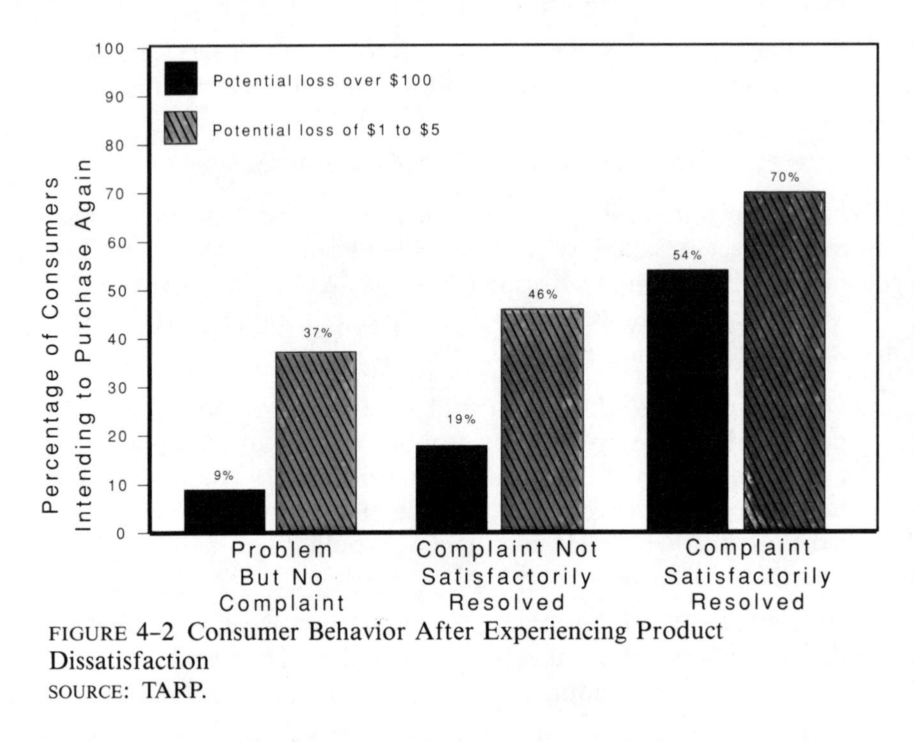

FIGURE 4-2 Consumer Behavior After Experiencing Product Dissatisfaction
SOURCE: TARP.

For fuller detail, see the full report. (United States Office of Consumer Affairs, 1985–86).

Keeping Customers Informed (Again)

Customers also have a need to be kept informed in cases involving product dissatisfaction. There are many situations in which an interruption in service will force customers to wait for an indefinite period until service is restored. Obvious examples are power outages or delays in public transportation. In all such cases the customers become restive. They are unable to solve the problem—they must leave that to the supplier. Yet they want to be kept informed as to the nature of the problem and especially as to the likely time of solution. Many suppliers are derelict in keeping such customers informed and thereby suffer a decline in their quality image.

> The New York subway system rules require conductors to explain all delays lasting two minutes or more. One survey reported that this rule was followed only about 40 percent of the time. A City Hall report concluded that ''shortage of

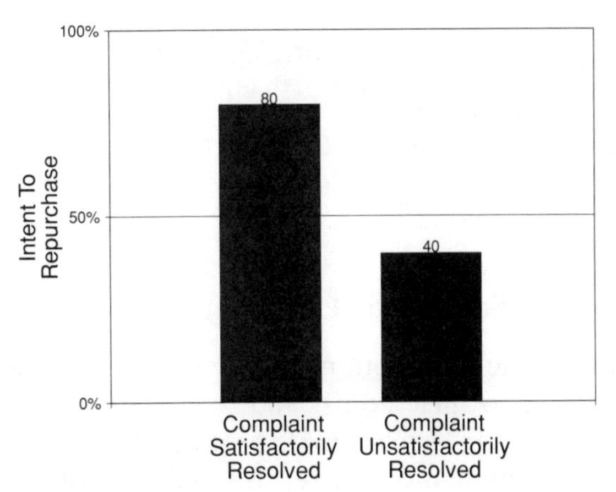

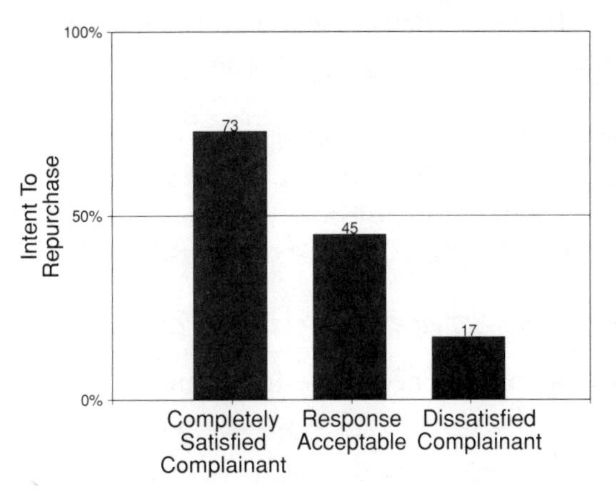

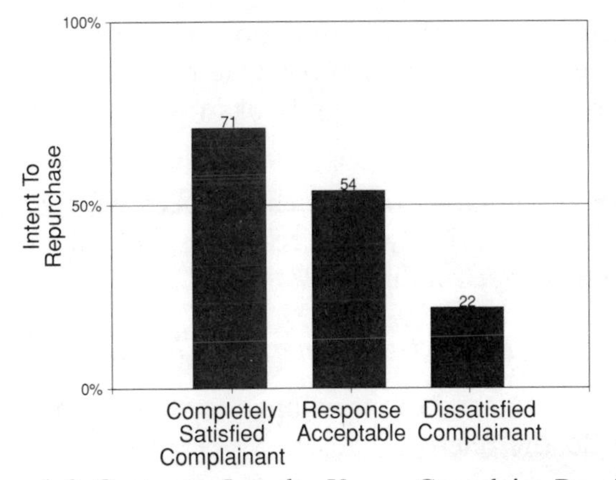

FIGURE 4–3 Customer Loyalty Versus Complaint Resolution
SOURCE: TARP.

> information is a significant source of public antagonism toward the Transit Authority'' (Levine, 1987).

In contrast, some airlines go to pains to keep their customers informed of the reasons for a delay, and of the progress being made in providing a remedy.

Sources of Customer Needs

The most simplistic assumption is that customers are completely knowledgeable as to their needs, and that market research can be used to extract this information from them. In practice, customer knowledge can be quite incomplete. In some cases the customer may be the last person to find out. It is unlikely that any customer ever expressed the need for a ''Walkman'' (a miniature portable audiotape player) before such devices came on the market. Once they became available, however, many customers discovered that they needed one.

These gaps in customer knowledge are filled in mainly by the forces of the competitive market and by the actions of entrepreneurs. It is useful to examine some of these forces and actions before looking at the methodology used to discover customer needs.

Available Services Is Regarded as Inadequate

In such cases customers' needs are for something better, whether a better product or the same product from a superior source of supply.

> The number of licensed New York taxicabs has remained frozen for years. The resulting vacuum in service has been filled by unlicensed cabs, limousines, and so on.

> Government instructions for filling out tax forms have been less than clear to many taxpayers. One result has been the publication of some best-selling books on how to prepare tax returns.

> The service provided by tradesmen has been widely regarded as expensive and untimely. One result has been the growth of a large do-it-yourself industry.

Relief from Onerous Chores

There seems to be no end to the willingness of affluent people to pay someone to do the onerous chores. Much former kitchen work is now being done in factories (soluble coffee, canned foods, and a lengthy list of etc.'s). The prices of the processed foods are often several times the prices of the raw food. Yet to do the processing at home involves working for a very low hourly rate. Cleaning chores have been extensively transferred to household appliances. The end is not in sight. The same kinds of transfer have taken place on a massive scale with respect to industrial chores, for example, data processing and materials handling.

Reduction of Time for Service

Some cultures exhibit an urge to "get it over with." In such cultures those who can serve customers in the shortest time are rewarded by higher share of market. A spectacular example of this urge is the growth of the "fast food" market. In other industries a major consideration in choice of supplier is the time spent to get served. An example is choice of automobile filling stations (see Ackoff, 1978, Fable 5.4, p. 108). This same need for prompt service is an essential element in the urge to go to "Just in Time" manufacture.

Changes in Customer Habits

Customer habits can be notoriously fickle. An obvious example is fashions in clothing. The existence of such variation in needs gives rise to a proliferation of offerings by suppliers along with some unpredictable responses by customers. Concerns over health have reduced the consumption of beef and increased that of poultry. New types of beer, promoted by extensive advertising, have resulted in large shifts of share of market. The taste for pizzas has created a surge in volume of sales, along with a proliferation of kinds of pizza. These shifts in fashions are not limited to consumers. Industrial companies launch drives, most of which briefly take center stage and then fade away. The associated "buzz words" similarly come and go.

Role of the Entrepreneur

The entrepreneur plays a vital role in providing customers with new versions of existing products. In addition, the entrepreneur identifies new products, some of them unheard of, which might create customer needs where none have existed previously. It is a risky way of life, since those new products have a shocking rate of mortality.

However, the rewards can be shockingly high, and this is what attracts the independent entrepreneur. Moreover, the entrepreneurs can make use of the power of advertising and promotion, which some do very effectively. The legendary Charles Revson, founder of Revlon, stated it somewhat as follows: "In our factory we make lipstick. In our advertising we sell hope." (For additional discussion, see Juran, 1988, "Discovering Market Opportunities," pp. 12.20–12.24.)

How to Discover Customer Needs

We now turn to the processes used to discover customer needs. The principal methods include:

Be a customer

Study customer behavior

Communicate with customers

Simulate customer use

Note that a great deal of discovery of customer needs does *not* come directly from customers. Much of it comes through indirect means. However, the confirmation of those needs will in due course come from customer decisions to buy or not to buy the product features developed in response to the presumed needs.

Be a Customer

The best way to discover customer needs is to be a customer.

To an astonishing degree, people *are* their own customers. The most obvious form is the independent craftsman. Consider the village cooper—let's call him Coop. He starts with an oak tree and ends up with a barrel. To do so he performs a long series of tasks: product design, process planning, selection of materials, numerous production operations, maintenance of tools, product inspection and test, marketing, customer service, billing and collection, and so on. As the work progresses *Coop becomes his own customer, over and over again*. There is no surer way of discovering what the needs of customers are. And there is no shorter feedback loop. All those direct, multiple feedbacks go far to explain why Coop has become so surefooted in meeting customers' needs.

We can generalize Coop's case to represent any situation in which a worker performs a series of interrelated tasks: physicians, nurses, maintenance workers, many office workers, housewives. A major commonality is that they all are their own customers, over and over again. The benefits to quality are considerable. These benefits become more obvious when processes are changed so as to enable people to become their own customers.

Every telephone company produces numerous telephone directories, one for each city served. In one telephone company the directories were prepared for publication using a sequence of twenty-one clerical steps, each step being performed by a separate employee. (Some steps required more than one person's full time, so the total department consisted of thirty-three employees.) A reorganization gave each employee the job of preparing a complete telephone directory, i.e., each person performed all the twenty-one clerical steps needed to do the job. The results of the change were stunning:

	Before	*After*
Annual turnover of employees	28	0
Absenteeism rate	2.8%	0.6%
Errors per 1,000 lines	3.9%	1.1%

Similar results have been observed when a factory assembly line is abolished, and the workers then assemble complete units from bits and pieces. Still other cases involve setting up self-supervising teams, whether in the office or in the factory. Here *the team* is its own customer, over and over again.

In all these cases, being one's own customer provides multiple benefits to quality:

The feedback loop for detecting symptoms of problems involves only one person.

The discovery of cause-and-effect relationships is simplified—the symptom of trouble is conveyed to a person who presides over many potential causes.

The climate for taking remedial action is favorable since there is direct benefit to the person taking the action.

Being a customer also provides direct information on how customers spend their time, which activities demand most of their assets, which are the disagreeable chores, and which are the unsolved problems. As we saw, knowledge of such matters is a major input to those who are on the lookout for marketable new products.

> Decades ago housewives prepared coffee from green coffee beans. They first roasted the beans. They then ground the roasted beans in a mill. Then the coffee had to be brewed, after which the residue had to be disposed of. Whether the final product was always superior is briskly debated. At any rate, every housewife knew that all this work was time consuming; that sometimes the beans were poorly roasted; that the brews varied; and that there was always a mess to clean up. The food processing companies also knew these things. Hence the stage was set for the development of soluble coffee.

Study Customer Behavior

Customer behavior is a better predictor of future customer actions than what customers say. So it becomes important to distinguish between customer behavior and customer opinions. Customer behavior consists of deeds carried out in real time and in the real world of push and pull. Customer opinions are leading indicators that are subject to revision later when the realities are faced.

Customer Actions Related to Dissatisfactions

One category of such actions consists of the familiar complaints about product deficiencies such as incorrect billing or field failures of goods. Another example is employee grievances, some of which are related to dissatisfaction. Public dissatisfactions are evident in letters to the editor, protest meetings, and lawsuits.

In such cases it is common practice to verify the validity of the complaint and, if valid, to satisfy the complainant. What is much less common is to analyze the complaints *collectively* to discover whether there is some underlying cause that is inherent in the system, remains in place, and will breed a continuing procession of dissatisfactions in the future. *Such inherent causes were planned that way,* and the remedy is replanning, starting with reviewing what the needs of the customers are.

Customer Actions Relating to Sales Income

Much customer behavior gets translated into an effect on supplier income:

Sales for certain product lines decline or increase

Price premiums are resisted or are accepted

Success in bidding declines or rises

Such fluctuations are usually the result of customer behavior. In some cases that behavior is quality-related. If this is verified by analysis, it requires going back to the quality planning road map.

There are numerous other forms of customer behavior that provide suppliers with a basis for initiatives in quality planning or replanning. For example:

Some customers require that their suppliers comply with certain mandated features of a quality system. Failure to comply risks loss of the business.

Sale of spare parts is typically a source of generous profits for suppliers. At the same time it is a major irritation for customers, since it is associated with product failures, down time, or costly maintenance. Increasingly the profitable spare parts business is discovered to be a fool's paradise, since the market in due course is taken over by competitors whose products do not fail.

Customer purchase of options is a leading indicator of what should become standard equipment in the future.

Direct Observation

In still other cases the study of customer behavior is based on direct observation.

> Marriott Hotels observed that guests were ignoring complimentary bath crystals. So the company dropped them in favor of another free feature—cable television—which was far better received.

In some cases it is feasible to conduct direct observation by nonhuman means. The television industry makes wide use of electronic devices that record the viewing habits of a sample of the public. The resulting data are the basis of "rating" the programs as to extent of viewer participation. In turn these ratings are decisive as to the salability of the associated advertising.

A delightful example of study of customer behavior takes place in playrooms used by toy companies for testing new toys. Children are turned loose in these rooms while engineers with clipboards and stopwatches observe the play from behind one-way mirrors. Later the engineers study the damage done. From these observations the companies are able to answer questions relating to:

Risks of injury

Ease of use; manner of use and misuse

Length of the attention span

Damage during use

(For additional cases, see Sellers, 1989.)

Still another kind of study of customer behavior consists of *terminating services* in order to see whether anyone protests. For example, reports that once served a useful purpose may no longer be needed because conditions have changed. One way to discover this is to stop publishing the reports and then see who protests.

> Some newspapers have stopped publishing certain features (such as comic strips) only to be overwhelmed by complaints from loyal fans. These complaints reflected the existence of a level of customer behavior to an extent which required reinstatement of the comic strips (Hughes, 1988).

Analyze Available Field Intelligence

The term "*field intelligence*" is used here in the generic sense of any information that relates to product performance and to its impact on customers.*

Some of this information routinely comes to companies from personnel who have regular contact with customers: sales personnel, technical representatives, and so on. Some customers regularly evaluate supplier performance and send the evaluations back to the re-

**A note on nomenclature:* The term "market research" has often been used as a label for the process of securing information from *clients*. The word "market" has usually been regarded as synonymous with *potential sales*. In our use of the term "field intelligence" the word "field" is used in the broader sense of the area occupied by all customers, whether clients or not, whether external or internal.

spective suppliers. Some data are available from government bodies acting in their capacity as regulators or as purchasers. Some independent laboratories make comparative tests of quality of competing products and publish the results.

These and other data sources require analysis to convert them into useable form. Some companies are organized to make such analyses; others are not. We shall shortly look at this critical need for organization.

Create New Field Intelligence

The information that "comes naturally" seldom provides adequate field intelligence. To fill the gap it is necessary to create supplemental sources tailored to the special needs of the company. The first step in creating such sources is to identify the questions to which answers are needed. Some questions appear in virtually all lists:

Which product features are of major importance to you?

As to these key features, how does our product compare to that of our competitors?

What is the significance of these quality differences to you, in money or in other ways that might be important to you?

Beyond such basic questions the list can broaden considerably. It may include such matters as:

Environments of use

Failure data, including exact failure modes

Information on users' costs

The answers to such questions are needed by various functional departments of the supplier: product development, process development, operations, marketing, customer service, and so forth. As a corollary, these same functional departments are the proper source of the list of questions to which answers are needed. A usual organized approach is to appoint a multifunctional team to design the data plan. The team identifies the questions to which answers are needed. In addition the team identifies those existing data which, upon analysis, can provide some answers. As to the rest, the team is faced with creating new sources of data.

Note that under the Big Q concept, *the "field" includes internal customers.* For these internal customers there is the same need to identify the questions to which answers are needed, the available sources of answers, the new sources required, and so on.

Data Sources

There are numerous ways of creating new sources of field intelligence. Here are some examples:

Enlarge the data-collecting responsibilities of personnel who are already in contact with customers.

Establish "controlled use" of the product. The data sources get free use of the product but must pay in data.

Establish data systems at captive service centers.

Buy data from customers. For example, contract with a sample of customers to provide field performance information under an agreed data recording plan.

Design automated data monitors to record operating data.

Note: Data sources should include former clients and nonclients. The "exit interview" can be used to secure information from departing clients. In the case of nonclients, the basic purpose is to discover why they are someone else's clients.

Tools of Data Collection

Many such tools have been specially designed to serve the needs of field intelligence. The more widely used include:

Mailed questionnaires. The responses are normally only a few percent of the total, but this sample may nevertheless include information of a decisive nature.

Feedback questionnaires. These are widely used in hotels, restaurants, and elsewhere to secure feedback from patrons who have just received service.

Telephone calls. These are used on a sampling basis to secure information in depth.

Visits to customers. Such visits have long been made by personnel from Sales, Customer Service and other traditional channels of contact. Visits to the vital few customers have often been made by upper managers.

> In one company, upper managers regularly visit complaining customers who have been chosen at random. (Such visits expose the manager to the "passion" as well as the facts, as in the case of a visit to a highway police officer whose "handie talkie" failed during a critical situation). These upper managers then "own" the problem and must get it resolved by working in the system without invoking rank. Their exposure to the system then leads to improvements in the system.

Partnerships. If the need for field intelligence is mutual as between supplier and customer, it becomes useful to establish *joint teams.* Some of these partnerships have led to solution of long-standing problems that would otherwise remain unsolved (see, for example, Kegarise and Miller, 1985).

Focus groups. These are variously called panels, advisory groups, advisory committees, etc. They are organized to provide companies with a source of customer group opinion. Such groups have consisted of consumers, merchants, hospital nurses, etc. They meet face to face with a skilled moderator. Part of the time they address a prepared agenda. Thereafter they take up whatever is on their minds. (For examples, see Bennett, 1986).

Use of Sampling

A common mistake in planning is to go after all relevant data when sampling could provide an adequate basis for decision making. Many well-intentioned comprehensive plans have been introduced only to fall of their own weight. They fail through sheer bulk—they become a new major problem. They also fail because much added work is imposed without providing added resources. Use of sampling reduces both of these risks of failure.

The sampling concept provides a practical, economic way for securing information, especially from the useful many customers. For example, we may contact all of the useful many customers through a questionnaire that focuses on selected quality needs. Alternatively, we may select a sample of the useful many customers, contact each in depth, and then draw broad conclusions from the results of the sampling.

Application of the sampling concept requires the use of certain special tools and skills in matters such as:

Choice of sample (the "panel"), whether at random, stratified, etc.

Conditions prevailing during collection of information, whether natural or controlled

Sample sizes that assure statistical significance

Avoidance of bias during data collection

The Influence of Who Is the Customer

Customers vary in multiple ways. They may be external or internal. They may be merchants, processors, or ultimate users. They vary extensively in economic importance. These and other variations influence not only the kind of intelligence needed but also the methods of securing that intelligence.

Vital Few Customers

Obvious examples include large original equipment manufacturers (OEMs), large merchant chains, government regulatory bodies, the media, and labor unions. Vital few internal customers include the upper managers.

Many of these customers take the initiative in stating their needs; some of them are quite assertive. Nevertheless the supplier should take steps to go beyond the stated needs. The goal should be customer satisfaction rather than mere conformance to stated needs.

The great importance of the vital few customers demands that each be contacted in depth, using (usually) any of several approaches:

1. "Make the rounds" to visit each customer and to secure that customer's perception of needs.

A quality manager undertook to update the company's package of managerial reports on quality. A part of his planning consisted of sitting down with each corporate officer to raise such questions as "What information do you need on quality in order to carry out your responsibility as a corporate officer?" The resulting inputs were helpful in establishing a consensus on what should be the contents of the report package.

2. Conduct an in-depth review of proposals with a sample of the customers.

From time to time the Bureau of Labor Statistics (BLS) proposes changes to the basis for computing the consumer price index (CPI). For example, BLS may propose to reflect population shifts by revising the list of cities from which price information is gathered; or BLS may propose to measure the cost of housing by rental cost rather than asset cost. As BLS prepares its proposal for revisions, it meets with a number of its customers (i.e., users of the CPI) to review the proposed revisions.

3. Convene a conference of such customers, a few at a time, to discuss in depth their perception of the needs.

While preparing the first edition of this book, the author convened a conference of trainers and quality managers from some twenty-five companies. Each of the companies was a potential customer for the completed text; each invitee was a potential trainer/facilitator. An agenda, distributed in advance of the conference, consisted of a large number of specific questions on the content and its application. The questions were designed to elicit specific information and to stimulate discussion. The conference proved to be a valuable aid to discovering the needs of potential customers and to shaping the text to meet their needs.

Processors

These customers are also *users.* They employ our product in their processes. In their capacity as users, their needs include worker safety, high productivity, low waste, and still other forms of internal goals. The processors then sell their products to *their* customers, whose needs may be quite different. In effect *there are two lists of customer needs,* and our product may impact some of the items on each list. In cases involving multiple successive processing companies, our product may impact multiple lists.

Our customers usually supply us with some information relative to certain of their customers' needs that must be met by our product. However, this information is sometimes limited to product dissatisfaction, or is otherwise incomplete. In such cases we may need to go beyond our customers and conduct research to determine more fully the needs of the subsequent levels of customers.

Merchants

As with processors, our product impacts multiple levels of customers: our clients, our clients' clients, and so forth. If we sell to many merchants, it can become prohibitive to contact each one in depth. Instead, resort can be had to sampling through a "Dealers' Council."

In some cases the "merchants" buy for ultimate use, e.g., hospitals who buy medical devices and supplies. There the council typically consists of specialists (e.g., physicians and nurses) from a variety of disciplines, and is designated by a broad name such as Professional Council.

Nonclients

It is easy to be fooled if we confine our data search to clients.

> A chemicals manufacturer asked its clients to rank the company relative to its competitors on various aspects of performance: product innovation, quality, promptness of delivery, technical assistance, among others. The company was quite pleased to learn that it was ranked first, second, or third in virtually all aspects of performance.
>
> Then someone noted that the study was biased: *it included no nonclients.* So a supplemental research was conducted, with special attention to former clients: Why had they stopped buying? This time the research findings were not so pleasing but were most informative.

Failure to include former clients and nonclients in such studies has led to serious errors in judging competitive status.

Consumers

To some degree, we can secure information about consumer reaction from intermediaries such as merchants or salespersons. However, these intermediate sources can and do introduce bias into the data. In consequence, if there is enough at stake, we should arrange to secure information direct from consumers.

Contact with consumers is carried out using some of the tools described above under "Tools of Data Collection."

An example is Qantas Airlines' survey of 2,500 passengers to secure their views on priority of "essential needs." The results (see box) contained surprises as well as confirmations. For example, the company managers had given high ranking to on-time departures and arrivals. It came as a surprise that these needs were not given high priority by the passengers surveyed.

	Qantas Airways *Survey of Passenger Needs* *Order of Priority*
	"Essential Needs"
1.	No lost baggage
2.	No damaged baggage
3.	Clean toilets
4.	Comfortable seats
5.	Prompt baggage delivery
6.	Ample leg room
7.	Good quality meals
8.	Prompt reservation service
9.	Friendly/efficient cabin crew
10.	Clean and tidy cabin
11.	Comfortable cabin temperature/humidity
12.	Assistance with connections
13.	Being kept informed of delays
14.	Transport to cities
15.	Accurate arrival information to relatives/friends
16.	Well-organized boarding
17.	Quick/friendly airport check-in
18.	Self-service baggage trolleys
19.	One-time arrival
20.	Provision of pillows/rugs
21.	Assistance with customs/immigration
22.	On-time departures

The Public

The public is impacted by companies' actions, and hence the public is a customer. Most of the needs of this customer are negative in nature—the need is for the company to refrain from certain actions that have a negative impact. The public makes these needs known by taking initiatives: direct communications to the company, letters to the editor, and protest meetings. In some cases these initiatives give a distorted picture: they represent only a small vocal minority.

In other cases, however, a broad problem may be in the making. In that event it may be well to conduct a structured public opinion survey to secure a more balanced, quantified understanding of the public's perception. (Some companies do not wait for matters to reach a problem state. They conduct periodic public opinion surveys to discover trends long before they grow into crises.)

Public opinion surveys are carried out in much the same way as any other search for field intelligence. Identify the questions to which answers are needed. Then contact a sample of the public to secure the answers. The sampling methods follow those used for discovering the needs of any large population.

Internal Customers

Internal customers also have needs, and these vary depending on level in the hierarchy, functional responsibilities, and so on.

1. *Upper Managers.* Their principal needs closely resemble the quality goals of the company: products that are salable, quality leadership, low cost of poor quality. Each upper manager also has personal needs: to be respected as a successful manager, to progress as to responsibility, and so on. Meeting the company goals is usually a prerequisite to meeting those personal goals.
2. *Middle Managers and Supervisors.* They typically represent about 10 percent of the employee population, but their influence on quality is considerable. This great influence demands that these customers be consulted in depth as to the needs of their respective organizations with respect to quality. Determining the needs of these managers is done in two major ways:
   i. *A multidepartmental team.* Such teams are quite effective for determining the needs of internal customers. The team members are of course experts as to their respective areas of the flow diagram, the inputs to those areas, the processes carried out in those areas, the resulting products, and the immediate customers for those products. However, the team members are not necessarily expert with respect to other areas of the flow diagram and the resulting mutual interactions. A multidepartmental team makes it possible for all members to broaden their view. In doing so they are able to propound questions which, when answered, clarify the mutual needs.

A manufacturer of instruments created a multidepartmental team to replan the process for developing new products. For some team members the project was a revelation. They learned things they had never known about the process. They appreciated being consulted about matters that had long been troublesome. The end result was improved teamwork as well as an improved process.

Most companies formalize the findings of such teams by writing them into the procedures. Some companies go further. Written *contracts* are prepared to record the agreements, much like service contracts between separate companies. (Putting the needs into written contract form forces the parties to think them out with greater thoroughness.)

Quite often the impacted departments are in *different companies.* In theory the same team concept should be applied. In practice this is difficult, especially in an adversary environment. The most common forms of such collaboration include:

Joint teams of supplier and customer personnel

Customers' visits to suppliers' locations to learn about suppliers' problems while providing information about customers' needs

Suppliers' visits to customers' locations to acquire information concerning needs

Trained specialists' visits to locations of both suppliers and customers, later to report for the information of all

ii. *Making the rounds.* In this approach a specialist is assigned to contact those departments which are significantly impacted by the project undergoing planning. Based on the findings, the specialist prepares a draft which is then sent to the managers for review.

3. *The Workers.* This is a large body of internal customers with much expertise relative to their jobs. This expertise can be a valuable input to quality planning, but special steps are needed to overcome certain inherent biases which may be present:

   An atmosphere of blame. If present it always inhibits the free flow of communications.

   The supervisor–subordinate relationship. The fact that the boss asks the question tends to influence the answer given by the subordinate.

Conflict in loyalties. Workers may be wary of communicating information that might create problems for their colleagues, for the union, etc.

These same biases also interfere with upward communication of employee needs and ideas. Among the tools used to get through this interference is the employee survey. Through this survey the methods used to gather field intelligence from external customers are applied to internal customers (for some examples, see Reibstein, 1986).

Design of the workplace is obviously something of great importance to employees. Some companies have taken special precautions to assure customer satisfaction on so sensitive a matter. When Union Carbide was constructing its Corporate Headquarters in Danbury, Connecticut, it faced the problem of design of offices for the personnel. The company constructed fifteen models of offices to provide a range of choice of furniture, colors, etc. (Becker and Hoogesteger, 1986).

Discovery of the needs of internal customers requires special alertness to the *cultural needs* discussed earlier under that heading.

Simulate Customers' Needs

An additional way to identify needs of customers is through simulation.

Numerous product quality comparison tests are conducted by trained specialists under controlled laboratory conditions, rather than by a consumer panel under conditions of actual use.

Automobiles undergoing crash tests are inhabited by lifeless dummies.

Many product design ideas are first worked out through mathematical simulation. Then a model is constructed in the model shop to be tested in the laboratory.

Simulation is also widely used in the service industries. A well-known example is the training of aircraft pilots, both civilian and military. Much of that training is carried out in simulated cockpits under simulated flying or combat conditions. In a related application, simulated automobiles are "driven" by a panel of motorists to test various configurations and color combinations for driver recognition, responses, and comfort (Holusha, 1985).

The opportunities for ingenuity are boundless. A bookstore owner pretends to be an oversized customer (or an undersized one) in order to judge the adequacy of the physical layout of the store (Galante, 1987). An industrial designer in her twenties adopts the dress, makeup, and limitations of a woman in her eighties in order to experience the problems encountered by older women (Bluestone, 1984).

Simulation has certain advantages over study during actual use. During simulation we are able to exclude unwanted variables. Such exclusion enables us to determine with greater precision the effect of specific quality features on overall fitness for use. In addition, simulation is less costly than market research under actual field conditions.

Simulation also has limitations. Laboratory conditions do not fully represent operating conditions—they are "an imitation of the real thing." (That is the literal meaning of simulation.)

Customers' Needs: A Moving Target

Customers' needs keep changing. There is no such thing as a final list of customers' needs.

Some of these changes are responses to powerful forces that keep coming over the horizon: new technology, market competition, social upheavals, and international conflicts. These changing forces may create new customers' needs or may change the priority given to existing needs.

> In the early 1970s an international cartel was able to raise the price of crude oil nearly tenfold. As a result, the need for "low fuel consumption" rose remarkably in the scale of priorities. In turn, this cascaded down to raise the priority of such customers' needs as fuel efficiency of engines, weight of motor vehicles, weight of components, and so on.

Of these powerful forces the most insistent is the force of competition. This force is all-pervasive in the marketplace, within any human hierarchy, in sports, among biological species, and so on. Examples in the market place are legion.

> Over the centuries communication systems have evolved from smoke signals to modern telephones, wireless, and satellites. During the 1980s the competition continued into linking communication systems with information processing systems, and into systems compatibility.

> When Ford Motor Company established its goal of Best in Class for the Taurus model, it discovered that it was in competition on more than four hundred product features (Veraldi, 1985; *Business Week,* 1986).

Failure to remain competitive has done extensive damage to the health of companies.

> A maker of household appliances was competitive with respect to product features, price, and delivery dates. However, it was not competitive with respect to field failures and warranty costs, and this became a major source of customer complaints. Within several years the company (B) lost all of its leadership in market share, as shown in the boxed table.

	Companies Who Were Leaders in Market Share During:			
Product Model	*Base Year*	*Base Year Plus One*	*Base Year Plus Two*	*Base Year Plus Three*
High price	A	C	C	C
Middle price	B	B	C	C
Low price	C	C	C	C
Special	B	B	B	C

The boxed table became influential in stimulating the upper managers of company B to take action to improve product reliability

Responsibility for Securing Field Intelligence

The chief reason for lack of needed field intelligence is vague responsibility. Many organization units are well poised to acquire some segment of the needed information as a by-product of their assigned function. However, their superiors judge them on how well they carry out that assigned function, not on how well they produce the by-product.

Some companies have faced squarely the question: How shall we assign responsibility for securing field intelligence? Most have opted for one of the following approaches:

Establish an interdepartmental team. Such a team consists of members from the pertinent departments—those who need field intelligence and those who are in a position to provide it. The team is given the responsibility for identifying the needs for field intelligence, and the means to be used to satisfy those needs.

Assign coordination responsibility. In this approach some department is designated to be the coordinator for field intelligence. Such a designation creates a sort of sponsor who also has a degree of legitimacy for stimulating action. Nevertheless, such a sponsor soon finds that there remains much need for "selling" and persuasion.

Create a special department whose mission includes provision of field intelligence. Such a department is especially effective when the need is to make a sweeping improvement of the approach to securing field intelligence.

No matter which organization form is chosen, it is useful to think through and publish the pattern of responsibilities, both in the respective job descriptions and in matrix form, as in Figure 4–4.

This matrix, prepared by a chemicals company, related specifically to field intelligence needs for the new product development cycle.

Systematic Organization of Customers' Needs

Expressions of customer needs are usually in broad terms such as needs for good health, effective transportation, etc. Response to these needs is by means of goods and services. To provide such responses, however, requires very precise expression of needs. This precision is achieved by "breakdown." The broad needs are "broken down" into secondary, tertiary, and still further subclasses. This breakdown continues until a point is reached where the expression of needs is so precise that a specific response becomes possible.

One result of this breakdown is a proliferation of needs into very large numbers. Despite these large numbers, every one of those needs requires specific quality planning. Each requires means of measure-

Responsibility Matrix for Analyzing Fitness for Use Needs					
Actions	*Marketing*	*Technical Service*	*Production*	*Development and Control*	*Research*
Contact customer to learn needs	R	C			
Identify critical properties		C		C	R
Learn process capability			R	C	
Identify critical measurements			C	R	
Determine if measurements reflect fitness for use	C	R			
Collect cost information		C	R	C	
Integrate all information and finalize specifications		C	C	R	
Key: R = primary responsibility C = contributing responsibility.					

FIGURE 4–4 Responsibility Matrix for Securing Field Intelligence
From Juran, 1988, p. 12.9, Table 12.5.

ment, a goal, a product design, and a process design. To simplify life for the planner, and to assure that nothing is missed, the masses of information relating to the needs should be organized in some orderly fashion.

Planners have evolved various approaches for organizing such large masses of information. Some of those approaches are in graphic form: pyramids, tree diagrams, and so on. Others are in tabular form.

The Spreadsheet

The most convenient form of orderly arrangement is the spreadsheet (matrix, table, "house of quality," etc.). In the spreadsheet, the customers' needs are listed in the left-hand column so that each horizontal row is devoted to a single need. Distinction among primary, secondary and tertiary needs (and so on) is made by differences in the amount of indentation from the left-hand margin.

The vertical columns of the spreadsheet then are used to record the successive inputs from the planning decisions. Figure 4–5 is an example of a spreadsheet showing customer needs in the horizontal rows and planning decisions in the vertical columns.

Note: Spreadsheets must be prepared for the needs of *internal* customers as well as external customers. Many quality planning projects are concerned with internal processes and procedures whose impact is mainly on internal customers.

As we proceed with our journey down the quality planning road map, we shall see how the spreadsheet accumulates its information and how the planners are aided by having all this information in well-organized form.

Translation

Customer needs may be stated in any of several languages:

The customer's language

Our language

A common language

When customer needs are stated in the customer's language, it becomes necessary to translate such needs into either our language or a common language. This necessity applies to internal customers as well as to external customers.

Vague Terminology

Translation within and between companies is plagued by the limitations of language. Identical words have multiple meanings. Descriptive words do not describe with technological precision. Various company functions employ local dialects, which often are not understood by other functions. The concept of what is important varies widely from function to function.

An everyday example of vague terminology is that faced by physicians when examining patients. Diagnosis of ailments requires an understanding of the symptoms. In some cases the diagnostic instruments provide extensive and even conclusive information as to the nature of the ailments. In other cases some essential information must come from the patients. The patients must describe, in words,

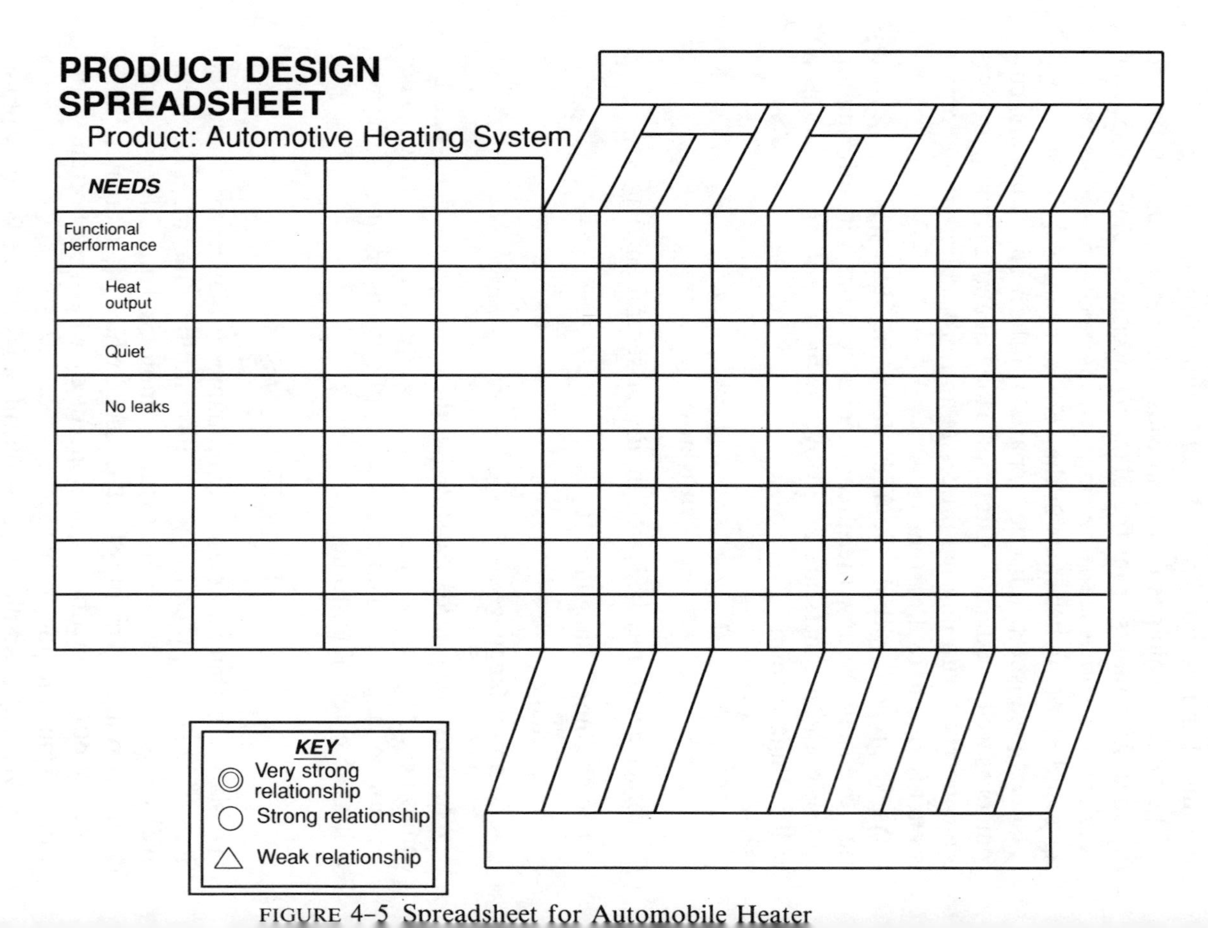

FIGURE 4–5 Spreadsheet for Automobile Heater

phenomena that to them may be unprecedented, and for which descriptions in words seem hopelessly inadequate. Yet the physician is faced with translating such vague descriptions into useful information.

At a different level is the translation problem faced by designers of aircraft during debriefing of test pilots. The engineers need information in technological, quantified language. The test pilots (who are the advance guard for ultimate users) describe the performance in terms of human sensing: vibration, bounce, yaw. Together the designers and test pilots can have some memorable dialogues.

Multiple Dialects

Within any company there are multiple functions: finance, personnel, technology, operations. Each function evolves its own dialect. The company also has multiple levels in the hierarchy, and again there are multiple dialects. At the bottom is the common language of things; at the top is the common language of money. Those in the middle need to be bilingual. Figure 4-6 shows this hierarchy in graphic form.

The situation becomes worse when *multiple companies* are involved.

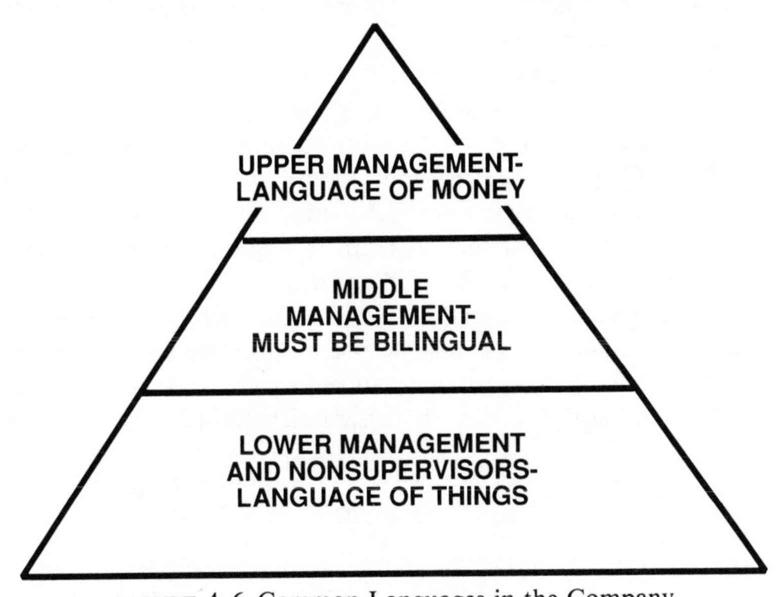

FIGURE 4-6 Common Languages in the Company

> The frequent traveler soon learns that his concept of "medium" as applied to a cooked steak is not the same as those of various restaurant chefs.
>
> Some industrial companies require that suppliers adopt "Self-certification," "Just-In-Time," "Statistical Process Control," and the like. Such terms have widely different meanings in various companies.

Aids to Translation

Numerous aids are available to clear up vagueness and to bridge across languages and dialects. The most usual are:

- The glossary
- Samples
- Special organization to translate
- Standardization
- Measurement

The Glossary

This remedy consists of agreeing on the precise meanings of key terms and then publishing the agreements. The publication takes the form of a glossary—a list of terms and their definitions. The publication may be embellished by other forms of communication: sketches, photographs, videotapes.

An example is the Glossary for this book.

A glossary does not evolve as a by-product of day-to-day communication. Instead, it is the result of a specific project to create a glossary. (Typically, the vagueness goes on and on until such a project is set up.) In addition, such a project is inherently multidepartmental in nature. A multidepartmental team is required to help assemble complete inputs and to assure full agreement.

The organization machinery for such a team project often employs a specialist to make the rounds, secure inputs, and summarize them for team review. This approach can reduce the time spent in team meetings while still securing the essential benefits of the team approach.

Samples

Samples take such forms as textile swatches, colored chips, and audio cassettes. They serve as specifications for such product features as appearance of textiles, color of printing, and noise of room air conditioners. They make use of human senses beyond those associated with word images. There are many cases in which such human senses provide better communication than is possible through words.

The concept of samples is not limited to physical goods. Some service companies use video recordings to demonstrate "samples" of good service—courtesy, thoughtfulness, and so forth.

As with the glossary, creating samples normally requires specific projects and multidepartmental teams. Some require industry teams and even multi-industry teams.

Special Organization to Translate

In the case of external customers, the volume of translation may require setting up a special organization to do the translation.

A common example is the Order Editing Department, which receives orders from clients. Some elements of these orders are in client language. Order Editing translates these elements into our language, e.g., product code numbers, our acronyms. The translated version is then issued as an internal document within our company.

A second example is the Technical Service Department. The specialists in this department are knowledgeable as to our products. Through their contacts with customers, they learn of customer needs. This combined knowledge enables them to assist both companies to communicate, including assistance in translation.

These and other organized forms of translation serve essential purposes. However, they are costly and, in varying degrees, error-prone. The costs and errors can be reduced by standardization and by establishing units of measure.

Standardization

As industries mature they adopt standardization for the mutual benefit of customers and suppliers. This standardization extends to language, products, processes and so on.

> An air traveler needs to fly from Cleveland to Chicago: late in the evening, economy class, in a nonsmoking area, and window seat if possible. The airline translates that into flight 455 Y, seat 8A.

In the case of physical goods, standardization is very widely used. Without it a technological society would be a perpetual Tower of Babel.

All organizations make use of short designations for their products: code numbers, acronyms, words, phrases, and so on. Such standardized nomenclature makes it easy to communicate with internal customers. If external customers adopt the nomenclature, the problem of multiple dialects disappears.

Measurement

The most effective remedy for vagueness and multiple dialects is through measurement—to "say it in numbers." The next chapter is devoted to measurement of quality. Note, however, that *measurement of quality is needed at every step* along the quality planning road map. That road map (Figure 1–10) shows measurement in the column at the left, and shows it as applying throughout the journey.

Application to Managerial "Products"

A critical problem in translation is "products" of a managerial nature. These include policies, objectives, plans, organization structure, orders (commands), advice, reviews, incentives, and audits. The customers are mainly internal, across all functions and all levels. The problem is to ensure that internal customers interpret these products in ways intended by the internal suppliers. In turn, there is the problem of ensuring that the responses are made in ways that minimize misunderstanding.

It helps to put these "products" into writing. The thought processes that precede writing are more thorough than those which precede oral communication. It also helps to hold face-to-face briefings, which provide an opportunity for two-way exchange. And it is a big help if work has been done to establish glossaries, standardization, and measurement.

Fitting the Translations into the Spreadsheet

This can be done by entering the translations into the vertical column adjacent to the list of customer needs. (In some cases no translation is needed: The customer needs are already stated in our language.) Figure 4–7 shows how the translation is fitted into the spreadsheet.

We are not finished with translation. Each of those customer needs requires a response in the form of product features. Most product features are expressed in technological terms. To the extent

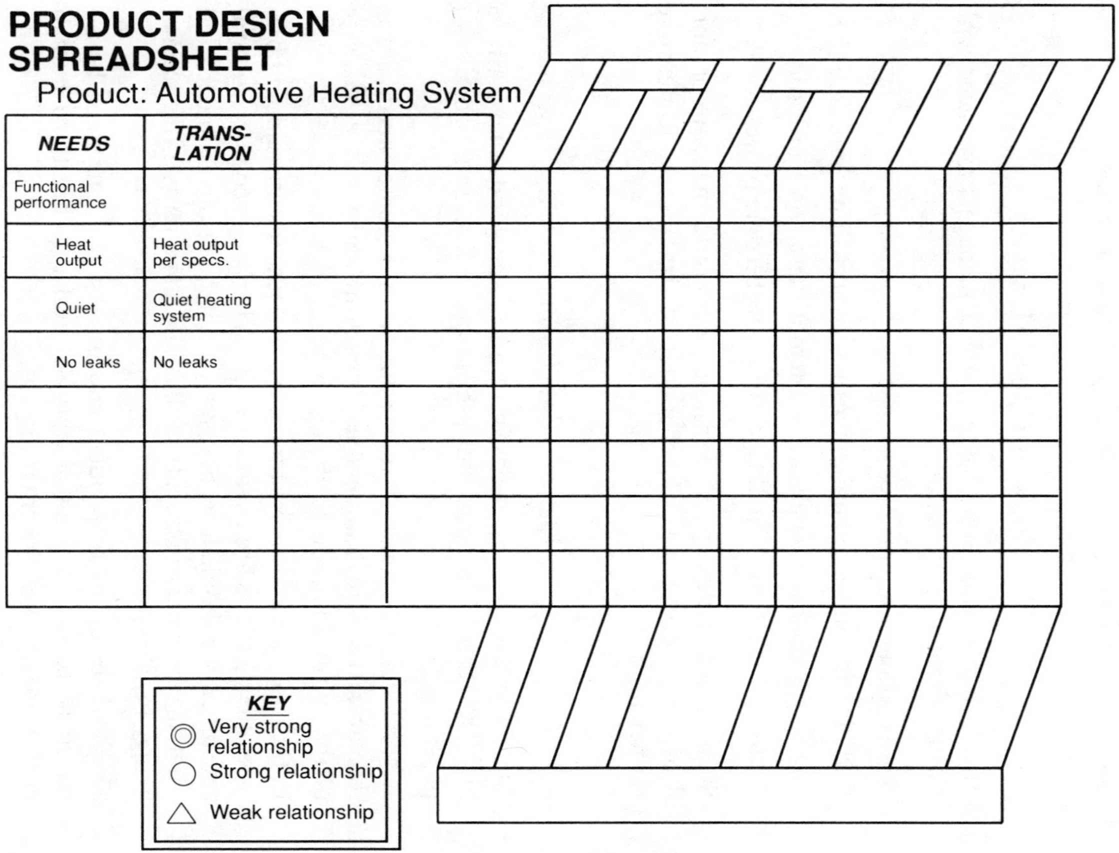

PRODUCT DESIGN SPREADSHEET

Product: Automotive Heating System

NEEDS	*TRANS-LATION*
Functional performance	
Heat output	Heat output per specs.
Quiet	Quiet heating system
No leaks	No leaks

KEY
- ◎ Very strong relationship
- ○ Strong relationship
- △ Weak relationship

FIGURE 4–7 Spreadsheet After Entering Translation

that customers do not express their needs in the language of technology, it is necessary to do further translation. We shall encounter this when we get to Chapter 6, "Develop Product Features."

The Roles of Upper Managers

In this chapter, as in several others, upper managers are faced with deciding whether to mandate:

A formal planning process to replace empiricism

Participation in the planning by those who will be impacted

Use of spreadsheets as an aid to memory and communication

Training the amateur quality planners to become professionals

Such an upper managers' decision (whether to mandate or not) will of course affect the subject matter of this chapter: Determine customer needs.

List of High Points

Clients may state their needs in terms of the goods they wish to buy. However, their real needs are for the services those goods can provide.

A great deal of failure to determine what customer needs are is traceable to failure to understand the nature and even the existence of the cultural pattern of the customers.

In the case of cultural resistance, the real reasons are seldom obvious—the disguises are usually subtle. When we encounter cultural resistance, we should look beyond the stated reasons to understand what are the potential threats to the cultural patterns of the human beings involved.

Much of the effort of product and process planning must be directed at reducing to an acceptable level the threats to human health, safety, and the environment.

The urge for prompt service requires including the time element when planning to meet customer needs.

Failure to keep customers informed is usually due to default: failure to raise the question, What shall we tell the customers?

Use of warranties as a tool for competition has intensified.

Relative to customer needs, the most simplistic assumption is that customers are completely knowledgeable as to their needs, and that market research can be used to extract this information from them.

The best way to discover customer needs is to be a customer.

Customer behavior is a better predictor of future customer actions than what customers say.

The starting point in creating new field intelligence is to appoint a multifunctional team to design the data plan.

The goal should be customer satisfaction rather than mere conformance to stated needs.

Customers' needs are a moving target.

The chief reason for lack of needed field intelligence is vague responsibility.

Despite large numbers, every one of the needs of customers requires specific quality planning.

The most convenient form of orderly arrangement of quality planning information is the spreadsheet.

Tasks for Upper Managers

Decide whether to mandate:

A formal planning process to replace empiricism

Participation by those who will be impacted

Spreadsheets to aid memory and communication

Training the amateurs to become professionals

] 5 [

Provide Measurement

Purpose of This Chapter

The purpose of this chapter is to show how to measure quality throughout all the steps of the quality planning road map. Figure 5–1 shows, by example, how measurement of quality applies to each of those steps.

The Need to Measure

Good quality planning requires precise communication among customers and suppliers. Some of the essential information can be adequately conveyed by words. However, an industrial society increas-

Steps on the Quality Planning Road Map	*Examples of Use of Measurement*
Establish quality goals	Analysis of prior performance Competitive analysis Benchmarking
Identify customers	Pareto analysis of customers Sampling of useful many customers
Determine customer needs	Market research on customer needs Analysis of customer behavior Analysis of customer dissatisfaction
Develop product features	Failure analysis Reliability analysis Optimization of product goals
Develop process features	Process capability analysis Failure analysis Optimization of process designs

FIGURE 5–1 Examples of Use of Measurement During the Quality Planning Process

ingly demands higher and higher precision for communicating quality-related information. This higher precision is best attained when we "say it in numbers."

In earlier chapters we encountered numerous instances in which quality-oriented matters were described in vague terms.

Chapter 2, "Establish Quality Goals," included such phrases as quality leadership, best in class, competitive quality, and market quality.

Chapter 3, "Identify Customers," included such phrases as significant impacts and key interfaces.

Chapter 4, "Determine Customer Needs," also included many vague terms.

Vague terminology is unable to provide precise communication. It becomes necessary to "say it in numbers." In future chapters we shall encounter further needs for saying it in numbers, especially in the chapters on product development and process development.

To "say it in numbers" requires that we create a system of measurement. Such a system consists of:

A unit of measure—a defined amount of some quality feature—that permits evaluation of that feature in numbers. Obvious examples are: *hours* of time to provide service; *kilowatts* of electric power.

A sensor—a method or instrument—that can carry out the evaluation, and state the findings in numbers, that is, in terms of the unit of measure. Obvious examples are: a *clock* for telling time; a *thermometer* for measuring temperature.

Units of Measure for Deficiencies

There are two kinds of quality, so there are two kinds of units of measure. One is for product deficiencies, and the other is for product features.

For most product deficiencies the unit of measure is expressed by a simple generic formula:

$$\text{Quality} = \frac{\text{Frequency of deficiencies}}{\text{Opportunity for deficiencies}}$$

In this formula the numerator (frequency of deficiencies) takes such forms as number of defects, number of errors, hours of rework, dollar cost of poor quality, and number of field failures.

The denominator (opportunity for deficiencies) takes such forms as number of units produced, total hours worked, dollars of sales, and number of units in service.

The resulting units of measure take such forms as percent defective, percent errors, percent rework, cost of poor quality per dollar of sales, and ratio of field failures to units in service.

The above examples represent the application of the generic formula in its simplest form. Actually, this formula has been around for a long time and is widely used in all functions. That wide use has generated a great many elaborations, as shown in the boxed table.

Functional Department	*Examples of Units of Measure*
Product development	Percent of drawings revised
Purchasing	Cost of poor quality (from suppliers) per dollar of purchases Percent of reorders due to poor quality
Manufacture	Cost of poor quality per dollar of manufacturing cost
Materials management	Percent stock-outs
Sales	Percent of orders canceled
Credit	Ratio of bad debts to sales
Field service	Percent of service calls requiring a second call

Units of measure for deficiencies typically start in simple form, such as percent errors. For example, a merchant faced with customer quality complaints began to inspect the goods before delivery to customers. To see which models were causing the most trouble, the merchant established a measure based simply on percent requiring repair. The data were as shown in the numerical table.

Model	*Number of Units*	*Repairs*	*Percent*
A	20	6	30
B	32	8	25
C	10	2	20
D	26	1	4
E	27	0	0
F	16	0	0

Measures of quality are widely used as a basis for making judgments and decisions. Those who are being judged will understandably study the unit of measure to see whether it provides a fair basis for judgment. If not, they will propose changes. A widespread example is the demand that the unit of measure take into account the *seriousness* of the deficiency. This leads to systems based on defining levels of seriousness, assigning weights (demerits) to each level, and ending up with units of measure such as *demerits per unit of product*.

Cost of Poor Quality

There are many situations in which it is useful to summarize the effect of all deficiencies through a single unit of measure. One way of doing so is to convert the effect of all deficiencies into money. The end result of such conversion goes by various names: Cost of Quality, Quality Costs, Cost of Poor Quality.

The terms Cost of Quality and Quality Costs are quite confusing, since they include two very different things:

1. Investments to make products salable
2. Wastes due to deficiencies

Such confusion is minimized if we focus on the Cost of Poor Quality (COPQ). Our definition becomes:

> Cost of poor quality (COPQ) consists of those costs which would disappear if our products and processes were perfect.

Those costs are huge, but the amounts are not known with precision. In most companies the accounting system provides only a minority of the information needed to quantify this cost of poor quality. It takes a great deal of time and effort to extend the accounting system so as to provide full coverage. Most companies have concluded that such an effort is not cost effective.

What can be done is to fill the gap by *estimates,* which provide managers with approximate information as to the total cost of poor quality and as to where the major areas of concentration are. These concentrations then become the target for quality improvement projects. Thereafter the completed projects do provide fairly precise figures on costs of poor quality before and after the improvements.

The popular classifications of these costs have been in the "categories" of failure costs, appraisal costs, and prevention costs. Failure costs are clearly part of COPQ. Appraisal costs and prevention costs are a mixture that includes investments to make products salable as well as elements of COPQ. To separate out this mixture requires getting into the subcategories of these costs. (For elaboration, see Juran, 1988, Section 4, "Quality Costs.") The basic test for what goes into COPQ remains as in the above definition: What costs would disappear if our products and processes were perfect?

Units of Measure for Product Features

For product features there is no known convenient, generic formula to serve as the source of many units of measure. The number and variety of product features is simply enormous. In practice, each product feature requires its own unique unit of measure.

A good starting point is to ask the customers what *their* units of measure for evaluating product quality are. If the supplier's units of measure are different, the stage is set for customer dissatisfaction.

> An airline sold unused cargo space by promising overnight delivery to customers. The customers' unit of measure was based on hours of time to make delivery. The airline's unit of measure continued to be based on percent of cargo space utilized. The natural result was customer dissatisfaction (Carlzon, 1987, pp. 107–110).

Application to Goods

Units of measure for quality features of goods make extensive use of "hard" technological units. Some of these are well known to the public: time in minutes, temperature in degrees, electrical current in amperes. Many others are known only to the specialists.

There are also areas of softness. Food technologists need units of measure for flavor, tenderness, and still other properties of food. Household appliances must be handsome in appearance. Packaging must be attractive. Dog fanciers pay out substantial sums based on judgments in the absence of units of measure. To develop units of measure for such features involves much effort and ingenuity.

Application to Services

Evaluation of service quality includes some "hard" units of measure. A widespread example is promptness, which is measured by time in days, hours, and so forth. Environmental pollutants (noise, radiation) generated by service companies are likewise measured using technological units of measure.

Service quality also involves such features as courtesy of service personnel, decor of surroundings, and readability of reports. Since these features are judged by human beings, the units of measure (and the associated sensors) must be shown to correlate with a jury of human opinion.

Some aspects of service quality involve numerous features, which collectively provide a basis for decision.

> Evaluation of which are the best (or worst) cities requires consideration of such features as crime rates, health facilities, economic affluence, educational facilities, atmospheric pollution, and cultural facilities. Statistics are readily available for most of these features. By assigning weights to each feature, it becomes feasible to arrive at a composite (Louis, 1975). However, the assignment of weights gets controversial (Becker *et al.,* 1987).

Numerous indexes make use of such composites: the consumer price index, the index of leading economic indicators, and the cost of living index.

Units of Measure: Other

The various units of measure are all interconnected; they constitute a sort of pyramid. If we dissect this pyramid, the layers will look somewhat like those in Figure 5–2.

At the base of the pyramid are the myriad technological units of measure on individual units of product and on individual elements of service.

In the second layer of the pyramid are units of measure that serve to summarize the basic data, e.g., percent defective for specific processes, documents, product components, service cycles, and persons.

Next are units of measure that serve to express quality for entire departments, product lines, and classes of service. In large organizations there may be multiple layers of this category of units of measure.

At the top of the pyramid are the financial measures, indexes, ratios, and so forth that serve the needs of the highest levels in the organization: corporate, divisional, functional.

As quality has moved to the highest levels of priority in management, it has also become necessary to evaluate the quality performance of managers (see p. 152, under ''Measures of Managers' Performance'').

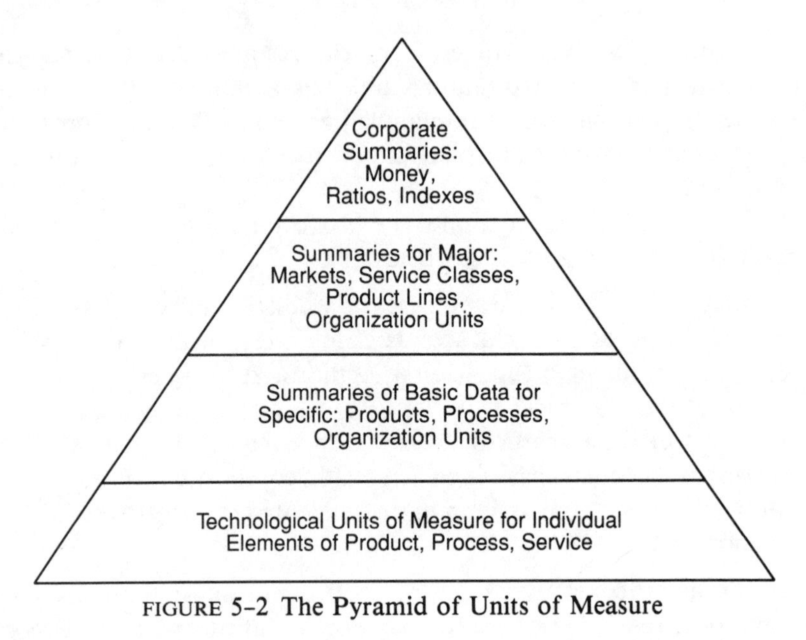

FIGURE 5-2 The Pyramid of Units of Measure

Units of Measure in Practice

To reduce units of measure to practice requires a good deal of detail in the form of precise definition and other formalities. Unless this detail is provided, the units of measure can create as many problems as they solve.

Precise Definition

All units of measure require precise definition. In the case of the technological units of measure, much research has gone into defining, with extreme precision, a meter of length or a second of time. For most other units of measure, we need not go to extremes, but we do need enough precision to ensure good communication.

Most of what we measure comes in subspecies. Errors may be critical, major or minor, they may be avoidable or unavoidable; they may be traceable to customer error, product design, purchased services or components, worker error, and so forth. If a unit of measure contains the word "error," we must define the word "error" with enough precision to enable us to agree on what to count and what to omit.

In some cases there are multiple definitions—one for the insiders and another for those outside. "On-time departure" has one meaning for those who use the dictionary. In the case of the Department of Transportation and the airlines, "on time" means not more than fifteen minutes after scheduled time.

Attributes and Variables

Many evaluations of quality are based on a count of the presence or absence of some condition: the promise was kept or not; the diameter conformed to specification or it did not; yes or no; go or no-go. Such evaluations are called measurement by attributes.

In contrast, other evaluations of quality are based on measurement along a graduated scale: delivery time in days, annealing temperature in degrees. Such evaluations are called measurement by variables.

In general, measurement by variables provides much more information per evaluation than measurement by attributes. Recognition of this fact has revolutionized the kinds of measuring instruments used in industry. Early in the century these instruments were predominantly of the attribute type. Now the variables instruments dominate.

Abstractions

Some quality features seem to stand apart from the world of physical things. Quality of service often includes courtesy as a significant quality feature. Even in the case of physical goods, we have quality features such as beauty, taste, aroma, feel, sound. How do we establish units of measure for such abstractions?

One answer is to quantify the number of violations of the abstraction. Safety is an abstraction, but we can count the known instances of lack of safety, that is, the number of accidents. Similarly we can count the instances of lack of courtesy, lack of beauty (presence of blemishes), and so on. In such cases it is quite common to go a step further and establish an index—a ratio of the number of such instances of "lack of" to the opportunity for such instances, e.g., accidents per million man-hours of exposure. (Note that in such kinds of quantification there is still need to define what constitutes "lack of.")

Another approach for dealing with abstractions is to break them up into identifiable realities. Hotel room "appearance" is certainly a quality feature, but it also seems like an abstraction. However, we can dig in and identify those specifics which collectively constitute "appearance": the condition of the carpet, lavatory, linens, windows, ashtrays, etc. Identifying these specifics also simplifies the job of establishing units of measure.

The Ideal Unit of Measure

Our extensive experience in establishing units of measure enables us to list the main criteria to be met by the ideal unit of measure. The ideal unit of measure:

1. *Is understandable.* This is seldom a problem at the technological level, where the meanings of the words have been highly standardized. However, many units of measure at the managerial level involve terms that lack standardized meanings, e.g., world-class quality. Local dialects may be understood by insiders but not by outsiders, e.g., on-time arrival. Any such vagueness or confusion becomes a natural source of divisiveness. Those who lack understanding of the unit of measure become suspicious of those who possess that understanding.

2. *Provides an agreed basis for decision making.* One purpose of measurement is to provide factual assistance for decision making by diverse human minds. The greater the validity of the measurement concept, the greater the likelihood of securing a meeting of those minds.

> A widespread problem in decision making is interpretation of observed differences in performance. Which of the differences are false alarms due to random variation in the data? Which are the result of real differences in performance? An agreed basis for decision making is statistical significance, as determined by Shewhart control charts, which use "standard deviation" as a unit of measure.

3. *Applies broadly.* Measures of quality features are widely used as a basis for comparative analysis. We need answers to such questions as: Is our quality getting better or worse? Are we competitive with others? Which one of our operations provides the best quality? How can we bring all operations up to the level of the best? Units of measure that have broad applicability can help us answer such questions. Meeting this criterion at managerial levels usually requires use of ratios and percentages. For example:

Ratio of cost of poor quality to sales

Percent of man-hours devoted to rework and repair

4. *Is conducive to uniform interpretation.* Identical numbers can nevertheless result in widely different interpretations. What is critical is whether the units of measure have been defined with adequate precision.

> Many efforts to compare performances have resulted in divisiveness due to failure to meet this criterion. Error rates are not comparable if the errors are not of comparable seriousness. Ratios of cost of poor quality are not comparable unless the underlying processes are comparable.

5. *Is economic to apply.* A balance must be struck between the cost of making evaluations and the value of having them. The most basic question is whether it is worthwhile to measure at all. If so, then the next question relates to precision of measurement. The precision needed is whatever enables us to make valid decisions from the data. To go beyond this adds cost without adding value.

> Many companies put much effort into expanding their accounting systems in order to quantify with precision their costs of poor quality. The resulting data had value but had little effect on managers' decisions. They would have made the same decisions had they simply estimated the figures.

6. *Is compatible with existing designs of sensors.* Measurement of quality is wonderfully simple if there exists a ready-made instrument that we can plug in to read the result in terms of the unit of measure. Such simplicity is widely prevalent at the technological level of the pyramid of units of measure. However, as quality grows in importance, we are faced with creating many new units of measure (see below).

Creating New Units of Measure

A frequent question raised by managers at training courses is "How can we measure the quality of XXX?" In such cases XXX is often a major process such as the process for developing new products. The reality is that *the answer will not be found in a book.* Instead, it is necessary to:

Define a mission of establishing means for measuring the quality of XXX

Assign the mission to an appropriate team (The team will usually recommend multiple units of measure.)

Prepare and publish performance reports based on the recommended units of measure

Acquire experience in using the measures, and then make revisions based on feedback from the users

Development of new units of measure is an evolutionary process, and the experience of the users is an essential input to the evolution.

For a case example of developing new units of measure (for the product development process), see p. 146, under "Measures for Operating Processes," the subheading "Application to Performance."

The Sensor

To "say it in numbers," we need not only a unit of measure; we need also to evaluate quality in terms of that unit of measure. A key element in making that evaluation is the sensor.

A sensor is a specialized detecting device. It is designed to recognize the presence and intensity of certain phenomena and to convert this sensed knowledge into "information." In turn, the resulting information becomes an input to decision making, since it enables us to evaluate actual performance.

Technological instruments are obviously sensors. So are the senses of human beings and of other animals. Trends in some data series are used as sensors. Shewhart control charts are sensors. "Anything that can sense is a sensor."

With growth of technology, the functions of many sensors have been expanded to include

Recording the resulting data to permit data processing

Data processing to arrive at summaries, trends, etc.

Comparing data on performance with goals and standards

Actuating changes in processes to bring performance into conformance with standards

Precision and Accuracy of Sensors

The *precision* of a sensor is a measure of the ability of the sensor to reproduce its results on repeat test.

For most technological sensors this reproducibility is high and is also easy to quantify.

At the other end of the spectrum are the cases in which we use human beings as sensors: inspectors, auditors, supervisors, appraisers. Human sensors are notoriously less precise than technological sensors. Such being the case, managers are well advised to understand the limitations inherent in human sensing before making decisions based on the resulting data (see below, under the heading "Human Sensors").

The more critical the quality features which are the subject of quality planning, the greater the need to evaluate the precision of the sensor, whether technological or human. On critical quality features it is necessary to keep human sensing to a minimum.

> The *accuracy* of a sensor is the degree to which the sensor tells the truth—the extent to which its evaluations of some phenomenon agree with the "true" value as judged by an agreed standard. The difference between the observed evaluations and the true value is the "error," which can be positive or negative.

The relationship between accuracy and precision is evident from Figure 5-3.

For technological sensors it is usually easy to adjust for accuracy—to recalibrate. A simple example is a clock or watch. The owner can listen to the time signals provided over the radio. (In this case the

Readings

Instrument A - Precise, but Not Accurate

.014	.015	.015	.017	.015
.015	.016	.014	.016	.015
.015	.016	.014	.016	.016
.017	.017	.016	.014	.016
.015	.015	.016	.014	.017

Instrument B - Accurate, but Not Precise

.008	.010	.009	.007	.010
.008	.010	.008	.016	.011
.007	.011	.013	.008	.010
.009	.012	.013	.011	.011
.009	.012	.014	.010	.012

Instrument C - Accurate and Precise

.009	.010	.010	.010	.009
.009	.010	.011	.011	.010
.009	.009	.011	.011	.009
.010	.011	.010	.011	.010
.010	.009	.011	.010	.010

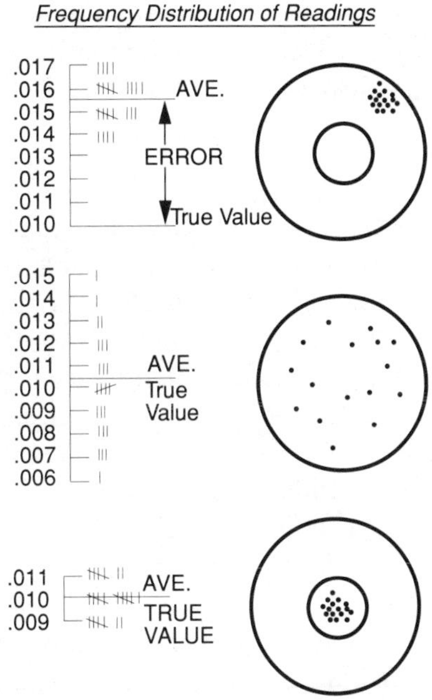

Frequency Distribution of Readings

FIGURE 5-3 Accuracy and Precision

time signals are the standard.) The owner then makes a correction, i.e., a change that offsets the error. In industrial dialect the owner has "recalibrated the instrument."

In contrast, the precision of a sensor is not easy to adjust. The upper limit of precision is inherent in the basic design of the sensor. To improve precision beyond this upper limit requires a redesign. (The sensor may be operating at a level of precision below that of its capability because of misuse, inadequate maintenance, etc. In that event removal of those causes can allow the sensor to regain its inherent precision.)

Sensors for Manufactured Goods

In the industrial societies we encounter sensors at every turn. In the home we have clocks to tell time, thermometers to measure temperature, scales to weigh ourselves, meters to measure usage of electricity. The automobile has a small instrument panel, which keeps the motorist advised on the fuel supply and such. Airplanes are much more complex. The numerous meters in the cockpit are just the visible fraction of the total. Not visible are the numerous microswitches, antennas, and so on, including the critical "black box" flight recorder.

The factory that builds automobiles or airplanes has instruments that are more numerous by orders of magnitude. Some of these are intriguing, such as the dummies used to record the effects of crashes on vehicle occupants.

Sensors for Services

The service industries also make extensive use of sensors, and some of these overlap those used for goods. Hospitals are part of the health service industry, but they make extensive use of diagnostic instruments of all sorts. In addition, many service industry sensors consist of data systems rather than technological devices.

In the home, many householders' incomes are keyed or "indexed" to the Consumer Price Index. The affluent ones may use the Dow Jones Industrial Index as a sensor of the state of the stock market. In the schools there is wide use of examinations to measure the performance of students and to judge their capability for advanced study.

The offices make extensive use of card files, clock cards, requisitions, accounting systems, and the like for collecting and analyzing data to be used for decision making at all levels. Similar devices are used in the factories. In fact, the term "support operations" is used to describe "indirect" activities that are common to all industries, whether service or manufacture.

In manufacturing and service industries alike, use is made of such sensors as market surveys, employee surveys, "mystery shoppers," and focus groups to provide managers with information for decision making. What all these have in common is their reliance on human beings as sensors. This wide dependence on human sensors requires a close look at the merits and limitations of human sensing.

Where to Plug In

The results of sensing depend on where the sensing is done—where the sensor is plugged in. Many processes consist of a series of sequential steps. A sensor designed to measure the volume being processed will give different readings depending on where it is plugged in. To illustrate, a data system is designed to measure volume of sales. In this example, volume might apply to any of a number of stages of progression, based on the respective key documents:

Stage	*Key Documents*
Bidding for business	Bid proposals
Contracting	Signed contracts
Performance of services	Interim invoices
Completion of work	Final invoices
Collection	Remittances
Issuance of credits	Credit vouchers

A similar pattern is found in measuring volume of goods produced:

Stage	*Key Documents*
Requisitioning	Requisitions
Production	Delivery tickets
Inspection and test	Inspection reports
Delivery	Shipping tickets
Installation	Installation reports
Final acceptance	Inspection reports

The term "volume" will mean different things to different people unless there is a clear definition—volume at which stage.

Human Sensors

Human sensing takes place at all levels of the hierarchy of measurement. At the basic data level, human beings must decide: How should this field failure be classified? Which account should be charged with these hours of labor? At higher levels there are corresponding questions relative to preparing summaries, indexes, and so on. In addition, we must contend with human errors that arise from a variety of causes: inadvertence, lack of technique, conscious errors. The extent of human sensing is so great that we should take positive steps to attain credible sensing. These steps are well known. Each is designed to be responsive to some particular species of human error.

Figure 5-4 summarizes the various types of human error and the usual associated remedies. The discussion that now follows elaborates on these error types and remedies.

Error Types	*Remedies*
Misinterpretation	Precise definition; glossary Checklists Examples
Inadvertent errors	Aptitude testing Reorganization of work to reduce fatigue and monotony Fail-safe designs Redundancy Foolproofing (errorproofing) Automation; robotics
Lack of technique	Discovery of knack of successful workers Revision of technology to incorporate the knack Retraining
Conscious errors:	
coloration	Design review of data collection plan
bias	Removal of atmosphere of blame
futility	Action on reports, or explanation of why not
	Depersonalize the orders Establish accountability Provide balanced emphasis on goals Conduct quality audits Create competition, incentives Reassign the work

FIGURE 5-4 Human Error Types and Remedies

Misinterpretation

Words are notoriously subject to a variety of interpretations. To secure uniform interpretations, precise definitions should be supplied, supplemented by such aids as checklists and examples. Similarly, detailed instructions should be provided on how to summarize, calculate, and so forth, including examples. In critical matters, formal training should be provided along with examinations to verify the "process capability" of the human sensors-to-be.

Inadvertent Errors

These errors are unintentional, unpredictable, and often unwitting, that is, the person making the error is not at the time aware of having done so.

> A depositor receives his or her monthly statement from the bank and discovers that the checkbook balance differs from that reported by the bank.
>
> Analysis then shows (usually) that the depositor had unwittingly made some inadvertent error due to a lapse of attention.
>
> Tests conducted by the Federal Aviation Administration have found that the process of screening passengers for weapons at the boarding gate detected on the average about 80 percent of the weapons. Some of the failures were attributed to inadvertent errors (Molotsky, 1987).

The unpredictable feature of these errors produces a randomness in the data. (We cannot predict which depositor will have the next unbalance, when it will take place, what type of error will be involved.) Such randomness helps us to identify that the errors are of the inadvertent species. However, we are limited in choice of remedy because the root cause of inadvertent errors is an inherent weakness in the human organism—an inability to maintain attention indefinitely. (If the inattention is intentional, that is a conscious error.)

To some degree, inadvertent errors can be reduced by

Aptitude testing to identify persons best suited for the tasks in question, and

Organizing work so as to reduce fatigue and monotony, e.g., rest periods, task rotation

However, in those cases where we cannot endure these inadvertent errors, e.g., matters affecting human safety, we must resort to technological solutions: fail-safe designs, errorproofing, automation, redundancy, etc.

> Use of barcodes for writing and reading identification numbers has greatly reduced the associated human errors (Sandberg-Diment, 1985).
>
> Software is now available for automatically proofreading documents to find spelling errors.

Lack of Technique

One widespread species of human error is traceable to incomplete knowledge on the part of the human sensor. Some persons have acquired a knack, a small difference in method that accounts for a large difference in results. Those who possess the knack get superior results; those who lack the knack get inferior results.

The remedy is to study the methods used by both superior and inferior performers. Usually such study discovers the knack, which can then be transferred to all workers through training. Alternatively, it may be feasible to incorporate the knack into the technology.

An interesting example of a knack was that devised by the eminent cardiologist, the late Dr. Paul Dudley White. (He was the leader of the team appointed to treat President Eisenhower's heart attack.)

Early in his career Dr. White established a spreadsheet system of record keeping to assist him in follow-up of the progress of his patients. He described the system in his autobiography (White, 1971):

> I had printed for me large sheets. . . . These sheets contained two horizontal lines for each patient, divided by vertical columns with the serial number, the name, the age, the sex, the diagnosis arranged according to etiology (both cardiac and noncardiac), the structural change and the functional condition of the circulation, and a special column at the end of the lines devoted to some unusual reason why this patient might be particularly important to be followed up. Now, after all these fifty years, I find these volumes of great value; they hardly require a computer, because of the organization of this original tabulation, which has proved so useful. This type of follow-up can apply to any particular field in medicine or surgery, or any science as a matter of fact, or any other activity of life, but as the years have gone by and the organization of my material has become so helpful I have

> emphasized more and more the importance of this relatively simple technique in the practice of medicine and in the collection of information otherwise [White, 1971].

In the dialect of practitioners in quality, Dr. White's knack consisted of a structured system of data recording to facilitate finding relationships between process variables (patients' symptoms) and product results (treatment and subsequent progress).

Conscious Errors

These are intentional and witting. The person making the error knows it at the time and intends to keep it up. Conscious errors come in a variety of subspecies:

Defensiveness against real or imagined grievances. For example, an atmosphere of blame stimulates subordinates to hide information which might become the subject of blame.

Coloration. This is a deliberate distortion of the sensed data, for a variety of (usually) self-serving human purposes: reduction of workload, avoidance of unpleasant tasks, self-aggrandizement, fear of being punished as the bearer of bad news.

> Airline pilots evidently have engaged in a good deal of underreporting of "near misses" in flight. The asserted reasons include becoming involved in lengthy investigations which might damage their careers. When the Federal Aviation Administration (during 1968 to 1971) gave immunity to pilots filing such incidents, it received 2,230 near collision reports (Dahl, 1987).

The following is an example of coloration that took place in a company whose product line included electric and gas ranges.

> The Vice President at Headquarters phoned the Works Manager in the hinterlands. "How many ranges are you shipping today?" The Works Manager asked the Production Manager, who asked the Assembly Superintendent, who asked the Shipping Room Foreman, who asked Pete. Pete, being low man on the totem pole, had no one to ask. So he went out to the shipping platform and counted the ranges—in the freight cars, in the trucks, and on the platforms. There were 400 in all.
>
> Pete was no fool. He remembered that yesterday they had shipped 440 ranges. He also knew someone would ask "Why is today below yesterday?"
>
> He found the answer. There were 40 more ranges in a hold area.

> They had been assembled today, but they couldn't be shipped, because they lacked electric clocks. "We're just out of electric clocks. A truckload is on the road now, and is due here at 11 A.M. tomorrow." In Pete's mind everything dropped into place. Those 40 ranges in the hold area were as good as shipped.
>
> So he reported—440 ranges. And this information sped up the line. 90 percent message and 10 percent coloration (Juran, 1964).

Reduction in coloration can in part be achieved by establishing a climate that favors forthright communication. Creating such a climate demands leadership from upper management—leadership by setting the example. A good deal can also be done to convert to nonhuman channels of communication. The computer has opened up extensive possibilities for processing basic data and communicating the results directly to the users with minimal human coloration.

Bias

Bias is one of the most troublesome sources of error in human sensing. Bias has some resemblance to coloration, but there are subtle differences. In coloration the human sensor knows the facts but consciously adds distortion. In bias the distortion is not necessarily conscious. There may be inner forces that influence the response of the human sensor. The bias may even be inherent in the design of the sensing plan. A classic example was the case of the shave test for razor blades.

> During the 1940s a manufacturer of razor blades made extensive use of human beings as sensors. Many male employees would forgo their morning shave at home. Instead they shaved themselves in special washrooms on the company premises. They recorded the results of these shave tests on data sheets such as Figure 5-5.
>
> Under the prevailing procedure the panelist was issued a razor blade to be tested. (The blade might be: a sample from current product, a competitor's blade, a new product under development.) The panelist used the blade day after day, recording his rating after each shave. Once the rating reached "poor," the panelist would discard the blade.
>
> A critical analysis of the resulting data sheets disclosed the existence of two major deficiencies in the shave test:
>
> 1. For any blade the ratings invariably either declined from day to day or remained the same. No rating ever

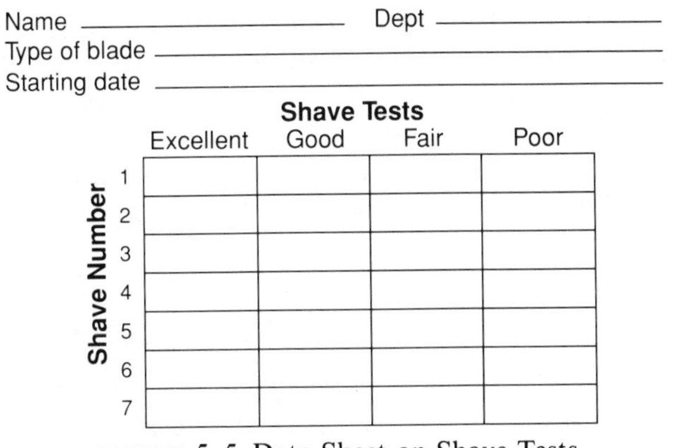

Name ______________ Dept ______________
Type of blade ______________
Starting date ______________

Shave Tests

Shave Number	Excellent	Good	Fair	Poor
1				
2				
3				
4				
5				
6				
7				

FIGURE 5–5 Data Sheet on Shave Tests

improved. This invariability was challenged by those who doubted that human evaluation of a shave could discriminate so precisely.

2. Every blade reached the rating of "poor" on or before the fifth shave, i.e., no blade was ever used more than five times. Again the skeptics doubted the ability of human sensors to appraise ultimate blade life so precisely.

The theory of the skeptics was that the panelists' data were biased due to their prior knowledge of how many times the blade had been used. A new shave test was then designed so that the panelists would be unaware of the number of prior uses of the blade. The resulting shave test data differed radically from the past, in two respects:

1. Shave test ratings wavered more widely. It was not unusual for ratings to improve during successive shaves with the same blade.
2. The life of the blades rose remarkably. Blades were often used ten times or more instead of the prior maximum of five. The previous life of the blade had been determined by psychological considerations, not by metallurgical capability.

Futility

Yet another source of human bias is a sense of futility. In many industries the work force is potentially a sensor relative to conditions in the workplace. Through their daily intimate contacts with those conditions, the workers are in a position to identify opportunities as well as deficiencies. For example, in a hotel the housekeepers, bellmen, and others are in a position to report on the conditions prevailing in the hotel rooms, reactions of hotel guests, and so on. If the workers discover that their reports are not acted on, they stop reporting.

The situation of futility is at its worst if the workers learn that their reward for acting as sensors is unwarranted blame.

> For years the hospital industry had only the vaguest idea of the extent of errors in the process of giving medication to patients. All hospitals posted rules requiring nurses to report medication errors promptly to the hospital administrator. However, in many hospitals the nurses had learned that when they made such reports they were often subjected to unwarranted blame. Hence they stopped making such reports. In due course a classic study made by a qualified outsider showed that (a) about 7 percent of the medications involved errors, some quite serious, and (b) the bulk of the errors were management-controllable, not worker-controllable. (For elaboration, see Juran, 1988, Section 33, under "Control of Hospital Medication Errors.")

The case examples suggest the means to be used to minimize the bias of human sensors.

> Provide for a design review of the data collection plan. In complex designs the design review team should include someone who is skilled in statistical designs and in communicating with persons who lack such skills.
>
> Approach the occurrence of errors constructively, i.e., What can we do together to reduce such errors in the future? Above all, avoid instant blame.
>
> When urging employees to act as sensors, either take action on their reports, or explain why not.

Errorproofing

The wide prevalence of human error has stimulated a great deal of effort to errorproof (also "foolproof") operations. Errorproofing can be applied to virtually any type of human error.

Managers usually do understand that these human sources of error exist, and that they can be serious obstacles to good quality. Managers also have a keen interest in reducing these errors. What is often missing is the analysis to discover the precise nature of the errors so that the appropriate remedy can be applied. Managers should inform themselves as to the nature of these species of error and the associated remedies. Otherwise they are engaging in fighting a war without knowing who the enemy is. (For an extended discussion of error-proofing, based on an analysis of nearly one thousand case examples, see Nakajo and Kume, 1985.)

Time of Sensing

Sensing is done in three time frames relative to operations:

Before operations

During operations

After operations

The purposes and uses of these forms of sensing are shown in Figure 5-6.

An example of an early warning sensor is the "design review." Under the design review concept, those who will be impacted by the plan are given the opportunity to review the plan in its early stages, meet with the planners, and supply early warnings: "If you plan it that way, here will be the consequences in our area." We shall encounter applications of this concept in the next two chapters.

The major benefit of sensing after operations is "lessons learned." We shall look at this concept in some detail in Chapter 12, where it goes by such names as retrospective analysis and the Santayana Review.

Measures for Maintaining Control

A major reason for measuring quality is to provide the information needed for making decisions relative to maintaining *control* of quality—keeping operations on a stable and predictable basis. These decisions are made by numerous people in various functions and at all levels in the hierarchy. However, all of these people use a common control process which is based on the universal feedback loop. Figure 5-7 shows this loop in graphic form.

	Before Operations	*During Operations*	*After Operations*
Purpose of sensing	To secure early warning of impact of quality planning on subsequent operations	To keep operations in a state of conformance to goals	To discover "lessons learned" as an input to future planning
Type of sensor	Special, early warning sensors	Usually, the "regular" sensors needed to generate data for control of operations	Mainly a summary of data that are a by-product of prior cycles of operation
Analysis of the sensed information is by:	The quality planners	The operating forces	"Historians" who may be planners or full-time analysts
Use of the sensed information is by:	The quality planners	The operating forces	The quality planners

FIGURE 5–6 Sensing Before, During, and After Operations

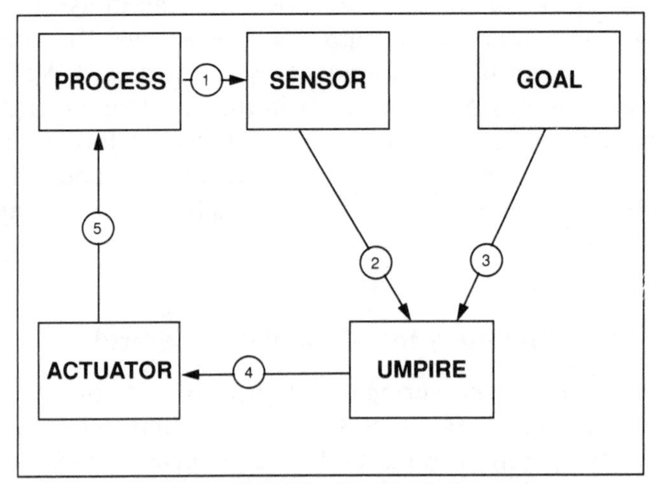

FIGURE 5–7 The Feedback Loop

It all starts with choosing the quality goals. Each quality goal becomes a "control subject" around which the feedback loop is built.

For each quality goal a system of measurement is designed, consisting of a unit of measure and a sensor which can evaluate quality in terms of the unit of measure.

The sensor is plugged into the operating process in order to evaluate the actual quality performance.

An umpire compares the actual performance to the goal, and makes a decision on whether there is adequate conformance.

In the event of lack of adequate conformance, the umpire energizes an actuator to restore conformance.

Application of this universal feedback loop to matters of quality was, until the 1980s, largely confined to manufactured goods and manufacturing processes. Since then, companies have begun to extend the application to "Big Q." The experience of these companies has shown that such extension requires a good deal of creative thinking as well as much trial and error.

Operational Controls Versus Managerial Controls

While the feedback loop is universal, the assigned responsibilities are not. Figure 5–8 shows how application of the feedback loop to the lower levels of the hierarchy differs from application to the higher levels.

Measures of Economic Consequences of Quality

Quality affects company economics in two major ways

- The effect on costs
- The effect on sales income

These are quite different conceptually, although they interact in some respects.

The Effect of Quality on Costs

Methods are available for quantifying the effect of quality on costs. These methods involve evaluation of various categories of costs of attaining quality as well as categories of costs of poor quality. The

Element	*Application to Lower Levels*	*Applicaton to Higher Levels*
Control subjects	Physical, chemical, specification requirements	Summarized performance for product lines, departments, etc.
Units of measure	Natural physical, chemical (ohms, kilograms, etc.)	Various: money, indexes; ratios
Sensing devices	Physical instruments, human senses	Summaries of data, human senses, statistical analyses
Who collects the sensed information	Operators, inspectors, clerks, automated instruments	Various statistical departments
When the sensing is done	During current operations	Days, weeks, or months after current operations
Standards used for comparison	Engineered specifications; specified procedures	History; the market; the plan
Who acts on the information	Servomechanisms, nonsupervisors, first-line supervisors	Managers
Action taken	Process regulation, repair, sorting	Replanning: quality improvement; motivation

FIGURE 5-8 Contrast, Application of Quality Controls to Lower Versus Higher Levels in the Hierarchy

evaluation may be done through enlarging the accounting system (a lengthy, time-consuming process). Alternatively, the evaluation may be done by estimates (see generally, Juran, 1988, Section 4, "Quality Costs").

The Effect of Quality on Sales Income

Measuring the effect of quality on sales income has very little in common with measuring the effect of quality on costs. In the case of sales income, "quality" refers mainly to *product features:* their presence or absence, and their competitiveness in the marketplace. In the dialect of the quality specialists, this form of "quality" is "grade" or "quality of design"—very different from "quality" in the sense of conformance to standards.

Sales income results from numerous factors, including the perceived value of the product features. The respective contributions of these factors cannot be determined with precision, but methods are available to establish some useful relationships. We shall have a look at these methods in Chapter 6, "Product Development," under the heading "Salability Analysis."

Some useful relationships can also be derived from a study of history—what happened in prior product launchings. See, in this connection, Chapter 12, under "The Data Base; The Santayana Review." See also Juran (1988) Section Three, "Quality and Income."

Interaction

The two different kinds of quality interact with each other. Each contributes to the quality reputation of the company, positively or negatively. Products that are failure-prone can easily result in the loss of future sales. Useful, innovative product features can help sell products even though predecessor products have a history of nonconformance.

Measures of Quality at the Highest Levels

As used here, the "highest level" includes not only the corporate level; it also includes the division level—that organization unit which is led by a general manager and which has virtual autonomy for running a subcompany. We shall first look at some examples in active use by companies. Then we shall generalize from those examples.

Florida Power & Light Company (FPL)

During the 1980s FPL undertook an extensive array of improvements in quality, more than a thousand significant projects. As experience was gained, there evolved the concept of enlarging the company's business plan to include quality and quality improvement. This same enlargement brought measures of quality into the company's system of key operating indicators. Figure 5–9 shows the key operating indicators for the Western Division (Brunetti, 1986).

Texas Instruments, Inc. (TI)

TI is a multinational manufacturer, mainly in the electronics field. During the 1980s TI mounted a major and successful effort to accel-

Operating and maintenance cost per customer
Customers per employee
Operating and maintenance cost—percent change versus Consumer Price Index
Customer/employee improvement index
Credit memos per 1,000 customers
Extension costs per new service account
Public Service Commission inquiries per 1,000 customers
Average hours vehicle utilization
Service unavailability index
Service interruptions per 100 miles

FIGURE 5-9 Key Operating Indicators for a Division of Florida Power & Light Company

erate improvement of quality. A part of that effort included establishing a revised system for reporting quality and quality improvement. Figure 5-10 shows the revised report contents, which are grouped under four category headings.

For elaboration, see Onnias (1986). Onnias notes that implementing the data base for cost of quality ran into cultural resistance from some of the operating managers. In retrospect it was found that the ease of implementation correlated strongly with the extent to which the managers had participated in the planning.

Commercial Nuclear Fuels Division, Westinghouse

The Commercial Nuclear Fuel Division of Westinghouse Electric Corporation (a National Quality Award winner) has reported that during 1989 its quality measures included the list set out in Figure 5-11.

Other Sensors

Beyond the evaluations made by the data systems, the upper managers make use of other sources:

Reports from committees, project teams, research teams, etc.

Audits conducted within the company and by external auditors

Personal observation by upper managers

Visits by upper managers to customers, to conferences, etc.

These and other sources provide upper managers with a broader data base and with help in interpreting the reports, which can be vague or even conflicting.

Commonalities at the Highest Levels

From the above case examples and others, several conclusions emerge:

1. At the highest levels the emphasis should be on: meeting customer needs, meeting competition, responding to customer complaints, continuing to improve quality, reducing the cost of poor quality.

It is all too easy to perpetuate the traditional focus on conformance to internal goals.

Leading indicators. These contain reports relative to the quality of inputs received from suppliers. Examples include: Parts per million defective (PPM) Purity level Functional test results Use test Visual/mechanical inspection results
Concurrent indicators. These relate to quality within TI's own processes, quality of finished goods, and quality of service to customers. Examples of process reports include: Rework at various steps Dust count average Final test yield Lot rejection rate Cycle time
Reports on finished units include information on: PPM electrical PPM visual/mechanical Operating life test Thermal shock
Reports on service given to customers include: Shipping performance, percent Delinquency over 30 days Warehouse errors Returned material cycle time Number of customers with direct to stock programs

FIGURE 5-10 Quality Measures Which Are Included in Texas Instruments Inc.'s System of Reports on Quality (*continued on p. 144*)

Still other concurrent indicators relate to the manufacturing equipments: Mean time between failures Mean time to repair Mean time between assists
Lagging indicators. These relate to feedbacks from customers, both in the form of material rejected and in the form of data feedback. The rejection categories include: Returns due to electrical, mechanical, or visual problems Returns due to administrative errors Unjustified returns
Customer data feedback is regarded as a reflection of customer perceptions. The categories include: Product quality and reliability as seen by the customer TI's ranking on quality and reliability versus competition TI's quality of service
Cost of Quality. TI also enlarged the cost data base so that cost categories measured include: Cost of conformance Cost of nonconformance Total cost of quality Total cost of quality as a percent of total manufacturing cost

FIGURE 5–10 *Continued*

Some years ago American Express Company conducted its measurements based on performance against budgets. In those days it took thirty-five days to decide on whether or not to issue a credit card. The company then changed its focus to

Subject Matter	*Unit of Measure*
Customer satisfaction	A composite measure
Fuel reliability	Number of plants with coolant activity below limiting value
Software errors	Percent error-free
Software delivery	Percent on time
Fuel assembly yield	Percent once-through
Tubeshell yield	Percent once-through
Cladding yield	Percent once-through
Total quality costs	A ratio

FIGURE 5–11 Quality Measures Reported by Quality Council in 1989 Quality Improvement Plan, Commercial Nuclear Fuel Division, Westinghouse Electric Corporation

quality as perceived by the customers. New goals were established, and within several years the time to issue credit cards was cut by more than 50 percent (Hicks, 1983).

Hospitals define a medication error as "a deviation from the physician's order"—a nonconformance to specification. The patient's definition of an error is in terms of any failure to provide a cure.

2. Upper managers should become concerned with the performance of the major business processes, such as: the new product development cycle, the order processing cycle, the process of bidding for business. (We shall look at this problem shortly.)
3. Upper managers should extend the system of evaluating performance of managers to put greater emphasis on quality and quality improvement. (We shall also look at this problem shortly.)
4. To choose the proper quality parameters requires a special design, tailor-made to the special needs of the company.
5. Design of the system for evaluating the performance of managers should provide for participation by those managers whose work will be evaluated.

Measures for Operating Processes

Much of the work of organizations is carried out through structured processes or systems. Some of these processes are relatively narrow in scope, involving tasks or steps conducted within a single functional organizational unit: opening the mail, machining gear teeth. We shall call these "microprocesses." Other processes are multifunctional in nature, consisting of numerous interconnected microprocesses. We shall refer to these multifunctional processes as "macroprocesses." Macroprocesses produce such end results as accounting reports, invoices, color television sets, bids for business, new products.

Measures for Macroprocesses

The performance of the key macroprocesses is obviously of critical importance to the company. For matters of such importance, there should be quality goals and measurement of performance against the goals. In practice, the use of such quality goals and measures has been selective. There has been extensive measure of those macroprocesses which generate products that are sold to clients. However, there has been only limited measure of those macroprocesses whose products are not sold, or are used only by internal customers. The recent move to adopt the concept of Big Q is stimulating initiatives to extend measurement of quality to the macroprocesses, many of which are business processes.

Application to Deficiencies

The universal formula for measuring deficiencies is the ratio:

$$\text{Quality} = \frac{\text{Frequency of deficiencies}}{\text{Opportunity for deficiencies}}$$

This formula is widely applicable to business processes. For example, a list of measures used in a bank includes ratios of:

- Errors to items processed
- Adjustments to items processed
- Charged-off loans to total loans outstanding
- Failed deliveries to total deliveries
- Dissatisfied users to total users

For elaboration, see Aubrey (1985).

Application to Performance

Measures of performance for some macroprocesses can make use of standard units of measure and sensors. A widespread example is timeliness of service. This can be measured in absolute units such as hours or days. The applications of this measure are legion: time to recruit personnel, time for launching new products, time to deliver goods, etc.

For other macroprocesses the measures of performance must be specially designed. For example, a maker of scientific instruments undertook to measure the performance of the product development process. To do so, a multifunctional team was organized, with a mission of designing an appropriate measurement system. Figure 5–12 shows the team conclusions.

Note that *the team did not find these measures in a book. The team had to create them.*

The number of engineering changes, cumulative over the life of the product
The number of months elapsed, from first pilot unit made to steady state production
The number of units installed without major trouble. (The unit works after normal installation time.)
The number of iterations of the printed circuit board schematic
The design for assembly Total assembly Total labor cost Total number of operations Number of parts Theoretical minimum number of parts
Percent of software bugs found during the development phase
Number of lines of software code
Predicted MTBF versus actual MTBF
Number of levels of product structure
Number of qualified suppliers
Manufacturing cost targets: First run cost versus goal at steady state Goal and actual versus predecessor product

FIGURE 5–12 Measures of Performance for the Product Development Process

Measures for Microprocesses

The comparative homogeneity of the microprocess makes it easier to establish measurement. There are fewer categories of deficiencies and hence fewer ratios (of deficiencies to opportunities for deficiencies). Similarly, there are fewer categories of performance and hence fewer units of measure. It is of course necessary to find out how the customers evaluate performance, but there are fewer customers as well. In addition, it is usually easy to identify who is the "owner" of a microprocess, since the scope of the microprocess typically lies within the boundaries of a single function.

Measures for Functions

Many companies measure the quality of the work done by the functional units of organization. The companies do so in order to:

Provide essential feedback for budgeting, managerial control, etc.

Provide an essential input to evaluating the performance of the respective supervisors.

Most of these measures have focused on deficiencies. In the case of microprocesses, the work performed is usually homogeneous, so deficiencies can be expressed by use of ratios such as error rates. For macroprocesses the measures are more complex. Any one functional unit carries out only a part of the macroprocess; the rest is done by other functional units.

The usual way of dealing with this limitation has been to identify the key measures—those which are strongly influenced by the functional activity. Figure 5–13 lists examples of actual measures employed by some companies.

To combine a wide variety of measures into summaries for use at higher levels requires use of such devices as arbitrary weighting, conversion into natural units of measure, or conversion into statistical equivalents (see below, under "Summary of Nonhomogeneous Measures").

Measures of Product Performance

Product performance is measured for multiple reasons, mainly to ensure that the product will meet customer needs. At lower levels in the hierarchy, the personnel often lack direct exposure to customer

Functional Department	*Examples of Measures*
Product development	Months required to launch new products
Purchasing	Cost of poor quality (from suppliers) per dollar of purchases Percent of reorders due to poor quality
Manufacture	Cost of poor quality per dollar of manufacturing cost
Materials management	Percent stock-outs
Sales	Percent of orders canceled
Credit	Ratio of bad debts to sales
Finance	Percent of documents in error
Field service	Percent of service calls requiring second call

FIGURE 5–13 Examples of Quality Measures for Functions

needs. For such personnel the measures are usually based on the degree of conformance to specifications or to procedures.

Application to Goods

Goods exhibit enormous numbers of features requiring suppliers to carry out enormous numbers of measures using numerous technological measuring instruments. In contrast, the customers usually focus on a relative few key performance features. For these key features the performance measures are often oriented to business goals rather than to technological goals. Similarly, the purchase decision includes various elements beyond technological quality: price, value, delivery date, courtesy, etc.

> The aircraft engine exhibits large numbers of technological features, requiring extensive technological measurement. The airlines are concerned with a relative few features: reliability, fuel efficiency, maintenance hours, etc.

> In like manner the technological features of an automobile run to many tens of thousands. Only several hundred can be sensed by consumers.

It is evident that suppliers of goods should identify those features which are at the top of the customers' priority list and should also discover the performances as perceived by the customers. The suppliers' measures must be correlated with those of the customer.

Competitive Performance of Goods

> In the case of the supplier of stainless steel (see Chapter 4, under "Perceived Needs"), competitive performance was equal with respect to the technological properties of the steel. However, the cleanliness of the packaging was not competitive, and in that case it had a major impact on share of market.

The above case example brings in the need to evaluate competitive performance, since the customer may take the initiative. In some cases it is feasible to evaluate competitive features through laboratory testing. In other cases it is necessary to acquire the measures in the field. (For a case example, see Utzig, 1980). In still other cases comparative data are available from government researches (e.g., product safety tests) or from independent testing performed by consumer service organizations. For elaboration, see Juran (1988), Section 12, "Field Intelligence," especially under "Competitive Evaluation by Field Studies."

Application to Services

Measurement of service quality has in the past concentrated on deficiencies—error rates and the like. The emergence of the Big Q concept has expanded the use of measures of product features. This same Big Q concept has also stimulated an expansion of measures for those service qualities which impact internal customers, a category previously underemphasized.

As in the case of goods, it is necessary for evaluation of product quality to relate closely to the customers' basis of evaluation. The airline cargo space example was a case in point (see above, under "Units of Measure for Product Features").

A major feature of service quality is timeliness. This is readily measurable, but first there must be agreement on the definition of timeliness. It is quite common for these definitions to deviate from the dictionary, as in the case of airline "on-time" arrival.

A further major feature of service quality is the treatment given to *consumers.* Most service industries have far more direct contact with consumers than most manufacturing industries. Direct contact with consumers requires patience, courtesy, sympathetic understanding, a spirit of helpfulness, and so forth. For such features there are no agreed units of measure and no widely accepted sensors. Instead, recourse is had to other means of evaluation. Samples of actual performance may be recorded: audio recording of telephone transactions, video recordings of face-to-face service transactions. (Any such sampling is done only with the prior agreement of the workers involved.) Subsequently the performances are critiqued to see what was well done and what are the opportunities for improvement.

In some cases the need for accuracy is extreme. The Consumer Price Index of the Bureau of Labor Statistics is referenced in many escalator clauses. Huge sums—many billions of dollars—flow in response to the monthly changes in the figures. Maintaining the accuracy of the Index is an exacting task and requires participation by those who are impacted.

On occasion someone comes up with a new measure. A British journalist visiting a Disney amusement park measured how his time was spent. He came up with data as follows:

Waiting in queues	110 minutes
Walking between attractions	28 minutes
On rides	12 minutes

The resulting ratios are of interest to the managers of the park as well as to the public (Hoggart, 1988). For an extensive discussion of quality in service industries, including measurement of service quality, see Juran (1988, Section 33, "Service Industries").

Competitive Performance of Services

Regulated service industries are usually required to report their performance on certain product features of importance to their customers and to the public. In turn, the regulatory bodies may publish the resulting competitive performance data.

> The Federal Department of Transportation publishes comparative data on airline performance with respect to on-time arrivals, passengers denied boarding ("bumped"), passenger complaints, baggage lost, and so on. Since these comparisons involve multiple features, it is possible for multiple companies to claim to be the "best." Each *is* the best for some feature, but not for other features. (The claims are silent as to those other features.)

In some industries data banks on product performance are maintained by the industry association, by independent researchers, and by other parties. Data banks for hospitals publish mortality statistics. Media researchers publish figures on circulation and readership for newspapers and other publications.

In launching new services it is most important to acquire reliable intelligence on competitive performance. To do so often requires thorough study in the field.

> A major hotel chain contemplated going into the economy hotel business. To secure field intelligence, a team of researchers spent six months living in various economy hotel chains and evaluating the service features provided (Dumaine, 1988).

A great deal of service is provided to internal customers in such forms as payroll preparation, internal transportation, and recruitment of personnel. Often such services are in the form of internal monopolies. Even in such cases it is often feasible to secure competitive performance data from outside companies that offer such services for sale.

Measures of Managers' Performance

Managers' performance with respect to quality has traditionally been evaluated on the basis of:

The performance of the process for which the manager has the principal responsibility (the manager is said to "own" the process) or, alternatively

The quality of the product produced by that process

Until the 1980s, measures of quality did not have top priority in judging the performance of managers. Other parameters had higher priority, and the prevailing concept was strongly oriented to Little Q. Since then companies have begun to rethink the entire approach used to evaluate the performance of managers. The reasons are compelling:

For quality to have top priority requires that quality receive the greatest weight during evaluation of the performance of managers.

To go from Little Q to Big Q requires new thinking in how to deal with activities not previously subject to quality evaluation.

Going into annual quality improvement requires new thinking on how to evaluate the contributions made by individuals to team projects (McGrath, 1986).

The new attention being given to macroprocesses requires new thinking, because there is no obvious "owner" of the macroprocess.

As of the 1980s some progress had been made in testing out revised methods of measuring managerial performance. Some of these methods are quite innovative. One company uses three categories for classifying people with respect to performance on quality. These can be paraphrased as follows:

1. Sets an example through understanding of quality; uses the tools; is a role model.
2. Is competent; understands quality, but is not yet a role model.
3. "Needs work."

Evidently a level of competence relative to quality is prerequisite for promotion (Kearns, 1989).

The published case examples have been few. Even the unpublished material has been scanty. We shall have to wait into the 1990s to reach a consensus.

The Report Package

To enable managers to "know the score" relative to quality, it is necessary to design a special report package. The case examples summarized above (in Figures 5-9, 5-10, and 5-11) illustrate some of the diversities and commonalities of such reports.

Contents

The report package consists of several conventional components:

Quantitative reports on performance, based on data systems

Narrative reports on such matters as threats, opportunities, pertinent events

Results of audits conducted

These conventional components are supplemented as required to deal with the fact that "each company is different." The end result should be a report package that assists managers to meet the quality goals in much the same way as the financial report package assists the managers to meet the financial goals.

The quality council has the ultimate responsibility for the design of such a report package. In large organizations, this design requires inputs from the corporate offices and divisional offices alike. At the division level the inputs should be from multifunctional sources.

Summary of Nonhomogeneous Measures

Summarization for executive reports often requires combining units of measure that are unlike. There are several ways of doing this:

1. *Arbitrary weighting.* For example, defects are classified as to seriousness, and each class is assigned a weight (demerits). This makes it possible to use demerits per unit of product as a new unit of measure.
2. *Conversion into a common natural unit.* A well-known example is the use of money as a common measure of scrap, re-

work, service work, and so forth, despite wide differences in products and processes. Another example is the concept of "opportunities for failure" used as the denominator of indexes of performance. Brainard (1974) proposed summations in the form of defects per 100 (labor) hours and defects per thousand dollars of labor. Some companies use failures per million dollars (of sales) as a universal unit of measure across multiple product lines.

3. *Conversion into statistical equivalents:* In this approach, the historical performance in natural units is equated to 100 percent (for example). A 10 percent departure from this level results in a score of 90 percent, regardless of what the natural unit is. This method also permits preparation of composite scores through weighting of the components.

Format; Frequency

The report package should be specially designed to read at a glance and to permit easy concentration on those exceptional matters which call for attention and action. Reports in tabular form should present the three essentials: goals, actual performances, variances. Reports in graphic forms should show minimally the trends of performances against goals. The choice of format should be made only after learning what the preferences of the customers are.

For reports to read at a glance, it helps to standardize the subject matter and units of measure as much as possible. During the 1980s General Dynamics Corporation (GD) revised its reporting on quality. The revised reports included twelve quality parameters on a corporate basis—they were common to all divisions of the corporation. They consisted of the following:

Avoidable engineering changes

Deviations/waivers

First-time yield

Scrap (labor hour content)

Scrap (material value content)

Repair and/or rework (labor hour content)

On-time delivery by Production

Purchased item acceptability

Service report response time

Material review actions

Inspection escapes

Overtime

For elaboration, see Talley (1986).

Publication of managerial reports on quality is usually on a monthly or quarterly basis. The schedule is typically established to synchronize with the meetings schedule of the Quality Council or other key reviewing body. The editor of the quality report package is usually the Director of Quality (Quality Manager, or however named), who is usually also the secretary of the Quality Council.

In some companies the format of the new managerial report on quality has intentionally been designed so as to resemble existing managerial reports.

> The revised quality reporting system of Texas Instruments, Inc., (see Figure 5-9, above) was published as the *Quality Blue Book* (*QBB*). The blue color of the cover was deliberately chosen to be the same as that of the traditional financial report package.

TI's *Quality Blue Book* is reviewed monthly during operational reviews and is the basis for the annual appraisal of the key managers' contribution to quality. TI's Corporate Quality Policy statement includes the following provisions:

> A manager's performance on the quality and reliability of his products is a key criterion in the evaluation of his overall performance.
>
> TI will not attempt to measure a manager's commitment to quality and reliability. Only his results will be measured. Commitment is assumed and is not enough.

For elaboration, see Onnias (1986).

Adding Measurement to the Spreadsheet

As units of measure and sensors are finalized, they are added to the vertical columns of the spreadsheet. Figure 5-14 shows these columns in place in a model spreadsheet.

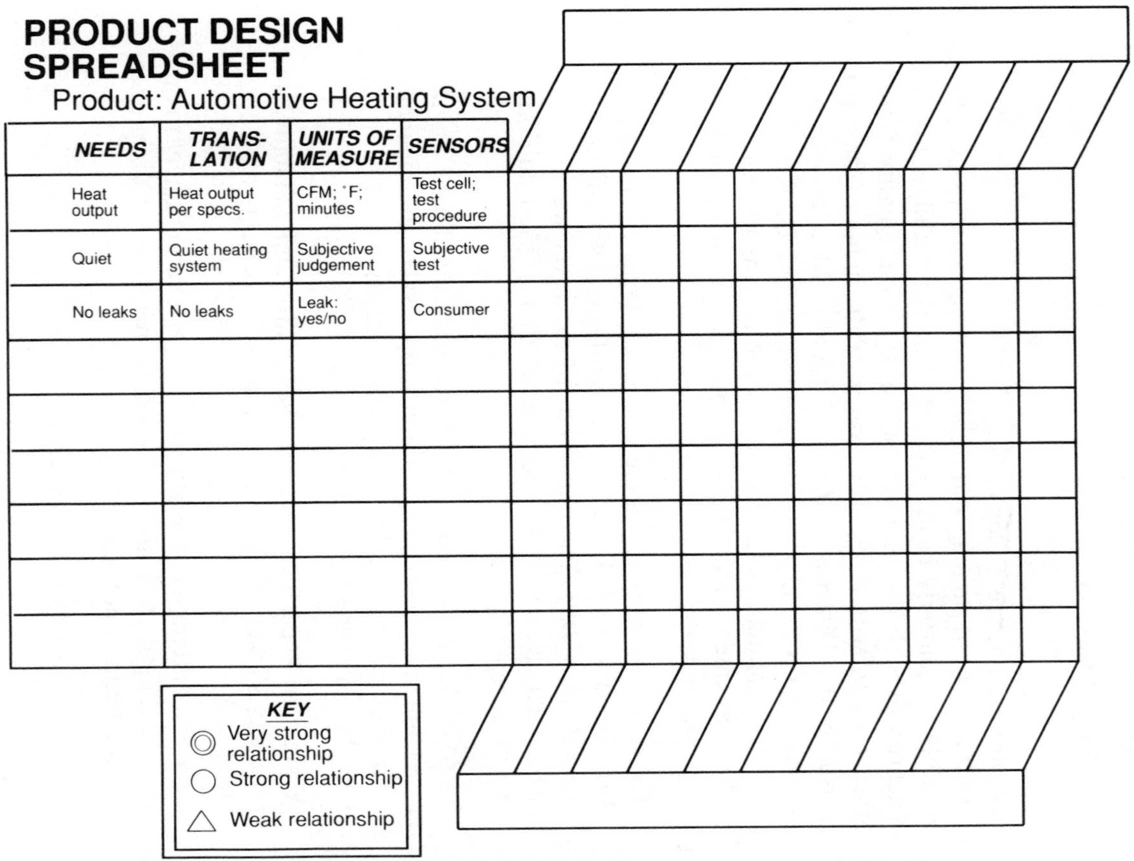

PRODUCT DESIGN SPREADSHEET

Product: Automotive Heating System

NEEDS	TRANS-LATION	UNITS OF MEASURE	SENSORS
Heat output	Heat output per specs.	CFM; °F; minutes	Test cell; test procedure
Quiet	Quiet heating system	Subjective judgement	Subjective test
No leaks	No leaks	Leak: yes/no	Consumer

KEY

◎ Very strong relationship

○ Strong relationship

△ Weak relationship

FIGURE 5–14 Spreadsheet Showing Units of Measure and Sensors

List of High Points

Precision for communicating quality-related information is best attained when we "say it in numbers."

To "say it in numbers" requires that we create a system of measurement.

Every system of measurement requires a unit of measure and a sensor.

A unit of measure is a defined amount of some quality feature that permits evaluation of that feature in numbers.

All units of measure require precise definition.

The ideal unit of measure:

- Is understandable
- Provides an agreed basis for decision making
- Applies broadly
- Is conducive to uniform interpretation
- Is economic to apply
- Is compatible with existing designs of sensors

For most product deficiencies the unit of measure is expressed by a simple generic formula:

$$\text{Quality} = \frac{\text{Frequency of deficiencies}}{\text{Opportunity for deficiencies}}$$

For measuring product performance a good starting point is to ask the customers what are *their* units of measure for evaluating product quality.

Development of new units of measure is an evolutionary process.

A sensor is a specialized detecting device, designed to recognize the presence and intensity of certain phenomena, and to convert this sensed knowledge into "information."

The *precision* of a sensor is a measure of the ability of the sensor to reproduce its results on repeat test.

The *accuracy* of a sensor is the degree to which the sensor tells the truth.

Human sensors are notoriously less precise than technological sensors.

The extent of human sensing is so great that we should take positive steps to attain credible sensing.

Quality affects company economics in two major ways:

The effect on costs

The effect on sales income

Suppliers should identify those features which are at the top of the customers' priority list and should also discover the performances as perceived by the customers. The suppliers' measures must be correlated with those of the customer.

Design of the system for evaluating the performance of managers should provide for participation by those managers whose work will be evaluated.

For quality to have top priority requires that quality receive the greatest weight during evaluation of the performance of managers.

The report package on quality should assist managers to meet quality goals much as the financial report package assists the managers to meet financial goals.

Task for Upper Managers

The emphasis in measurement should be on meeting customer needs, meeting competition, responding to customer complaints, continuing to improve quality, reducing the cost of poor quality.

Measures should be established for the performance of the major business processes.

Upper managers should regularly review the performance of the major business processes.

Upper managers should extend the system of evaluating performance of managers to put greater emphasis on quality and quality improvement.

Upper managers should understand the limitations inherent in human sensing before making decisions based on the resulting data.

] 6 [

Develop Product Features

Purpose of This Chapter

The purpose of this chapter is to show how to respond to customer needs by developing product features that will meet those needs. Implicit in that response is the concept of optimizing, of meeting the needs of suppliers as well as customers, and doing so at a minimum combined cost. Figure 6–1 shows the input–output diagram.

The input is the list of customer needs.

The process consists of developing the product features required to meet those needs. (Optimizing is implied).

The output is the list of product features and the associated product goals.

Definitions

The terminology associated with product development has not yet been standardized. The definitions that follow explain the meanings of certain key terms as used in this book.

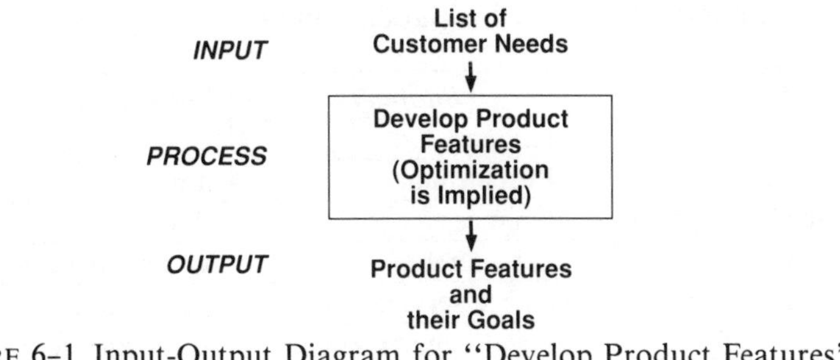

FIGURE 6–1 Input-Output Diagram for "Develop Product Features"

Product

Product consists of goods and services. (This is also the economist's definition). In addition, this book uses the word "product" in its broad sense as the end result of *any* process—anything that is produced.

An office team works up a business process for preparing invoices. Their product is the *business process.*

An office department then uses that business process to prepare invoices. Their product is *invoices.*

A team of engineers prepares a design for a gear box. Their product is a *design.*

A factory department then makes gear boxes to that design. Their product is *gear boxes.*

A company prepares next year's business plan, which includes a list of quality-related objectives to be met. The product is a *business plan.*

During the following year the company carries out the plan and meets the objectives. Here the product is *performance.*

A departmental supervisor undertakes a review of the departmental activities and prepares a proposal for revision. The product is a *proposal.*

The supervisor then receives approval to carry out the proposal. Upon completion, the resulting product is a *revision of departmental activities.*

Categories of Products

The single most important product is that which brings in the company's income. In industrial companies this consists of the goods and services produced by the operating departments and sold to clients.

There are also many other products that go to external and/or internal customers. Here are some examples, along with the identities of the suppliers and the principal customers.

Products	*Suppliers*	*Principal Customers*
Invoices	Finance	Clients
Purchase orders	Purchasing	Suppliers
Financial statements	Finance	Managers
Recruits	Personnel	All departments
Office space	Office service	All office departments
Legal advice	Legal department	All departments

When the Product Is a Business Process

One form of product is a business process. Every company needs systems and procedures for such purposes as:

Recruiting employees

Preparing financial statements

Preparing the payroll

Paying suppliers' invoices

Each such system or procedure is generated through planning. The end result is something produced—a product.

Concept to Customer

All products are created by a progression of events like that depicted in Figures 6–2a and 6–2b, "The Spiral of Progress."

Figure 6–2a generalizes this progression as applied to goods. Figure 6–2b shows this progression as applied to a support service, the creation of training courses.

There is no standardized name for this progression of events. AT&T calls this entire progression the "Product Realization Process." Ford Motor Company calls it "Concept to Customer." We shall call it either "Concept to Customer" or "one turn of The Spiral."

The Phase System

Once a product starts its journey around The Spiral it can run into unforeseen obstacles. These obstacles may become so severe that the planned product is no longer worth having. However, the journey, once started, develops a momentum of its own, with the risk of overruns in costs and schedules.

To guard against such overruns, some companies use a "phase system" (or "stage system"). The phase system divides the progression from concept to customer into segments or phases. Each phase sets out the criteria to be met—the activities to be carried out and the results to be achieved—for completion of that phase.

One example of such a division is as follows (Schmidek, n.d.):

Product concept identification

Product definition and requirements

Design, verification, and preproduction qualification

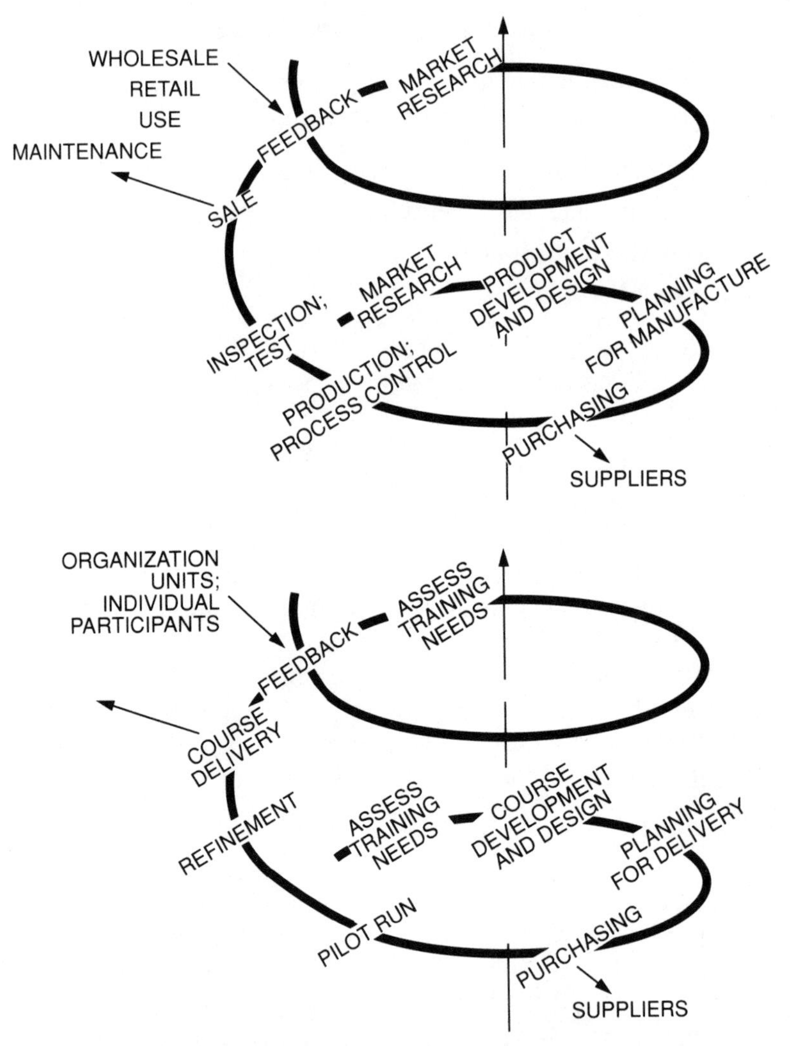

FIGURES 6–2a and 6–2b The Spiral of Progress in Quality
a. Application to Goods Production
b. Application to Support Service

Product general market release

Postmarket release evaluation

The phase system also provides for *business decisions* to be made at several key points or ("gates") during the progression, as for example, after model test. In this way, the phase system is a managerial tool for stimulating and controlling the progression of events. It defines work segments, establishes criteria to be met, and provides for a business team to decide whether to proceed to the next phase or to stop. Figure 6-3 graphically illustrates the phase system.

In addition the phase system designates which function (or group of functions) is responsible for carrying out the activities and meeting the criteria. The phase system also provides indications of the sequence in which the activities are to be carried out.

Product Development

A part of the progression from concept to customer consists of choosing the product features that are to be the means of meeting customer needs. To choose these features, companies make use of a series of steps, which includes:

Examination of the alternative product features available for meeting customer needs

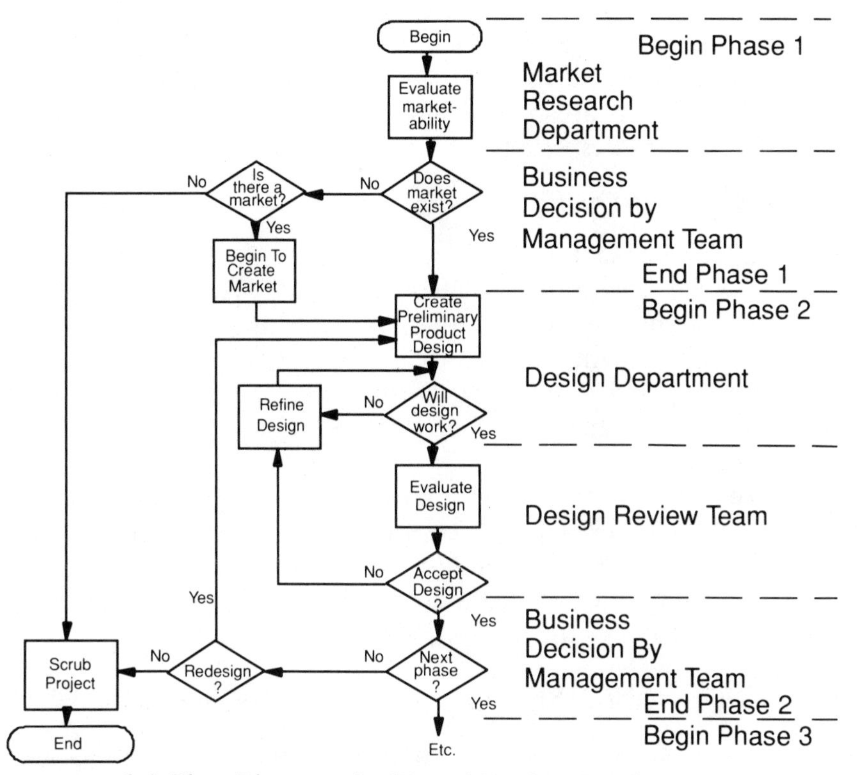

FIGURE 6-3 Flow Diagram of a Phased Product Development Process

Creation of new alternatives

Experimentation and test of the alternatives in order to choose the optimum

Definition of the chosen product features

This series of steps is often called product development. The terminology is not standardized. In some companies one entire turn of The Spiral (Figure 6–2) is called product development. In this book we shall use the definition:

Product development is the experimental process of choosing the product features that respond to customer needs.

Product Design

An essential part of product development is product design. As used here,

Product design is the process of defining the product features required to meet customer needs.

Product design is a creative process based largely on technological or functional expertise. The designers are design engineers, systems analysts, operating heads, and still other planners. The end results of product design are procedures, specifications, flow diagrams, spreadsheets, and, especially, goals for the product features.

Relation of Quality Planning to Product Development

Product development involves planning for multiple parameters: cost, schedule, quality, and so forth. The quality parameter involves meeting customer needs by choosing and defining product features, including defining the product goals. These quality-oriented activities are better carried out through use of the quality-oriented methodology and tools that collectively are the basis of modern quality planning.

The subject matter of this book is quality planning—establishing quality goals and developing the products and processes required to meet those goals. The focus in this chapter is therefore on the way in which quality-oriented methodology and tools can assist product development to meet the quality parameter.

The Need for Structure in Product Development

When companies are small and products are simple, it is feasible for product developers to keep track of everything in their heads. Then, as companies grow, and as complexity sets in, everything multiplies; the numbers proliferate. A larger market means more customers, a broader spectrum of human needs, and hence more product features. That same larger market attracts more competitors and hence stimulates more models, colors, options, and so on. The companies become larger, employ more people, use more specialities, generate systems of greater complexity, and hence have more internal customers and needs to satisfy.

The resulting combinations (of customers and needs) not only require development of large numbers of product features, but also require a systematic approach to product development. It takes a structured approach to deal with all those numbers of combinations and the resulting complexity.

Product developers have varied in their response to this proliferation of combinations. Some have continued to keep track of everything in their heads. Other product developers have resorted to "structure."

What Constitutes Structure?

Structure is many things. The more obvious include spreadsheets, countdowns, and checklists to back up human memory, guard against human error, and so on. In the case of product development, structure may also include:

Mandated use of quality-oriented methodology to improve quality planning

Various kinds of mandated analyses, which we shall examine shortly

Mandated forms of participation with customers

Recent Pressures Urging Structure

There is now a growing suspicion that deficiencies in the product development process are somehow related to lack of structure. Product development has been a slow process which creates costly wastes, mostly in other functions. There are numerous design changes, unforeseen internal crises, field failures, and the like. A product may be developed "several times" before all is "debugged." This suspicion has raised questions that are increasingly being addressed by upper managers:

Does proliferation require a structured approach to product development?

Should a structured approach be mandated?

In increasing numbers of companies, the emerging answer to both questions is "Yes." As a result, upper managers are faced with deciding whether to mandate a structured approach to product development.

The Pros and Cons of Structure

The decision as to whether or not to mandate a structured approach should be made only after first understanding the pros and cons, and the resulting effect on those impacted.

THE CONS. It is a lot of extra work to prepare the spreadsheets (and other elements) of the structured approach. Moreover, to prepare the spreadsheets requires extensive collaboration with external and internal customers, again adding to the work of product development and to the length of the cycle time. The instinctive reaction of most product developers is to avoid such structured approaches. Generally they feel that their training and experience have qualified them to carry out their function, and that all that structure largely adds cost and delay without adding value.

THE PROS. The benefits of a structured approach include:

An aid to human effectiveness: a major supplement to human memory and a guard against human error

An aid to participation in quality planning, i.e., to complete the spreadsheets requires inputs from the impacted departments.

Documentation that provides essential information to subsequent activities, as well as maintaining a record for reference and continuity

What is most persuasive to practicing managers is an emerging belief that use of a structured approach results in (a) products that outperform those developed by traditional empirical methods and (b) a shorter time interval from concept to customer. This belief is not based on any research in depth; rather it is based on the statements and publications of certain observers who have had the opportunity to see both structured and unstructured systems in action.

The "extra work and delay" during product development is a fact

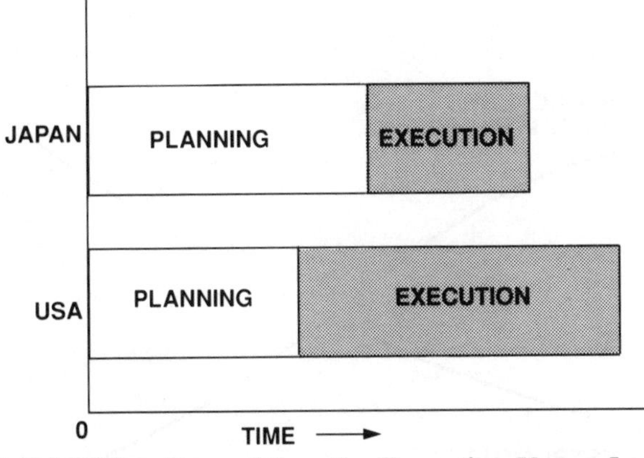

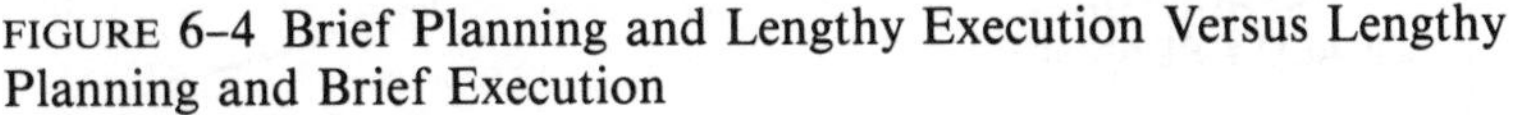
FIGURE 6–4 Brief Planning and Lengthy Execution Versus Lengthy Planning and Brief Execution

that is obvious to the product developers and should be taken seriously by everyone else, including upper managers. The expectation of a net gain is usually explained by a model such as Figure 6–4.

Figure 6–4 has often been used to explain the difference in the approach to product development, United States versus Japan. Note, however, that this model is not necessarily persuasive to product developers. To many of them the model is an unproved theory.

Another model used to explain the difference in approach is Figure 6–5.

In this model the emphasis is on the costs incurred. Greater thoroughness in the early planning phases increases the costs during those phases. However, the costs in later phases are lower because of fewer crises to be resolved. (For case examples of product development employing various elements of structure, see Iwahashi, 1986, and Fosse, 1987.)

More on the Quality Planning Spreadsheet

The spreadsheet (also matrix, quality table, etc.) introduced in Chapter 1 is the major tool used during a structured approach to quality planning.

Use of Standardized Symbols

Experience with spreadsheets has resulted in the creation of symbols to express relationships. (Some of these symbols are undergoing

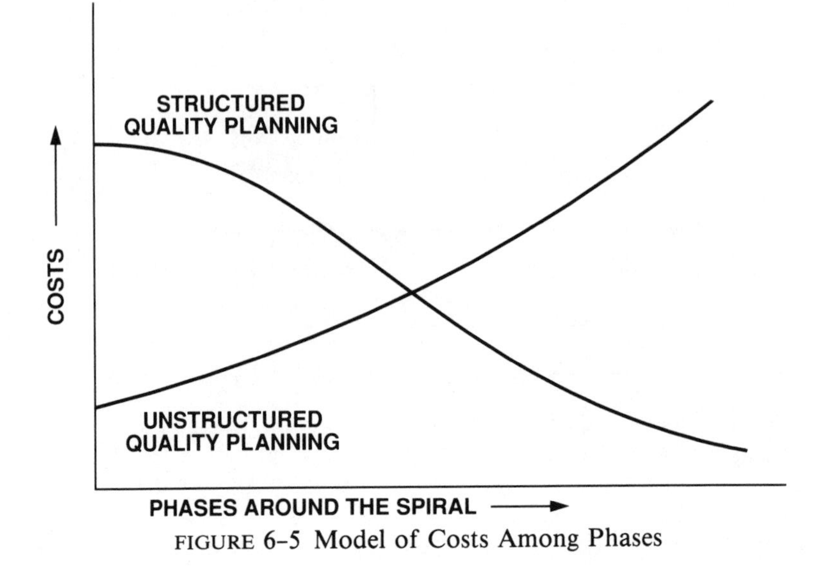

FIGURE 6–5 Model of Costs Among Phases

standardization.) Figure 6–6 shows a segment of the relationship of customer needs to product features (quality characteristics) for ink used in pens (Iwahashi, 1986).

For complex products the totality of information (customer needs, product features, etc.) becomes huge and extends over many spreadsheets. Planners and operations personnel are required to tune into and out of this array of information, over and over again. They are helped considerably if the spreadsheets use standardized symbols and formats as in Figure 6–6 (see Figure 4–5 for the key to the symbols).

Limitations of Spreadsheets

It is a fact that the spreadsheet assembles a great deal of information into condensed, convenient form and is clearly an aid to a systematic approach. Through judicious use of symbols, a great deal of information can be compressed into a small space.

It is also easy to be carried away by the elegance and convenience of the spreadsheet. The spreadsheet *does not provide answers;* it is mostly a depository for answers. However, the spreadsheet does make it much easier for the planners to:

Keep track of large arrays of information

Focus on the vital few elements

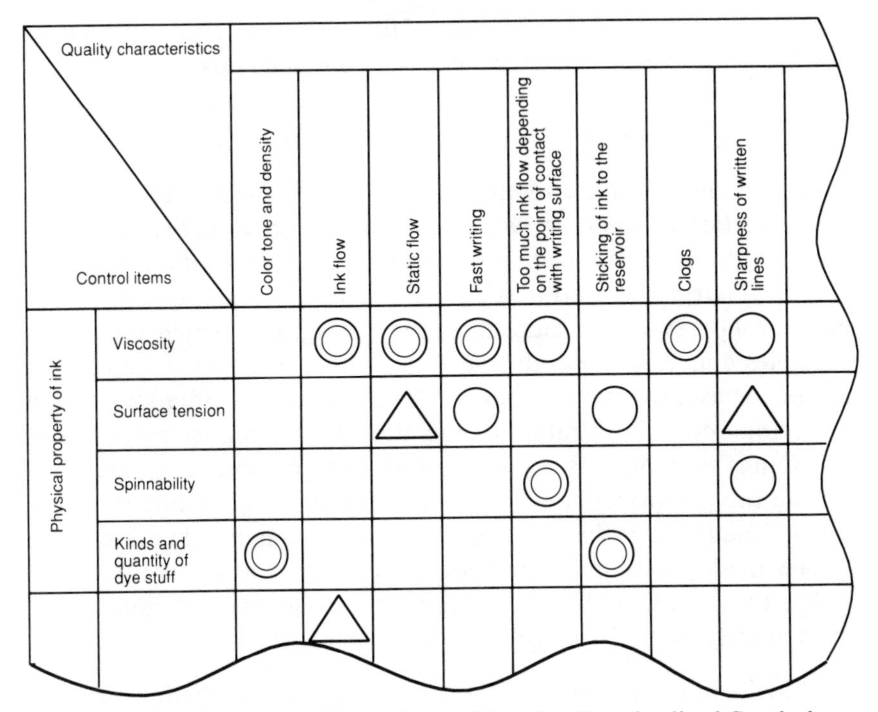

FIGURE 6-6 Example of Spreadsheet Showing Standardized Symbols

Secure ready reviews from those impacted

Write the subsequent procedures

Concept of the Optimum

Ideally every product feature, whether for goods or services, should meet certain basic criteria. These criteria include:

Meet the needs of the customers. "Needs" includes all customer needs: stated, perceived, real, cultural. "Customers" includes internal customers and others impacted.

Meet the needs of the supplier

Meet competition. The fact that a product meets customer needs does not assure that customers will want it; a competitor's product may be better or may give better value. "Competition" includes alternative suppliers for monopolistic internal services.

Minimize the combined costs. Customers and suppliers incur costs when they use or supply the product, and each tries to keep their respective costs to a minimum. However, the true optimum as viewed by society is to minimize the combined costs.

The Quality Disciplines are Essential

To attain the optimum requires use of much functional expertise. This functional expertise, while necessary, is not sufficient. Additional expertise is needed, and much of it consists of a body of quality-related know-how, which we shall call the "quality disciplines." For example, there are many designs in which numerous variables converge to produce a final result. Some of these designs are of a business nature, such as design of an information system involving optimal utilization of facilities, personnel, energy, capital, etc. Other such designs are technological in nature, involving optimizing the performance of hardware. Either way, finding the optimum is made easier through the use of certain quality planning tools.

The quality disciplines include an extensive array of methods, skills, tools, and so forth, of which the following are among the more widely used during product development:

Models and data systems for evaluating and predicting product reliability and maintainability

Models and data systems for analysis relating to criticality, salability, failure proneness, carryover of prior designs, etc.

Design of experiments for discovering the optimum result attainable from multiple converging variables

Process capability studies for evaluating and predicting producibility

Spreadsheets for assembling numerous interrelated data into condensed, easy-to-grasp forms

Flow diagrams, decision trees and still other aids to quality analysis and decision making

For a more complete list of quality-oriented tools and methodology, see Chapter 12 under "The Quality Disciplines; Tools and Methodology."

Collectively the quality disciplines can be of considerable help to product developers. However, there has been no mandate requiring the developers to use these disciplines. In practice the developers have made little use of them. The reasons have been numerous. To name a few, the developers have been:

Unaware of the existence of these disciplines

Unaware of the potential value

Untrained in how to use the disciplines

Unwilling to use the disciplines

The more experienced developers tend to accumulate an acquaintance with these disciplines by being exposed to them during successive cycles of product development. This exposure has seldom been accompanied by training in depth, however, so most of these experienced developers have remained in the category of experienced amateurs with respect to the quality disciplines.

Who Does the Quality Planning?

This question was answered in Chapter 1, under the heading "Quality Planning Has Been Done by Amateurs." It was pointed out that product developers, while possessing expertise in their function, have lacked expertise in the quality disciplines. Efforts to overcome this lack by providing consulting assistance to the developers have not worked very well.

Meanwhile, during the second half of the twentieth century, Japanese industries surprised the Western world by taking over quality leadership in many important product lines. A distinguishing feature of the Japanese quality revolution was their approach to quality planning:

They assigned responsibility for quality planning mainly to the operating managers and line specialists.

They carried out massive training programs to enable the operating managers and line specialists to understand and use the new quality concepts and tools. In effect, *they trained the amateurs to become professionals* with respect to the quality disciplines.

The Japanese results have caused Western companies to reexamine their assignment of responsibility for quality planning. These companies are in the early stages of shifting more and more of this responsibility to the operating managers and line specialists, while providing the training needed to convert the amateurs into professionals.

The Numerous Kinds of Analysis

Product development involves many kinds of analysis. Each makes use of multiple disciplines, including the quality disciplines. What now follows is a brief discussion of some of the principal kinds of these analyses, with emphasis on the role played by the quality disciplines.

Analysis Based on Functional Expertise

The central know-how required for product development is functional expertise. Developers of business systems need to be well grounded in the nature of business processes. Developers of information systems need to be well grounded in how information flows and how to employ modern information-processing facilities. Developers of manufactured goods or manufacturing processes need to be well grounded in the underlying technology—the properties of materials and the formulas for stress versus strain.

Knowledge of How the Product Will Be Used

Use of the product can involve a broad spectrum of practice. A part of functional expertise consists of acquiring the data base that includes this spectrum.

> Airfield runways in developing countries are shorter than those in developed countries and are commonly built of asphalt rather than concrete. These differences require making design modifications in the aircraft to adapt them to the conditions of use (Kupfer, 1988).

The presence of intermediate users can require much elaboration in product development, even extending to "system design" rather than product design. For example, the pharmaceutical industry devotes much effort to producing various medications to exacting quality standards. In addition, the industry devotes much effort to the problems created by the presence of intermediate users. This effort has taken such forms as:

- Development of means for uniquely identifying individual doses (tablets, capsules, etc.) to reduce the risk of mixups due to look-alike products
- Design of packages that are convenient to open, spillage resistant, readily disposable after use, etc.
- Provision of dose amounts that are convenient for pharmacists to issue and for nurses to administer

Design of containers that establish traceability and display identity of contents in various storage conditions

A major form of intermediary is the internal customer who carries out "subsequent processing" on the product design. A well-worn example is the manufacturing department, which is faced with producing the design. The frequency and intensity of this problem has led design departments to become knowledgeable about the principles that govern efficient assembly (Boothroyd and Dewhurst 1987).

Exposure to Human Fallibility

As a product design progresses through its various phases, it is subjected to all sorts of human influences. These are notoriously fallible and in some cases willfully so.

> The so-called all-terrain vehicle has the ability to travel in many areas otherwise inaccessible to vehicular traffic. Use and especially misuse of these vehicles has resulted in many injuries along with demands for legislation to ban or restrict their use. A critical decision is whether to do the designing based on how the product *should* be used or based on how the product *will* be used. Note that this decision is not merely a decision in technology. It is a business decision involving legal, marketing, financial, and still other inputs (Ross, December 1987).

Chapter 5 (Figure 5-4) showed that human performance is subject to many error types, some of which are inherent in the design of the human organism. Guarding against the effects of such errors is best done at the product development stage. The quality disciplines can provide the developers with much assistance to this end.

It is evident that while functional expertise is fundamental in product design, there is considerable interaction with the quality disciplines. This will be seen over and over again in the kinds of analyses which follow.

Hierarchies of Product Features

We saw in Chapter 4 (under "Systematic Organization of Needs") how human needs can be classified into a sort of hierarchy: primary, secondary, tertiary, etc. This hierarchy of needs then requires a hierarchy of product features to respond to those needs. For product design purposes this hierarchy must be subdivided or "broken down" to the very lowest level. Every feature, however tiny, requires its own design.

The terminology used to designate the successive levels in the product hierarchy differs from industry to industry. In the case of business processes, the terms often used are system, subsystem, process, activity, operation, and task. In the case of physical goods, the usual terms are system, subsystem, component, module, assembly, piece, and part.

The process for going from the system design level down to lower levels in the product hierarchy is called product subdivision, product breakdown, or the like. For large systems the constituent elements can run into huge numbers—thousands, and even hundreds of thousands. For such numbers, the need for structure becomes absolute. The spreadsheets become numerous, and they are crammed with high-density information.

Criticality Analysis

The purpose of this analysis is to identify the "vital few" features so that they will receive priority of attention and assets. A product feature may be classified as critical for a variety of reasons:

Essential to human safety. Product features may pose direct threats to human health or safety, or to the environment. Other threats may arise from user ignorance or misuse of the product. The aim of criticality analysis is to identify such threats so that steps can be taken to eliminate them.

Legislated mandates. Many of our laws impact product features. Product safety is an obvious area of such legislation, but there are others, e.g., restrictions imposed to conserve energy.

Essential to salability. In the case of the Ford Taurus automobile, about 400 product features were judged to be critical for product salability. The total number of product features (primary, secondary, tertiary, etc.) in an automobile runs into many tens of thousands.

Demanding as to investment. Some proposed product features may require substantial investment in facilities, inventories, special processes, and so forth. The challenge to the product developers is to come up with alternatives that are less demanding as to investment.

Demanding as to continuity. The industrial society is dependent on the continuing performance of technological goods and services. This dependence has given birth to a new family of product features, all related to continuity of performance: reliability, failure rate, uptime, maintainability, etc. For some goods and services, these features of continuity require quite as much emphasis from product developers as the more traditional product performance features.

Long lead time. Some product features may necessitate long lead times in subsequent processes, e.g., developing a source of supply, establishing an adequate operating process, training and certifying workers. Again there is a challenge to the product developers to find alternatives.

Ethically sensitive areas. Some actions can create unfavorable publicity all out of proportion to the amount of money involved: favoritism, expense account cheating, various kinds of unethical conduct. The financial controls are usually designed in ways that apply strict safeguards to such sensitive areas.

Instability. Some product features are inherently unstable because of failure-proneness (e.g., susceptibility to misuse, low shelf life, numerous components. The most economic remedies may lie in developing product features that are inherently more stable.

Note that criticality is viewed from the standpoint of *both the customer and the supplier.* For example, in the case of salability, the priority given to product features is based on analysis of customer views and behavior. Other forms of criticality, e.g., investment, are based on realities faced by the supplier.

Criticality Analysis Spreadsheet

To assure that appropriate action is taken with respect to all critical features, use can be made of a criticality analysis spreadsheet. Figure 6–7 shows the Critical Component Register, a form of spreadsheet used by Rank Xerox Limited. In this example the application is to product components. Each component is listed on a horizontal row. A total of twenty-seven categories of criticality are listed in the vertical columns. The analysis then identifies which types of criticality are applicable to which component.

In the same company, a more detailed analysis is then carried out for each instance of criticality. Figure 6–8 is the Component/Assembly Criticality Analysis, which shows the actions planned to respond

ISSUE NO: 1

DATE: 9/9/83

PRODUCT: Printer

SHEET: 1 of:

CRITICAL COMPONENT REGISTER

Function							Critical Process						SAFETY				Critical Tooling			Critical Handling			Critical Inventory					Critical Sourcing			
Comm Ops					O	O	O	O	O			O	O	O			O	O		O	O	O	O	O	O	O	O	O	O	O	O
Quality					O	O	O	O	O		O	O	O	O	O	O	O	O	O	O	O				O			O			
MED					O	O	O	O	O	O		O	O	O	O	O	O	O	O	O	O	O	O	O	O		O				
COMM CODE	PART NO.	DESCRIPTION	SUB SYST	ISSUE DATE	1 Problem History	2 New Technology	3 Tight Tolerances	4 Critical Parameters	5 Rigid Standards	6 Operator Certification	7 Inspector Certification	8 Complex	9 Mech Safety	10 Elec Safety	11 Environmental Safety	12 Spec. Clothing/Apparel	13 High Cost	14 Long Lead	15 Requires Calibration	16 Handling Sensitivity	17 Special Toting	18 Spec Vendor Packaging	19 High Unit Mfg Cost	20 Long Lead	21 Shelf Life	22 Storage Bulk	23 Weight	24 New Vendor	25 S.P.P.S	26 I.P.O.	27 Proprietary Part
570	2S93801	Bookwell Mldg	17.00	8237													o	o		oo		oo	o	o		o		oo			
570	2S93816	Platen Cover	17.00	8237													o	o		oo		oo	o	o		o		oo			
180	9P90864	Gas Strut	17.00	8237	oo																										
1100	30594134	Elev. Mot. Bracket	16.30	8237				o																						o	
210	130P90307	Sensor	•	8237				o						o																	
230	140S91354	Stk. Sensor Pwb	•	8237																o		o				o				o	
250	127P91103	Disc Drive Motor	•	8237				o														o				o				o	
260	121S90607	Disc Clutch	•	8237				o						o																	
1400	101S91216	Chassis Elec Assy	•	8237																											
570	5P90486	Disc Stacker	•	8235			o	o									o				o										

FIGURE 6–7 Critical Component Register, a Form of Criticality Analysis Spreadsheet
Courtesy: Rank Xerox Limited, Mitcheldean Plant.

RME: M.E. Payne	MODEL: Printer	PART NO. 2S93816
Delete as applic.	SS:	DESCR: Platen Cover

	Med Affected	Quality Affected	Comm Ops. Affected	REF	ITEM	
				1	Problem History	
				2	New Technology	
Critical Process Make/Assy/Vendors				3	Tight Tolerances	
				4	Critical Parameters	
				5	Rigid Standards	
				6	Operator Certification	
				7	Inspector Certification	
				8	Complex	
SAFETY				9	Mech Safety	
				10	Elec Safety	
				11	Environmental Safety	
				12	Spec. Clothing/Apparel	
Critical Tooling				13	High Cost	
				14	Long Lead	
				15	Requires Calibration	
Critical Handling				16	Handling Sensitivity	
				17	Special Toting	
				18	Spec Vendor Packaging	
Critical Inventory				19	High Unit Mfg Cost	
				20	Long Lead	
				21	Shelf Life	
				22	Storage Bulk	
				23	Weight	
Critical Sourcing				24	New Vendor	
				25	S.P.P.S	
				26	I.P.O.	
				27	Proprietary Part	

	MED Planned Actions
16	Process instructions to indicate handling sensitivity and plant damage
18	Monitor packaging for sufficient protection
	Quality Planned Actions
16	Planned inspection for damage
24	Ensure vendor is fully conversant with RX procedures lr. 88P9
	COMM OPS Planned Action
13	Monitor tool scheduled for progress
18	Special toting must be stipulated with purchase order
19	Del'y date/price critical
20	Need close monitoring
24	Ensure vendor has all relevant
22	Bulk storage must be considered

FIGURE 6-8 Component/Assembly Criticality Analysis: Details
Courtesy: Rank Xerox Limited, Mitcheldean Plant.

to the several types of criticality. Some of these actions impact other processes: purchase of materials, materials transport, packaging, storage.

Competitive Analysis

Competitive analysis is essential in an industrial market-based society. The forces of technology keep creating new opportunities and threats, while competition makes quality a moving target. Competitive analysis is best done in the early stages of the phase system, since customer needs are influenced by what is available competitively.

Product Features

Evaluation of competitiveness of product features is essential because clients make such evaluations when deciding which products to buy.

It is quite common for companies to tabulate their product features alongside those of competitors. The resulting comparison identifies the *presence or absence* of specific features and is an essential first step in competitive analysis.

For many product features the competitive analysis should go further. It should evaluate *performance,* e.g., comfort, fuel consumption, millions of instructions per second. Such evaluations can in part be made in the laboratory, but some must be done from data based on actual performance under operating conditions. Such data must be acquired from those who actually use the products under operating conditions.

For some consumer products it is necessary to make consumer preference tests, using the human consumers as instruments. (See Schuon, 1989, for an example involving automobiles.) Such tests are subject to all the risks of human error and hence require special care in design of the test programs. (See, in this connection, Figure 5–4 and the associated discussion).

In some product lines the competitors are so numerous that full-scale competitive analysis can become very costly. Companies solve this problem by use of the Pareto principle: they concentrate on the key product features, or on the key competitors, or both.

> One electronics company conducts competitive analysis with respect to its three principal competitors in each product line. ‘‘Principal’’ is based on share of market.

> In the case of the Ford Taurus automobile, the competitive analysis concentrated on about four hundred key features.

In some cases the company is a monopoly, e.g., the local school district or electric power company. In such cases the comparison should be made with similar monopolies. In most industries there exist professional societies, industry associations, and other agencies, which have established systems for pooling, analyzing, and publishing data on performance, including performance as to quality. There are also numerous companies in which internal monopolies exist, such as Payroll Preparation, or Components Manufacture. In such cases it is often possible to secure competitive information from outside suppliers of similar services.

Aside from objective determinations of competitive quality, there is also the need to determine *customer perceptions* of competitive quality. Where these perceptions differ significantly from reality, steps should be taken to bring the two into closer agreement, whether by product changes or by marketing methods aimed at changing customer perceptions.

Product developers use a separate column of the spreadsheet to record the results of competitive analysis.

Process Features

A second level of evaluation of competitive quality is the features of the *process* used by competitors to produce their products. Generally, analysis of the product also tells a good deal about the process used to make that product. (Additional information is sometimes volunteered by suppliers of equipment, tools, consumables, etc.) The respective process capabilities can then be estimated, as well as the process costs, leading to an estimate of the unit costs.

There is a further, though subtle, aspect of competitive process features that is quite useful if it can be learned. This aspect relates to the competitive *process yields*. There have been numerous instances in which two companies using the "same" processing facilities have nevertheless differed remarkably in yields. These differences have usually been traced to the respective rates of quality improvement. Those competitors who are the most active in quality improvement projects are also those who acquired the deepest understanding of the relationships between process variables and product results.

Salability Analysis

As used here, "salability" is the extent to which the product features stimulate customers to be willing to buy the product. This definition applies to internal as well as external customers. (Internal suppliers often refer to the need to "sell" their proposals to their internal customers.)

In the case of potential products based on new technology, ("technology driven" products), the first and most basic question is, "If we had it, could we sell it?"

Evaluation of Salability—A Contrast

For many decades, marketing managers have studied how to evaluate, quantify, and predict salability. A great deal has been learned about how to interpret economic indicators so as to provide predictions of purchasing power and affluence.

In contrast, there has been only limited progress in understanding the relationships between product quality and product salability. Some studies, called "Profit Impact of Market Strategies" (PIMS), have broadly related quality to profit (see Schoeffler *et al.,* 1974). Some of the needed tools have already been invented. However, to apply these tools (and to invent others) requires new levels of collaboration among the major company functions. This opportunity should not be missed.

The Methods of Salability Analysis

There are many of these methods, but we shall limit ourselves to those which seem to be the vital few. Each involves study of some combination of the following phenomena:

Product differences
Customer behavior
Customer perceptions
Customer opinions

Product Differences

Competitive products can differ in quality along a spectrum that runs from obvious to no difference. At the "obvious" end of the spectrum are quality differences that can be sensed directly by the customers. Such differences can by themselves be decisive in product salability. At the "no difference" end, it is the marketing skills that become decisive.

The use of bar codes on goods sold in supermarkets has provided superior accuracy and promptness in such functions as billing and inventory control. The concept is being extended into the automotive industry for related reasons (Ross, August 1987).

Quality Differences Translatable into User Economics

The spectrum includes cases in which there is a real quality difference, but the difference is not known to, or understood by, the customers. In such cases the technologists and marketers must join forces to demonstrate the quality differences in terms which can be understood by customers.

DuPont's Kevlar. Kevlar is a high-strength fiber that exhibits other valuable technological properties as well. It has been applied widely, but each application has required persistent effort on the part of the technologists and marketers (Hays, 1987).

The power tool case. A maker of power tools succeeded in improving their reliability to a level well beyond that of competing tools. A team was then sent to secure field data, from users, on the costs of using these high-reliability tools versus those of competitors. Those data enabled the maker to convert the differences in reliability into differences in operating costs. The cost data were then publicized, and it became feasible to secure a premium price.

These and similar cases are found on analysis to exhibit the following commonalities:

There is in fact a quality difference among competing products.

This difference is technological in nature so that its significance is not understood by many users.

It is possible, by experimental application, and by appropriate data collection in the field, to translate the technological difference into the language of money or into other terms that can be understood by customers.

To stimulate action by users, the results must be presented in terms of the users' system of values, not the manufacturer's.

Where the product differences do in fact lead to higher salability, the supplier has the option of striving for a higher share of market, or premium prices, or a combination of both. Generally, to strive for a higher share of market seems to optimize the supplier's financial results.

Quality Differences Minor but Demonstrable

> A company making sugar-coated chocolate candies came under the control of a knowledgeable marketer. He used television commercial messages to dramatize a small difference: the sugar-coated chocolates were less likely to smear the clothes and hands of children than uncoated chocolates. His share of market soared.
>
> A manufacturer of ball bearings carried out an in-depth study of the process capabilities of his machines. He succeeded in making bearings much more precise than those made by competitors using similar machinery. The superior precision was in most cases not really needed by the (industrial) clients. Nevertheless, they preferred to buy the more precise product since there was no price differential.

In these and similar cases, the quality differences might be dismissed by some as minor. Yet the engineers and purchasing managers who could get greater (though unneeded) precision at the same price were strongly influenced. In like manner the television message was so successful in dramatizing a relatively rare occurrence that consumers remembered it and acted accordingly.

Quality Difference Not Verifiable but Accepted on Faith

> Some years ago Schick, a manufacturer of electric razors, published the results of tests conducted by an independent test laboratory. During the test, users shaved themselves twice, using two electric razors one after the other. On one day the Schick razor was used first and a competing razor immediately after. On the next day the sequence was reversed. In all tests the contents of the second razor were weighed precisely. The data assertedly showed that when the Schick was second, the weight of its contents was greater than those of competitors. The implication was that Schick gave a cleaner shave. Within a few months the Schick share of market rose from 8.3 to 16.4 percent.

The most striking feature of the above case is the fact that the consumers had *no way to verify* the validity of the published account. They had the choice of accepting it on faith, or not. Many accepted it on faith.

Customer Behavior

Customer behavior is a factual phenomenon. It consists of deeds—what customers did or did not do. This past behavior is a useful leading indicator, a predictor of future behavior. It therefore can also be used as an input for prediction of product salability.

Customer behavior is exhibited in such forms as:

PRODUCTS PURCHASED OR NOT PURCHASED. This form of customer behavior is widely evaluated in terms of "share of market." It is an important measure of product salability.

There are enormous variations in product salability for such products as books, greeting cards, songs, and moving pictures. Sales of "hits" can be many orders of magnitude greater than sales of "duds."

> One study undertook to discover what were the major variables that influenced the salability of songs. One finding was that repetition of nonsense syllables was a favorable influence.

DEMANDS FOR OPTIONS. Some product lines are marketed on the basis of a standard product supplemented by options. Analysis of the purchase of options then leads to decisions as to which options to offer as standard features in future models.

DEMANDS FOR "SPECIALS." In like manner, customer demands for products that differ from standard can lead to changes in what is regarded as standard.

> A company in the health industry was processing seven hundred special orders annually, with delivery intervals averaging three months. Analysis showed that a relative few catalog numbers accounted for 95 percent of the special orders. The remedy was to convert these frequent specials into standard products. The delivery interval dropped dramatically: 85 percent of the orders were now delivered within two days. The number of special orders dropped from seven hundred to two hundred a year. All this was done at a substantial cost reduction (Engle and Ball, 1986).

BIDS: SUCCESSFUL AND UNSUCCESSFUL. In some industries the unsuccessful bids dominate the successful bids by a wide margin. It is useful to analyze the results retrospectively in an effort to discover what features of the bids dominated in success or failure.

Figure 6–9 shows the results of such an analysis involving twenty unsuccessful bids to sell and install heavy industrial equipment.

The analysis identified installation price as a leading reason. Further analysis then disclosed a weakness in the cost estimating process. This weakness required a revision in the size of the contingency factors.

PRODUCTS USED OR NOT USED. In the service industries there are many instances in which it is easy to evaluate the extent to which customers make actual use of the product features provided.

A hotel chain introduced a feature that enabled guests to check out by use of the television set, rather than by waiting in line at the cashiers' desk. It was easy to evaluate the actual customer use of the new feature.

Contract Proposal	Bid not accepted due to				
	Quality of Design	*Product Price*	*Installation Price*	*Reciprocal Buying*	*Other*
A1	• • •	X	X	• • •	X
A2	• • •	• • •	XX	• • •	• • •
A3	XX	X	• • •	• • •	• • •
A4	XX	• • •	X	• • •	• • •
A5	XX	• • •	• • •	• • •	• • •
A6	XX	• • •	• • •	• • •	• • •
A7	• • •	XX	• • •	• • •	• • •
A8	• • •	XX	• • •	• • •	• • •
A9	• • •	• • •	XX	• • •	• • •
A10	• • •	• • •	XX	• • •	• • •
B1	X	• • •	X	• • •	• • •
B2	• • •	• • •	• • •	XX	• • •
B3	• • •	• • •	• • •	XX	• • •
B4	• • •	• • •	• • •	XX	• • •
B5	• • •	X	X	• • •	• • •
B6	• • •	X	XX	• • •	• • •
B7	XX	• • •	• • •	• • •	• • •
B8	• • •	X	X	• • •	• • •
B9	• • •	• • •	• • •	X	• • •
B10	X	X	X	• • •	• • •
Totals	7	8	10 (of14)	4	1

X = Contributing reason XX = Main reason

FIGURE 6–9 Analysis of Unsuccessful Bids

Customer Perceptions

In many cases, knowledge of customer behavior is not an adequate basis for decision making; it is necessary in addition to know *the reasons for that behavior.* Those reasons can come from supplementary information, such as customer perceptions and customer opinions. In the discussion that follows:

> Customer *perceptions* are customers' conclusions derived mainly from use of the product.
>
> Customer *opinions* are customers' assertions based mainly on judgment.

These definitions are not mutually exclusive; there is some overlap.

A common example of securing customer perceptions is the study of consumer preferences. Consumers are offered samples of competing products. After use of the products, the consumers state their preference.

> A classic case involved shaving systems. Some years ago the Schick Company marketed a new design featuring easy blade changing. The Gillette Company then conducted a defensive market research study to determine the impact of the new feature on consumers. Samples of the competing shaving systems were given to each of several hundred consumers. Each was asked to use each of the systems for an entire month. Then each consumer was asked to (a) rank the various qualities as to their order of importance and (b) rank the competing systems as to each of the qualities (see Figure 6–10). The study showed that:

	Users' Rankings			
Qualities	*Order of Importance*	*Gillette*	*Gem*	*Schick*
A Remove beard				
B Safety				
C Ease of cleaning				
D Ease of blade changing				
E -----				
F -----				
G -----				

FIGURE 6–10 Ranking the Shaving Systems

1. Ease of blade changing was the least important quality.
2. The competing systems were equal with respect to ease of blade changing.
3. The Gillette system was inferior with respect to a different and very important quality.

Note that in the above comparison of shaving systems the consumer panel was first *put into a state of experience* in order to provide a factual basis for their perceptions. Their use of the products, over and over again, qualified them to make credible perceptions. Without all that experience their conclusions would have been unsupported opinions rather than perceptions based on experience.

Putting customers into a state of experience may still end up with misleading results, since the new experience must compete with human fallibility as well as with all sorts of prior prejudices, cultural values, and so on. A hilarious example emerged from a newspaper's efforts to secure information relative to a furor over cola drinks.

> During the mid-1980s, after extensive testing, the makers of Coca-Cola changed their formula. Their customers protested the change so vigorously that the old formula was reinstated under the name Coca-Cola Classic. The new formula was also retained, under the name Coca Cola (and "Coke"). These two then competed in the market with Pepsi Cola as well as with each other. When the newspaper sponsored a battery of taste tests at a shopping mall, one of the findings was that 70 of the 100 panelists were mistaken in their identification of what they were drinking. Their preferences in the taste tests also extensively contradicted their prior stated preferences. When confronted with the facts, many became defensive and challenged the conduct of the tests (Morris, 1987).

Response to Customer Perceptions

Customers act on their perceptions. Collectively, the consequences can be enormous.

> A 1986 Business Week/Harris poll showed that users of long distance communications rated quality and reliability of service as more important than cost of the service. The same poll showed that the company that was the highest rated for its quality also commanded the highest share of market.

Since customers act on their perceptions, the product developers should use the customers' perceptions as inputs to decision making.

When Thomas Edison was working on the system design for electric lighting for homes, he adopted the policy that the new, unfamiliar electrical system must be made to resemble the prevailing, familiar gas lighting system as far as possible: appearance of the appliances, color of the light, intensity of the light, price of the service (Josephson, 1959).

Once customer's perceptions become known, the product developers may be able to revise the product features to respond to those perceptions.

A study of performance of oil company service stations found that customer choice of service station was strongly determined by the amount of time lost in stopping for service. Refinement of the study then established that the critical variable was the *perceived* lost time, and that waiting for an attendant accounted for much of this. One remedy was for unoccupied attendants to make themselves conspicuously visible in the service area (Ackoff, 1978, Fable 5.4, p. 108).

Some customers' perceptions have little or no validity, but the customers act on them all the same.

Many consumers believe that the price of a product is an indication of its quality—the higher the price, the higher the quality. Numerous investigators have examined this belief and have been unable to confirm it (see, in this connection, Juran, 1988, Section 3, under "Quality and Price").

Customers' Opinions

The urge to understand the reasons behind customer behavior stimulates a good deal of customer contact and market research based on asking customers for their opinions. Why do customers buy or not buy product X? Why do customers prefer product X over Y? The hope is that the customers will be able to identify those quality-related features that explain their behavior.

This is a treacherous area of inquiry. There are many product features to be evaluated amid various degrees of competition. In addition, numerous forces converge on the customers, some of which are of no help to rational decision making. So while the market research design may require customers to give answers, it does not follow that the answers provide a reliable guide to decision making.

The situation is at its worst when we ask for predictions: Would you buy this product, at this price? We can obtain answers, but the reality is missing, since the customers are not faced with making an actual choice, and with backing that choice by an actual expenditure of money.

Interaction: Product Development and Marketing

The spectrum of product differences has a profound impact on the source of salability, that is, whether salability is due mainly to the tools of product development or to the tools of marketing. An interesting study of the interplay between these two sources of salability is seen in Figure 6–11.

Each point on the diagram represents some food product: corn flakes, frozen potatoes, chocolate, and so on. The horizontal scale is consumer preference for the product of one company over the leading competitive product. The vertical scale is share of market.

The absence of points in the right and left hand zones of the diagram is mainly the result of quality differences created by product development. A high degree of consumer preference for one product

FIGURE 6–11 Study of Consumer Preference Versus Share of Market

soon becomes widely known and drives the competing product out of the market.

The vertical spectrum contains surprises. Some products hold over 80 percent share of market despite being neutral as to consumer preference. On analysis, these surprises were found to be mostly the result of marketing skills: getting to market first ("prior franchise"), attractive packaging, persuasive propaganda, and so on.

The diagram also contains some investment implications. An investment in product development to raise consumer preference for some product from (say) 47 to 53 percent would not be likely to create a significant change in salability. That investment might better be put into the marketing effort.

Analysis to Avoid Product Failures

The top priority in product development is product features that make the product salable. The second priority is to avoid product failures in service. If products fail in service, customers will turn to competing products that do not fail so often.

> The xerographic (dry) copier possessed a new and unique product feature: it could copy documents directly from the original. As a result the original producer of dry copiers enjoyed a remarkable growth in sales and profits during the years when its patents gave it a monopoly. However, its products were quite failure-prone. In due course competitors found ways around the patents, came out with products of distinctly lower failure rates, and took over much of the market.

Product failures take place internally as well as externally. The internal failures become evident in such forms as redoing of prior work, delays, and waste of material. Collectively these internal failures result in shocking increases in costs. The external failures also add to our costs and to our clients' costs as well. Thereby they become a threat to continued salability of the product.

The planned approach to product development should include specific provision for guarding against external failures. Such a planned approach involves taking preventive steps with respect to the principal sources of failures that are:

Inherent in the product design

Carryovers from prior models

Due to internal degradation

Design for Reliability

The need to reduce field failures has become acute. Service companies and business processes depend on the continuing operation of their equipment to provide prompt service. For manufacturing companies the field failure rate is a major element of competition.

That same need to reduce field failures has generated an extensive body of practice and a literature devoted to "reliability analysis" of product designs. The methodology includes preparation of reliability models, quantification of reliability; data banks of failure rates of various designs and components; and lists of approved designs, components, and sources of supply. Increasingly the resulting data base is becoming computerized and hence accessible to those product designers who are trained in the use of computer aided design.

The data base for reliability goes beyond the mathematical models. It includes the results of laboratory tests during which discoveries are made about the relationships of operating conditions to failure rates. The data base also includes the feedback of performance under the realities of operating conditions in the field.

A major benefit of using the modern methodology is that it forces the designers to quantify certain elements that in the past were often glossed over. It is easy enough to specify a reliability goal—a maximum failure rate or a mean time between failures. But designing to such a goal requires defining the operating conditions. Reliability is essentially the probability that the product will continue to operate for a specified time under specified operating conditions. To define these operating conditions, the designers are forced to learn, in unprecedented depth, what the environments of use are. The resulting depth of knowledge enables the designers to come up with superior designs.

(For some detailed methodology on reliability analysis, see Juran, 1988, Section 13, "Product Development." See also the selected bibliography on reliability at the end of this chapter.)

Carryover of Prior Product Designs

The product features that result from product development are a mixture of:

a. Features carried over from prior products
b. Features carried over but modified to correct prior weaknesses, or to adapt to new needs
c. Features newly developed

Within this mixture the carryover usually dominates the newly created by a considerable margin. This extensive carryover makes it important for the product developer to understand what the results of those predecessor features were, both as to performance and as to failures.

Carryover of failure-prone features has been a widespread cancer and has destroyed many product lines. The subtle reason is that in most companies the responsibility for diagnosis and remedy of chronic quality problems is so vague that such problems just go on and on. Moreover, the prime responsibility of the product developers has not been to remedy long-standing, chronic quality problems; their prime responsibility has been to develop new product features that can create new sales.

> In the case of the dry copier, analysis showed that the list of "top ten" field failure modes remained virtually unchanged, model after model. Such a phenomenon is strong evidence of lax discipline relative to the carryover of failure-prone features.

More recently upper managers have taken steps to provide greater assurance that reliability goals will be met. In some companies the stated quality policies require that new models of products may be put on the market only if their reliability (the opposite of failure-proneness) is at least equal to that of the models they replace, and of competitors' models as well. These policies are then enforced by requiring the product developers to prove, through laboratory and field test data, that the policies have been met. Another approach is to make the "product manager" responsible for field service costs that result from the carryover of failure-prone product features.

There is also a positive side to carryover of prior design features. Some of these features have been in operation for years, and their performance has met customer needs as well as competition. For unchanging customer needs, the carryover of such proven features may be the most efficient solution. In such cases carryover not only reduces design effort and the associated time interval but also reduces the costs and time required to conduct model tests and field tests for the new design.

> In the design of large-scale integrated circuits, the practice is increasingly to carry over modules and circuit elements that have already been proven during field use of previous designs (Sanger, 1988).

The "Sidewinder" missile was developed during the 1950s. It proved to be so reliable that it was still in use during the 1980s (Fialka, 1985).

Urging designers to make use of proven prior designs runs into some cultural resistance. Some designers prefer to be original. There is a tendency to regard using prior designs as lower-grade work than creating new designs. Some companies offer rewards to designers who do make efficient use of proven designs, e.g., "Thief of the Month."

Underachievement of Reliability

In general, actual reliability falls short of predicted reliability. Laboratory test results usually show values of reliability lower than those predicted by the mathematical models. Similarly, reliability attained in the field is usually lower than that predicted by the laboratory tests.

For the most part this progressive degradation is traceable to the differences between the "two worlds" of theory and practice. The mathematical models and laboratory tests are designed under conditions that differ extensively from those prevailing in the world of operations. There are differences in priorities, facilities, personnel, training, motivation, and so on. While these differences cannot be abolished, steps can be taken to minimize their adverse effect on reliability.

One of these steps is to provide for participation by the customers, the various suppliers, processors, and users who will be impacted by the product design (see below, under "Participation").

A more comprehensive step is to identify the specific tasks that must be carried out in order to achieve reliability and to assign clear responsibility: identify which organization unit is to carry out which tasks (see generally, Juran, 1988, Section 13, "Product Development").

Value Analysis

Value analysis is a process for evaluating the interrelationships among (a) the functions performed by product features, and (b) the associated costs. The aim of value analysis is to:

Provide the customer with the essential product functions

Optimize the cost of providing those essential functions

Identify the marginal product features that can be eliminated

The inputs to the value analysis process consist largely of:

The list of customers' needs and the associated order of importance

The corresponding list of product features

The estimates of the costs of providing the product features

Information on competing product features and their costs

Starting with such inputs, the value analysis process undertakes several activities:

Define the product functions with precision. Express each function in terms of a verb and a noun.

Break the primary product functions down into subfunctions: secondary, tertiary, etc.

For each subfunction estimate the cost of carrying it out.

Use the resulting cost estimates as an aid to judging the merits of the respective product development alternatives.

Practitioners have evolved a number of methods of analysis to aid in carrying out the above activities. Generally these methods are all built around a matrix or spreadsheet which establishes relationships between product functions and the costs of providing those functions. An example of such a spreadsheet is shown in Figure 6-12 (Withers, 1983).

In this spreadsheet each vertical column represents some function performed by a product feature. Each horizontal row represents some cost associated with the product feature—a component, an operation, a test, etc.

In this analysis the left-hand column lists the various elements that generate costs. Next the "Cost" column shows:

a. The total cost for each element (shown above the diagonal)
b. The ratio of that cost to the grand total cost for all elements (shown below the diagonal)

For example, in the top horizontal row the total cost for the comb elements is £11.58, which is 13.14 percent of the total of all costs (£88.15) for all functions.

VALUE ANALYSIS SPREADSHEET

Departments, Operations, Assemblies, etc.	Cost		FUNCTIONS (verb + noun)									
			Provide landing	Accept steps	Provide safety	Be durable	Be inter changeable	Provide rigidity	Be serviceable	Provide identity	Be adjustable	Assembly
Comb (4)	£ 11.58	13.14%	0.58	2.90	4.05	0.23	1.16		1.40		1.27	
Safety switch	£ 13.14	14.90%			5.26		4.60		1.31		1.97	
Comb bearer	£ 28.94	32.83%	11.57					14.47			2.89	
Tread plate	£ 3.22	3.65%	0.64		0.64	1.28	0.32			0.32		
Entry guide	£ 15.26	17.31%		5.34	3.81	1.53	1.53		1.53		1.53	
Logo	£ 1.01	1.15%				0.51				0.51		
Assembly	£ 15.00	17.02%										15.00
TOTAL COST (£)	88.15		12.79	8.23	13.76	3.54	7.61	14.47	4.23	0.82	7.66	15.00
% OF TOTAL COST	100%		14.51	9.33	15.61	4.01	8.63	16.41	4.80	0.93	8.69	17.02

FIGURE 6–12 Value Analysis Spreadsheet

The remaining columns then show the estimates of the extent to which the elements of cost are allocable to the various functions.

Once the matrix has been filled in, the totals for the columns show the estimated total cost for each function.

The estimated costs of the functions can then be compared to (a) the estimates of the salability of the associated product features and (b) the estimated costs and values of the competing product features. These comparisons become a useful input to the planning and business decisions relative to meeting customer needs.

The matrix also provides useful detail on the cost buildups. There are 28 "active" cost-function combinations within the matrix, adding up to a total of f88.15. However, these follow the Pareto principle, so that several of the combinations collectively account for the bulk of the costs. Any major reduction in costs will obviously have to come from these "vital few."

Note: No one should be fooled by the seeming precision of the numbers in the spreadsheet. They are carried out to the second decimal place, but the real precision of the figures depends heavily on the validity of the estimates. These estimates are usually made to the nearest 10 percent, and they have a range of error beyond that.

Design for Manufacture and Assembly (DFMA)

A further form of analysis increasingly used by designers is "design for manufacture and assembly." The 1980s witnessed a trend for designers to provide their internal customers with increased participation. The experience gained from this participation has increasingly been converted into "lessons learned." Applied to design as it affects manufacture, these lessons learned have provided designers with data bases, rules for decision making, and still other aids for optimizing their designs.

For an extended treatment of these lessons as they apply to design for manufacture, see Boothroyd and Dewhurst (1987).

The Sequence of the Analyses

On the face of it, the various analyses can be done in some logical consecutive order. The quality planning road map has an implication of planning in consecutive steps. Flow diagrams for the phase system are typically drawn in a way that suggests consecutive activities. The business decisions inherent in the phase system certainly are arranged in consecutive order. The various company functions have generally exhibited a preference for a consecutive approach in which each carries out its mission and then "hands off" to the next function in the sequence.

Nevertheless, experience has shown that the analyses should be done mainly on a concurrent basis. Strict adherence to a consecutive approach has resulted in handoffs by "throwing it over the wall" to the next department, with resulting costly crises. To attain the optimum (see below) requires "tradeoffs" among multiple customer needs and product features, some of which compete with each other.

In general, the market-oriented analyses (salability, competitive) are among the earliest to be done, while analyses relating to internal operations are done later. The lists of activities that make up the phase system usually follow such a sequence. However, those same activities are multifunctional in nature, requiring a team approach. In turn, a team approach tends to do things concurrently rather than consecutively. What we are witnessing is the emergence of a concept of concurrent planning, such as was done by "Team Taurus." Such concurrent planning is likely to become the dominant form during the next century.

An aid to concurrent planning is the design of the spreadsheet itself. Commonly the spreadsheet is provided with a separate column for each of the respective analyses.

To fill in those columns, the product developer needs the participation of many of the functions around The Spiral. Such participation then tends to favor a concurrent form of quality planning.

Optimizing Product Design

The goal in optimizing is to:

Meet the needs of customer and supplier alike

Minimize their combined costs

The goal is valid, but to reach it requires

Overcoming the traditional urge of customers and suppliers to *suboptimize*—to meet their separate goals

Securing the participation of those impacted

Acquiring the needed inputs and discovering the conditions that provide an optimum result

Resolving differences

The Urge to Suboptimize

The main cause of failure to reach the optimum is the pursuit of local goals. This suboptimization takes place between companies and also within companies.

Suboptimizing Between Companies

In market-based societies, the dominant tradition has been for each company to look out for its own interests: to meet its own quality needs and to minimize its own costs. The competitive society does contain forces that favor arriving at the optimum, but the pace can be agonizingly slow. (The concept of life cycle costing has been known for many years. It offers a major opportunity to improve our national quality and productivity. Yet application of this concept is still in its infancy).

In cases where companies do recognize the opportunities inherent in the optimum, the results can be stunning.

> The automatic teller machine is a convenience to bank customers while enabling the banks to provide service at less cost than through human bank tellers. However, bank customers could secure such service only from machines that belonged to their own bank.
>
> In March 1985, ten New York banks created the New York Cash Exchange (NYCE) to enable the banks to pool their teller machines in a shared network. Within a year the consortium grew to seventy-four financial institutions with more than double the original numbers of cardholders and teller machines, and with a rapidly expanding volume of transactions (Stevenson, 1986).

An optimal situation does not necessarily remain optimal. Changing conditions may require revision to restore the optimum.

> In metropolitan areas it is common for vehicular traffic to create severe congestion at the bridges and tunnels. In some cases the average seat occupancy of incoming cars is less than two. The usual toll charge is per car, irrespective of occupancy. One solution has been to revise the toll structure so as to encourage car pooling (Ackoff, 1978, Fable 3.6, p. 58).

Optimizing usually involves some degree of collaboration between supplier and customer. The initiative may be taken by either.

> A maker of instruments found that installation on the customers' premises was frequently delayed because of inadequate preparation of facilities (foundation, power supply, etc.). The company prepared a videotape explaining the preparations needed. The company also required customers to certify that preparations were complete before sending the installation personnel out to the site. The time to install was reduced from an average of about ten days to about two days.

> Another example of an initiative by the supplier involved a special size of ingot demanded by only one customer. To provide this special size was an annoying burden to the supplier. During a visit to the customer, the question was raised: "No one else requires a special size. Why do you need one"? The reply was, "Our storage chest is not big enough to hold the regular size." The supplier then built a bigger storage chest for the customer.

Suboptimizing Within Companies

Suboptimizing is also a widespread problem *within* companies. A major contributing cause is the practice of establishing departmental goals and then judging the performance of managers based on departmental performance against these goals. This practice is inherently sound. People get more done when they do have goals and are judged by their performance against goals. However, it is all too easy for a department to improve its performance and in doing so to damage company performance.

> A purchasing department reduced the cost of purchased materials by buying a year's supply rather than one month's at a time. However, the net result was a loss to the company. The material deteriorated gradually during storage. The effect over a month or two had been tolerable. Over a period of many months, it was not tolerable.

Internal Monopolies

Many internal departments are given specific jurisdiction over certain areas of decision making. This jurisdiction is enforced through a monopoly on the approval of the documents that can generate action. Various critical documents do not become official until they bear the approval of the departments recognized as having jurisdiction. For example:

Department	*Jurisdiction*
Product design	Approve specifications
Marketing	Sign sales contracts
Purchasing	Sign purchase contracts
Staff departments	Establish schedules; issue procedures manuals; interpret regulations

The provisions inherent in such documents can and do impact quality. Yet the associated jurisdictions are generally interpreted as having a degree of monopoly over the respective areas of decision making. Cases abound in which the monopoly departments, to meet their departmental goals, create problems for internal customers. Often these problems have their origin in a misuse of the monopolies—in a claim of exclusive jurisdiction.

The Claim of Exclusive Jurisdiction

Organization units often claim to have exclusive jurisdiction over certain areas of decision making: "*We* are responsible for quality" (or for cost, safety, design, etc.). To deal properly with such claims requires separating the asserted monopoly into its elements. Normally these elements consist of responsibilities relative to:

Choice of the inputs that are to enter the decision making

Making the decision

Signing the documents that make the decision official

Responsibility for signing the documents *should* be a monopoly, and usually such is the practice. (It is asking for confusion to authorize multiple organizations to sign specifications, sales contracts, purchase orders, etc.) However, this logical monopoly has a habit of extending itself into unintended areas. This extension then results in monopolies over choice of inputs and over decision making.

Choice of inputs should *not* be a monopoly. An optimal result is most unlikely unless those impacted have the opportunity to provide their inputs.

Making the decision (in the light of the inputs) may logically be a monopoly in some cases but not in others. Decisions that relate to optimizing company economics are ideally the result of a consensus among the impacted organizations. In contrast, there are cases in which we must rely on the judgment of the acknowledged experts. Here are two examples:

> Our planning requires preparation of a new form of product warranty. The wording of the warranty is critical. If poorly worded it may expose us to extensive costs in the form of unjustified claims. We rely on the lawyer's opinion as to how the wording would be interpreted by the courts.
>
> A new product involves potential safety hazards for ultimate users. What is critical is the factor of safety to be used in the design. We rely on the design engineer's opinion as to the factors of safety needed to ensure the structural integrity of the design.

In each case the reliance is on expertise derived from special training and experience. As to their areas of expertise, we give the experts the benefit of the doubt and the last word.

Special Expertise and Broad Planning

While we rely on the experts as to their area of expertise, we should distinguish carefully between areas of expertise and the broad planning of which these areas are a part.

> We look to the lawyer to provide the legal interpretation of the wording of the warranty. We do not look to the lawyer to determine what should be the features covered by the warranty, or what should be the duration of the warranty. Those are business decisions to be made by the managers who collectively run the business.
>
> We look to the product designer to provide expertise relative to using the laws of nature to attain structural integrity. We do not give the designer the last word on whether we should go to market with the product. That is a business decision.

Optimizing Through Participation

Finding the optimum involves balancing of needs, whether multicompany needs or within-company needs. Ideally the search for the optimum should be done through the *participation* of suppliers and customers alike.

Design Review

Under the design review concept, those who will be impacted by the design are given the opportunity to review the design during various formative stages. The reviewers are chosen based on their experience and expertise in the areas that will be impacted. They use this experience and expertise to make such contributions as:

Early warning of upcoming problems. "If you design it this way, here are the problems I will face."

Data to aid in finding the optimum. The various customers are frequently in a position to provide data in the form of costs that will be incurred, process capability of facilities, etc. Such data are of obvious help for optimizing overall performance.

Challenge to theories. Specialist departments are typically masters of their own specialty but seldom masters of the specialties of other departments. In the absence of participation by those other departments, the risk is that unproven theories or unwarranted beliefs will prevail. Participation by the customers provides an informed challenge.

Collectively these and other contributions make the whole greater than the sum of the parts. The equation takes the form 1 + 1 = 3.

Analysis of findings of prior design reviews can provide a data base, which in turn can assist the conduct of future design reviews. During the 1980s, General Electric evolved a quantitative method of rating product designs for ease of assembly. Design review teams were trained to use the method for rating new designs, after which the ratings became an input for the design review (Maczka, 1984).

(For elaboration, see Gryna, 1986. See also, Juran, 1988, "Design Review," pp. 13.7 to 13.11.)

Joint Planning

A second major approach for optimizing through participation is joint planning. Such joint planning has long existed in various forms. For example:

Some service companies prepare and publish information to help customers analyze their needs. A widespread example has been in the area of energy conservation.

Many manufacturing companies offer a service of "Technical

Representatives'' to visit with customers, analyze their needs, and provide consulting assistance.

In some instances, joint planning has resulted in extensive shift of work between independent organizations.

> A major activity in the Postal Service is sorting the mail based on destination. It was determined by joint studies that companies who send out large volumes of mail were in a position to presort such mail with less effort than the Postal Service, and with resulting speedier delivery. In turn, the Postal Service established a discounted price for presorted mail.

Joint planning is feasible even in cases where proprietary information is involved.

> The Aluminum Company of America (Alcoa) and the Eastman Kodak Company (Kodak) established a joint team to optimize performance of a photographic plate. Alcoa made the aluminum base, and Kodak applied the coating. The surface condition of the base was critical, and both companies made use of proprietary processes. Nevertheless the team was able to make significant improvements in the product quality, and at a cost reduction. How did they protect their proprietary secrets? They simply trusted each other (Kegarise and Miller, 1985).

Joint planning has been shown to be applicable to a wide variety of situations. Toy designers are able to secure inputs from very young children. An architect secures inputs from children on design of playgrounds, as reported on CBS News ''Sunday Morning,'' March 30, 1986). Computer networks link up computer-aided design with computer-aided manufacture (CAD/CAM), and create a common data base (Sterling, 1984).

The need for participation in quality planning is dramatized whenever an industry undergoes a consolidation or breakup of companies. A classic example of breakup was that of the Bell System ''divestiture.''

> Until the 1980s the Bell system had a virtual monopoly on all aspects of providing telephone service in the United States: designing, making, and installing the equipment; selling the telephone service; operating the telephone lines. There was no

> debate about the quality of the service, but there was much debate about the costs and prices.
>
> Then, as a result of government action, there was a divestiture. The regional operating telephone companies became completely independent. What followed was many months of utter chaos with respect to quality of service. The planning of the divestiture gave top priority to intracompany matters. However, some important aspects of quality of service to the paying customers had now become a multicompany problem, requiring joint quality planning. This lacked top priority, resulting in a scandalous decline in quality of service, which took many months to rectify.

An example of consolidation is seen in the wave of airline mergers that followed deregulation of that industry by the federal government. Some of the mergers were accompanied by severe declines in quality of service. Some of the decline was traceable to lack of standardization. The computers used for ticketing were not compatible; various physical facilities were not interchangeable; the personnel were not trained to service unfamiliar equipment. Ideally, joint quality planning should have been done prior to consolidation so as to ease the transition. Instead, many of the quality problems were left to be solved after the consolidation, resulting in numerous complaints by customers and a poor quality image for the companies (Thomas, 1987).

Another aspect of joint quality planning relates to the role of the "human factor" in attaining quality. As products become complex, the limiting factor often is the ability of human beings to operate and maintain those products. In such cases the joint planning team should include specialists from the pertinent behavioral sciences as well as personnel who will be faced with doing the operation and maintenance.

Some military weapon systems have become extremely complex. Nevertheless it is feasible to design such systems in ways that provide the operating personnel with controls and instructions that are comparatively simple and can be absorbed through training (Cushman, 1987).

Participative Teams: Concurrent Planning

During the 1980s a trend toward concurrent quality planning done by multifunctional teams emerged. This method became a challenge to the traditional approach. Under the traditional approach a manual is prepared, setting out the planning actions and decisions to be taken by each functional organization unit around The Spiral: Market Research, Product Development, etc. Thereafter, for each planning project, each of those functions carries out its work and then "hands off" the result to the next function. This sequential method has encouraged the development of a career concept within each function as well as functional expertise and loyalty to the function. However, in practice this same method has unilaterally created numerous quality problems and crises for the subsequent functions around The Spiral.

Under the new approach a team is organized with members from multiple functional organization units around The Spiral. The team then carries out the planning in a concurrent fashion. The very nature of such a team approach stimulates design reviews and the inputs needed to arrive at the optimum. In addition, the concurrent nature of the planning makes it possible to shorten the time cycle for the project.

> A major example of the new approach was "Team Taurus" organized by Ford Motor Company to plan the Taurus models of automobiles to be "best in class." To meet that goal required achieving best in class for more than four hundred product features of the cars. In turn that required more than four hundred planning teams. For the most part the goals were met, and the Taurus was a stunning success in the market (Veraldi, 1986).

The extent to which companies will adopt concurrent planning by multifunctional teams remains to be seen.

However, one widespread conclusion has been that the spirit of teamwork generated during the project does not stop with the end of the project; it carries over into the day-to-day operations as well.

Resistance to Participation in Planning

The opportunity to participate is generally welcomed by the customers—those who will be impacted by the plan. However, this opportunity is often *not* welcomed by the planners. Many planners, especially product developers, have resisted participative planning. Their stated reasons usually include the following:

> We are experienced product developers, and we are already well informed about the needs of those who will be impacted.

The participative process is time-consuming. It will add to the cost of product development and to the length of the development cycle.

Product developers should be free to use their creativity. The participative process suppresses that creativity.

Such are the usual stated reasons, and they have a degree of validity. Behind such stated reasons are unstated reasons that often are the real reasons for the resistance. They include:

The product development department has had a monopoly on much of the decision making associated with product development. That monopoly has been an important source of status for the product developers. Introduction of participation will break the monopoly and thereby reduce the status of the developers.

The benefits of participation (if any) will show up on the books of the company but not on the books of the product development department. The "scoreboard" will show that under participation the development department takes longer to do its work, and at a higher cost.

These and other reasons collectively make up what is called "cultural resistance," since the origin is the *"cultural pattern"* of (in this case) the development department. Managers who contemplate introducing the concept of participative planning should become familiar with the nature of cultural patterns and the way in which they affect human behavior. See in this connection Chapter 12 under "Human Behavior and Cultural Values" and under "Dealing With Cultural Resistance: Rules of the Road." For elaboration, see Juran (1964). The major, seminal work is Mead (1951). See also Kanter (1983), Argyris (1985), and Kotter (1985).

The process of resolving differences (see below) is made easier if the parties understand the nature of cultural resistance.

Resolving Differences

The validity of the concept of an optimum is absolute. Nevertheless, customers and suppliers are tugged by powerful local forces to an extent which can easily lead to a result other than the optimum. To avoid such a result requires an understanding of the interplay among these local forces. In the case of external customers, these forces are mainly of an economic and technological nature. In the case of internal customers, the forces of cultural resistance must also be understood and faced.

Essential Inputs

In some cases the main obstacle to resolving differences is lack of essential information. All the participants have pertinent information, but this is usually limited to their local areas of responsibility. In turn, their defined areas of responsibility urge them to optimize their departmental performances, which often means suboptimizing the overall performance. The missing "essential inputs" are usually those which cut across departmental lines: competitive analysis, salability analysis, value analysis, etc.

For those who have the responsibility to find the real optimum, it is tempting to "make do" with such information as is already available. This temptation should be resisted. An essential part of the job of finding the optimum is to identify what the needed inputs are. Once these have been identified, each poses questions of the sort:

Is this information now available?

If not, is it worthwhile to create it?

A further input to goal setting is derived from the processes needed to produce the product features. The optimal process design interacts with the optimal product design, which makes each an input to the other. We shall have a look at this interface in the next chapter.

Economic Analysis

The goal in economic terms is to minimize the combined costs of customers and suppliers. Arriving at this optimum requires that we determine:

What the alternative ways for meeting (or revising) customers' needs are

What are the associated costs, for customers and for suppliers

Preparation of such inputs requires digging well below the surface. A widespread example is life cycle costing for long-life goods. Design of these goods requires a decision of whether to:

a. Design for low original cost so as to permit a low selling price. Such designs often result in a high "cost of ownership"—a high cost of operating and maintaining the product over its lifetime. The high cost is in turn due to maintenance costs, downtime, high energy consumption, etc., resulting from design emphasis on low original cost.

b. Design for low cost of ownership over the life of the product. Such designs often result in a high original price, with associated selling problems.

The life cycle cost concept is sound and can contribute importantly to improving national productivity. The chief obstacle is cultural resistance. For most of human history, the major determinant in purchasing has been the original price. A good deal of creative product design and innovative marketing is needed to extend the life cycle cost concept throughout the economy (for elaboration, see Juran, 1988, "Life Cycle Costing," pp. 3.20 to 3.27).

Technological Analysis

Designers of technological products and processes face many complex problems of optimizing. Product designs consist of numerous bits and pieces, made of numerous kinds of materials, put together in numerous kinds of ways, programmed to operate under a variety of environments, and so on. The number of potential combinations is enormous, but the optimal combinations are few in number. Process designs similarly exhibit enormous numbers of potential combinations and few optimal combinations.

Designers have for many centuries been aware of the existence of these problems, but they lacked the tools needed to solve them. Then, during the twentieth century, two new families of tools were developed to make available to the designers the means for solving those problems of optimizing. These tools were:

1. Design of Experiments and Analysis of Variance, which provided the equations and algorithms needed to organize the variables into soluble form. Actually these tools have been available for decades, but the problem of solving the resulting equations was beyond the capability of the then-existing methods of calculation.
2. The electronic computer, which provided the computation capability for solving the resulting complex equations.

Application of these tools involves a great deal of detail, which is beyond the scope of this book. However, there is a considerable literature on the subject. For elaboration and bibliography, see Juran (1988) under "Design and Analysis of Experiments" (Section 26), "Product Development" (Section 13), "Process Industries" (Section 28), and "Computers and Quality" (Section 27).

The Coonley-Agnew Process

This process for resolving differences was set out in a paper published in 1941. It related to an attempt to establish national quality standards for cast iron pipe. The climate for agreement was decidedly unfavorable—the manufacturers and the ultimate users had for years been unhappy with each other. When a joint committee was set up to develop the quality standards, the chairman stipulated three conditions to be met during the deliberations:

1. They must identify their areas of agreement and their areas of disagreement. "That is, they must first agree upon the exact point at which the road began to fork." When this was done it was found that a major point of disagreement concerned the validity of a certain formula.
2. "They must agree on why they disagreed." They concluded that the known facts were inadequate to decide whether the formula was valid or not.
3. "They must decide what they were going to do about it." The decision was to raise a fund to conduct the research needed to establish the necessary facts. "With the facts at hand, the controversies disappeared" (Coonley and Agnew, 1941).

The Alternatives of Mary Parker Follett

Follett's writings included an analysis of resolving differences through the alternatives of dominance, compromise, and constructive conflict (Metcalf and Urwick, 1941).

Dominance is sometimes found in situations where superior product features are protected by patents. In such cases it is tempting for product designers to conclude: "We know best what the customer needs." But the customers resent such autocratic behavior. The result is an adversary relationship with associated suspicion and mistrust. Each party works to optimize its own results, not to find ways to improve results for both. The adversary relationship effectively shrinks the communication and teamwork needed to find the common optimum. The customers must nevertheless endure the autocratic behavior—for the time being. Then, as competitors find ways around the patents, the dominance is reversed, and the customers relish the opportunity to take their business elsewhere.

Dominance is also widely practiced between internal suppliers and internal customers. Most of this has its origin in internal monopolies. To illustrate:

> The Budget Office is given responsibility for preparing the budget. To simplify its work it imposes elaborate forms and procedures on all other departments. The end result is higher overall cost to the company.

> In like manner, Management Information Systems may impose unwarranted burdens on other departments. Marketing may demand perfectionism in quality with little effect on sales volume but with costly consequences. Product Development may come up with new product designs that are uneconomic to make.

As to internal customers, the rule must be: No one has the right, unilaterally, to make trouble for a customer.

Compromise is widely used in the negotiating process, but not necessarily to arrive at the optimum. In some design review meetings an impasse may get broken by methods similar to the "logrolling" used in the political process: "You vote for my bill and I'll vote for yours." Each party meets some desired goals, but at the price of taking some unwanted and even unpleasant actions.

The atmosphere of compromise is less abrasive than that of dominance. But compromise still falls short of arriving at the optimum. It satisfies no one in a fundamental way. It also lacks the basic spirit of teamwork that is essential to create the communication and joint effort needed to discover the optimum.

Constructive conflict is Follett's term for a teamwork approach to *discover some new solution* that outperforms those derived from dominance or compromise. The concept can be illustrated by case examples in which a major commonality is ingenuity:

> In large companies it is common for the divisions to sell to each other under a monopoly arrangement: the supplying divisions have a captive market; the buying divisions have a captive source of supply; the transfer prices are determined by negotiation. The numerous negotiations are time-consuming and are a frequent source of irritation, since trading with

outside suppliers or customers is precluded by the corporate insistence on the monopoly arrangement. Many companies have solved the problem by separating the pricing policy from the monopoly policy. The basis for pricing becomes the market price. Either the buying division or the supplying division may insist on retaining the monopoly, but only at the market price.

A classic example involving goods is the case of the household refrigerator door. The refrigerator door had to be right-handed or left-handed depending on the floor layout of the kitchen. Forecasts of total refrigerator sales were quite reliable, but not so for the door openings. As a result, manufacturers were forced to maintain two sets of inventories of refrigerators. The size of these inventories was a constant source of controversy. The marketers wanted ample inventories of both models. The factory managers wanted minimal inventories. The new solution was a redesign of the appliance as to make the door reversible either in the factory or in the field. Now the inventories became minimal, and the marketers acquired maximum flexibility (Ackoff 1978, Fable 4.5, p. 91).

Product Features as Goals for Process Developers

At the outset of product development, customer needs are stated in *qualitative* terms. Following product design the resulting product features are expressed in *quantitative* terms. To illustrate, Figure 6-13 lists some customer needs in qualitative terms (left-hand column), and the associated quantification (right-hand column).

The quantified product features (right-hand column) become the basis for setting quantitative product goals—goals in terms of aimed-at values and specification limits. Those goals then become the targets for the process developers and the operating forces.

To make matters more complicated, goals for many product features are established at two levels:

For product units individually

For product units collectively

To illustrate, a goal for promptness of service may be established at five minutes for any individual cycle of service. However, for the

Customer Needs (in qualitative terms)	Result of Quantification
Promptness	Delivery time
Freedom from errors	Error rate
No interruptions	Percent downtime
Roominess	Spatial dimensions
Reliability	Mean time between failures
Safety	Tensile strength
Purity	Parts per million of impurities

FIGURE 6–13 Qualitative Customer Needs and Quantified Product Features

cycles collectively the goal may be expressed as 85 percent of the clients shall be served within five minutes of entering the queue.

A similar practice is followed in the case of goods. A designer's specification for a mechanical component may define the dimensions in terms of nominal values and specification limits. That definition then applies to each and every unit of product. However, the purchase orders, sampling tables, and so forth may be designed to impose a limit on nonconforming units in terms of X parts per million.

Goals Based on Product Uniformity

Goals for product features have long been expressed in terms of an aimed-at target, with specification limits around that target. As product developers acquired knowledge about process capabilities, it became evident that the frequency distributions of the resulting products were not really compatible with the prevailing concepts of specification limits. Figure 6–14 shows the contrast.

In Figure 6–14 the specification limits are shown as vertical lines, whereas the frequency distribution often takes the form of the bell shaped curve.

The first large-scale effort to create a closer compatibility was probably the case of the L3 coaxial transmission system for multiple telephone or television channels (Dodge, Kinsburg, and Kruger, 1953). In that system, specification limits for the key product features of components were established on the basis of:

A maximum for the standard deviation of the frequency distribution of the product feature

A limit on the average, equal to ± one-third of that standard deviation

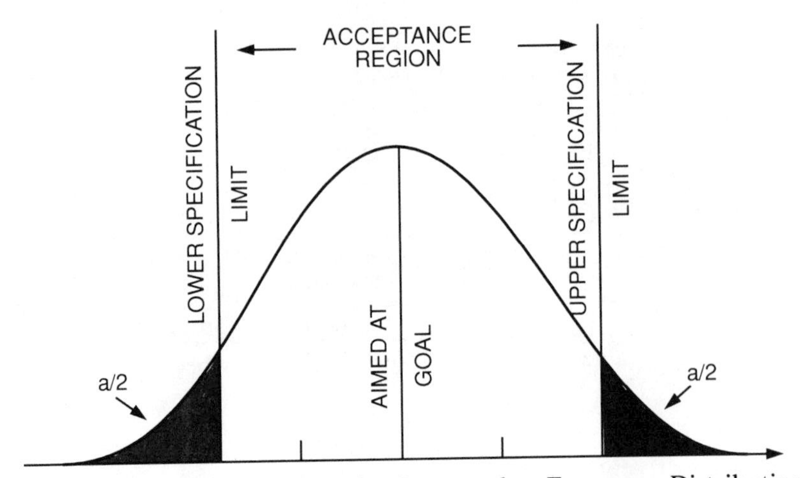

FIGURE 6–14 Specification Limits Compared to Frequency Distribution

During the next few decades, the concept of product goals based on uniformity remained largely dormant. Then during the 1980s a renewed interest emerged, involving a concept of specification limits based on:

An aimed-at target

Continuing reduction in process (and product) variability

Behind this concept is the realization that for some kinds of products, reduction in variability of the components can significantly improve the performance of the system. The Ford Motor Company found that transaxles made from high-uniformity components resulted in warranty charges much lower than transaxles made from components of conventional uniformity (Ford, 1981).

The potential applications for this concept are very numerous, and the authors believe the concept is inherently sound. However, it remains to be seen whether it will be widely adopted. The application (in the 1950s) to the L3 coaxial system was also inherently sound, but there was no rush to apply the concept more broadly.

Completing the Documentation

The results of product development are officially transmitted to other functions through various kinds of documentation. These include the specifications for the product features and product goals, as well as the spreadsheets and other supporting documents. All this is supplemented by instructions, both written and oral.

Completing the Spreadsheets

Filling out the spreadsheets is an ongoing process throughout product development. As the various analyses progress, the results are entered into the appropriate columns. The process of optimizing the product features concludes with a list of product goals for those features. The establishment of those product goals also completes the spreadsheet (which relates product features to customer needs).

Publication of Goals for Product Features

Publication of goals for product features is a natural monopoly. If there is more than one publisher, there will inevitably be confusion as to which publication is official. This publication actually involves two separable functions:

1. *Authentication.* This is the job of certifying what the official goal is. The authenticator may be that specialist department which has "the benefit of the doubt and the last word." The authenticator may also be some coordinating department that secures a consensus and then in effect certifies: "Here is the consensus that was reached."
2. *Issuance.* This is the administrative job of preparing duplicate copies of the official product goals and distributing them to the customers. Here again, the issuing department may be the same as the authenticator, or it may be a separate service.

There is nothing trivial or demeaning about the job of publishing quality goals. A great deal of damage can be done and has been done as a result of publication errors in product design specifications, operating instruction manuals, maintenance manuals, and the like. The publication job should be in the hands of people whose training and experience qualify them to carry out such exacting work.

Some aspects of publication of goals are influential in meeting the criteria for what "a goal should be."

Goals should be written out. This discipline helps to assure that the goals are *understandable.*

Goals should be approved by the appropriate authority. This helps to assure their *legitimacy.*

Publication of Associated Know-how

During the work of product development, the developers acquire a great deal of know-how about the subject matter. Much of this know-how gets put into the documentation, and thereby gets transferred to the process developers and other functions. Some of this acquired know-how is undocumented but gets communicated through design reviews and other forms of participation. Additional undocumented know-how does not get communicated through usual channels, but nevertheless has value to other functions, and should be communicated to them. This can be done by setting up meetings for the specific purpose of briefing the process developers and other functions, as needed.

Quality Characteristic

Many quality specialists, especially in manufacturing industries, use the term "quality characteristic" to mean any property of a product or process. In this book we have avoided use of the term "quality characteristic." Instead, we have been using the word "feature" to designate such a product or process property.

The reason for not using the term "quality characteristic" is that it is seldom used within service industries and is used hardly at all by the general public. In contrast the word "feature" is universally used and understood.

On to Process Development

The next chapter is "Develop Process Features." It starts with the product features and product goals. It then develops the processes needed to meet those goals.

A Note on Quality Function Deployment (QFD)

QFD is a quality planning tool that has been recently popularized in the United States. The essence of QFD is a series of interlocking matrices that start with customers' needs and then deploy these down to the process control characteristics. The nature and use of QFD matrices is very closely related to the generic spreadsheets shown in Figure 1–11a–d. In fact, the "house of quality" is a specialized adaptation of a generic spreadsheet.

The QFD spreadsheet (known as the "house of quality") was first developed at the Kobe, Japan, shipyards in the early 1970s and was also used for specific applications by Toyota in the mid-1970s. The "house of quality" spreadsheet allows for the additional information to be added to the generic spreadsheet, including competitive technical data, customer survey data, and importance factors.

Published examples of QFD have mainly related design of goods and focus on the successful deployment of customer needs into the technical design aspects of the goods. The emergence of QFD supports the importance of interlocking spreadsheets to aid the quality planning process.

For details on the QFD matrices, see Hauser and Clausing (1984), Sullivan (1986), and Morrell (1987).

List of High Points

The single most important product is that which brings in the company's income.

The numerous combinations of customers and needs require a structured approach to product development.

The spreadsheet (also matrix, quality table, etc.) is the major tool used during a structured approach to quality planning.

The spreadsheet *does not provide answers;* it is mostly a depository for answers.

Product development requires not only functional expertise; it also requires use of a body of quality-related know-how—the quality disciplines.

There has been no mandate requiring product developers to make use of the quality disciplines.

Companies are in the early stages of providing the training needed to convert the amateur planners into professionals.

Criticality should be viewed from the standpoint of both the customer and the supplier.

In case of internal monopolies, it is often possible to secure competitive information from outside suppliers of similar services.

For product developments based on new technology, the first and most basic question is, "If we had it, could we sell it."

Past behavior of customers is a useful leading indicator, a predictor of future behavior.

Product developers should use customers' perceptions as inputs to decision making, since customers act on their perceptions.

The planned approach to product development should include specific provision for guarding against external failures.

A major benefit of modern methodology is that it forces the designers to quantify certain elements that in the past were often glossed over.

Carryover of failure-prone features has been a widespread cancer, and has destroyed many product lines.

Concurrent planning is likely to become the dominant form during the next century.

Responsibility for signing critical documents should be a monopoly.

Choice of inputs should not be a monopoly.

The spirit of teamwork generated during completion of a project does not stop with the end of the project; it carries over into the day-to-day operations as well.

An essential part of the job of finding the optimum is to identify what are the needed inputs.

As to internal customers the rule must be: No one has the right, unilaterally, to make trouble for a customer.

Goals should be written out.

Goals should be approved by the appropriate authority.

Tasks for Upper Managers

Upper managers should face the question of whether to mandate a structured approach to product development.

Upper managers should take steps to provide assurance that reliability goals will be met.

Managers who contemplate introducing the concept of participative planning should become familiar with the nature of cultural patterns and the way in which they affect human behavior.

Selected Bibliography on Reliability

Bajaria, H. J. "Integration of Reliability, Maintainability and Quality Parameters in Design." Paper SP-533. Warrendale, Pa.: Society of Automotive Engineers, n.d.

Feigenbaum, Armand V. *Total Quality Control.* 3d edition. New York: McGraw-Hill Book Co., 1983.

Groocock, J. M. *The Cost of Quality,* New York: Beekman, 1974.

Juran, J. M., and F. M. Gryna. *Quality Control Handbook.* 4th edition. New York: McGraw-Hill Book Co., 1988.

Kapur, K. C., and L. R. Lamberson. *Reliability in Engineering Design.* New York: John Wiley & Sons, 1977.

Lloyd, D. K., and M. Lipow. *Reliability Management, Methods and Mathematics.* 2d edition. Published by the authors, 1977.

Nixon, Frank. *Managing to Achieve Quality and Reliability.* New York: McGraw-Hill Book Co., 1971.

O'Connor, Patrick D. T. *Practical Reliability Engineering.* New York: John Wiley & Sons, 1981.

] 7 [

Develop Process Features

Purpose of This Chapter

The purpose of this chapter is to show how to develop processes that are able to produce the product features required to meet customer needs. The input-output diagram is shown in Figure 7-1.

In Figure 7-1:

The *input* is the product features and goals.

The *process* is process development.

The *output* is a process capable of meeting product goals under operating conditions.

The product features and quality goals have already been defined through study of who are the customers and what are their needs. The goals are set out in such forms as product specifications, mission statements, objectives, and so on. The job of process development is to create the means for meeting those goals.

Definition of "Process"

We have already begun to use the word "process." That word will come up over and over again throughout this book. It will give us a

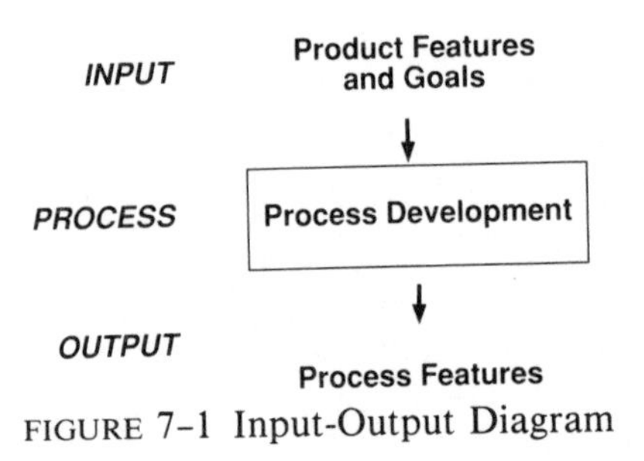

FIGURE 7-1 Input-Output Diagram

lot of trouble, because it has so many meanings that confusion is almost assured. To help minimize that confusion, we shall at this point list the principal ways in which we will be using the word process, along with a brief explanation of the associated nuances. We start with the basic generic definition:

A process is "a systematic series of actions directed to the achievement of a goal."

That generic definition covers a wide assortment of processes:

The overall process of managing a business. This is the responsibility of the Chief Executive Officer (CEO). There is no agreed name for this process.

The broad functional activities carried out within major functions such as Finance or Customer Service. We shall call these *functional processes.* When mapped out on the organization chart, they assume a mostly vertical direction.

The broad multifunctional systems through which the major affairs of the company are conducted. Examples are processing customer's orders or billing. We shall call these *macroprocesses.* When mapped out on the organization chart, they assume a horizontal position.

Macroprocesses are made up of departmental operations (steps, tasks, etc.) sometimes called subprocesses or procedures. Examples are opening the mail or assembling gear boxes. We shall call these *microprocesses.*

That same generic definition of a process also covers the processes used to carry out the various steps of the quality planning road map:

Identify who are the customers. Some call this a part of the market research process.

Determine customer needs. This has long been regarded as a part of the market research process.

Develop product features. This process is often called product development.

Develop process features. This is widely called process development, or process engineering.

Establish process controls. This lacks a widely used name but is a recognized process all the same.

Still other classifications of processes are based on the goals toward which they are directed. Processes directed at producing goods in factories are usually called *manufacturing processes*. Processes directed at producing services in offices are usually called *office processes*. However, the terminology has not been standardized.

A Hierarchy of Terminology

The existence of processes at various hierarchical levels gives rise to a corresponding hierarchy of processes. Here are some of the terms that are widely used:

Level in the Hierarchy	*Term Used for "Process"*
Company or division	System or process
Major function	Subsystem or subprocess
Subfunction or department	Activity or unit process
Basic organization unit	Task or operation

Quite often the design of processes must be fitted into broader functional or hierarchical processes. To illustrate:

A process for employee selection, training and motivation for quality must be woven into the broader human relations structure.

A process for qualifying suppliers as to quality must be woven into the broader purchasing process.

A process for administering quality warranties must be woven into the broader customer service process.

It might seem that no two processes are alike, that each is "different." That is true as to the functions, the technology, etc. However, the managerial approach to process quality planning is largely common to all processes.

In view of these numerous meanings of the word "process," the authors have tried to write the text so as to make clear just which kind of process is under discussion. However, there will remain a residue of usages of the word process in which the reader will be faced with deducing the finer shades of meaning from the surrounding context.

Criteria for a Process

As used here, the term "process" includes the human components as well as the physical facilities. In addition, a process (as used here) meets the following criteria:

Goal oriented. We cannot plan in the abstract. We can plan only if we know what the goal is. To plan for quality we must first establish the product quality goals we are trying to reach.

Systematic. The activities that make up a process are all interconnected through a coherent concept.

Capable. The proper end result of quality planning is a process able to meet the product quality goals under operating conditions.

Legitimate. The process is evolved through authorized channels. It bears the approval of those to whom the associated responsibility has been delegated.

Related Definitions

As used here, *process development* is a comprehensive term which includes the activities of: product design review, choice of process, process design, provision of facilities, and provision of software (methods, procedures, cautions). Our emphasis in this chapter is on *process design.*

Process design is the activity of defining the specific means to be used by the operating forces for meeting the product quality goals. The resulting definition includes:

The process features that collectively make up the means for meeting the product quality goals

The physical equipment to be provided

The associated software (methods, procedures, cautions, etc.)

Information on how to operate, control, and maintain the equipment

Does Process Quality Planning Require Prior Product Quality Planning?

A question often raised is whether process quality planning must be preceded by product quality planning. For example, a decision is made to plan (or replan) the process for producing invoices. Is it necessary to go through the steps of identifying customers, determining customer needs, and developing product features before tackling the job of planning that process?

The answer is: Yes, it is necessary. There is no known way of planning an invoicing process without knowing who will be impacted by the invoices and by the process; what are the needs of those who will be impacted; and what are the product features of the invoices that the process must be designed to produce.

In some cases it may be felt that all those things are already known, and that there is no need to redo all that work. If that assumption is valid, then of course there is no need to duplicate what has been done previously. However, such assumptions are usually not valid—the prior knowledge was not derived by following the quality planning road map in a structured way.

> Such an invalid assumption took place for many years relative to environmental impacts. Many companies failed to recognize the public as customers. The result was stringent laws to protect the environment.

Process Quality Planning by "Experienced Amateurs"

As in the case of product development, the quality planning component of process development has been largely carried out by "experienced amateurs."

At the multifunctional level these planners often include full-time systems analysts, process engineers, procedures analysts, and master mechanics. In addition these planners may include teams of managers acting as a committee, task force, or the like. At the departmental level the planners may include full-time departmental planners or departmental supervisors. At the base of the hierarchy (tasks and operations), the planners may include workers at the nonsupervisory level.

An essential step toward improving process quality planning is to provide these amateur process developers with the quality-oriented training needed to convert them into professionals. The nature of that training will be discussed in Chapter 12.

Process Design

Process design is the activity of defining the specific means to be used by the operating forces for meeting the product quality goals. To be able to define those means requires inputs such as:

Knowledge of the product quality goals

Knowledge of the operating conditions

Knowledge of the capability of alternative processes

These inputs exhibit a good deal of commonality despite wide variation in technology. Additional commonality exists in the quality-oriented skills and tools used during process design. These include understanding of the concept of process capability, the anatomy of processes, and the nature and use of flow diagrams and spreadsheets.

Process Design and Redesign

The term process *redesign* is usually applied to situations in which there has been no change in the product goals. In such cases any further process design work becomes redoing of prior work, and hence is called process redesign.

In contrast, design work done to provide the means for meeting new product goals is commonly called process design.

Review of Product Quality Goals

Ideally, the product quality goals have been established with the prior participation of those who will be impacted. Failure to provide such participation reduces the available options. Alternatives that could have been readily adopted in earlier stages become more expensive, or even prohibitive. In addition, those who have set the goals develop a vested interest in their decisions and exhibit cultural resistance to proposals for change.

Despite these complications the process designers should start by review of the product quality goals. Some of the findings will turn out to be usable. Other findings will turn out to be academic—it is too late to use them.

An obvious reason for review of product quality goals is to assure that they are understood. In addition the review is used to help achieve the optimum. The process designers are able to present the product designers with some realities relative to the costs of meeting the product quality goals. The review process should provide a legitimate, unobstructed path for challenging costly goals. "If you could ease up on this goal by X amount, you would make it possible to reduce the cost by Y."

> In one company the captive tool room was obliged to bid against outside tool shops for each job of building a new tool needed by the company. For the most part the captive tool room's bids were significantly lower than those of the outside tool shops. A study then showed why. The captive tool room

had much easier access to the company's product designers and was therefore better able to secure design changes that would reduce the cost of the tools.

As the process design evolves, new challenges to product quality goals may evolve as well. In this way, review of the product quality goals can continue for the life of the project.

Knowledge of Operating Conditions

By definition the process should be able to meet the product quality goals under operating conditions. It follows that the process designers should be knowledgeable about what the operating conditions are. These conditions exist in several dimensions.

Users' Understanding of the Process

By users we mean those who will be employing the processes to meet goals. These users consist in part of internal customers (organization units or persons) who have the responsibility of running the processes to meet the quality goals. Users also include external customers who run the processes to meet *their* goals.

Users vary greatly in their capability for unaided use of the process. Some users have the training and skills needed to use sophisticated technological processes. Other users may be able to acquire supplemental training to bridge any deficiency. Still other users—e.g., the general public—occupy a wide spectrum of technological literacy. The process design, along with the software (manuals, etc.), should ideally be such that the entire spectrum of users can use the process successfully.

Consumers are a class of users who present special problems because of their wide range of knowledge and ignorance about technological goods and services. Some appliance makers report that over 25 percent of consumer complaints involve cases in which there is nothing wrong with the product. Many consumers fail to follow the instructions, lose or discard the owner's manual, and so on. Increasingly, manufacturing and service companies are placing higher priority on errorproofing the use of products and services, providing self-maintaining designs, offering training courses in how to use the products, and so forth.

How the Process Will Be Used

The process designer always knows the intended use of the process, but not necessarily the actual use (and misuse). However, there are ways for the designer to find out about actual use:

Personally acquire firsthand experience in actual use. Some training courses are designed to provide such experience.

Make the rounds, i.e., observe users' behavior during use and try to learn the reasons behind that behavior.

Secure knowledge indirectly, e.g., through participation by those who are familiar with actual use.

The choice of whether to plan for intended use or actual use is not purely a technological decision. For example, misuse of some processes poses risks to human safety or health. In such cases the decision (plan for intended use versus actual use) involves legal, marketing, and other business expertise as well as technological expertise.

The Environments of Use

Process designers can learn about these environments in the same way they learn about how the process is actually used:

Firsthand experience

Make the rounds

Secure knowledge through participation

Designers are well aware that their designs must take account of environments that can influence process performance. Designers of physical processes usually do take account of such environmental factors as temperature, vibration, or dirt.

Designers of processes that depend heavily on human responses should similarly take into account the way in which the environment can affect human performance. A remarkable example involved the loss of an important football game played on December 26, 1982, between the New York Giants and the St. Louis Cardinals (Anderson, 1982).

> The Giants were leading by a score of 21 to 17, with 67 seconds remaining to be played. Then, with 34 seconds to go, the Giants were in a defensive huddle, anticipating a forward

pass. The Giants' process design for defense against a forward pass included:

A "man-to-man" defense. For this type of defense, the signal was the phrase "five green," but actually only the word "green" was being used.

A "zone" defense. For this type of defense, the signal was the phrase "stack three," but actually only the word "three" was being used.

The Giant's defensive quarterback called out the signal "green," but one of the players thought he heard "three." As a result, in the words of the Giants' defensive coach, "At the snap, we had three guys playing man-to-man like they were supposed to, and another guy playing zone."

The journalist who reported the event tended to assign blame to the player who "misunderstood" the call. However, neither the journalist nor the coach discussed the design of the signaling system relative to the environment.

The most audible portion of the two signals ("green" and "three") consists of the identical letters "ree." The two signals are close to "sound-alikes." The environment in a football stadium is inherently hostile to oral communication. The spectators are in any case a noisy lot. In this case, circumstances combined to raise the noise level to a deafening pitch: it was an important game, with tens of thousands in attendance; it was a close game, with the ultimate winner still in doubt; the game had reached its climax, with only 67 seconds remaining. It is understandable that the noise tended to drown out the signal.

Environment is not simply a matter of the physical conditions that impact on the operating forces. Environment also includes such factors as:

Job stresses: multiple goals to be met, the boss, peer pressure

Outside stresses: personal health, family problems, the social community

These and other nonphysical aspects of "environment" abound. They have plagued human beings throughout history. That is why one of the criteria of a good process design is that it be capable of meeting the goals *under operating conditions.*

Additional Customers: Additional Needs

As process designers acquire knowledge of operating conditions, they may also discover the existence of customers who had previously not been identified.

> For example, prospective process designs may pose risks for the work force—eyestrain traceable to long hours in front of computer terminals; toxic fumes in factory departments. Alternatively, the additional customers may be external to the company.

Such additional customers also have needs, so the process design should provide for meeting those needs.

Carryover of Process Designs

Much process design is directed at broad macroprocesses—broad systems, procedures, and so on. A broad office procedure consists of a series of specific "steps" or "tasks." A broad chemical process consists of a series of "unit processes." A broad factory process consists of various specific "operations."

Virtually all macroprocesses are made up of a mixture of:

- Designs carried over from existing processes
- Designs carried over but modified to correct weaknesses or to adapt to new needs
- Designs newly created

The questions raised for the carryover decision include:

- Which of the existing designs (if any) should be carried over into the new process?
- If new designs are to be created, should they be of an evolutionary nature, or should they be state-of-the-art designs?

The advantages of carryover are considerable. The cost of process design becomes minimal. The performance is predictable, i.e., the prior performance can be evaluated. The operating forces are already on familiar ground. Because of such advantages, carryover is the dominant ingredient in most process designs.

Carryover also includes a potential uninvited, unwelcome guest. The process feature may include chronic quality problems that have never been solved.

> In the early days of computer installations, it was common practice to design the new data processing systems to do electronically what had previously been done manually by clerks and paperwork. However, the manual processing often included deficient features and chronic wastes, which then were carried over into the electronic data system. The "manual mess" became locked into an "automated mess."

To defend against such uninvited guests, process designers should inform themselves as to the prior performance of the potential carry-over. Once informed, they face the alternative: reject, revise, or adopt as is.

Design of Macroprocesses

The term macroprocess refers to multifunctional processes at the higher levels of company hierarchies.

Process Subdivision

A common early stage of design for macroprocesses is a subdivision (or breakdown) into major segments variously called subsystems, procedures, etc. This subdivision is quite similar to a "black box" design for goods. Each box has a broad label identifying its contents (power supply, sensor, actuator), but the details of the contents of each box have not yet been worked out. As the planning progresses there is further subdivision, and in due course all details do get worked out.

It is the same with process design. The macroprocess is subdivided into the equivalent of black boxes. At this stage the functional contents of each segment (or box) of the subsystem (or procedure) are set out broadly, along with the interfaces. The breakdown continues into narrower subdivisions, which we shall call microprocesses. Meanwhile the planning becomes more and more detailed, getting into very specific product features and associated process features.

Reasons for Process Subdivision

A compelling reason for this subdivision is the need for concurrent planning. Breakdown into multiple black boxes enables the managers to assign each black box to a different team, thereby securing concurrent planning instead of sequential planning.

A further reason for this progressive subdivision is to permit flexibility in assigning responsibility. One planning team may have responsibility for the planning at the macro-level. Other teams may then be assigned to planning for the various black boxes. And so on.

For example, one company designed a series of macroprocesses, each oriented to some major aspect of planning for quality: supplier relations, internal quality controls, customer service, and so forth. The macroprocess for customer service then set out subsidiary processes as follows:

Customer contact. This identified the employee categories that have contact with customers. It then made their superiors responsible for assuring that performance goals were defined and that the employees were qualified to meet those goals.

Customer interfaces. This singled out those categories of employees which interface with clients and set out more specifically the nature of those interfaces. It also defined the supervisory responsibilities for assuring that the employees were trained to be able to meet the established goals.

Visits to customers. This dealt with the plan for making visits to customers. It defined the objectives, along with the responsibility for choosing who is to be visited, and by whom.

Advertising, sales promotion, and field feedback. These boxes similarly set out objectives, broad plans, and responsibilities.

Coordination of Interfaces

The broad planning should make provision for coordinating the interfaces among microprocesses. Such coordination is most acutely needed in macroprocesses that are multifunctional; they have no obvious "owner." Lacking such coordination, it is easy for some functions to be duplicated and others to be omitted.

> In one company, finished telephone switching equipment was packed into boxes, sealed up, and sent on to shipping. There are boxes were opened up to enable the inspectors to carry out their function. A process redesign changed the sequence so that inspection could be performed prior to packing (Bowen, 1986).

Advances in technology are making it easier to establish close linkages between macrosystems and their subsidiary microsystems. Examples have included:

Processing enormous volumes of paperwork with the aid of optical imaging systems (Markoff, 1988)

Integration of multiple factory processes through computer networks

Use of such linkages has a tie-in with process design to reduce cycle time. This has become a major subtopic of process design and is discussed below, under "Process Design to Reduce Cycle Time."

Design for Critical Processes

As used here, "critical processes" are those which present serious dangers to human life, health, and the environment, or which risk the loss of very large sums of money. Some of these processes involve massive scales of operations: airport traffic control systems, huge construction projects, systems of patient care in hospitals, and even the process for managing the stock markets (Stewart and Hertzberg, 1987).

Planning for such processes should obviously include: ample margins of safety as to structural integrity, fail-safe provisions, redundancy, multiple alarms, and still other safeguards of modern technology. Additional safeguards can be provided by such methods as:

A basic process design that provides the operating personnel with ample time to deal with crises

Training and qualifying examinations for the operating personnel

Rigorous, structured maintenance procedures, enforced by audits

Systematic feedback and investigation of "critical incidents"

Beyond providing such safeguards for the process, *planning for critical processes should also include planning of the operating quality control system.* This is quite different from what is done in less critical processes. There the planning of the quality control system is largely left to the operating forces.

Design of the quality control system should stress self-control by the operating forces. Such a design provides the shortest feedback loop but also requires the designers to ensure that the process capability is adequate to meet the product quality goals (see below, under "Process Capability—the Concept" and subsequent headings). It is also essential to reduce the opportunity for human error to a minimum (see below, under "Design to Reduce Human Error").

Design to Reduce Human Error

Human beings are by nature error-prone. They are unable to maintain attention 100 percent of the time, to continue muscular exertion 100 percent of the time, to recall all past events, or to make 100 percent good decisions. Human beings also vary in their capabilities. Some develop a knack that enables them to outperform those who lack the knack. Some consciously violate company rules, e.g., fail to report errors because they feel there is an atmosphere of blame. Some are not aware that innocent looking shortcuts can do damage to users. Some are rebels who deliberately violate the rules in order to take revenge on society for real or imagined grievances. Collectively the extent of human errors is large enough to require that the process design provide for means to reduce and control human error.

The starting point is to analyze the data on human errors and to apply the Pareto principle. The vital few error types become candidates for special process design on an individualized basis.

> For example, some workers persistently outperform others on specific quality features. The likely reason is possession of a special knack. In such cases the need is to study the methods used by the respective workers in order to discover the differences in methods. These differences usually include the knack—a small difference in methods that produces a big difference in performance. Once the knack is discovered, the process designers can arrange to include the knack in the technology. Alternatively, the knack is brought into the workers' training program so that all workers are brought up to the level of the best.

A useful principle in designing human tasks is to provide instant feedback to the worker so that the *performance of the work conveys a message to the worker.* For example, a worker at a control panel pushes a switch and receives three feedbacks: the *feel* of the shape of the switch handle, the *sound* of an audible click signaling that the switch went all the way, and the *sight* of a visual illumination of a specific color and shape.

Another useful principle is that of designing human work in ways that require human attention as a prerequisite, that is, the task cannot be performed unless the person doing it devotes attention to it and to nothing else. A widespread case in point is "checking" or inspection of documents, products, or whatever. Human checking is done in two very different ways:

1. By *passive* deeds: listening, looking, reading. Such deeds are notoriously subject to lapses in human attention. Also, such deeds leave no trail behind them; we have no way of knowing whether the human being in question is really paying attention or is in a state of inattention.

2. By *active* deeds: operating a keyboard, writing, speaking. Such deeds cannot be performed at all without paying attention to the task at hand, and to the exclusion of all else. These active deeds do leave a trail behind them.

   To illustrate, telephone companies have the problem of ensuring that subscribers' listings in the telephone directory correspond to the original copy approved by the subscriber. The conventional approach for providing this assurance was passive checking: a clerk visually compared the printer's proof with the approved original. A later approach, using the active principle, is as follows:

   a. Working from the basic subscriber data, a data entry clerk uses a keyboard to put this information on magnetic tape.
   b. Subsequently the proofreader, also working from the basic subscriber data, uses a keyboard to put this information into a computer.
   c. The computer compares the two inputs to see if they are alike. If so, the verified tape is used to produce the directory.

The underlying principle is the low probability that two clerks will independently make identical errors on the same element in the listing.

It is also possible to reduce human errors at the low end of the Pareto distribution—the numerous error types each of which is comparatively rare. Here the designers look for some generic remedy that is applicable to a wide assortment of error types.

For example, office work has long had the annoying problem of misspelled words. Most of these misspellings are inadvertent errors scattered over a wide assortment of different words. Now, some word processing programs include a dictionary in their memory as a means of detecting misspelled words. The designers found a way to deal with numerous error types each of which is comparatively rare.

Similar planning approaches can be found in the factories.

In design of assembly line conveyers, each work station is designed to give the worker enough time to perform the operation under normal operating conditions. Occasionally an abnormality arises: an input component doesn't fit, the worker fumbles, a passerby creates a distraction, etc. In such cases the worker may be unable to complete the operation before the conveyor has taken the unit out of reach. Some assembly conveyors now provide means for the workers to detach the product from the conveyor in order to complete the operation. Here again the designers have found a way to deal with numerous error types each of which is comparatively rare.

Inadvertent human errors can also be reduced, but the means involve "errorproofing": building safeguards into the technology, fail-safe designs, automation, robotics, or self-checking systems to secure prompt detection of errors. Nonhuman processes do not have lapses in attention, do not become weary, and do not lose their memory (so long as they are properly maintained).

Bar codes are increasingly used to reduce human errors in identifying goods.

Some utility companies guard against incorrect invoices going to customers, by programming the computers to reject invoices that show charges out of line with prior history. Rejected invoices are then checked out by human means.

In like manner, some factory operations are provided with automated instruments that check the product and/or the process, and sound the alarm when things go out of control.

Principles of Errorproofing

Two Japanese authors have recently generalized the principles of errorproofing. They reviewed nearly one thousand case examples of errorproofing—steps taken to guard against the effects of human error. From these cases they established a classification of errorproofing methods as set out below.

ELIMINATION. This consists of changing the technology so as to eliminate operations that are error-prone. For example, in some materials-handling operations, the worker should insert a protective pad between the lifting wire and the product so that the wire will not damage the product. Elimination could consist of using nylon bands to do the lifting.

REPLACEMENT. This method retains the error-prone operation but replaces the human worker with a nonhuman operator. For example, a human worker may install the wrong component into an assembly. A robot avoids such errors.

FACILITATION. Under this method the error-prone operation is retained and so is the human worker. However, the human worker is provided with means to reduce error-proneness. Color coding of parts is an example.

DETECTION. This method does nothing to prevent the human error from happening. Instead, it aims to find the error at the earliest opportunity in order to minimize the damage done. A widespread example is automated testing between processes.

MITIGATION. Here again the method does nothing to prevent the human error from happening. However, means are provided to avoid the damage done. A common example is providing a fuse to avoid damage to electrical equipment.

Classes of Errors

The authors have also classified human errors, as follows:

Errors of memory

Errors of perception

Errors of motion

Having provided bases for classifying human errors and methods of errorproofing, the remainder of the paper goes into detail to show how the various errorproofing methods are applied to the various categories of human error. A great many case examples are presented to illustrate these applications.

The case examples will be quite familiar to the experienced practitioner. However, the organization of the subject of errorproofing is mostly new, and entirely enlightening. It is a useful research, and it should become a classic in its field (Nakajo and Kume, 1985).

The Anatomy of Processes

One of the major decisions facing the process designer is choice of the "anatomy" of the process. There are several major options.

The Autonomous Department

This process form receives basic "materials" and converts them into finished goods and services, all within a single self-contained department. A schematic diagram is shown in Figure 7-2.

> A widespread example is the self-employed professional, e.g., physician or artisan. In the factory, a well-known example is a tool room. It starts with tool steel and ends up with punches, dies, fixtures, gages, etc.

For such autonomous departments much of the process design is done by the departmental supervision and by the workers. Additional process design may be acquired from outside sources. For example, the self-employed physician may purchase equipment and other designed processes from supply houses, pharmaceutical companies, etc.

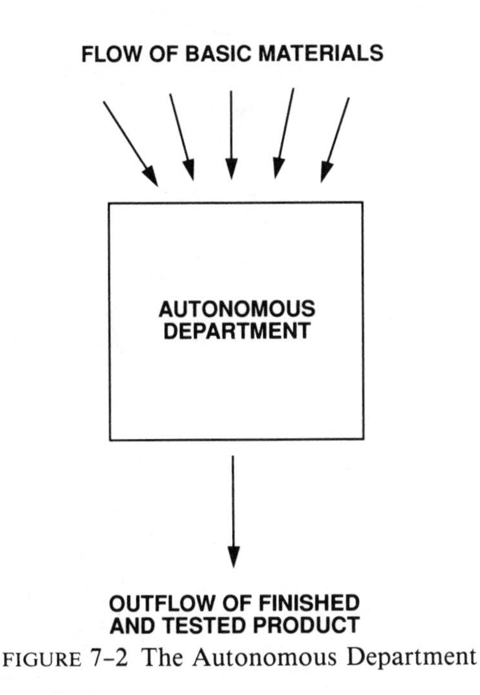

FIGURE 7-2 The Autonomous Department

The Assembly "Tree"

This familiar process is widely used by the great mechanical and electronic industries that build automotive vehicles, household appliances, electronic apparatus, and the like. The roots (or leaves) of the tree are numerous suppliers or in-house departments making parts and components. These elements are assembled by still other departments. Figure 7-3 shows this process schematically.

In the office certain processes of data collection and summary also exhibit features of the assembly tree. Preparation of major accounting reports (e.g., balance sheet, profit statement) requires assembly of myriad bits of data into progressively broader summaries, which finally converge into the consolidated reports.

The assembly tree requires process designs of two very different kinds: multifunctional and departmental. In large operations, it is virtually mandatory to use staff specialists to design at the multifunctional level. However, it is not mandatory to use staff specialists for departmental design as well, though this is often done.

The Procession

In this form, there are again numerous in-house departments (with occasional supplier departments). However, all the product pro-

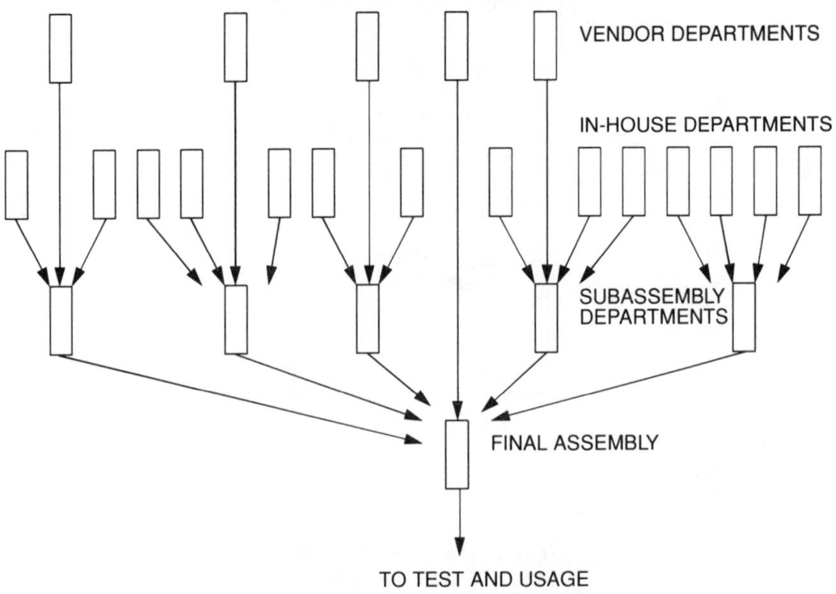

FIGURE 7-3 The Assembly Tree

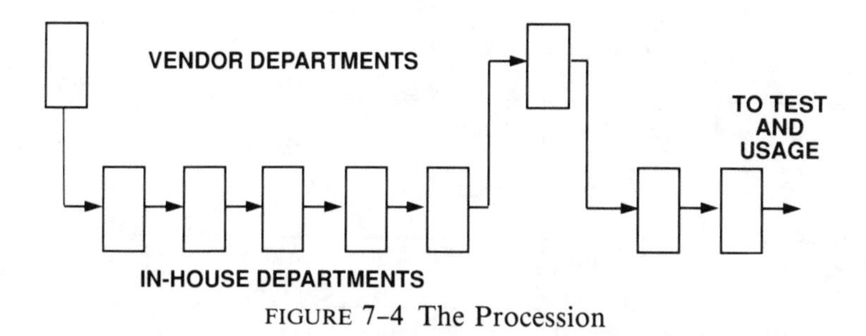

FIGURE 7–4 The Procession

gresses sequentially through all departments, each performing some operation that contributes to the final result. This form is exhibited by the bulk of the "process" industries. It is also exhibited by many office processes in which documents move sequentially from desk to desk. Figure 7–4 shows the schematic.

As in the assembly tree form, an extensive procession requires both multifunctional and departmental process design. For the former, it is usually mandatory to make use of staff specialists. For departmental designs it may be feasible to use departmental planners, departmental supervisors, or nonsupervisory workers.

The Biological Process

In this form a cell divides into multiple cells, which differentiate to create organisms, each coordinated by a nervous system. An enterprise created by a single founder and then "franchised" follows a similar process of growth.

Figure 7–5 shows some examples of the above processes in various industries.

Revisions in Process Anatomy

For many processes there are alternative ways of designing the anatomy. In addition, it is often possible to revise the anatomy from one form to another. An example was the "job enlargement case" involving telephone directories (see Chapter 4, under "Be a Customer"). In that case an office procession was converted into an autonomous process, with results which are worth repeating:

	Before	*After*
Annual turnover of employees	28	0
Absenteeism rate	2.8%	0.6%
Errors per 1000 lines	3.9	1.1

Industry	*Autonomous Department*	*Assembly Tree*	*Processions*	*Biological*
Hotel	Bar	Assembling buffet	Assembling kitchen meal	
Military	Ranger/unit	Invasion	Basic training	Insurrection
Publishing	Pamphleteer	Handbook	Printing & binding	Experimental newsletter
Transport	Independent taxi	Assembling a freight train	Guided Tour	
Computer	Personal computer	Complex computer installation		Building an unmanaged user system
Training	Plato plus a student	Training for an astronaut mission	College curriculum	Training in an emerging "discipline"
Construction	Henry Thoreau at Walden Pond	Building construction	Laying pavement	Shanty town
Communi-cation	Ham operator	Network election returns	Relay repeaters	
Health Care	Dr. Schweitzer	Heart surgery	Physical examination at army camp	Home remedies
Food Service	Family kitchen	Restaurant table service	Cafeteria	Franchised chain

FIGURE 7–5 Anatomy of Various Processes

A related change in anatomy of the process is the creation of autonomous "cells" in which self-supervising teams of workers produce products which previously were produced by processions involving numerous "handoffs."

An insurance company (Kemper) computerized its process (a procession) for issuing insurance policies. This change had little effect on productivity. Subsequently the company changed the anatomy of the process by creating cells of three workers each. It gave each team responsibility for performing all the steps needed to issue policies.

The result was a revolutionary increase in productivity. In

this case the gain from redesigning the anatomy of the process was much greater than the gain from new technology (Bowen, 1986).

The insurance operations of another organization (Aid Association for Lutherans) underwent a similar change in process design. Self-supervising teams were created, each capable of performing the numerous (over 160) tasks formerly spread over multiple functional departments. The processing time per case was reduced dramatically while the productivity was increased significantly (Hoerr, 1988).

Factory processes have also been undergoing revisions in process anatomy. The most widely publicized examples have featured replacement of assembly lines by cells involving self-supervising teams of workers. In some cases the process design has reverted back to the autonomous process in which a skilled craftsman assembles a complete product from bits and pieces. The name sometimes given to such revisions in anatomy of the process is "job enlargement."

In virtually all such cases (replacing the assembly tree with self-supervising teams or with skilled craftsmen) the resulting product quality has improved significantly. A major reason undoubtedly is the fact that the team (or the craftsman) *is its own customer, over and over again.* The resulting intimate knowledge (of the interrelationship among the many tasks) enables the team to identify the existence of quality problems and, in many cases, to solve those problems.

The Legacy of the Taylor System

Many of the existing cases of outdated anatomy of the process are traceable to the late nineteenth century Taylor System of separating planning from execution. The planning became the responsibility of engineers. The execution was left to the line supervisors and workers. The planners then designed processes that consisted of numerous simple, short-cycle tasks. Such tasks could be performed by semiskilled or unskilled workers. In this way it became possible to increase production without an increase in the supply of skilled craftsmen.

The system worked brilliantly. It was widely adopted and became a major contributor to bringing the United States to world leadership in productivity. However, the system was based on the premise that the supervisors and the work force lacked the education—the technological literacy—needed to do the planning. That premise was largely valid in Taylor's time, when education levels were very low. Since then there has been a remarkable rise in education levels, thereby undermining the basic premise of the Taylor system. One result is that a major *underemployed asset* of the economy is the education, experience, and creativity of the supervisors and the workers. (All those cases of changing the anatomy of the process to create self-supervising teams of workers involve extensive reunifying of planning with execution.)

The trend is now unmistakably toward enlarging the participation of the line supervisors and workers in the planning process. The nature of that participation was discussed in Chapter 6, under the heading "Optimizing Through Participation." The application of participation to process design is based on similar principles. The pace is slow simply because all those decades of separation have built up vested interests, which exhibit strong cultural resistance. In many companies the extent of those vested interests is such that an initiative by the upper managers is needed in order to make use of that underemployed asset.

(For elaboration on the nature of the Taylor system and its effect on quality, see Copley, 1923, and Juran, 1973).

Process Capability—The Concept

A far-reaching concept in process and product design is the concept of process capability. All processes have an *inherent* ability to produce quality products. This ability can be evaluated through data collection and analysis. The resulting evaluation becomes a valuable aid during process design, and also during the subsequent conduct of operations.

The ability of the process to produce quality products actually consists of two different abilities:

The ability to meet the product quality goals. We shall call this "target achievement."

The inherent ability to reproduce its results consistently. This ability has been widely called "process capability."

The concepts of target achievement and process capability are closely related to the concepts of accuracy and precision, which are used to evaluate measuring instruments. The relationship can be tabulated as follows:

	Name of the Ability, as Applied to:	
Nature of the Ability	*Measuring Instruments*	*Operating Processes*
To hit the target	Accuracy	Target achievement
To reproduce its own results	Precision	Process capability

Target Achievement

The concept of evaluating target achievement goes back for centuries. Ancient planners measured the load-carrying capacities of animals (and of human slaves) along with their food consumption, in order to make process design decisions. The early steam engines were used to pump water out of mines. The planners evaluated competing steam engines in terms of "duty," that is, coal consumed per unit of work done. These measures were influential in managerial decision making and in stimulating engine development.

The service industries for centuries have used the concept of target achievement, but without calling it target achievement. A widespread example is "credit rating." Most companies do their selling on credit, but some buyers do not pay up. This risk of bad debts has led to a demand for early warning information that can predict creditworthiness. The best known basis for such prediction is information on (a) whether prospective debtors currently have the means and (b) whether they have in the past had the inclination to pay their debts. For centuries this information was acquired empirically, through gossip in the marketplace, and so on. Today there is a formal data bank (Dun & Bradstreet), which compiles and publishes data on creditworthiness.

There are also data banks that "rate" bonds and other securities as to creditworthiness. All these ratings are predictions of target achievement. The companies or securities being rated are regarded as a financial process. The published ratings constitute a target achievement data bank. These data banks are widely used as planning tools by credit managers, purchasing managers, financial managers, and others.

Industrial societies make extensive use of evaluation of target achievement. The units of measure take such forms as:

Cycle time for providing service

Load-carrying capacity of industrial equipment and household appliances

Fuel consumption of vehicles

Process Capability

The term process capability is widely used to designate the *inherent reproducibility* of a process, the ability to repeat its results during multiple cycles of operation. A high degree of such reproducibility is required by modern industrial societies to meet certain exacting needs: interchangeability on a massive scale, predictable performance, standardization, and so on. The greater the degree of industrialization, and the more advanced the technology, the greater the demand for uniformity in products. In turn, uniformity in products demands uniform processes to produce those products.

The technical term for reproducibility is "variability" (or "dispersion"). The higher the variability or dispersion, the lower the reproducibility. We shall shortly be discussing variability, since it has become the basis for quantifying process capability.

"Performance Index"

There have been efforts to combine target achievement and process capability into a single "performance index" (see Kane, 1986; see also Juran, 1988, p. 16.24).

The Urge to Quantify

In nonquantitative terms, the definition of process capability is as follows:

> Process capability is the inherent variability of the products that emerge from a process.

The growing demands for greater and greater uniformity of products has stimulated an evolution of ways to quantify process capability. Until recently, evaluation of process capability was done empirically: estimates, rule of thumb, cut and try. What is new is the trend to *quantify process capability based on data collection and analysis.* In addition, what is new is the trend to *standardize the quantitative evaluation methods* to make them applicable to a wide variety of processes.

Life Without Quantification

Quantification of process capability requires added work to be done in the form of data collection and analysis. Yet the great majority of process design has been done empirically, without quantitative evaluation of process capability, and certainly without standardized methods of quantifying. Why then do we now need to go to all that extra work? The reason is that *organizations that have adopted such methods of quantification have significantly outperformed those which have not.*

To illustrate, in the U.S. automotive industry the activities of manufacturing planning had for decades been carried out without quantifying the capability of manufacturing processes. During those same decades a notorious situation existed: manufacturing processes were unable to meet the product quality goals. The planners of those processes were intelligent, competent engineers. They certainly had training in the technology of the processes. In addition they had practical experience derived from having engaged in prior cycles of process design. This training and experience made them competitive with other planners who relied on similar training and experience.

In due course these quality planners found that they were being outperformed by a new level of competition. The new superiority in planning was found to be due, in part, to use of quantification of process capability. It then became imperative to adopt quantification as a tool for competition in quality planning. The U.S. automobile companies did so under such names as "Statistical Process Control."

Another way of describing the situation is in terms of the resulting percent defective. Empirical ways of quality planning typically resulted in processes that yielded 80 percent to 90 percent good product; the defects were in terms of parts per hundred. The scrap, rework, detailed inspection, and so forth were a price paid for the deficiencies in planning. It worked for as long as competitors conducted their affairs in the same way. It could not work when competitors came up with ways to drive defect levels down to parts per million.

The Effect of Incapable Processes

Processes that are excessively variable are incapable of meeting the product quality goals. Such processes generate waste in the form of work redone, material scrapped, and so on. The effect of such excessive variability is shown graphically in the contrasting Figures 7–6a and 7–6d.

In these figures the specification limits are identical. The aimed-at value is also identical. What differs is the process variability and the resulting extent of nonconforming product.

Less obvious is the damage done in other forms, some of which are below the surface:

> The supervisors and workers learn soon enough that the process is incapable, and that the remedy may have to come from higher managerial levels.

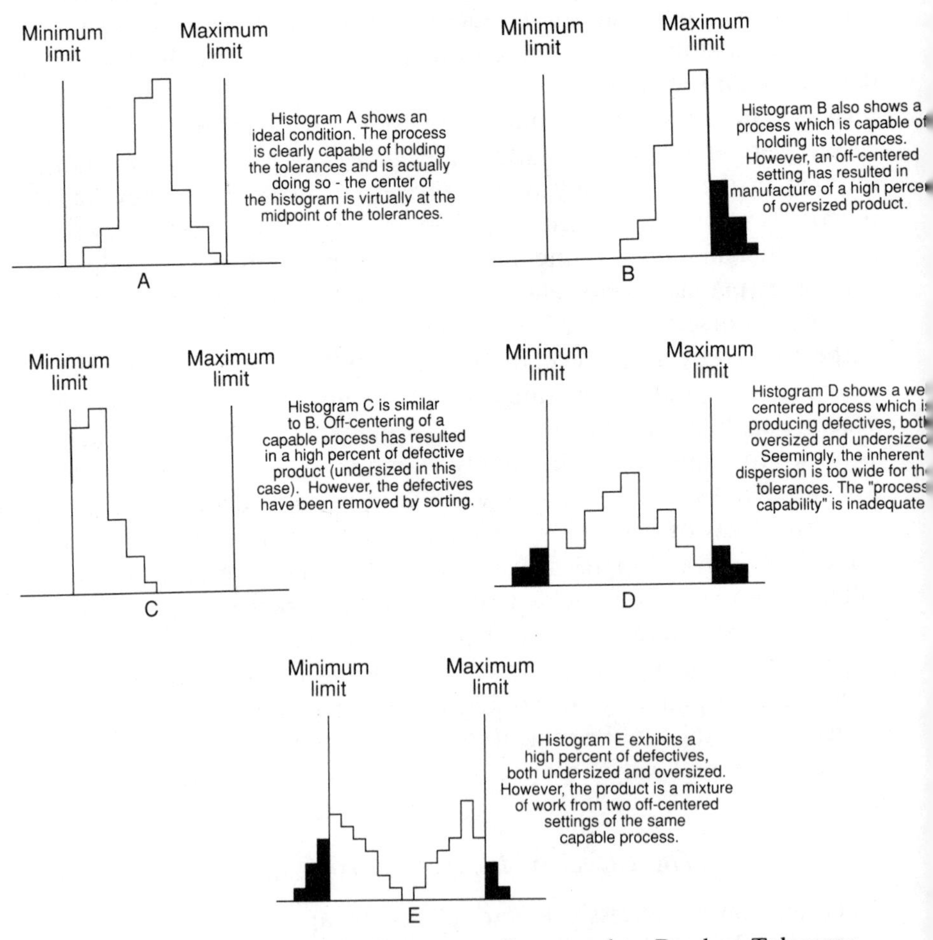

FIGURE 7–6 Frequency Histograms Compared to Product Tolerance

If the managers then push for higher quality, divisiveness sets in. The lower levels feel that the managers have not come to them with clean hands.

The damage is compounded in those cases where the top priority is meeting the goals for productivity or delivery dates. The work force may consciously play loose with the process controls while the supervision looks the other way.

Evaluating Process Capability—The Methods

The principal method for evaluating process capability is through analysis of data collected under operating conditions. (Other methods include mathematical models and simulation.)

The term "under operating conditions" means that:

The process is already in existence.

Operations are being conducted under "regular" conditions, not "laboratory" conditions.

The personnel conducting operations are the regular operating forces.

Process capability for such an existing process may be evaluated by collecting data on either:

The quality features of the *process* itself, or

The quality features of the *product* turned out by the process. (The product "tells" on the process.)

Evaluating Process Capability from Operating Data

Let's start with an office process: preparation of insurance policies. The process consists of a "policy writer" armed with a keyboard. The inputs are mainly the customer's order, a blank policy form, the company manuals, and the training of the workers. The output is insurance contracts ready for signature.

The policy writers fill in the blank policy forms with data from the various inputs. The filled-in forms then go to a checker, who reviews them for errors. During a certain time period, the checker reported eighty errors, as shown in Figure 7–7.

Those eighty errors represent the *performance* of the process—what the process actually did. That is not the same as the *capability*

	POLICY WRITERS						
ERROR TYPE	A	B	C	D	E	F	TOTAL
1	0	0	1	0	2	1	4
2	1	0	0	0	1	0	2
3	0	16	1	0	2	0	19
4	0	0	0	0	1	0	1
5	2	1	3	1	4	2	13
6	0	0	0	0	3	0	3
28							
29							
TOTALS	6	20	8	3	36	7	80

FIGURE 7–7 Matrix of Errors by Insurance Policy Writers

of the process—what the process *could* do. We can, however, by analysis of the data, evaluate the process capability.

The total of eighty errors when divided by the six workers results in an average of 13.3 per worker. However, the workers varied widely in their error-proneness. Four were well below the average; their errors numbered 6, 8, 3 and 7, respectively. Two (workers B and E) were well above the average: 20 and 36, respectively. *None was close to the average.*

In the case of worker B, her total of twenty errors is inflated by sixteen errors of a single error type. This was found to be due to her misunderstanding of a part of the procedure. Her performance is represented by twenty errors, but her inherent capability is represented by 4 errors.

In contrast, worker E made thirty-six errors, and made them in virtually all error categories. So the number thirty-six does reflect the error-proneness of worker E on this type of work. This number was so high compared to the rest that it suggested worker E was misassigned to this type of work.

Still another significant phenomenon is the thirteen errors of type 5. Every worker made one or more errors of this type. The total was significantly above the average for all error types. Analysis showed that the policy writers' interpretation of the instruction differed from that of the inspector. When this difference was cleared up, the abnormality of error type 5 disappeared.

To arrive at process capability, it is necessary to exclude the abnormal performances: the type 3 errors by worker B; the type 5 errors; the errors of worker E. The numbers of errors for the remaining five policy writers becomes 4, 3, 5, 2, and 5 respectively. The average becomes 3.8, and each worker is close to the average. The number 3.8 then represents our best estimate of the capability of this process.

Performance and Capability; Significant Differences

Process performance is what a process *actually does.*

Process capability is what a process *could do* if we removed the significant causes of poor performance.

In the case of the policy writers, the actual process *performance* was represented by eighty errors for six workers, or an average of 13.3 per worker. Based on the analysis, the process *capability* was 3.8 per worker.

Note that the definition of process capability (what a process *could do*) includes the proviso: "If we removed the *significant* causes of poor performance." In some cases it becomes important to define how big is "significant."

In the case of the insurance policies, we had no trouble. For Worker B the presence of twenty errors was obviously significantly different from the capability of four. For Worker E the number thirty-six was obviously significantly greater than the number for any of her colleagues.

However, in many cases the differences are not so obvious. In addition there are cases where the differences between performance and capability are smaller but nevertheless important. In such cases statistical tools are available to help determine what is significant.

The distinction between process performance and process capability has wide application to all functions. Ideally, goals should be set based on process capabilities. Projects should be undertaken to upgrade processes so that their performance matches their capability. However, many operating goals continue to be based on past performance rather than on process capability.

Process Variability

All processes exhibit variability. The extent of this variability is a critical input to process design.

The errors of the insurance policy writers varied from one writer to another. Had a second set of such data been collected, the numbers of errors for the respective workers would have been similar to the first set of data, but would not have been identical.

Other human beings, e.g., athletes, similarly vary in performance among each other as well as from time to time.

Nonhuman processes also exhibit variability. Input materials vary as to their properties. Variations in environmental conditions affect the performance of equipments. So do progressive changes due to depletion, wear, age and so on.

All these and other sources of variation are a fact of life for the operating forces. Their responsibility is to meet the product goals, but the reality is that they must do so under variable operating conditions.

In consequence, the process designers have the responsibility of determining, in advance, what the operating conditions will be, including the nature and extent of variations. Process designers who lack such information may be able to develop a process that works under "laboratory conditions," but not necessarily under operating conditions.

Process Capability Based on Variability

During the last few decades, many manufacturing industries have gone heavily into evaluating process capability through analysis of process variability. This approach has considerable merit, and it is here to stay.

Also, it is very likely to spread to other industries. So it is worthwhile for planners to understand the concept of variability and its application to process design and process capability.

Unit of Measure for Variability

Every quality feature has its own unit of measure, such as temperature in degrees or speed in revolutions per minute. However, we are now able to express variability in *universal* units of measure—units that are applicable to *any* quality feature. The most widely used of these universal units of measure is called the "standard deviation." We represent it by the lower-case Greek letter σ (sigma).

The methods of computing standard deviation have been widely disseminated by courses in "Statistical Process Control" and will not be repeated here. Once the standard deviation has been computed, it becomes possible to express process capability in terms of standard deviations.

The widest application of evaluating process capability in terms of standard deviations has been in manufacturing industries, and especially in the automotive industry. Many manufacturing processes make units of product for which quality is evaluated on a *variables* basis, e.g., length in millimeters, resistance in ohms. For such manufacturing processes, the usual method of expressing process capability has become:

$$\text{Process capability} = 6\ \sigma$$

(In the absence of data by variables, process capability may be expressed in such units of measure as percent yield or percent error.)

Process Capability Index

Adoption of six standard deviations as a universal unit of measure has greatly simplified communication and goal setting. To illustrate, in the automotive industry it is common to require that process capability (6 σ) should be no greater than 0.75 of the distance between specification limits—the "tolerance width." Stated in reverse the rule requires that the ratio of tolerance width to process capability should be a minimum of 1.33. This latter ratio is sometimes called Process Capability Index (also Capability Index, Performance Index, etc.).

Establishment of such a quantified minimum for Process Capability Index provides a quantitative goal for process designers. As data on process capability are worked up for various processes, the planners can use the data in multiple ways. The principal use has been to predict whether a process will be able to meet the product quality goals. This prediction is made by comparing the process capability with the product tolerance width. Figure 7-6 shows some simple comparisons of data on product variability with product tolerance width.

(For elaboration on the use of the ratio of process capability to product tolerances, see Juran, 1988, "Relation to Product Tolerance," pp. 16.18 to 16.21.)

In cases where the frequency distribution is "normal" (follows the bell shaped curve), knowledge of the process capability index permits an estimate of the yield of the process, in accordance with Figure 7-8.

Process designers make additional uses of process capability data, such as:

Number of Standard Deviations Within the Tolerance Limits	Resulting Process Capability Index	Resulting Defects per Million
4	0.67	46,000
5	0.83	12,000
6	1.00	3,000
7	1.17	500
8	1.33	60
9	1.50	7

FIGURE 7–8 Yields of Processes at Various Levels of Process Capability Index (Assumes Stability and Centering)

To judge the relative merits of alternative processes

To communicate the needs for precision to suppliers of processes

Note that process capability tells us only what is the inherent uniformity of the process. It does *not* tell us whether the process is *able to meet the product quality goals.* The latter is a matter of target achievement. A business process may provide twenty-four-hour service to customers, very uniformly. However, the customer needs may be to get service in eight hours. A manufacturing process may produce batteries that uniformly have a life of thirty days, whereas competitive batteries have a life of ninety days. In such cases the processes are uniformly *incapable* of target achievement.

Application to Nonmanufacturing Processes

The concept of six standard deviations as a measure of process capability is applicable to any process, provided we are able to acquire an adequate data base. Some cases involving business processes have in fact made such applications. However, the published nonmanufacturing cases have been few. They have also had difficulty in separating out (a) what the process did do, from (b) what the process could do. Lacking such separation, the planners run the risk of perpetuating poor performances through carryover of poor yields, carryover of failure-prone features, and so forth.

A good deal remains to be done to study a broad spectrum of nonmanufacturing processes and to evolve a standardized method of quantifying process capability that is widely applicable.

Data Banks: Process Capability and Target Achievement

A data bank on process capability is an organized collection of evaluations of process capabilities. Once such a data bank has been prepared, process planners can use the information in various ways, such as:

Predict results in advance of conducting operations

Secure early warning of deficiencies

Choose the best from the available alternatives

Outside of the Company

Data banks on process capability abound in the world outside of the company.

In the world of sports, there are extensive records of past performance of teams and individual athletes. These records are widely used to assign teams to various league classifications, determine handicaps and seedings for individuals, predict future performance, establish pay scales, and so on.

Within the Company

Within the company, data banks on processes cover a mixture of process capability and target achievement. These data banks are found in all functions. To illustrate:

Function	*Data Banks*
Product design	Tables of properties of materials
	Lists of approved components (those which may be specified without further qualification testing)
Purchasing	Creditworthiness of suppliers
Manufacture	Tables of inherent uniformity of production processes
Marketing	Sales potential of various territories Creditworthiness of potential clients
Industrial engineering	Work standards for tasks and operations
Human relations	List of workers certified as qualified to perform various tasks

Units of Measure

Creation of data banks also requires the creation of units of measure. These units of measure vary among company functions. See generally Chapter 5, especially under "Measures for Functions."

As Seen by Ultimate Users

Many products sold by manufacturers become processes in the hands of ultimate users. Examples of such products include office copiers, machine tools, trucks, and computers. To users of such products, target achievement may be expressed in positive terms: percent uptime, copies per minute. Alternatively the expression may be in negative terms: percent downtime, failure rate, spare parts usage.

Such evaluations are the modern equivalent of the "duty" of the early steam engines. As in those early days, these modern evaluations are influential in deciding whose products will be bought. It is obviously useful for manufacturers to acquire the information in those data banks.

Procedure for Creating Data Banks

Establishing data banks on process capability requires an organized approach such as is used for improvement projects. A team is appointed to guide the project. This team is given the responsibility to:

Determine the scope of the data banks—what processes should be included

Define and standardize the basic terminology

Establish the conceptual approach: definition of process capability, essential input data, units of measure, method of evaluation, etc.

Prepare the instruction manual for evaluating process capability: forms for data collection and analysis, criteria for precision of measurement, sample sizes, etc.

Provide a training course to guide those who will collect and analyze process capability data

Establish a procedure for publishing the data bank: format, distribution list, etc.

Provide for audit to ensure adherence to the plan.

Process Capability Data Not Available

In many cases the process designer lacks information on process capability. The data may be nonexistent, or it may exist, but not in usable form. In such cases the process designers can nevertheless create sources of usable information. They can:

1. Assemble information on prior performance of like or similar facilities, materials, etc., and estimate process capability from this information. Such information is a form of "lessons learned" (see Chapter 12, under "The Data Base: The Santayana Review").
2. Conduct competitive tests of alternatives
3. Acquire or buy data from users or data banks
4. Use simulation to estimate process capability

Simulation to Estimate Process Capability

"New" processes normally consist of a mixture of:

Features carried over from predecessor processes for which we have operating experience

Features for which there is no prior operating experience

As to carryover features it is generally feasible to evaluate process capability by direct data collection and analysis. In the case of truly new process features, such an approach is not available. The process features in question have not yet been in service under operating conditions. In consequence, the process designers must resort to other forms of evaluating process capability. One of the most widely used of these other forms is simulation.

The literal meaning of simulation is *an imitation of the real thing.* Our planning may contemplate a new process that involves considerable investment. Since the process is new, such an investment is at risk: we have no proof that it will be able to meet our goals under operating conditions. However, we can reduce our risk by simulation. We can design a scaled-down process and then test it out. We can then use the test results to predict what the results will be under full-scale operation.

Examples of Simulation

The concept of simulation is applied widely. To illustrate:

A market survey asks the question: Would you buy this product? The answers are an imitation of the real thing—no money is being spent.

The armed forces stage maneuvers to test out operational readiness.

The theater troupe conducts rehearsals.

The office building holds fire drills.

Trainees work out exercises before applying the new tools to their jobs.

Product designers create prototypes, which they test in the laboratory.

Process designers create pilot plants to secure a prediction of what to expect if they scale up to the real thing.

Mathematical Models

A special form of simulation is through mathematical models, which deal with symbols rather than with physical things. In the design of many kinds of processes and products, use can be made of reliability models to aid in quantifying reliability, predicting reliability, identifying likely weaknesses in the designs, and so forth. Numerous special tools have been evolved to enable designers to understand and use these models.

The designers' acceptance of these mathematical models has been less than enthusiastic. Designers do not want their designs to fail. However, their long-standing method for judging fitness for use has been by test of the hardware, either in the laboratory or in service. A design that failed on test was an alarm signal, which designers heeded. (They still do.) In contrast, a design that "failed" a mathematical analysis was not regarded as an alarm signal, since no hardware had failed on test.

All this is undergoing change. Increasingly, designers are acquiring training in the use of reliability models as an extension of the simulation process.

Limitations and Risks in Simulation: Two Worlds

Simulation is a tool of great value provided we understand the limitations and risks. We can better understand these limitations and risks by noting that simulation and full-scale operation are carried out in two different "worlds"—the "laboratory" and the "real world." The existence of these two worlds means that we are dealing with two versions of process capability:

Process capability in the laboratory

Process capability in the real world

These two worlds can differ extensively in several critical aspects.

Scale of Operations

When we progress from the laboratory to the world of operations, we commonly scale up by orders of magnitude. We are then faced with extrapolating from small numbers in order to predict the effect on the subsequent large numbers.

Small numbers are a treacherous basis for decision making. They do exhibit the effect of the treatment they received in the laboratory, but they also exhibit considerable variation due to chance. These chance variations can and should be quantified so that their statistical meaning is evaluated. The technologists should learn how to do this. Until they do learn how, someone else should do it for them.

Technology

In part the two worlds differ because of the demands of technology. In the laboratory we may take pains to exclude the effect of certain variables in order to secure adequate data on relationships between cause and effect. In the real world it may be impractical to exclude those variables.

The Mission

In the laboratory the mission is to produce the plan: the system design, the procedure, the product design, the process design, or whatever. In the real world the mission is to meet the various operating goals. This difference in mission creates other differences, such as:

The priorities assigned to the various goals

The type and intensity of supervision provided

The integrity of data collection and analysis

Personnel

A further consequence of the difference in mission is various differences in personnel practices, such as:

The educational background of people recruited

The supplemental training and experience

The career concept

The choice of incentives

The above differences make clear that *extrapolation from laboratory findings should be based on input from both worlds.* The technologists are quite competent to interpret what happened in the laboratory. However, they are not necessarily able to extrapolate—to predict what will happen in the real world—unless they have adequate knowledge of how life is lived in that world. Lacking such knowledge, they must acquire it from inhabitants of the real world through such team efforts as design review or joint planning.

Process Redesign

Process redesign consists of work that is quite similar to the work of process design. The main difference is the newness of the product quality goals. Work done to provide the means to meet *unchanged product quality goals* is called process *redesign.* Work done to meet *new or changed product quality goals* is called process *design.*

The need for process redesign arises from a variety of reasons, such as:

A new process design turned over to the operating forces proves to be incapable, and hence must be revised.

A quality improvement project discovers that the remedy for the problem is to redesign the process.

A plan known to be deficient has nevertheless been competitive. However, because of competitive pressures it can no longer be endured.

Process not Capable

In some cases the designers transfer a process to the operating forces only to discover that the process is not capable of meeting the quality goals. In such cases there are multiple options available to the planners:

1. Look closely to see whether the "incapability" is really based on inadequate process *capability,* or is due to evaluation based on process *performance.* If the basis has in fact been process performance, attempt to evaluate process capability.
2. Analyze the scope of incapability. The process may be capable as to some quality goals but not as to others. Such analysis identifies the incapable residue and thereby narrows the problem.
3. Improve process capability by digging deeper to discover new relationships between process variables and product results. Concentrate on the dominant variables to simplify the analysis.
4. Review the product quality goals associated with the process incapability to see if the optimum is best served by revising the goals.
5. Endure the incapability and the resulting chronic waste. In that event it is necessary to provide for an adequate level of customer service for both external and internal customers.

The last of those options (endure the incapability) should always be regarded as a temporary measure. Future planning projects, as well as the annual improvement process, should keep reviewing such cases to see whether the march of technological and managerial progress has found ways to solve the problem.

Redesign Through Change in Anatomy

An extensive opportunity for improvement through process redesign lies in changing the anatomy of the process. We saw some case examples above, under "The Anatomy of Processes: Revisions in Process Anatomy." The cases below, (under "Reduction of Cycle Time") also involve some degree of change in the anatomy of the process.

Reduction of Cycle Time

Reduction of production cycle time has long been a goal of designers of *factory processes.* During the 1980s designers of *business processes* intensified their efforts toward that same goal. The targeted business processes included launching of new products, providing service to customers, recruiting new employees, and response to customer complaints, among others.

Reduction of cycle time requires diagnosis to identify causes and opportunities for improvement, followed by remedies. The diagnosis proceeds along several lines:

Collecting and analyzing basic data relating to "what takes so long"

Analysis of the process design, both at the macro-level and at the micro-level

Analysis of the major background influences.

Diagnosis of Cycle Time

This diagnosis follows a series of steps which are applicable to a wide variety of processes.

1. The starting point is to secure data on the time consumed during the processing of a number of prior cycles. These data include:

   The time consumed by each of the steps that make up the cycle

   The total time required to carry out the entire cycle

2. In addition, data are acquired on the total cycle time taken by other organizations that perform similar work. Some of these organizations are "friendly"; others are competitors. Special means may be needed to acquire such data.*
3. These data are then plotted as a frequency distribution such as the diagram shown in Figure 7-9.

In Figure 7-9 the horizontal scale is time—hours, days, months or whatever. The vertical scale is the frequency—the number of cycles processed in that interval of time. The frequency distribution is usually unsymmetrical: there is a long tail stretching off to the right. As a result, the average is well to the right of the peak frequency.

**A note on data collection for diagnosis of cycle time:* The choice of number of prior cycles to be studied (the sample size) is arbitrary at the outset. The subsequent analysis will disclose whether the sample was adequate for the intended confidence level.

Acquiring market data may require "deals." Some customers are also clients of competitors, and hence are a potential source of data on competitive performance. In the case of internal monopolies there are usually external suppliers who offer competing services, and therefore are a potential source of data on market performance.

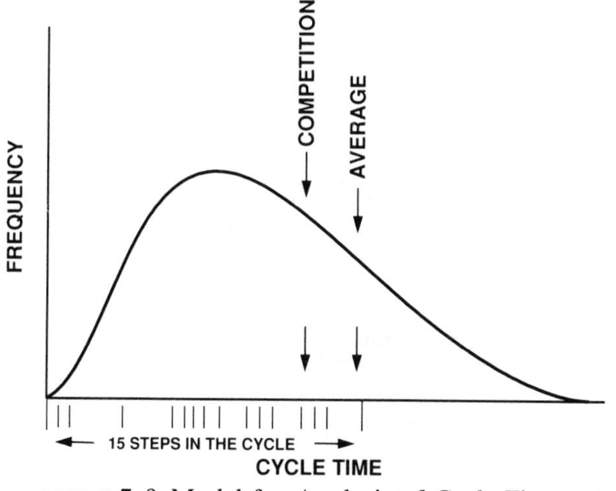

FIGURE 7–9 Model for Analysis of Cycle Time

4. In addition, the data on the individual steps are entered in graphic form. In the model of Figure 7–9, there are fifteen steps within one complete cycle. The diagram shows these steps in their chronological order. The horizontal distance covered by each step is the average time consumed in carrying out that step. The total time for all steps is of course the average for one complete cycle.

The data analysis then focuses on (a) the total cycle time, and (b) the time consumed by the "vital few" steps.

The adequacy of the total cycle time is judged based on:

The performance of others, i.e., market performance. "If they can, why can't we?"

The degree of customer satisfaction with present cycle times. Customers may be unhappy with the market cycle time as well as with our performance.

If the total cycle time is regarded as excessive, then the remedy is likely *not* to come solely from taking action on specific steps. Instead, some sweeping changes will be needed in the basic design of the macroprocess itself.

Diagnosis of the Process

This part of the analysis concentrates on how the process has been designed and operated. A good beginning is to prepare a flow diagram in order to understand:

The number of handoffs that take place, both vertically within the same function, and horizontally between functions

The number of functions that are impacted

The extent to which the same macroprocess is used for the vital few customers and the useful many

The existence of redoing of prior work

The extent and location of bottlenecks such as numerous needs for signatures

Additional analysis is made of the vital few individual steps (microprocesses). Here the analysis focuses on:

Is there a customer for the work done in this step?

Can this step be performed after serving the customer rather than before?

What can be done to reduce the time to perform this step?

Diagnosis of Major Influences

As used here, "major influences" refers to powerful forces that are all-pervasive and must not be ignored: they must be dealt with even if this means changing the culture.

THE INFLUENCE OF FUNCTIONAL ORGANIZATION. Any multifunctional process is handicapped with respect to cycle time. For many functional managers the function is a source of status, and they place high priority on that status and the associated symbols—monopolies, territory, jurisdiction, and so on. The priority on functional jurisdiction often takes priority over the needs of the multifunctional process. The functional managers own the functions, but they do not own the multifunctional processes.

The mismatch between the functional hierarchy and the multifunctional process gives rise to conduct that seems logical to functional managers but not to those who try to optimize operations. A case in point was the opening of sealed boxes to inspect and test the product (see above, under "Design of Macroprocesses: Coordination of Interfaces"). In that case the optimal process design would be for the testing to be done "at the end of the line" within the production area. Such a design would avoid the unpacking and repacking of goods, reduce waiting time, minimize transportation costs, and so on. However, the Quality Department may urge that the testing be carried out in its territory. The Production Department may well support this idea because it prefers not to be a landlord to other departments.

The resistance to "concurrent engineering" similarly is traceable, in part, to giving priority to jurisdictional rights. The functional managers tend to prefer carrying out their work without "interference" by others. Then, when their work is finished, they tend to prefer a clean transfer—over the wall.

THE INFLUENCE OF THE ANATOMY OF THE PROCESS. The choice of anatomy of the process has a major influence on cycle time. A long procession involves numerous steps with associated handoffs, waiting time between steps, jurisdictional boundaries, and the time-consuming rest.

Many of these processions are outdated residues of the Taylor system of separating planning from execution. The subsequent rise in education levels has made it possible to assign broader responsibilities to supervisors and workers. In turn, such assignments make it possible to create self-supervising teams to carry out multiple steps and to minimize the number of handoffs. The reduction in number of steps not only reduces the overall cycle time; it also improves quality through the phenomenon of the team becoming its own customer, over and over again.

THE INFLUENCE OF NEW TECHNOLOGY. New technology keeps coming over the horizon, and some of it offers new opportunities for reducing cycle time. The analysis should include a look at these opportunities. We shall shortly look at some examples of successful use of new technology to reduce cycle time.

Remedies to Reduce Cycle Time

Numerous ways have been found to shorten the cycle time for macroprocesses. These have included:

1. *Provide a simplified process for the useful many.* In a surprising number of cases, the planners design one comprehensive process to serve all applications, the useful many as well as the vital few. The comprehensive process is needed for the vital few but is too burdensome for the useful many, which typically represent over 80 percent of the applications. The remedy is to provide a simpler process for the useful many.

The simpler process usually involves delegating greater responsibility to lower levels of organization, and training in how to carry out that responsibility. In some cases there may be need to create new forms of "ownership".

> Numerous functional departments are involved in enabling an airplane to depart on time: maintenance, baggage handling, cabin cleaning, food service, check in, and still others. Each has functional goals and a culture which can delay departure. Some airlines have dealt with this problem by designating a gate manager, a sort of "owner" for each departure. The gate manager is given decision-making responsibilities over the departure.

2. *Reduce the number of steps and handoffs.* Handoffs take place vertically as well as horizontally. Either way they introduce multiple handling, waiting time, sources of error, etc. Reduction of the number of handoffs has been done in various ways:

   Delegate more approvals to lower levels. This reduces the number of vertical handoffs.

   Establish self-supervising multifunctional teams to replace consecutive functional processing. (For some examples, see above, under "The Anatomy of the Process: Revisions in Process Anatomy.")

   Combine multiple steps to create jobs of broader scope. Now the workers hand off to themselves, and are their own customers, over and over again.

   Establish self-contained "cells" to reduce handoffs between departments.

3. *Eliminate wasteful "loops."* These loops consist of numerous forms of redoing prior work. The loops become evident from the flow diagram as well as from the analysis of the operation of the process. Each such loop becomes a nomination for an improvement project.

4. *Reduce changeover time.* Some processes require frequent change in "setup" in order to adapt to revisions in customer orders. In such cases the time to make the changeover may be a major source of long cycle time. One of the remedies is to create dedicated facilities that involve no changeover.

   > Some hospital operating rooms are utilized to only about 20 percent of capacity. The bulk of the time is consumed in changeover from one type of operation to another.

Creation of operating rooms dedicated to just one type of operation has resulted in a remarkable rise in percent of capacity utilized, as well as reducing the cost of doing the operations.

A further remedy is to find ways of reducing changeover time.

Some factories have made much progress in reducing changeover time. A major element in this progress has been standardization of the pertinent features of the machine tools, conveyors, dies, fixtures, etc. Some changeover time cycles have been reduced by orders of magnitude, such as from eight hours to a few minutes (Holusha, 1987).

5. *Change from consecutive to concurrent processing.* The opportunities here are found at high managerial levels as well as at operational levels.

   In a case of preparation of bid proposals, a total of twenty-eight signatures was required from various managers. These signatures were secured mostly on a consecutive basis, with serious delays in getting the bids out.

   A remedy is suggested by the process followed during the closing of the sale of a house. There is extensive formality in this process, requiring the signing of numerous documents by numerous persons. The process is carried out concurrently. There is a gathering of all the parties: the seller and spouse; the buyer and spouse; the respective lawyers; the lenders; the insurers; etc. Following mutual discussion, the papers are signed. The process is completed in an hour or two. Were it done sequentially it would take weeks or months.

Remedies Through Change in Technology

Some stunning reductions in cycle time have come from adoption of new technology. A widespread example is use of computers to provide instant display of the information needed to give service to customers, or to request service from suppliers (Wessel, 1987).

Networking of information for multiple functions has also contributed to reductions in cycle time. Computerized microprocessors have been able to make changeovers in shorter time and at lower error rates. The computerized communication also reduces transmission time. For elaboration and case examples, see Dumaine (1989). Dumaine presents data on reductions in cycle times for product development and for order-to-finished-goods, as shown in the boxed table.

		Product Development Time	
Company	*Product*	*Old*	*New*
Honda	Cars	5 Years	3 Years
AT&T	Phones	2 Years	1 Year
Navistar	Trucks	5 Years	2.5 Years
Hewlett-Packard	Computer Printers	4.5 Years	22 Months
General Electric	Circuit Breaker Boxes	3 Weeks	3 Days
Motorola	Pagers	3 Weeks	2 Hours
Hewlett-Packard	Electronic Testing Equipment	4 Weeks	5 Days
Brunswick	Fishing Reels	3 Weeks	1 Week

Companies that have gone all out to make judicious use of modern technology have in some cases greatly outperformed their competitors in terms of cycle time.

> An apparel marketer makes use of multiple technologies: computers to provide real time information on the status of sales and inventories; satellite communication to transmit orders to suppliers; chartered aircraft to bring back the ordered goods; automated sorting and pricing at the distribution center; and so on. The cycle time from placing the order to putting the goods on sale becomes sixty days, whereas most competitors require a six-month cycle (Main, 1988).

A caution is in order when replacing human processes with technology, that is, automating human processes. It is essential first to "debug" the human process. Otherwise the problems become locked into the technology, which often makes it harder to solve them later.

Remedies for Microprocesses

There are also opportunities to reduce cycle time for the individual steps—the microprocesses. Figure 7-9 identifies the "vital few" steps in terms of the time consumed. The focus on these vital few then considers such options as:

Eliminate the step. Prior events may have made this step obsolete so it no longer has a customer.

Change the sequence so that this step is performed after serving the customer rather than before. In some cases customer service is held up until the internal paperwork is complete, whereas it may be feasible to change the sequence.

Adopt modern technology to shorten the time required to perform the step.

Goals for Process Features

As the process design progresses, the specific process features through which it becomes possible to meet the product quality goals emerge. *These same process features also become goals to be met.*

Some of these process goals are directly related to the product goals. Process equipment must be maintained and serviced. Input information and materials undergo audits and tests. The operating conditions must be maintained at specified levels. Failure to meet such process goals risks failure to meet the product goals. Setting quality goals for these product-related process features may require the same kind of experimental work as is required for setting product quality goals.

Other process goals are unrelated to the product goals. They must nevertheless be met, because the process, once established, creates various effects of its own, such as a hazard to the work force, a threat to the environment, or a showplace for visitors.

No matter what the nature of the process goals, the process planning must provide for recognizing their existence and for meeting them. The design of the process controls (See Chapter 8) must provide for meeting all process quality goals, whether product-related or not. The process quality goals get entered on the spreadsheet and become the targets for the process control step of the quality planning road map.

The Spreadsheet for Process Features

As process design progresses from the macro-level down into details, a long list of very specific process features emerges. Each of these features is directly aimed at producing one or more product features. For example:

Product feature X (for an invoice) requires a process feature that can perform calculations in arithmetic

Product feature Y (for a gear wheel) requires a process feature that can bore precise holes in metal

Such process features are entered into the vertical columns of the process design spreadsheet (Figure 7–10). In due course each of these process features becomes the focal point of a system of process control, as discussed in the next chapter.

Optimizing Process Design

Our travels along the quality planning road map have included looking at various forms of optimizing:

During product development we tried to meet our needs as well as customers' needs.

We looked at value analysis as a means of providing needed functions at minimal cost.

We looked at life cycle costing as a means of optimizing cost of ownership for long-life products.

We noted the use of designed experiments to optimize product and process performance.

These and other forms of optimization have generally related to our external customers. There are additional areas that also require optimization, especially:

Our relationship to our external suppliers

The planners' relationship to the operating forces

Optimization Relative to External Suppliers

Each external supplier is an extension of our operating forces. Viewed in this way, everything we have said about our "operating forces" applies to the external suppliers as well. However, some things are different:

The external supplier is a separate legal entity; there is no common boss.

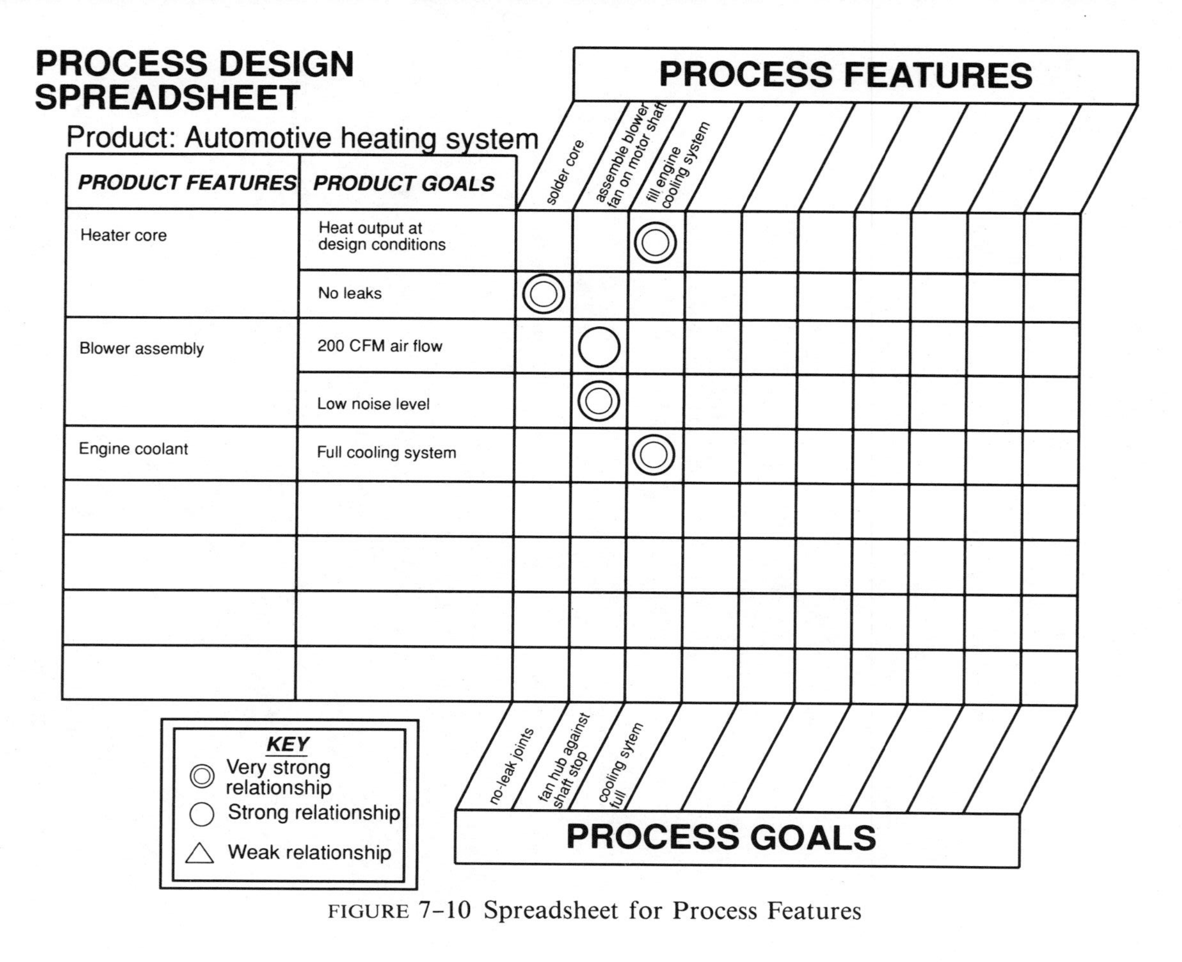

FIGURE 7–10 Spreadsheet for Process Features

External suppliers seldom have a monopoly. They have competitors, and there is wide use of competitive bidding.

External suppliers may supply product design and process design as part of their services.

The traditional adversary relationship has stimulated the urge to suboptimize.

Nevertheless, the potential gains from optimizing are considerable:

The assignment of work can be based on who is best qualified to perform the tasks.

Quality improvement by suppliers can lead to lower costs as well as to further improvements, e.g., "Just In Time" operations.

An emerging teamwork spirit can lead to joint planning.

An emerging mutual trust can lead to reduced duplication of facilities, instruments, tests, reports, and so on.

The key to achieving such gains is teamwork, which takes such forms as design review and joint planning. Creating such teamwork is a delicate task in an adversary relationship. Such a relationship breeds suspicion and mistrust, the worst possible climate for optimization.

One way to break out of the adversary relationship is to experiment. All organizations have multiple external suppliers. Invariably these include some with whom a long-standing, comfortable relationship has existed. Such suppliers become the testing ground for optimization. The results of these tests then provide an experience base for extending the concept.

Optimization Internally

Here the main problem is to strike the optimum balance between the work of planning and the subsequent work of operations—carrying out the plan. Planners are always under pressure to meet their schedules and budgets. Yet shortcuts in planning usually result in far greater burdens on operations, in such forms as incapable processes, frequent firefighting, and high maintenance costs. The key to internal optimization is the team approach.

Suppose we ask an audience of upper managers: Do you favor teamwork within your organization? The answer is a unanimous: Of course! Yet many of those same upper managers act otherwise:

They establish structured departmental goals and structured merit rating systems to reward departmental managers for meeting departmental goals. Such reward systems *inherently tend to suboptimize* unless well coordinated.

Those same upper managers fail to establish the organization structure needed for coordination.

The point is that exhortations to work as a team are not enough; it is also necessary to provide the structures that *inherently favor optimization.* In the chapter on product development, we discussed two such structures: design review and joint planning. These same structures are applicable to process design.

Design Review

Applied to process design, design review involves creating a *design review team,* to include membership from those areas which are heavily impacted by the process design, the areas that will produce the product, test the product, use the product, maintain the product, and so on. The team review of process designs provides early warning to the designer: "If you design it this way, here are what the consequences will be in our area."

Under the design review concept, the responsibility for action on early warnings rests with the process designer. The other members of the design review team are there to provide inputs and early warnings, not to make decisions. These warnings are often heeded. Where they are not heeded, the team members have a channel for appeal to higher authority through the regular chain of command.

Joint Planning

The joint planning concept also involves creating a team that includes those impacted as well as the process designers. However, under this concept the team (rather than just the process designers) bears responsibility for the final design. (In some elaborate undertakings, e.g., a major new product development program, there are even migratory teams that remain with the program as it progresses through its phases.) Such team responsibility stimulates communication and participation among team members, and thereby contributes to optimization.

Tasks for Process Designers

During this chapter we have discussed the basic tasks of process designers: acquire the needed inputs, design the process features with the aid of various quality-oriented concepts and tools. Beyond these there are additional tasks. Some relate directly to the process design function itself. Others relate to the design of process controls and to transfer to the operating forces (see Chapter 8).

Establish the Relationship of Process Variables to Product Results

For simple processes the simple process capability study goes a long way toward establishing this relationship. The histograms of Figure 7-6 illustrate how helpful such simple studies can be.

For complex processes, the simple process capability study, though still useful, is not sufficient. The process designers should in addition evolve an understanding of the relationships between the multiple variables of the complex process and the associated product results. This understanding is needed not only during process development in the laboratory; it is needed also by the operating forces who, in due course, must deal with those same variables. In this connection, see Chapter 8, under "Stages of Process Control: Corrective Action—Remedy."

To establish those relationships requires designed experiments. Statisticians have come up with a variety of ways to design such experiments: Evolutionary Operation and Response Surface Methodology are examples. What these have in common is a planned, systematic collection of data on multiple process variables and the associated product results. The data are then systematically analyzed to establish the relationships. The resulting relationships provide multiple benefits: operations can be conducted at optimum yields and costs; process controls can be designed for optimum effectiveness; the work force can be provided with a deeper understanding of the variables they are to keep under control.

Provide Measurement Capability

This task is closely related to the tasks of "establish process capability" and "design process controls." Measurement is a vital part of the feedback loop.

Measurement capability depends mainly on precision of measurement—the ability of the sensor to reproduce its results on repeat test. For technological instruments this repeatability is relatively easy to quantify. In addition, instrument designers have made astonishing progress in improving precision of measurement.

For other types of sensors, notably use of human beings as sensors, progress in precision has been less than astonishing. (See above, under the heading "Design to Reduce Human Error.") This comparative lack of progress requires that the process designer establish measurement capability through designed experiments.

Provide Adjustment Capability

This task relates to the corrective action segment of the feedback loop, which we shall discuss in the next chapter, under the heading "Stages of Process Control: Corrective Action—Remedy." Failure of the process designers to perform this task often leaves the operating forces with a residual burden of cut and try when they attempt to take corrective action.

For an uncommonly useful elaboration on tasks for process designers, see the paper "Approving a Process for Production" (Bemesderfer, 1979).

Transfer to Operations

The transfer of responsibility from planners to the operating forces is a major step along the quality planning road map. We shall take this up in the next chapter.

List of High Points

"Process" includes the human components as well as the physical facilities.

A process design should meet the following criteria: goal oriented, systematic, capable, legitimate.

The quality planning component of process development has been largely carried out by "experienced amateurs."

An essential step toward improving process quality planning is to train the "amateur" process developers to become "professionals."

Process design should start with review of the product quality goals.

Process designers should be knowledgeable about what the operating conditions are.

Whether to plan based on intended use or actual use is a broad business decision rather than purely a technological decision.

Carryover of prior process designs features may bring in a potential uninvited, unwelcome guest. The process feature may include chronic quality problems that have never been solved.

Broad process planning should make provision for coordinating the interfaces among microprocesses.

Planning for critical processes should also include planning of the operating quality control system.

The process design should provide means to reduce and control human error.

Design of human tasks should provide feedback to the worker. The performance of the work should convey a message to the worker.

Human work should be designed in ways that require human attention as a prerequisite, so that the task cannot be performed unless the person doing it devotes attention to it and to nothing else.

Inadvertent human errors can be reduced through errorproofing.

For many processes there are alternative ways of designing the anatomy of the process.

In some process redesign cases, the gain from changing the anatomy of the process has been much greater than the gain from new technology.

Many of the existing cases of outdated anatomy of the process are traceable to the late-nineteenth-century Taylor System of separating planning from execution.

One result is that a major underemployed asset of the economy is the education, experience, and creativity of the supervisors and the workers.

Organizations that have adopted quantification of process capability have significantly outperformed those which have not.

The principal method for evaluating process capability is through analysis of data collected under operating conditions.

Quality goals should be based on process capabilities rather than on prior process performance.

All processes exhibit variability.

Evaluation of process capability through analysis of process variability has considerable merit, and is here to stay.

The technologists should learn how to extrapolate from small numbers to large numbers. Until they do learn how, someone else should do it for them.

Extrapolation from laboratory findings should be based on input from the world of operations as well as from the world of the laboratory.

Numerous ways have been found to shorten the cycle time for macroprocesses:

- Provide a simplified process for the useful many transactions
- Reduce the number of steps and handoffs
- Eliminate wasteful loops
- Reduce changeover time
- Change from consecutive to concurrent processing

One way to break out of the adversary relationship with suppliers is to experiment.

Exhortations to work as a team are not enough; it is also necessary to provide the structures that inherently favor optimization.

Tasks for Upper Managers

In process development, as in the other chapters, upper managers are faced with deciding whether to mandate:

- Structured quality planning to replace empiricism
- Participation by those impacted
- Spreadsheets to aid memory and communication
- Training the amateurs to become professionals

A special question to be faced relates to the residue of the Taylor System: Should upper managers take the initiative to make use of the underemployed asset—the education, experience, and creativity of the supervision and the workers?

] 8 [

Develop Process Controls: *Transfer to Operations*

Purpose of This Chapter

The purpose of this chapter is to show how to develop the process controls needed to keep a process in a stable state so that it continues to meet the product and process quality goals. The chapter also shows how to transfer the planned process plus the associated process control plan to the operating forces.

The input-output diagram is shown in Figure 8–1.

The input is the process design established during process development.

The process consists of (a) development of a system of process controls and (b) transfer of the process design and the system of process controls to the operating forces.

The output becomes the means to be used by the operating forces to meet the product and process quality goals.

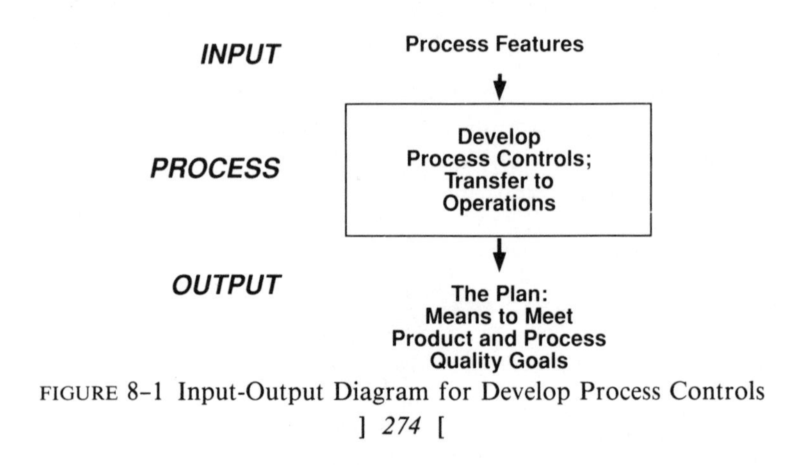

FIGURE 8–1 Input-Output Diagram for Develop Process Controls

Design for Process Control

"Process control" as used here consists of several activities:

Evaluate the actual performance of the process

Compare actual performance with the goals

Take action on the difference

The Feedback Loop

These control activities take place in a systematic sequence called a feedback loop. In its simplest form the loop can be diagrammed as in Figure 8-2.

The flow of information proceeds as follows:

The sensor (which is "plugged into the process") evaluates actual performance.

The sensor reports this performance to an umpire (also collator, comparator, etc.).

The umpire also receives information on what the goal is.

The umpire compares actual performance to goal. If the difference warrants action, the umpire energizes an actuator.

The actuator changes the process conditions so as to bring performance into line with goals.

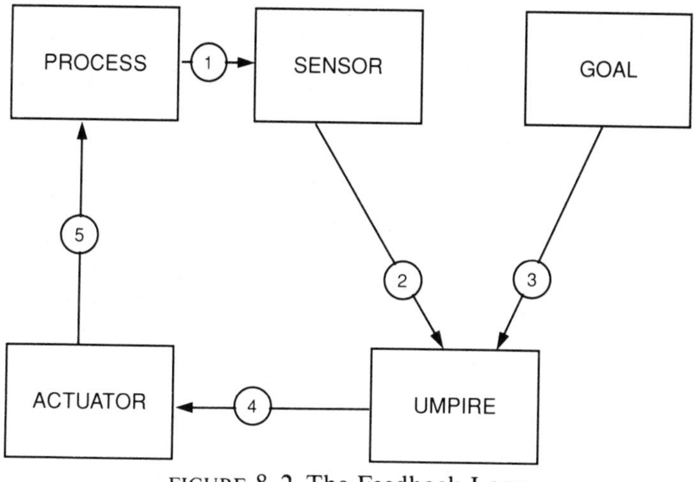

FIGURE 8-2 The Feedback Loop

Stages of Process Control

Process controls can take place at several stages of progression of operations. The following are the most frequent of these stages.

Setup (Startup) Control

The end result of this form of control is the decision whether or not to "push the start button." Typically this control involves:

A *countdown* listing the preparatory steps needed to get the process ready to produce (Such countdowns sometimes come from suppliers. Airlines provide checklists to help travelers plan their trips. Electric power companies provide checklists to help householders prepare the house for winter weather.)

Evaluation of process and/or product features to determine whether, if started, the process will meet the goals

Criteria to be met by the evaluations

Verification that the criteria have been met

Assignment of responsibility (This assignment varies, depending largely on the criticality of the quality goals. The greater the criticality, the greater the tendency to assign the setup tasks to specialists, supervisors, and "independent" verifiers rather than to nonsupervisory workers.)

Running Control

This form of control takes place periodically during the operation of the process. The purpose is to make the "run or stop" decision—whether the process should continue to produce product or whether it should be stopped.

Running control consists of closing the feedback loop, over and over again. The process and/or product performance is evaluated and compared with goals. If the product and/or process conforms to goals, and if the process has not undergone some significant adverse change, the decision is "continue to run." If there is nonconformance or if there has been a significant change, then corrective action is in order.

The term "significant" has meanings beyond those in the dictionary. One of these meanings relates to whether an indicated change is a real change or a false alarm due to chance variation. The design for process control should provide the tools needed to help the operating forces distinguish between real changes and false alarms (see below, under "Design for Evaluation of Performance: Interpretation; Statistical Significance").

Product Control

This form of control takes place after some amount of product has been produced. The purpose of the control is to decide whether or not the product conforms to the product quality goals. Assignment of responsibility for this decision differs from company to company. However, in all cases those who are to make the decision must be provided with the facilities and training that will enable them to:

Understand the quality goals

Evaluate the actual quality

Decide whether there is conformance

Since all this involves making a factual decision, it can in theory be delegated to anyone, including the workers. In practice, this decision is not delegated to those whose assigned priorities might bias their judgment. In such cases the decision is usually delegated to those whose responsibilities are free from such biases, e.g., "independent" inspectors or even automated instruments.

Corrective Action—Diagnosis

The design for process control should also provide the operating forces with the means for corrective action. "Corrective action" consists of *diagnosis* of the cause as well as provision of a *remedy.* Some process designs provide for ready diagnosis of the cause and for taking remedial action: turn this calibrated knob until the green light comes on; remove this battery and insert a replacement. In such cases the operating forces at the bottom of the hierarchy can be trained to carry out the corrective actions and restart the process.

The really troublesome problems of corrective action involve sporadic changes for which the causes are not immediately obvious. In such cases the main obstacle to restoring the status quo is diagnosing the cause. The diagnosis makes use of such methods and tools as:

Autopsies to determine with precision the symptoms exhibited by the product and process

Comparison of products made before and after the trouble began, to see what has changed; also comparison of good and bad products made since the trouble began

Comparison of the *process* before and after the problem began to see what process parameters have changed

Reconstructing the chronology. This consists of logging on a time scale (of hours, days, etc.):

a. The events that took place in the process before and after the sporadic change: rotation of shifts, new employees on the job, maintenance actions, and the like

b. The time-related product information: date codes, cycle time for processing, waiting time, move dates, etc.

Analysis of this chronology usually sheds a good deal of light on the validity of the various theories of causes. Certain theories are denied. Other theories survive to be tested further. (For elaboration, see Juran, 1988, Chapter 22, under "Troubleshooting.")

If the operating forces are not trained to conduct such diagnoses, they may be forced to shut down the process and call for assistance from some designated source: the technologists, the maintenance department, or someone else. (They may also run the process "as is" in order to meet schedules, and thereby risk failure to meet the quality goals).

Corrective Action—Remedy

The process designers should in addition provide the means for adjusting the process as needed to bring it into conformance with the quality goals. Such adjustments are almost always needed at startup of the process and are needed periodically during running of the process. This aspect of design for process control ideally should meet the following criteria:

There should be a known relationship between the process variables and the product results.

Means should be provided for convenient adjustment of the process settings for the key process variables.

There should be a predictable relationship between the amount of change in the process settings and the amount of effect on the product features.

To meet these criteria the process designers may need to conduct designed experiments. Such experiments not only can disclose the relationships between process variables and product results but can also provide the information needed to optimize product performance and process yields. If the designers lack such in-depth knowledge, the operating forces will in due course be forced to cut and try in order to carry out remedial action. The resulting frustrations become a disincentive to putting a high priority on quality.

> In one foundry an automated process design for controlling the amount of metal poured failed to provide adequate regulation. As a result, human regulation took over. The workers then played safe by overpouring, since underpoured castings had to be scrapped. The result was much waste until a new technology solved the problem (Burgam, 1985).

Facilities Control

Most processes include various physical facilities: equipment, instruments, tools. The trend has increasingly been to use automated processes, computers, robots, and the like. This same trend makes product quality more and more dependent on maintenance of the facilities.

The elements of design for facilities control are well known:

Establish a schedule for conducting facilities maintenance

Establish a checklist—a list of tasks to be performed during a maintenance action

Train the maintenance forces to perform the tasks

Assign clear responsibility for adherence to schedule

The weakest link in the above has been adherence to schedule. To assure strict adherence to schedule requires an independent audit.

In cases involving introduction of new technology, a further weak link is training the maintenance forces.

> During the 1980s the auto makers began to introduce computers and other electronics into their vehicles. It soon emerged that many repair shop technicians lacked the technological education base needed to diagnose and remedy the associated field failures. To make matters worse, the auto makers did not give high priority to standardizing the computers. As a result a massive training backlog developed (White, 1988).

Design for Evaluation of Performance

Throughout all those stages of process control, there is need to acquire and analyze the data required to evaluate product and process performance. This need gives rise to yet other areas of process planning: planning for

Inspection and test. Assigning responsibility for making the evaluations, and establishing procedures that provide sampling tables, criteria for decision making, etc. Some of the features of this plan will find their way into the process control spreadsheet (see Figure 8-4, "The Process Control Spreadsheet"). For elaboration see generally, Juran (1988), Section 18, "Inspection and Test."

Measurement control. Defining the sensors and the means for maintaining their precision—for both technological and human sensors. For elaboration, see Chapter 5, under "The Sensor," also under "Human Sensors." See also Juran (1988), Section 18, p. 18.63 to 18.97.

Data analysis and interpretation. Learning from the data what is going on in the process. Much of the methodology for this area of planning is derived from what is generally called Statistical Process Control (SPC). A major use of SPC is to interpret the data that evaluate performance (see below). There are also numerous other uses. For extensive discussion, see Juran, (1988), Section 24, "Statistical Process Control."

Statistical Process Control (SPC)

The term generally refers to the concept of applying statistical methodology to the problems of process control. The concept includes, among other things, collection of the basic data and use of the Shewhart control chart to distinguish real changes in the process from apparent changes.

These statistical methods and tools have been known for decades, but application was limited until the 1980s. The 1980s then witnessed a great expansion in the use of these tools and in their application to process control. In the opinion of the authors, these statistical methods and tools have contributed importantly to effective process control and to certain other aspects of managing for quality.

The SPC movement has also resulted in the training of a great many supervisors and workers in basic statistical tools. The resulting increase in statistical literacy has enabled these employees to understand better the behavior of processes and products. Many of them have learned that decisions based on data collection and analysis will outperform decisions based on empiricism.

Interpretation: Statistical Significance

A frequent problem in process control is to interpret observed differences. Any evaluation of the product or process usually differs from the previous evaluation. Such observed differences can result from:

a. A real change in the product or process
b. An apparent change arising from chance variation (such apparent changes abound when sample sizes are small). An apparent change is a false alarm. It is a waste of time to look for the cause: the cause is not "findable."

Because false alarms do abound, they should be distinguished from real changes before trying to discover the causes. An elegant tool for this purpose is the Shewhart control chart (or just control chart). Figure 8-3 shows a typical control chart.

In Figure 8-3 the horizontal scale is usually time, or some time-related variable. The vertical scale is performance. The plotted points show successive performances over time.

The chart also exhibits three horizontal lines. The middle line is the average performance over some earlier span of time. The other two lines are "limit lines." They are drawn to separate false alarms from real changes, based on some chosen level of odds, e.g., 1,000 to 1.

Point A on the chart differs from the historical average, but this difference could be due to chance variation (at odds of less than 1,000 to 1). Hence it is assumed that there has been no real change. Point B also differs from the historical average, but now the odds are heavily against this having been caused by chance—over 1,000 to 1. Hence it is assumed that there was a real change and that the cause is findable.

(For extensive discussion on the many types of control charts and on other graphic aids to process control, see Juran, 1988, Section 24, "Statistical Process Control.")

Self-control

Ideally, responsibility for control should be assigned to individuals. Such assignment is inherently clear. It also confers status—a form of "ownership"—which responds to some basic human needs.

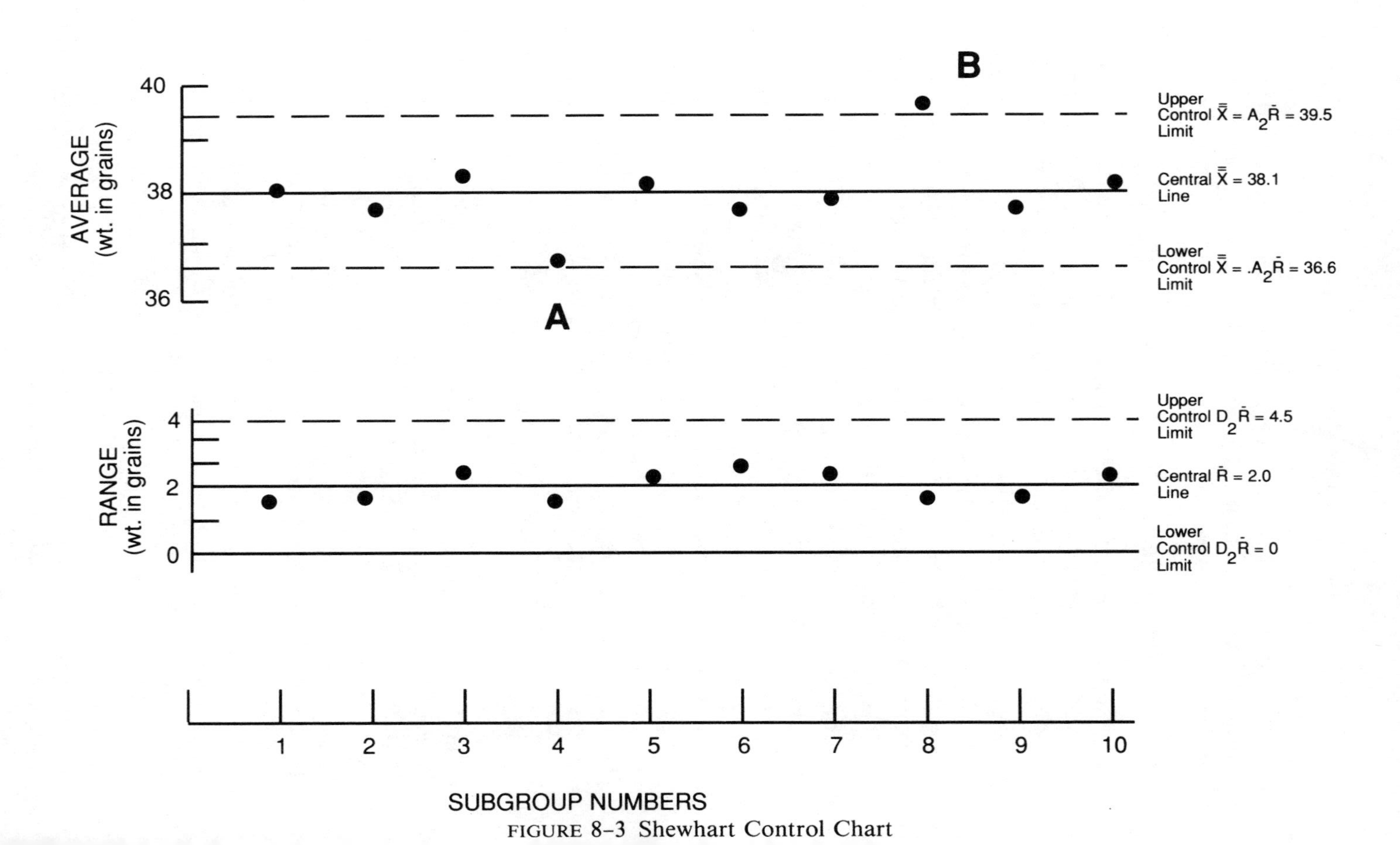

FIGURE 8–3 Shewhart Control Chart

Criteria for Self-control

Ideally also, responsibility should be coextensive with authority. Applied to quality control this requires placing the operating forces into a state of self-control, a state in which they are able to carry out all of the activities of the feedback loop. To create such a state of self-control, the process designers must provide the operating forces with:

The means of knowing what their target performance is. This criterion is met by establishing and publishing the quality goals.

The means of knowing what their actual performance is. This criterion is met by establishing the system of evaluation.

The means for changing their performance in the event that performance does not conform to goals. To meet this criterion requires an operating process that (a) is inherently capable of meeting the goals and (b) is provided with features that make it possible for the operating forces to change the performance as needed to bring it into conformance with the goals.

These criteria for self-control are applicable to processes in all functions, and all levels, from general manager to nonsupervisory worker.

It is all too easy for managers to conclude that the above criteria have been met. In practice there are many details to be worked out before the criteria can be met. The nature of these details is evident from checklists that have been prepared for specific processes in order to assure meeting the criteria for self-control. Examples of these checklists include:

Personnel Involved	*See Juran's Quality Control Handbook, Fourth Edition (1988), at Pages:*
Product designers	13.71
Production workers	17.12; 17.18; 17.21
Administrative and support personnel	21.13

The term *controllability* is often used to describe the extent to which the criteria for self-control have been met. The degree of controllability is closely related to the degree of responsibility for results. To hold someone responsible for results without having first met the criteria for self-control creates the risk of unwarranted blame and of divisiveness. In this way, one of the tests of completeness of design for process and product control is whether the criteria for self-control have been met.

Controllability and the Workers

Much product and process control is done by automated methods. Most of the residue is carried out by *the workers:* office workers, factory workers, salespersons, and others. Many of these have been put into a state of self-control, so they are able to detect and correct nonconformances. There are also a great many operations for which the criteria for worker self-control have not been fully met. In such cases it is risky for managers to hold the workers "responsible" for quality.

If all the criteria for self-control have been met at the worker level, any resulting product nonconformances are said to be *worker-controllable.* If any of the criteria for self-control have not been met, then management's planning has been incomplete: the planning has not fully provided the means for carrying out the activities within the feedback loop. The nonconforming products resulting from such planning deficiencies are then said to be *management-controllable.*

In the minds of workers and managers alike, responsibility for results should be keyed to controllability. However, in the past many managers have not understood the extent of controllability as it prevailed at the worker level. Numerous studies conducted in the 1950s and 1960s showed that for operations at the worker level the proportion of management-controllable to worker-controllable nonconformances was of the order of 80 to 20. That ratio helps to explain the failure of so many efforts to solve the companies' quality problems solely by motivating the work force.

Control Subjects

All control is centered on specific things to be controlled. We shall call these things "control subjects." Each control subject is the focal point of a feedback loop. Control subjects are a mixture of:

Product features. Some control is carried out by evaluating features of the product itself (the invoice, the gear wheel, the research report, etc.)

Process features. Much control consists of evaluating those process features which directly impact the product features, e.g., the state of the ribbon in the printer, the temperature of the annealing furnace, the validity of the formulas used in the researcher's report.

Side-effect features. These features do not impact the product but may create such troublesome side effects as irritations to employees, offense to the neighborhood, and threats to the environment.

Concept of Dominance

Control subjects can be very numerous. In such cases the process control designers are well advised to identify the vital few control subjects so that they will receive appropriate priority. One of the tools available for this purpose is the concept of dominance.

Operating processes are influenced by numerous variables: input materials, physical facilities, human skills, environmental conditions, and so forth. Often one variable is more important than all the rest combined. Such a variable is said to be the dominant variable. Once designers know which variable is dominant, they can confidently assign top priority to acquiring mastery over that variable. The more usual dominant variables include:

1. *Setup-dominant.* Some processes exhibit high stability and reproducibility of results over many cycles of operation. The design for control should provide the operating forces with the means for precise setup and validation before operations proceed. A common example is the printing process.
2. *Time-dominant.* Here the process is known to change progressively with time, e.g., depletion of consumable supplies, heating up, wear of tools. The design for control should provide means for periodic evaluation of the effect of progressive change and for convenient readjustment.
3. *Component-dominant.* Here the main variable is the quality of the input materials and components. An example is the assembly of complex electronic or mechanical equipments. For the short run it may be necessary to resort to incoming inspection. For the long run, the design for control should be directed at supplier relations, including joint planning with suppliers to upgrade the inputs.
4. *Worker-dominant.* In these processes, quality depends mainly on the skill and knack possessed by the workers. The skilled

trades are well known examples. The design for control should emphasize aptitude testing of workers, training and certification, quality rating of workers, and errorproofing to reduce worker errors.

5. *Information-dominant.* Here the processes are of a "job-shop" nature, so that there is frequent change in what product is to be produced. As a result, the job information changes frequently. The design for control should concentrate on providing an information system that can deliver accurate, up-to-date information on just how this job differs from its predecessors.

Control Stations

Organization for control usually starts by defining specific "control stations." In the lower levels of organization, a control station is usually confined to a single physical area. Alternatively, the control station takes such forms as a patrol beat or a "control tower." At higher levels a control station may be widely dispersed geographically, such as the scope of a supervisor's or manager's responsibility.

A review of numerous control stations shows that they are usually designed to provide evaluations and/or early warnings in the following ways:

At changes of jurisdiction, where responsibility is transferred from one organization to another

Before embarking on some significant irreversible activity

After creation of a critical quality feature

At the site of dominant process variables

At areas ("windows") that allow economical evaluation to be made

The Process Control Spreadsheet

For each control station the designers identify the control subjects over which control is to be exercised. Those control subjects are usually numerous. Each requires a feedback loop made up of multiple process control features. To keep track of all this detail, the designers make use of a process control spreadsheet, as in Figure 8-4.

In this spreadsheet the horizontal rows are the various process con-

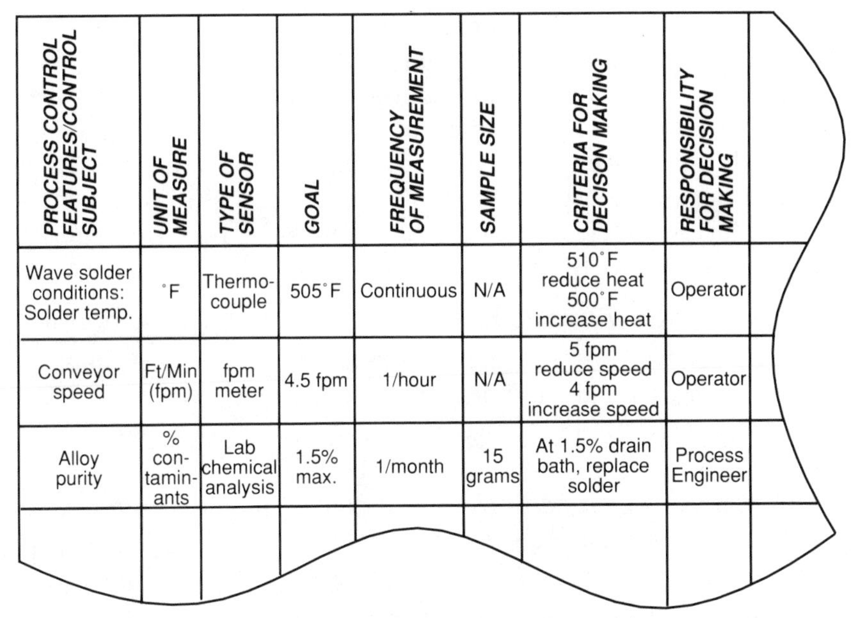

PROCESS CONTROL FEATURES/CONTROL SUBJECT	UNIT OF MEASURE	TYPE OF SENSOR	GOAL	FREQUENCY OF MEASUREMENT	SAMPLE SIZE	CRITERIA FOR DECISON MAKING	RESPONSIBILITY FOR DECISION MAKING
Wave solder conditions: Solder temp.	°F	Thermo-couple	505°F	Continuous	N/A	510°F reduce heat 500°F increase heat	Operator
Conveyor speed	Ft/Min (fpm)	fpm meter	4.5 fpm	1/hour	N/A	5 fpm reduce speed 4 fpm increase speed	Operator
Alloy purity	% con-tamin-ants	Lab chemical analysis	1.5% max.	1/month	15 grams	At 1.5% drain bath, replace solder	Process Engineer

FIGURE 8–4 A Quality Control Spreadsheet

trol subjects. The vertical columns consist of elements of the feedback loop plus other features needed by the operating forces to exercise process control so as to meet the product goals.

Some of the contents of the vertical columns are unique to specific process features. However, certain vertical columns apply widely to many process features, such features as:

Unit of measure

Type of sensor

Product goal (aimed-at value)

Product goal for uniformity (tolerance)

Frequency of measurement

Sample size

Criteria for decision making

Responsibility for decision making

Product Conformance or Not: Self-inspection

Company policies usually provide that products conforming to specification should be sent on to the next destination. The assumption is that product that conforms to specification is also fit for use. This assumption is valid in the great majority of cases.

Whether product features do conform to product goals involves myriad decisions, which, because of their great numbers, must be delegated to the lowest levels of organization. Ideally, the operating forces at the lowest levels of organization should make these numerous product conformance decisions. However, some prerequisite criteria must be met first:

Quality is number one. Quality must have undoubted top priority.

Mutual confidence. The managers must trust the workers enough to be willing to make the delegation, and the workers must have enough confidence in the managers to be willing to accept the responsibility.

Self-control. The conditions for self-control should be in place so that the workers have all the means necessary to do good work.

Training. The workers should be trained to make the product conformance decisions and should also be tested to ensure that they make good decisions.

In many companies these criteria are not yet met, so the product conformance decisions are delegated to a separate inspection or checking department rather than to the operating forces. The reason has generally been that quality has not had top priority. In such cases there is a risk that product conformance decisions made by the operating forces will be biased in favor of meeting the top priority parameter (whatever that is), rather than the quality parameter.

Disposition of Nonconforming Products

Many nonconforming products are so obviously unfit for use that they are discarded (or repaired) as a matter of course. Other nonconforming products are not so obviously unfit for use. For some of such cases, the optimal decision may be to use the product as is.

To make this "fitness for use" decision requires acquiring certain additional pertinent information, such as:

How will this product be used? What will be the environments of use?

Who will be the users?

Are there any potential dangers to human safety or health?

Are there any potential violations of obligations to society?

What is the urgency for delivery?

How do the available alternatives affect our economics?

How do these alternatives affect the users' economics?

Some companies must deal with numerous cases of nonconforming products. In such companies it is usual to establish a standing committee (Material Review Board, etc.) specifically to deal with disposition of nonconforming products.

Improper disposition of nonconforming products is a potential trouble area. Failure to use products that meet customer needs is a waste. Sending out products that do not meet customer needs is worse. In view of such potential problems, the companies' quality audit system should ensure that decisions on disposition of nonconforming products are made by persons armed with the information needed to balance the considerations of customer satisfaction and costs.

Definition of Work: Who Does What

The feedback loop involves multiple tasks. These include:

Evaluation of actual performance

Interpretation of the goals

Comparison of actual performance to goals

Decision as to conformance

Action to be taken

Usually there are multiple people associated with each control station: the workers, the supervision, planners (e.g., process engineers), inspectors, data collectors, and others. Even among the workers, there can be multiple categories: setup specialists, operators, maintenance personnel, etc. In such cases of multiple categories, it is necessary to agree on: Who should make which decisions? Who should take which actions? An aid to reaching such agreement is a special spreadsheet similar to Figure 8–5.

In this spreadsheet the essential decisions and actions are listed in the left-hand column. The remaining columns are headed by the names of the job classifications associated with the control station. Then, through multidepartmental discussion, agreement is reached on who is to do what.

The spreadsheet is a proven way to find answers to the long-

DECISIONS, ACTIONS	PRODUCTION			INSPECTION		OTHER
	SETTER	WORKER	SUPERVISOR	BENCH	PATROL	
PROCESS DECISIONS:						
SETUP						
SETUP VERIFICATION						
RUN						
RUNNING VERIF'N						
PRODUCT DECISIONS:						
CONFORMANCE						
FITNESS FOR USE						

FIGURE 8–5 Spreadsheet for Who Does What

standing question, "Who is responsible for quality?" This question has never been answered, because it is inherently unanswerable. However, if the question is restated in terms of decisions and actions, the way is open to agree on the answers.

Responsibility for Design of Process Controls

Design of process controls is done variously by:

Multifunctional staff planners

Multifunctional teams of staff planners and operating managers

Departmental planners

Departmental managers and supervisors

The workers

The assignment of this responsibility is complicated by the fact that process control consists of multiple tasks within the feedback loop. We looked at these tasks earlier in this chapter:

Choice of control stations

Allocation of control subjects to control stations

Choice of process control features

Establishment of the criteria to be met, such as rules for data collection and analysis, rules for decision making.

Establishment of the procedures required to meet the criteria: operations to be performed, sequence of operations, data to be recorded, etc.

Assignment of these tasks varies depending on such factors as: the criticality of the process, the traditions in the industry, the organization structure in the company, and so forth. The major question in assigning responsibility is whether to assign these tasks to the staff planners or to the operating heads, and which tasks to assign to whom.

In the case of critical processes, it is common for the process planners to plan the process controls as well. For example, the process planners may establish criteria for selection, training, and qualification of operating personnel.

For well-standardized processes it is quite common for much or most of the design for process control to be delegated to the operating forces.

There is also a widely used plan that involves joint responsibility and audit, as follows:

Activity	*Operations*	*Staff Planners*
Planning	X	X
Execution	X	
Audit		X

Under this allocation the responsibility for planning is joint. Each can nominate; each can veto. The responsibility for execution rests with Operations: run the process, meet the goals. However, an audit is established to provide added assurance that the execution follows the plan. (In some companies the audit is assigned to special auditing departments.)

Provision for Audit

Experience has shown that control systems are subject to "slippage" of all sorts. Personnel turnover may result in loss of essential knowledge. Entry of unanticipated changes may result in obsolescence. Shortcuts and misuse may gradually undermine the system until it is no longer effective.

The main tool for guarding against deterioration of a control system has been the audit. Under the audit concept an independent review is established to provide answers to the following questions:

Is the control system still adequate for the job?

Is the system being followed?

The answers are of course useful to the operating managers. However, that is not the main purpose of the audit. The main purpose of the audit is to provide those answers to people who, though not directly involved in operations, nevertheless have a need to know. If quality is to have top priority, those who have a need to know includes the upper managers.

△ It follows that one of the responsibilities of upper managers is to mandate establishment of an audit of the quality control system.

In practice, the upper manager's quality audit extends well beyond the system of quality control. See, in this connection, Chapter 9, under "Quality Audits."

Transfer to Operations

"Transfer to operations" includes a transfer of responsibility from the planners to the operating managers. These managers understandably do not want to accept responsibility for results if the process cannot do its intended job—in our dialect, if the process lacks process capability or lacks controllability.

Proof of Process Capability

In some cases, proof of process capability can be provided by direct measurement of the process, as described in Chapter 7, under the heading "Evaluating Process Capability—The Methods," and also under the heading "Process Capability Based on Variability." Where direct measurement is not feasible, there are other ways. These include:

THE DRY RUN. This is a test of the process under operating conditions. The purpose is to test the process. Any resulting product is not sent on to customers.

A bank data processing manager purchased computer software designed to replace manual processing of a complex data system. She tested the software by running the same input data through both systems—manual and computer—and then comparing the results.

THE PILOT TEST. This is a step intermediate between the planning phase and full-scale operations. The approach goes by various names:

A "test town" for trying out a new marketing plan

A "pilot lot" for testing out a manufacturing process

A "test department" for trying a new managerial concept, e.g., QC Circles

ACCEPTANCE TEST. This is a highly structured form of testing common in computer systems but applicable to other situations as well. A test plan is designed by a special team not directly involved in design of the process being tested. The test plan sets up the proper environmental conditions, inputs, relevant interventions, and operating conditions. The test is intended to stress, in relevant ways, the important functional and other features in which the process could fail. The test is then conducted either by a specific test group or by the operating forces. The process designers do not conduct the test.

SIMULATION. This takes such forms as prototype construction and test, market surveys prior to sale, rehearsals, or mathematical models. *Simulation is an imitation of the real thing,* with many benefits and risks. The risks can be reduced if the operating personnel participate in the simulation planning and in the subsequent interpretation of results.

(For additional discussion on simulation, see Chapter 7, under the heading "Simulation to Estimate Process Capability," and under the heading "Limitations and Risks in Simulation: Two Worlds".)

Process Validation

In some industries one of the meanings of "process capability" is conformance to specifications rather than ability to meet the needs of customers. Typical examples are industries in which:

The client is a government agency, e.g., the Department of Defense

Government regulators are given responsibility to protect human safety, health, or the environment

In such industries the clients and the regulators prepare product and process specifications that are presumed to reflect the needs of customers. The suppliers are then given the responsibility to:

Provide products that conform to product specifications

Provide processes that conform to process specifications ("Process" here extends to managerial processes as well as technological processes.)

These same government clients and regulators tend to stress quality assurance in the form of "process validation." The following is an example of a definition (from a guideline drafted by the Food and Drug Administration):

> Process validation is a documented program which provides a high degree of assurance that a specific process will consistently produce a product meeting its predetermined specifications and quality attributes.

The associated forms of quality assurance then include a review of all quality-related process activities to ensure that they do conform to the process specifications. These specifications take such forms as the Defense Department's MIL-Q-9858 or the FDA's Good Manufacturing Practice.

Proof That the Process Is Controllable

Transfer from Planning to Operations includes transfer of responsibility for control. The operating forces become responsible not only for producing the product but also for maintaining the process at its planned level of capability. To carry out the latter responsibility requires that the process be controllable—that the planning has provided the means for carrying out the activities within the feedback loop.

For many processes the design of the control system is left to the operating forces. In such cases, design for control should not wait until the process transfer has been made. Instead, the design for control should be done as the process design proceeds. Failing this, the risk is that the process will lack full controllability, and that discovery of this fact will come too late in the day. Our experience has been that such cases involve costly retroactive revisions.

For "critical" processes the design for control should properly be a part of the basic process design. There are indications that for various disasters and near-disasters there have been linkages to certain aspects of the design of the control system:

Time to respond to a crisis

Criteria for qualification of the operating forces

Simulation; rehearsal

Maintenance

In most cases the physical facilities have done what they were designed to do. The weaknesses usually seem to have been centered in the human component of the control systems.

Proof of human controllability is best provided by demonstration. In consequence, the planning should include defining the terms of the demonstration, that is, the criteria to be met by the operating forces when faced with crises of the type that might arise during conduct of operations. These criteria consist of such matters as time of response to alarm signals, accuracy of diagnosis, and adequacy of remedial action.

A similar approach can be used to design the system of independent audit needed to ensure that the operating forces carry out the control plan and maintain the integrity of the basic process.

Transfer of Know-how

During process design the planners acquire a great deal of know-how about the process. The operating forces could benefit from this know-how if it were transferred. There are various ways of making this transfer:

Process specifications. These set out the process goals to be met. The information is vital to the operating forces but is the barest minimum.

Procedures. These are a welcome elaboration. They can include instructions, cautions, and the why as well as the how. Being written, they become a reference base and an aid to the indoctrination of new employees. A well-written Owner's Manual serves similar purposes.

Briefings. These are meetings specifically set up for transfer of information. When well organized these briefings are most useful. The planners make a presentation built around a written statement, supplemented by visual aids. Questions and discussion are encouraged so that the transfer goes beyond the surface.

On-the-job training. In many cases the planners can usefully participate in the training given to the operating supervisors and the workers. The merits of this approach go beyond the transfer of know-how; there is an associated, valuable feedback to the planners. The supplier learns from the customers.

Formal Training Courses. These are needed in cases where the new process departs radically from the past. Examples have included introduction of word processors, computer aided design, QC Circles, laser drilling, and orthogonal arrays. Such formal training courses become essential if the new process is to be applied widely throughout the organization.

Prior participation. Transfer of know-how is a mixture of transfer before the fact and transfer after the fact. Both forms are needed, but the greatest damage is done by neglect of transfer before the fact. Such neglect loses the benefits of early warning and of the teamwork that results from participation.

Introduction of computer aided diagnostic equipment in repair shops has brought out some unanticipated side effects. Experienced mechanics may actually be slowed down by the need to go through the structured countdown. In addition, a mechanic with minimal experience may, aided by the computer's data base, acquire access to knowledge that took the senior mechanics twenty years to accumulate (Fisher, 1988).

Note that transfer of know-how is made to external customers as well as to internal operating departments. Many "products" made by suppliers become "processes" in the hands of external customers. These external "operating departments" also need know-how with respect to the product/process.

Transfer of know-how to many external customers takes place during installation of the process on the customers' premises and during the trial runs.

Another widespread example of transfer of know-how is through the owners' manuals provided to consumers.

(For elaboration on transfer of know-how, see Bemesderfer, 1979).

The Formalities of Transfer

In some companies, transfer of the process from Planning to Operations is structured and formalized. An information package is prepared, consisting of certain standardized essentials: goals to be met, facilities to be used, procedures to be followed, instructions, cautions, and so on. There are also supplements unique to the project. In addition, provision is made for briefing and training the operating forces in such areas as maintenance and dealing with crises. The package is accompanied by a formal letter of transfer of responsibility. In some of these companies, this transfer takes place in a near-ceremonial atmosphere. In other companies, formality is minimal.

The structured approach has value. It tends to evolve checklists and countdowns, which help ensure that the transfer is orderly and complete. (Formality is useful if it contributes to such orderliness and completeness.)

In companies that already have such a structured approach, the planners need only to adapt the project information package to conform with established practice. If the company has only a loose structure, or none at all, the planners must make their own decision as to the contents of the information package, and how far to go with formalities.

Application to the Hierarchy

Transfer to operations completes the journey down the quality planning road map. What has been discussed up to now is the universal quality planning process along with the methodology for carrying out the various steps.

The remaining chapters take up the application of the quality planning process to various levels in the hierarchy. While the road map is common to all levels, the problems of application are different. In addition, each level presents its own special problems relating to such critical aspects as motivation, training, and so on.

List of High Points

The design for process control should provide the operating forces with the means for corrective action.

The weakest link in maintenance of facilities has been adherence to the checking schedule.

To assure strict adherence to scheduled maintenance of facilities requires an independent audit.

Responsibility for control should be assigned to individuals.

A state of self-control consists of:

Knowing what the target performance is

Knowing what the actual performance is

Having the means for changing performance in the event of nonconformance

One test for completeness of design for process and product control is whether the criteria for self-control have been met.

Responsibility for results should be keyed to controllability.

The concept of dominance helps planners to concentrate on the major variables.

Organization for control usually starts by defining specific "control stations."

Product conformance decisions should ideally be made by the operating forces at the lowest levels of organization.

The question "Who is responsible for quality?" is inherently unanswerable.

Design for process control should be done concurrently with the design of the process itself.

Proof of human controllability is best provided by demonstration.

Tasks for Upper Managers

The quality audit system should ensure that decisions on disposition of nonconforming products are made by persons armed with the information needed to balance the considerations of customer satisfaction and cost.

One of the responsibilities of upper managers is to mandate establishment of an audit of the quality control system.

] 9 [

Strategic Quality Planning

The Purpose of This Chapter

The purpose of this chapter is to explain how to apply quality planning at the upper levels of the company hierarchy. These upper levels consist mainly of autonomous organization units. In the private sector such units are profit centers. The corporation is a profit center. So are the autonomous divisions. In the public sector the autonomous organization units usually include the agency, the autonomous regions, and the autonomous bureaus.

The Concept of Strategic Quality Planning

Strategic business planning is essentially a structured process for defining the broad mission and strategic goals for the company and then determining the means to be used to reach those goals. In the private sector the strategic goals are strongly income-oriented, and therefore typically include such financial goals as sales, net income, and return on investment. In the public sector, the strategic goals are strongly mission-oriented: national defense, administration of justice, tax collection.

Until the 1980s, strategic business planning seldom included planning for quality. Planning for quality did exist, but on the "Little Q" level. The scope was narrow, being confined to selected operating entities such as factories. The 1980s then witnessed a significant trend toward the adoption of the "Big Q" concept and an associated trend toward adoption of the concept of strategic quality planning. The authors strongly support these trends. They believe companies that should adopt the Big Q concept for competitive survival and should enlarge their business planning to include strategic quality planning. The authors also believe that these same trends will accelerate, and that in the decades ahead they will dominate all activities related to managing for quality.

The Terminology

Although there have been relatively few actual adoptions of the concept of strategic quality planning, there has been much groping in the general direction of somehow increasing the attention given to quality during the business planning process. This groping has generated a long list of terms used to describe what the companies are trying to do. The more popular terms have included:

Companywide Quality Control

Strategic Quality Management

Strategic Quality Planning

Total Quality Management

Total Quality Control

For the most part, the companies have not defined such terms with precision. As a result the personnel have been widely confused as to what change is supposed to be taking place. The confusion has been extensive in those companies where "Total" and "Companywide" did not seem to apply to the upper managers. (Many upper managers limited their role to setting vague goals and then exhorting everyone else to meet the goals.) The situation has been at its worst in the numerous cases of failure to make clear to the personnel just what they should do that is different from prior practice.

Confusion as to the meaning behind the banner is inherently divisive. Companies that embark on broad initiatives should define their terminology with precision. It is essential to give the company personnel a clear understanding of (1) what the intended changes from past practice are and (2) how they will be affected by those changes.

In this book the authors have elected to adopt the term Strategic Quality Management (SQM) as a name for strategic quality planning. As used in this book:

> Strategic Quality Management (SQM) is a structured process for establishing long-range quality goals, at the highest levels of organization, and defining the means to be used to reach those goals.

Notice that the term Strategic Quality Management differs from the title of this chapter. The choice has been deliberate. The term "quality management" is all-inclusive, relating to all the processes of the Juran Trilogy: quality planning, quality control, and quality improvement. This same term is appropriate at the upper management level, where there is a convergence of the responsibility for conducting all of those processes.

The remainder of this chapter is devoted to explaining in detail the concept of SQM, how to apply the concept to a going company, and how the concept impacts the company personnel.

The Financial Analogy

The structure of SQM is similar to that long used to establish and meet financial goals. The similarity is so striking that it is worthwhile to review briefly the well-known approach to strategic financial management.

Many companies manage for finance by use of a structured, coherent approach, which can properly be described as *strategic financial management.* The key elements consist of setting financial goals, determining the actions (or deeds) required to meet the goals, providing the needed resources, establishing measures of performance, reviewing performance against goals, and providing rewards based on results.

This approach is now sufficiently generic to be applicable companywide, throughout the hierarchy. It is also applicable to other functions, including the quality function. The generic features consists largely of:

A hierarchy of goals (The major financial goals, as reflected in the corporate budget, are supported by a hierarchy of financial goals at lower levels: divisional and departmental budgets, sales quotas, cost standards, project cost estimates, etc.)

A formalized methodology for establishing the goals and for providing the needed resources.

An infrastructure, which includes financial managers and supporting personnel

A control process, which includes systems for data collection and analysis, financial reports, and reviews of financial performance against goals.

Provision of rewards (Performance against financial goals is given substantial weight in the system of merit rating and recognition.)

Universal participation (The financial goals, reports, reviews, etc., are designed in hierarchical form to parallel the company's organization hierarchy. These hierarchical designs make it possible for managers at all levels to support upper managers in managing for finance.)

A common language, centered on a major, common unit of measure—money (There are also other common units of measure, e.g., ratios such as return on investment. In addition, the key words (such as budget, expense, profit, etc.) acquire standardized meanings, so that communication becomes more and more precise.)

Training (It is common for managers at all levels to undergo training in various financial concepts, processes, methods, tools, etc. Companies that have so trained their managers, in all functions and at all levels, will outperform companies in which such training has been confined to the finance department.)

Establishing SQM: The Quality Council

The elements that make up SQM are generally alike for all companies. However, each company's uniqueness will determine the sequence and pace of application as well as the extent to which additional elements must be provided.

A fundamental step in establishing SQM is the creation of the Quality Council (or Quality Committee, etc.). The Quality Council is the key element in the company's infrastructure for SQM. It exercises complete oversight with respect to establishment and maintenance of SQM.

The Quality Council membership properly consists of the senior managers. In many cases the Quality Council consists of the senior executive staff. At a given point in their staff meeting they declare: We have finished with that part of our agenda; now we take up quality. At that point they "change hats" and become the Quality Council.

In large organizations there may be quality councils at multiple levels of organization. In such cases the councils are "networked," that is, members of upper-level councils serve as chairpersons for lower-level councils. Figure 9-1 shows an example of networking as practiced in one large company.

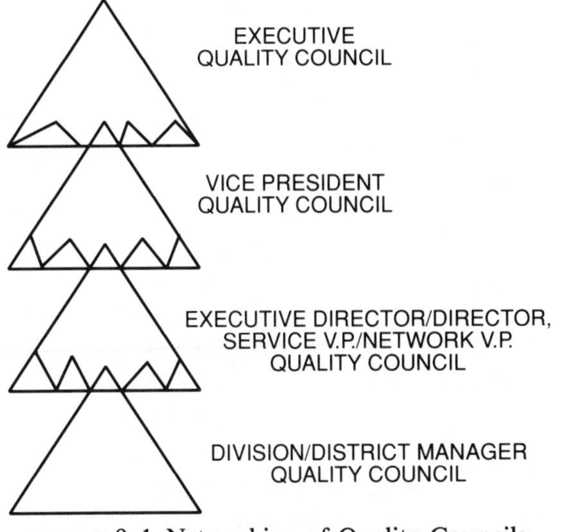

FIGURE 9–1 Networking of Quality Councils
SOURCE: AT&T Network Operations Group.

If there is a quality improvement council, it is identical with, or an arm of, the Quality Council.)

If the needed quality councils are not already in existence, the upper managers should create them.

Once created, the Quality Council has the responsibility to define and incorporate the elements of SQM into the company's strategic business planning. In addition the council has the responsibility to ensure that any needed associated infrastructure is created at subordinate levels of organization.

Quality Policies

The purposes of SQM include establishing guidelines for the actions to be taken in order to reach the quality goals. A major tool for establishing such guidelines is Quality Policies.

"Policy" as used here is *a guide to managerial action.* Published policy statements are the result of a good deal of deliberation in high places, followed by approval at the highest level. The Quality Council plays a major role in this process.

Policy declarations are a necessity during a period of severe change, and companies have acted accordingly. The 1980s have seen an unprecedented surge of activity of thinking through and publishing quality policies. While the details vary, the published policies have much in common.

Without exception, all published quality policies declare the intention to *meet the needs of customers.* The wording often includes identification of specific needs to be met, e.g., the company's products should provide customer satisfaction.

Most published policies include language relative to competitiveness in quality, e.g., the company's products shall *equal or exceed competitive quality.*

A third frequent area of published quality policy relates to quality improvement, e.g., the published statements declare the intention to *conduct improvement annually.*

Some quality policy statements include specific reference to internal customers, e.g., quality should *extend to all phases of the business.*

Enforcement of quality policies is a comparatively new problem because of the relative newness of written quality policies. In some companies provision is made for independent review of adherence to quality policies.

> In a major electronics company, there is a quality policy requiring that new models of products, at the time they become generally available, must have a reliability at least equal to the reliability of the models they replace, and also at least equal to the reliability of the models of competitors. The product development departments are required to demonstrate that this policy has been met. In addition, the Quality Assurance Department has the responsibility to review the demonstration.

As a part of introducing SQM, the Quality Council should make sure that the prevailing quality policies correctly reflect the company's intentions with respect to quality. If the policies are found to be out of date, the Quality Council should take steps to ensure that the quality policy statements are updated.

Strategic Quality Goals

As used here, a quality goal is an aimed-at quality target. A goal is specific. It is usually quantified and is to be met within a specific period of time.

An essential element of SQM is the establishment of broad quality goals as part of the strategic business planning. Here are some actual examples of high-level quality goals that companies have established and met:

Make the Taurus/Sable models at a level of quality that is best in class (This goal was established by Ford Motor Company.)

Cut in two the time to fill customer orders (Becton, Dickinson & Company)

Reduce the field failures on major appliances by 50 percent in the next three years (This goal was established in 1981 by the Swedish-based AB Electrolux. The goal was met. A second such goal was established in 1984, and also was met. A third such goal was established in 1987.)

Reduce billing errors by 90 percent (Florida Power & Light Company)

Note that all of the above goals involve broad, multifunctional activities.

Subject Matter of Quality Goals

Despite the uniqueness of specific industries and companies, certain quality goals are widely applicable:

PRODUCT PERFORMANCE. This goal relates to those product performance features which determine response to customer needs: promptness of service, fuel consumption, mean time between failures, courtesy, and so on. Such features directly influence product salability.

QUALITY COMPETITIVENESS. This has always been a goal in market-based economies, but seldom a part of the strategic business plan. The trend to bring quality competitiveness into the business plan is recent but irreversible.

QUALITY IMPROVEMENT. This goal may be aimed at improving product salability and/or reducing the cost of poor quality. Either way, the end result after deployment is a formal list of quality improvement projects with associated assignment of responsibilities.

REDUCTION OF THE COST OF POOR QUALITY. The goal of quality improvement usually includes a goal of reducing the costs due to poor quality. These costs are not known with precision, but they are known to be very high. Despite the lack of complete figures, it is feasible, through estimates, to bring this goal into the strategic business plan and to deploy it successfully to lower levels.

PERFORMANCE OF MACROPROCESSES. This goal has only recently entered the strategic business plan. The goal relates to the performance of major processes that are multifunctional in nature, e.g., new product launching, customer order processing, billing. For such macroprocesses, a special problem is: Who should have the responsibility for meeting the goal? We shall discuss this shortly, under the heading "Deployment of Quality Goals."

Nominations of Quality Goals

The quality goals that are to enter the strategic business plan are in all cases selected by the upper managers. In companies that practice participative management, this selection is preceded by a nomination process, which is open to all levels of the hierarchy. There may be many nominations, but only a few will survive the screening process and end up as part of the strategic business plan. Other nominations may instead enter the business plans of lower levels in the hierarchy. Many nominations will be deferred—they were unable to secure the necessary priority.

Upper managers have always received inputs that are helpful in selection of quality goals: inputs from customer contacts or from contacts with upper managers in other companies. As experience is gained with SQM, the upper managers receive added inputs from such sources as:

Membership on the Quality Council

Periodic reviews of performance against quality goals

Quality audits conducted by upper managers (see below, under "Quality Audits")

Deployment of Quality Goals

At the outset, a list of strategic quality goals is a "wish list." To convert this list into potential realities requires getting deep into specifics: what actions need to be taken in order to meet the goals, who is to take those actions, and so forth. The process for identifying these specifics will be called "deployment of quality goals."*

**A note on terminology:* Some companies use the term "policy deployment" to designate deployment of quality goals. This usage seems to be the result of difficulties in translation from the corresponding Japanese term.

As used here, "deployment" means subdividing the goals and allocating the subgoals to lower levels. Such deployment accomplishes some essential purposes:

The subdivision continues until it identifies the specific actions to be taken.

The allocation continues until it assigns clear responsibility for taking the actions.

Those who are assigned to take the actions then respond by determining the resources needed and communicating this back to higher levels.

Deployment proceeds through the sequence of events shown in Figure 9-2.

Subdivide the Goals

The strategic quality goals have already been established by the Quality Council. The need is to allocate these goals to lower levels. However, most strategic quality goals consist of broad-scope quality planning or improvement projects. (Also called "global" or "elephant-size" projects). The deployment process includes dividing up such broad goals into manageable pieces. For example:

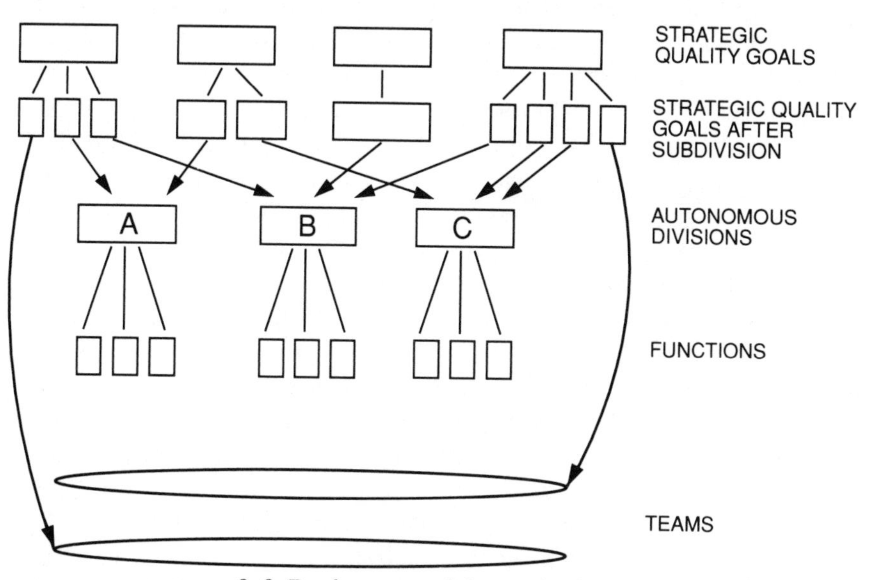

FIGURE 9-2 Deployment of Strategic Quality Goals

1. An airline goal of attaining X percent on-time arrivals may require subprojects to deal with such matters as:

   The *policy* of delaying departures in order to accommodate delayed connecting flights

   The organization for decision making at departure gates

   The need for revisions in *departmental procedures*

   The state of *employee behavior* and awareness

2. A quality goal to reduce the cost of poor quality by Y million dollars must first be subdivided and deployed to lower levels, and then broken down into manageable "bite-size" projects, using the tools of the quality improvement process.
3. Any goal of improving timeliness of customer service requires a subdivision of the customer service process into its components, identifying the vital few, and then considering each as an improvement project, along with the macroprocess itself.

In some cases the Quality Council has the information needed to do the subdividing. In other cases the Council may assign specific broad goals to subordinate units and leave it to them to do the subdividing.

Allocate to Subordinate Levels

Following subdivision by the Quality Council, the goals are allocated to appropriate organization units. Much of this deployment follows the hierarchical pattern: corporate to division, division to functional department, etc. For example, a broad goal to reduce the cost of poor quality by X million dollars may be subdivided by the Quality Council, and the pieces allocated to various general managers. Those general managers may then subdivide and allocate to their subordinates, and this process continues down to the action level.

Note, however, that this hierarchical arrangement fails if meeting the goals requires tackling multifunctional quality improvement projects. The prevailing practice is to assign such goals to *teams*.

Goals that relate to macroprocesses present a similar problem. The strategic goal may be to plan or replan a macroprocess. Usually a macroprocess involves many steps and multiple functions, so that there is no obvious "owner," hence no obvious answer to the question: Deployment to whom? The experience to data suggests that in such cases the deployment should be to a team rather than to some functional manager or to an arbitrary owner. However, this problem has only recently been under active study by companies. As of the late 1980s no clear consensus had emerged.

(We shall have a detailed look at ownership of macroprocesses in Chapter 10. Right now what is pertinent is that there should be no vagueness on the question, "Deployment to whom?")

Deployment to teams has taken on new dimensions as a consequence of the trend to establish teamwork relations with external suppliers. There are numerous cases in which the assigned team should include the impacted supplier(s) and still other external agencies. (For an example of a quality improvement project carried out by a supplier-customer team, see Kegarise and Miller, 1986.)

Identify the Needed Actions and Resources

The allocations establish responsibility but do not make clear what actions are to be taken. Only as these actions are identified does the wish list begin to have a flavor of reality. What happens next is that each organization unit or project team examines its mission and comes up with conclusions like this:

> Based on the available data, the vital few error types (five of them) account for 80 percent of all errors. In our judgment we should be able to bring the error rates of those five types down to levels that will result in an overall reduction of 50 percent. To do so we shall need resources as follows: . . .

At this stage the deployment process has already accomplished a major purpose: to assign responsibility and to define the actions to be taken.

Provide Resources

Now the direction of communication is reversed. The proposals from the action level flow upward to the Quality Council, along with the requests for resources. The proposals are then talked out. There may be much negotiation and revision. An agreement emerges: actions to be taken, resources to be provided, results to be achieved.

Note that the deployment process provides for participation by lower levels, as well as for communication both up and down the hierarchy. Strategic quality goals may be proposed at the top. The lower levels then identify the actions that, if taken, will collectively meet the goals. The lower levels also submit the bill: "To take these actions, we need the following resources." The subsequent negotiations then try to arrive at an optimum that balances the value of meeting the goals against the cost of doing so.

The two-way communication feature of the deployment process (a Japanese term is "catch ball") has turned out to be an important aid to getting results. Feedbacks from companies using this process suggest that it outperforms the process of unilateral goal setting by upper managers.

The work to be done at the action levels can reach formidable proportions.

> The Ford Taurus goal of "Best in Class" ended up with more than four hundred specific subgoals, each related to a specific product feature. The total planning effort was enormous.

(For a case example in a service company, see Brunetti 1987).

Train the Recipients

The deployment process requires that the recipients be trained in how to respond. Lacking such training, the wish list usually remains a wish list.

An essential prerequisite is training in the quality planning process. In addition, it has been the experience of the authors that extensive prior experience in quality improvement projects is a most valuable aid to those involved in the deployment process. Participation in such projects is a high-density form of exposure to all the processes of the Trilogy—quality planning and control as well as quality improvement. (We shall have a closer look at the subject of training in Chapter 12).

Resources for the SQM System

Resources are the price to be paid for the benefits of meeting the strategic quality goals. In part these resources are related to specific goals. Each goal requires certain actions to be taken and to take those actions requires resources. Providing those resources is done on a goal-by-goal basis, each on its merits.

In contrast there are other resources that are needed to establish and maintain the system of SQM. These resources parallel those required to establish and maintain the system of strategic financial management. More specifically, these resources include:

The effort needed to establish the basic infrastructure, including processes for goal setting and deployment, evaluation of results, and recognition and rewards

Training in the conceptual approach and in the operation of the system

The effort required, at all levels, to administer the system on a continuing basis

The damage done by lack of resources was widely demonstrated during the 1980s. During that decade many companies undertook initiatives to carry out quality improvement projects. To bring such projects to completion requires:

A basic infrastructure for the projects collectively

Support for the projects individually

With the exception of some aspects of training, those resources were seldom provided adequately. Lack of those resources then starved out many efforts to improve quality.

The SQM approach, being tied into strategic business planning, offers a more promising way to provide the resources. Strategic business planning has long included a positive approach to bringing out into the open the resources required to meet the strategic business goals. Those who are apprehensive about "corporate interference" (see below) should realize that SQM provides a channel for dealing with the problem of securing resources.

Corporate Interference

In most companies SQM faces resistance from the autonomous divisions (or from the functional departments) on the grounds of "corporate interference." It is a fact that adoption of SQM takes away some of the autonomy previously enjoyed by these divisions and departments. Such reduction in autonomy is never welcome, even if the associated human relations are harmonious. Where they are less than harmonious, the problem can become severe.

The nature of this reduction in autonomy becomes evident if we look sideways at the finance function. In virtually all large companies, the corporate headquarters office "interferes" in divisional financial affairs. The corporation mandates that it:

Approve the divisional financial budgets

Approve the divisional financial plans for meeting their budgets

Review the divisional financial performances against budgets

Under SQM a parallel "interference" may take place with respect to quality. The corporate headquarters may mandate that it:

Approve divisional quality goals

Approve divisional plans for reaching the quality goals

Review the divisional quality performances

In the case of finance, the practice of corporate interference is of long standing. Hence the problems of cultural resistance and of rejection by the immune system have been largely overcome. In the case of quality, the practice is just beginning. Hence the problems of cultural resistance and of rejection by the immune system have yet to be solved. SQM does in fact invade the autonomy of the divisions and functions, and the newness makes it all the more conspicuous.

The Infrastructure for Control

Strategic business management includes provisions for control—for evaluating the results of operations, comparing the results with goals, and taking action on the difference. This is the universal control process. It is extensively practiced in the case of financial management. It is also fully applicable to strategic quality management, but only if the necessary infrastructure has been built.

Building that infrastructure is the responsibility of the Quality Council. Many quality councils have asked the quality manager to assist them in carrying out that responsibility. The situation is similar to the practice in finance, where the executive staff looks to the financial controller for assistance in establishing financial controls.

Performance Evaluation

The starting point is to establish the means for evaluating performance relative to the strategic goals. This requires agreement on just what is to be evaluated, the units of measure, the methods of measurement, and so on. This agreement is properly reached as a part of the goal setting process—goals cannot be communicated with precision unless they are quantified. The methodology for such evaluation has been discussed in detail in Chapter 5, "Measurement of Quality." In that chapter the topics pertinent to SQM include:

Measures of Quality at the Highest Levels

Measures for Operating Processes

Measures for Functions

Measures of Product Performance

Measures of Managers' Performance

The Report Package

Performance Review

Adoption of SQM requires that the upper managers regularly review performance against strategic quality goals. This parallels what they have long done with respect to financial performance.

The practice varies, but generally the review of performance in quality is conducted by the upper managers during the same meeting that reviews other matters of strategic importance. This approach tends to send messages to the effect that quality has priority at the highest level and that the upper managers are personally participative. In effect, the emerging practice is one of regarding review of performance in quality as an extension of the traditional corporate review of performance relative to other matters of strategic importance.

Action on the Difference

The very fact that upper managers conduct regular reviews increases the likelihood that the performances will attain the quality goals. If performance falls short of goals, the usual managerial courses of action are open. Some of these relate to specific goals that are not being met: provide assistance, stimulate, and so on. A second course of action involves using the reward system to enforce the priority assigned to meeting the strategic quality goals. (The nature of that reward system, as it applies to meeting quality goals, will be discussed in Chapter 12 under the heading "Motivation Through the Reward System.")

Quality Audits

An essential part of upper managers' system of quality controls is quality audits. As used here:

A quality audit is an independent review of quality performance.

(To be "independent" the auditor should not have any close responsibility for the adequacy of the performance.)

The purpose of audits is to provide independent, unbiased information not only to the operating heads but also to others who have a need to know. For quality performance relative to strategic quality goals, those who have a need to know includes the upper managers.

Subject Matter

Traditionally, quality audits have been used to provide assurance that products conform to specifications and that operations conform to procedures. At upper management levels the subject matter of quality audits expands to provide answers to such questions as:

Does our quality provide product satisfaction to our clients?

Is our quality competitive with the moving target of the marketplace?

Are we meeting our responsibilities to society?

Are we making progress in reducing the cost of poor quality?

Are our quality policies and quality goals appropriate to our company's mission?

Is the collaboration among our functional departments adequate to ensure optimizing company performance?

Questions like the above are not answered by conventional technological audits. Moreover, the auditors who conduct technological audits seldom have the managerial experience and training needed to conduct business-oriented quality audits. In consequence, companies that wish to carry out quality audits oriented to business matters usually do so by using upper managers or outside consultants as auditors. The widest use of this concept has been in the major Japanese companies.

(Still another option for conducting these audits is by an all-purpose corporate audit function. To date, the feedback from the use of this approach has been too limited to permit confident evaluation of the option.)

An example of subject matter content for these audits is the list of criteria used in Japan to award the Deming Application Prize. This list has been in evolution since 1951. As of 1987 it could be summed up as follows:

Policies and objectives

Organization and its operation

Education and its dissemination

Information flow and utilization

Product and process quality

Standardization

Control and management

Quality assurance of functions, systems, and methods

Results

Future plans

For elaboration, see Ishikawa (1987).

In 1987 the United States government established a national quality award known as the Malcolm Baldrige National Quality Award. The first awards were presented by President Reagan in the White House in 1988.

The criteria for the Baldrige award, and the associated weights, are shown in the boxed table. A great deal of detail relative to the interpretation of these terms is available from The National Institute of Standards and Technology, Gaithersburg, MD, 20899.

Category	*Weight*
Customer satisfaction	30
Quality results	15
Human resource utilization	15
Quality assurance of products and services	14
Leadership	12
Planning for quality	8
Information and analysis	6
Total	100

Conduct of Audits by Upper Managers

Audits by upper managers should be scheduled with enough lead time for preparing the needed information base. The subject matter should likewise be determined in advance, based on prior discussions by the Quality Council.

Some of these audits are conducted on-site at major facilities or regions. In such cases local managers are able to be active participants through making presentations, responding to questions, guiding the upper managers during the tour of the facility, and so forth.

The President's Quality Audit

In some major Japanese companies, quality audits are conducted by managers at the highest levels of the company, either by the Companywide Quality Committee or by some other team of upper managers. Where the president personally participates in the audit, it is usually called The President's Quality Audit (Kondo, 1988).

Such audits, conducted by upper-level managers, can have major impacts throughout the company. The subject matter is so fundamental in nature that the audits reach into every major function. The personal participation of the upper managers simplifies communication among the various levels and increases the likelihood that action will be forthcoming. The very fact that the upper managers participate in person sends a message to the entire organization about the priority placed on quality and the kind of leadership being provided by the upper managers—leading, not cheerleading (Shimoyamada, 1987).

For elaboration on quality audits at upper management levels, see Juran (1988), Section 8, "Upper Management and Quality," under "Quality Audits by Upper Managers."

SQM: The Pros and Cons

Up to now, in this chapter on "Strategic Quality Planning," we have concentrated on:

The nature of Strategic Quality Management

The methodology for making SQM effective

It may all seem logical and natural. However, the experience of the 1980s showed that introducing SQM into a company involves profound changes, and much cultural resistance. While the climate of the 1990s will probably be more favorable to adoption of SQM, it is useful to examine the experience of the 1980s. What were the claims made by the advocates? What was the nature of the resistance encountered? How did companies bridge the conflicting views?

The Premises of the Advocates for SQM

Advocacy for SQM starts with some premises that have a sound factual base:

Many of our industries are no longer among the quality leaders in the marketplace

Some of our industries are in a crisis due in large part to lack of competitiveness in quality

All of our industries are enduring huge wastes resultant from redoing prior work

Assertions as to Causes

Explanations of why our industries are in this state usually center on the "methods of the past"—such past practices as:

Each department has been pursuing departmental quality goals, with resulting failure to optimize overall quality performance.

Quality planning has largely been done by untrained amateurs.

Multifunctional planning projects have suffered delays and wastes due to inadequate participation by those impacted.

There has been no clear responsibility for reducing the major chronic quality wastes. Companies disconnected the alarm signals by hiding the wastes in the standards.

Quality was assumed to apply only to manufactured goods and manufacturing processes ("Little Q").

From the above list of asserted causes there emerges an asserted *supercause:*

The deficiencies of the past have their origin in lack of a systematic, structured approach to managing for quality such as already exists in managing for finance.

This assertion then leads logically to a proposal for a remedy—a remedy that will put managing for quality on a strategically planned basis as is already being done to manage for finance. This strategic planning would consist essentially of the elements listed above under "The Financial Analogy," but applied to quality.

Objections to SQM

Prior to the 1980s the asserted benefits of SQM were generally not persuasive to managers. Their objections were a mixture of stated reasons and real reasons, most of which fell into the categories set out below.

"HERE COMES ANOTHER ONE". Some managers had endured prior experiences in which logical-sounding proposals did not come up to what the advocates had promised. Such managers regarded the benefits of SQM as untested theories where their companies were concerned.

IT WILL BE TIME-CONSUMING. These objections related to the time required to participate in the annual goal setting and deployment, to make the subsequent periodic reviews of results, and so on.

IT WILL CAUSE DISRUPTIONS. Fitting in the added work load is an obvious disruption. So is the change in priorities—higher priority for quality means lower priority for other things. (An unstated objection is the disruption of career patterns caused by the change in priorities.)

IT WILL BRING CORPORATE INTERFERENCE. Of course it will, in much the same way as already exists in the financial area.

Cultural Resistance

Introduction of change into any human society also encounters resistance from what is called the cultural pattern—the collection of beliefs, practices, habits, status symbols, and the like, accumulated by that society during its life span. That cultural pattern includes values that are important to the society. Hence each society carefully examines any proposed changes to see if they contain a threat to those values.

Introduction of SQM does include threats to the cultural patterns of the multiple societies which make up the company. For example:

Adoption of Big Q in place of Little Q is an obvious disturbance to long-standing beliefs and habit patterns.

A shift of responsibility for planning (from a functional level to a divisional or corporate level) readily runs into cultural resistance from the function that previously "owned" the responsibility.

Mandating a structured planning approach can be disturbing to those planners whose status is derived from long experience with empirical methods.

The behavioral scientists have provided managers with some helpful explanations about the nature of cultural patterns. In addition, they have developed some useful rules of the road for dealing with cultural resistance to change. For elaboration, see Chapter 12, under the heading "Human Behavior and Cultural Values" and under "Dealing with Cultural Resistance."

Rejection by the Immune System

Large organizations exhibit some of the features of a biological organism. One of those features is the immune reaction when something alien is introduced. The organism senses the intrusion of the alien and mobilizes to reject it. The introduction of SQM is analogous to an alien transplant. It may be of great value to the company, but it stimulates an immune reaction nevertheless. This reaction can be dealt with in ways similar to those used for the biological organism:

Design SQM so it becomes part of something familiar, i.e., it becomes part of the existing business planning structure

Revise the reward system in ways that will change the managers' receptivity to the new quality goals

Bridging the Viewpoints—Pilot Tests

Efforts to introduce SQM bring out two contesting schools of thought:

1. The advocates point to the benefits to be derived from SQM.
2. Conservative managers point out that these benefits are unproven in this company and hence it may all end up as just another unsuccessful drive.

This contest is seldom resolved by debate or by an edict from the upper managers. More often it is resolved by the results achieved in a pilot test conducted at some test site. If the results of the pilot test are favorable, the new approach gets scaled up, because the results attract other managers.

The pilot test takes place in the area of some venturesome manager—an "explorer"—who is willing to make that area a test site. In any organization of substantial size, there are always some managers who are willing to participate in a pilot test.

When companies change direction they seldom do so by moving across a broad front. Instead, they move in single file: one division after another, one department after another, one product line after another. This tends to be true even if there has been an upper management mandate requiring all to move simultaneously. In part, the single file results from bottlenecks in essential services, e.g., capacity for training. In part, the single file results from differences in priorities and enthusiasm among the various managers in the organization.

The single file phenomenon means that little is lost by deliberately designing a pilot test to be conducted in the organization units of the "explorers." These explorers are likely to be at the head of the single file anyway. The results of the pilot tests in due course become the means for converting the skeptics into believers.

Embarking on SQM—The Scenario

Companies that have successfully instituted SQM have done so through a series of phases. Figure 9-3 shows the progression of these phases in graphic form.

The First Phase: Choice of Strategy

The first phase has usually consisted of the managers collecting their wits and adopting a strategy, a scenario that could lead the company to SQM. This choice has not been easy for these reasons:

There are numerous strategies from which to choose.

Each has been urged by persuasive advocates.

Those faced with deciding which strategy to adopt usually have lacked the expertise needed to judge where the various alternatives would actually lead.

This first phase has commonly consumed a minimum of six months. Sometimes it has taken much longer as a result of false starts.

Project-by-Project Improvement at a Test Site

The most successful choice of strategy has been to go first into project-by-project improvement. This is itself a structured approach; quality improvement is one of the processes that make up the Juran Trilogy.

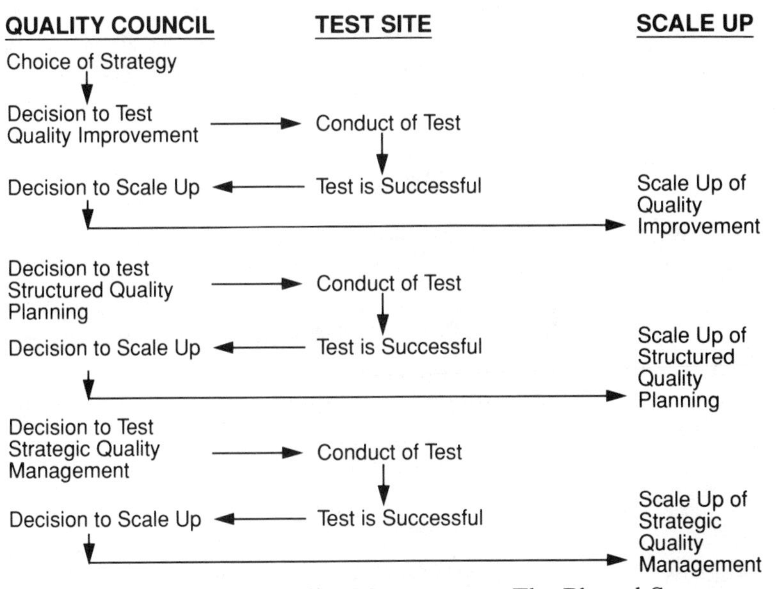

FIGURE 9–3 Strategic Quality Management: The Phased Sequence

Companies that adopted this strategy did not undertake project-by-project improvement throughout the entire company simultaneously. Instead they tried the concept out at some test site. The test site results then became the basis for scaling up companywide.

The pilot test of project-by-project improvement and the associated evaluation of results have commonly consumed about a year of calendar time. Scaling up then consumed an additional year or two of calendar time.

A major by-product of all those improvement projects is a dramatic rise in the quality-oriented training and experience of the managers who have served on the quality improvement teams. The learning experience from multiple improvement projects is profound:

> For most quality improvements the remedy is to replan the product and/or the process. As a result the teams learn much about the quality planning process.
>
> For most quality improvement projects, controls much be established in order to hold the gains. As a result the teams learn much about the quality control process.

Still another by-product of the improvement projects is a growing atmosphere of teamwork. Major quality improvement projects are inherently multifunctional in nature, requiring multifunctional teams and teamwork for their completion. The resulting spirit of teamwork then carries over into the traditional work of conducting operations.

Scaling Up

The results achieved at the test site open the way for scaling up into quality improvement on a companywide basis. Meanwhile, the experience gained has demonstrated that most quality problems were planned that way. This leads to testing out a more structured approach to quality planning in order to avoid creating new quality problems. Projects are undertaken to plan/replan specific processes, especially multifunctional processes.

Finally, SQM

As experience is gained with structured quality planning, there emerges an interest in bringing quality goals into the company's business plan. That concept then also undergoes a pilot test before being scaled up to the corporate level.

Figure 9-3 shows also how the phased approach provides managers with the experience needed to go into full-scale SQM.

Other Sequences Are Possible

The sequence described above (and depicted in Figure 9-3) is the actual sequence most widely followed by companies that have been "stunningly successful" in quality improvement and in reaching a state of SQM. Other sequences are possible, but they all require the participating managers to be trained in the basics and to acquire experience in actual quality planning as well as quality improvement. If this experience and training are lacking, the result will be failures to meet the strategic goals during the first few years. The managers will of course learn from their failures. However, there is a strong likelihood that the managers meanwhile will become discouraged and will abandon the effort as not being cost effective.

The Total Calendar Time

Managers are dismayed to hear that attainment of SQM runs into years of calendar time. Yet such are the realities, based on experience. The typical intervals have been about as follows:

Phase	*Interval*
Choice of strategy	6–12 months
Quality improvement at a test site, plus evaluation of results	One year
Scaling up to companywide quality improvement; initiating structured quality planning	Two years
Scaling up into SQM	Two years

In all, a minimum of about six years will elapse before SQM is comfortably in place.

The Quality Department

An essential resource for SQM is a quality department—the quality equivalent of the financial controller's office. The need for such a department is better understood if we first look sideways at the roles played by the financial controller's office.

The Financial Analogy

The finance function includes the organization structure needed to:

a. Establish the strategic financial goals. These goals are the end result of the budgetary process. A controller (the titles vary) presides over this budgetary process.

b. Evaluate performance against financial goals. The accounting system provides the factual basis for the summarized financial reports. The controller is importantly involved in editing and interpreting these reports.

c. Conduct audits. Auditors (both internal and external) are assigned to determine (1) whether the system if followed will result in meeting the company's financial goals, and (2) whether the system is being followed.

To carry out the above activities requires resources in the form of a controller, along with a budget officer, accountants, and others. In those companies which establish a Finance Committee (at the board level or the upper management level), the controller sometimes provides a "secretariat" service.

The Quality Equivalent

Virtually all sizable companies already have an organization unit or units devoted full time to quality. These organizations have such names as Quality Control or Quality Assurance. In manufacturing companies their activities have been strongly oriented to technological matters, such as inspection and test of products and processes—the traditional focus on Little Q. However, in all companies (including manufacturing companies) some of the activities of the quality department parallel those of the controller's department. How to establish more broadly the quality equivalent of the controller's office has not yet been widely thought through, since most companies have not yet gone into SQM.

The Quality Department of the Future

The indications are that the present functions and structure of the quality department will undergo substantial change in those companies which are successful in converting to SQM.

PRODUCT EVALUATION. This function is now carried out by inspectors, checkers, and testers, most of whom are in the quality department. In the future this function is destined to be carried out by the operating forces, and especially by nonsupervisory workers, provided some essential criteria are met:

Quality really has top priority among all parameters.

The operating forces are placed into a state of self-control. For elaboration, see Chapter 8 under the heading "Self-control: The Criteria."

Mutual trust is established between the managers and the work force with respect to the new delegation.

The operating forces are trained to carry out the newly delegated function.

CONSULTING SERVICES. This function consists mainly of the specialties of reliability engineering and quality engineering. The clear trend is to transfer this function to line department specialists. A prerequisite to such transfer is training of the line department specialists. To do this training and to provide consulting assistance will require some residue of quality specialists, whether within the quality department or from the outside.

SERVICE TO THE QUALITY COUNCIL. Companies that adopt SQM require some form of secretariat to do the detailed work of the Quality Council. A logical choice for secretary of the Quality Council is the quality manager. Such a choice adds a significant business orientation to the quality manager's activities.

MEASURES OF PERFORMANCE. The adoption of SQM greatly broadens the scope of quality-oriented activities, and therefore demands a corresponding expansion of measures of performance. For elaboration, see Chapter 5, "Measurement of Quality," especially under the heading "Measures of Quality at the Highest Levels" and under the subsequent major headings.

QUALITY AUDITS. The traditional quality audits conducted by the quality department have little relation to the audit needs created by the adoption of SQM. In addition, most of the quality auditors of the past have lacked the business training and experience required to conduct broad business-oriented audits. As a result, much of the quality auditing required by SQM must be done by upper managers themselves. (See above, under "Quality Audits.") However, these high-level audits require extensive preparatory work, and some of this work will logically be delegated to the quality manager.

The Transition Process

Converting the present quality department to the quality department of the future should be done on a phased basis. Most of the changes are contingent on meeting prerequisites that have lengthy lead times.

The conversion lends itself readily to establishing goals (or milestones) and then defining the steps required to reach the goals.

The Emerging Job of Quality Manager

This emerging job will differ radically from the pattern prevailing during the 1980s. This difference is mandated by the array of unprecedented strategic quality goals. One way of summing it up is to say that the emerging job will be business-oriented rather than oriented to technological or departmental goals.

That is a profound change, and many, perhaps most, quality managers will face a considerable problem of adaptation. Some will have difficulty in conceptually grasping the broader role. Some will be reluctant to delegate so many of their familiar functions to the line organizations. Some will be well advised to take supplementary training in business management.

Upper managers should likewise realize that a profound change is involved. The quality manager has a key role to play in SQM. Appointment to this key role should not be automatic. Appointment to the role of quality manager should go to someone who is able to grasp the role conceptually and who in addition is willing to put forth the effort needed to become qualified to carry it out.

Upper Managers' Roles in SQM

Before discussing these roles it is a good idea to *discard some diversionary baggage.* There are schools of thought that try to define the roles of upper management by skillful choice of a label: upper managers should become committed, involved, aware, and so on. Choice of such labels is an exercise in futility. None of those labels makes clear to upper managers what they should do that is different from what they have been doing. What is required is a setting out of specifics: just what actions are to be taken, just what decisions are to be made. Discarding the diversionary baggage makes it easier to concentrate on those specifics.

Serve on the Quality Council

Membership on the Quality Council exposes the members to essential inputs relative to the quality problems requiring solution, to the resources needed, and so on. The council is seldom effective if the members lack decision-making power over the subject matter. In addition, the rank of the council membership sends a message to the rest of the organization as to the priority of quality.

Participate in Policy Formation

This participation takes several forms:

Help to identify the need for quality policies (A major symptom of such need is repeated requests from below for guidance on broad issues.)

Assign responsibility for drafting the policy statements and checking them out with the impacted organization units

Review, revise, and approve

Participate in Goal Setting and Deployment

Establishing the broad quality goals is inherently an upper management responsibility. It is also an exercise in futility if the "plans" for reaching the goals consist of exhorting the subordinates. Instead, it is essential to deploy the goals to subordinate levels and then to review/revise/approve their proposals.

Provide the Needed Resources

The resources are a price to be paid for meeting the goals. A major failing of upper managers has been the failure to provide those resources. Not only will the performance suffer; such a failure also sends a negative message to the lower levels.

Establish the Organization Infrastructure

The major elements in organizing the SQM consist of:

The quality council(s)

The quality manager (director of quality, etc.)

The multifunctional teams

Multifunctional teams are needed principally to:

Plan multifunctional processes such as the new product launching cycle

Tackle the vital few quality improvement projects

Such teams require legitimacy, priorities, resources, training, etc., which much be provided through upper management action.

Review Progress

Reviews of progress are an essential part of assuring that goals are being met. The very fact that upper managers do review progress sends a message to the rest of the organization as to the priority given to the quality goals.

Much of the data base for these reviews comes from:

Summarized reports of actual performance against quality goals

Audits of the processes in use, especially the broad business processes

Give Recognition

Recognition consists mostly of "ceremonial" actions taken to acknowledge meritorious performance publicly. These ceremonial actions focus on improvement activities rather than on the control of operations.

It is common practice for upper managers to preside at ceremonial awards of certificates or plaques to persons who have completed training courses. In some companies, upper managers personally and prominently participate in dinner meetings specifically organized to honor teams that have completed their quality improvement projects. Similar meetings are organized to recognize outstanding contributions made by suppliers. Still other companies establish special awards for teams or individuals whose contributions are judged to be outstanding. These awards are made by upper managers at ceremonial occasions and are publicized through various media: the company's newsletter, the bulletin boards, the local press, and so forth.

Revise the Reward System

The reward system (merit rating, salary changes, promotions, bonuses, etc.) serves the basic purpose of rewarding performance against operating goals. It also serves to inform all concerned as to the upper managers' priorities. If additional goals are imposed by adoption of SQM, but without revising the reward system, then the perception of the subordinate levels is one of conflicting signals. Most subordinates resolve this conflict by following the traditional priorities associated with the unchanged reward system.

Establish the Necessary Quality Audit

The approach for this is set out above under the heading "Quality Audits."

Efforts to Avoid Upper Management Participation

The above is a formidable list of roles to be assumed by upper managers. Most upper managers would prefer to delegate managing for quality to lower levels of management and to the workers. However, the quality function has grown in importance to a point where *the grand strategy is no longer delegable;* the upper managers must take charge personally.

A Widespread Failure

A widely tested effort to delegate has consisted essentially of:

1. Goal setting by upper managers. Some of these goals have been specific, e.g., Let's cut the cost of poor quality in two. More usually the goals have been vague, e.g., Do it right the first time.
2. Exhortation to subordinates to increase "awareness," and to reach the goals.

The Reasons for Failure

Such approaches are doomed to failure because they lack the substantive content needed to compete with the existing order.

> A number of upper managers, disappointed that such an approach had failed, have complained bitterly to one of the authors (Juran) that their subordinates had "let them down." The author offered a rather different explanation, which is summarized in Figure 9–4.

Influences on Performance	*The Existing Order*	*The "Doomed Approach"*
Goals	Clear: budgets, schedules, specifications, etc.	Usually vague Suspect due to being part of a new drive: "Here comes another one"
Plans for meeting goals	In place; specific	Vague
Definitions of responsibility	Clear; in job descriptions	Vague
Resources	Provided	Seldom provided
Progress review	In place: standardized reports, scheduled reviews	Vague
Motivation	In place through: supervisory review of progress reports; reward system	Exhortation

FIGURE 9–4 Why Many Efforts to Delegate Have Been Doomed to Failure

It is evident from Figure 9-4 that the existing order has long imposed on the subordinates a clear system of responsibilities based on specific goals, plans, organization structure, resources, progress reviews, rewards, and so on. These responsibilities do not change when the new approach (the "doomed" approach) is applied. The subordinates are still expected to meet their schedules, budgets, etc. The vagueness of the new approach cannot possibly compete with the existing order.

SQM or Not: The Decisive Element

Whether the upper managers should take the company into SQM is a unique decision for each company. What is decisive is the importance of quality relative to the future health of the company. The potential benefits of SQM are clear:

The goals become clear—the planning process requires clarification of vagueness and provides a coherent interrelationship among goals at various levels.

The planning process then makes the goals achievable.

The control process helps to ensure that the goals are reached.

Chronic wastes are reduced through the quality improvement process.

Creation of new wastes is reduced through revision of the quality planning process.

Training

To make SQM operative requires extensive training in managing for quality. This need for training impacts the entire company hierarchy. Among the most important training needs are those for:

UPPER MANAGERS. Here the training concentrates on basic concepts and on the specific roles of upper managers for integrating managing for quality with the company's business plan.

PLANNERS. The term "planners" includes full-time planners as well as operating managers to the extent that they participate in the quality planning process. The purpose of the training is to minimize the extent to which quality planning is done by experienced amateurs, resulting in quality problems thereafter for the customers, external and internal.

QUALITY IMPROVEMENT TEAMS. These teams are assigned specific projects aimed at improving product quality and reducing chronic costs of poor quality. The training serves to arm them with the methodology on quality improvement: the process, the skills, the tools.

We shall have a closer look at training in Chapter 12.

On to Multifunctional Quality Planning

SQM is by definition concerned with the highest levels of organization. Of added concern to upper managers is the performance of certain essential processes, such as those which put new products on the market, fill customers' orders, collect the income, and recruit personnel.

The approach to planning and replanning such processes is the subject of Chapter 10.

List of High Points

Companies that embark on SQM should define their terminology with precision.

The structure of SQM is similar to that long used to establish and meet financial goals.

A fundamental step in establishing SQM is the creation of the Quality Council.

An essential element of SQM is the establishment of broad quality goals as part of the strategic business planning.

Prevailing practice is to assign multifunctional goals to teams.

There should be no vagueness on the question of "Deployment to Whom?"

Deployment to teams has taken on new dimensions because of the trend to establish teamwork relations with external suppliers.

The deployment process requires that the recipients be trained in how to respond.

Failure to provide resources has starved out many efforts to improve quality.

Adoption of SQM requires that the upper managers regularly review performance against strategic quality goals.

An essential part of the upper managers' system of quality controls is quality audits.

Introducing SQM into a company involves profound changes, and much cultural resistance.

Conflicting views on whether to go into SQM are usually resolved by the results achieved in a pilot test conducted at some test site.

Companies change direction by moving in single file: one division after another; one department after another; one product line after another.

A minimum of about six years will elapse before SQM is comfortably in place.

The emerging job of the quality manager will be business-oriented rather than oriented to technological or departmental goals.

The roles of upper managers cannot be defined though simplistic labels. The need is to make clear what they should do that is different from what they have been doing.

Exhortation to meet vague goals cannot possibly compete with the existing order.

Tasks for Upper Managers

If the needed quality councils are not already in existence, the upper managers should create them.

The Quality Council should ensure that the prevailing quality policies correctly reflect the company's intentions with respect to quality.

Building the SQM infrastructure for control is the responsibility of the Quality Council.

Adoption of SQM requires that the upper managers:

Serve on the quality council

Participate in policy formation

Participate in goal setting and deployment

Provide the needed resources
Establish the organization infrastructure
Review progress
Give recognition
Revise the reward system
Establish the necessary quality audit

] 10 [

Multifunctional Quality Planning

Purpose of This Chapter

The purpose of this chapter is to explain how to plan multifunctional processes in ways that will meet the needs of customers while minimizing the creation of chronic wastes during the subsequent operations.

Macroprocesses

Companies and their autonomous divisions conduct their principal affairs through major, repetitive-use systems that are inherently multifunctional in nature (also called "cross-functional" or "interfunctional"). We shall use the term "macroprocess" to designate such a multifunctional process.

Roles of Macroprocesses

Most macroprocesses are business processes with roles within the Big Q concept: bring out new products, process customers' orders, collect income, recruit employees. Other macroprocesses have roles that are closely associated with the concept of Little Q: plan for manufacture, purchase materials, produce goods.

To carry out these roles, the macroprocesses receive inputs from suppliers, process the inputs, produce specific products, and deliver those products to customers, external and internal. The processing done conforms to our definition of a process: a systematic series of actions directed to the achievement of a goal.

As companies grow, the macroprocesses become very numerous. For example, in one large company, the major business processes associated with the office of the corporate controller were by themselves a lengthy list, as seen in Figure 10-1.

The Anatomy of Macroprocesses

A macroprocess consists of multiple segments, which we shall call "microprocesses." Each microprocess is typically carried out within a single functional organization unit, often presided over by a first-line supervisor. The activities of a microprocess consist of closely focused operations (steps, tasks, etc.) such as opening the mail or assembling gear boxes. (We shall discuss the planning for microprocesses in Chapter 11.)

The "anatomy" of macroprocesses varies, but most of them consist of a "procession" like that shown in Figure 10-2 (this is the same as Figure 7-7 but is reproduced here for convenience).

Another major form of macroprocess is the "assembly tree," as depicted in Figure 10-3 (the same as Figure 7-6, reproduced here for convenience).

Relation to Functional Organizations

Companies and their autonomous divisions are usually organized along functional lines. Organization by function starts with separating the overall workpile into logical functional groupings: finance,

Payment to suppliers
Time reporting and payroll
Reimbursement of employee expenses
Transfer/billing within the company
International financial services
Enhancement of financial collections
Cost allocation within company
Financial planning
Budget preparation
Financial reports preparation and analysis
Fixed asset information preparation
Inventory management information preparation
Financial and management accounting policies and standards
Common support functions

FIGURE 10-1 Major Business Processes Associated with a Corporate Controller's Office

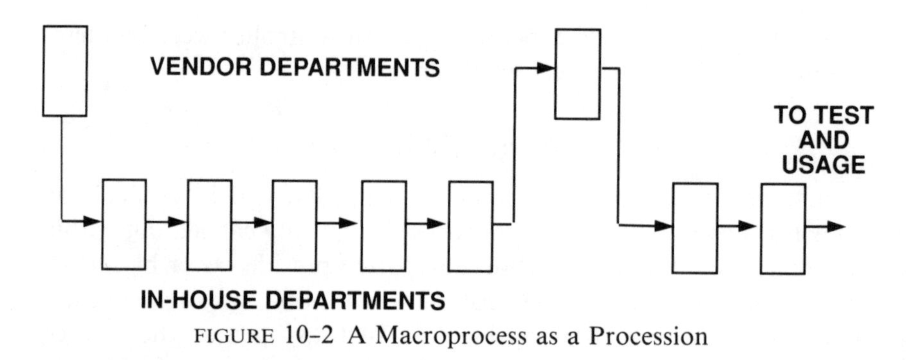

FIGURE 10–2 A Macroprocess as a Procession

marketing, human relations, and so on. Following this separation, each function is assigned to a functional manager. That manager then has the responsibility to carry out that function.

While such is the conventional way to organize, the company does its work primarily through macroprocesses. These macroprocesses are made up of microprocesses scattered here and there among the functional departments. As a result a macroprocess moves into and out of multiple major functional organizations. This interrelation between the "vertical" functions and the "horizontal" macropro-

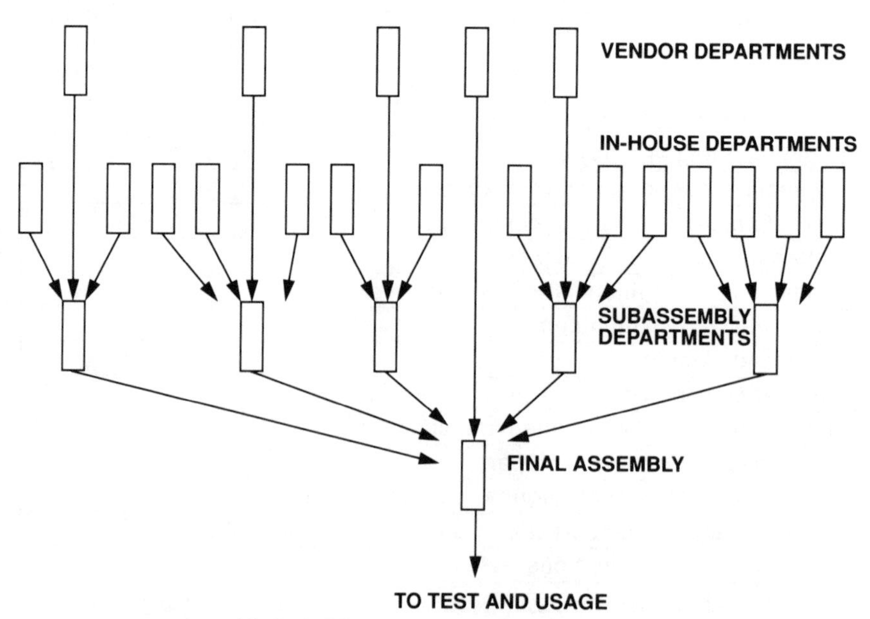

FIGURE 10–3 A Macroprocess as an Assembly Tree

cesses often follows a pattern like that shown graphically in Figure 10–4.

The striking fact is that *the anatomy of the macroprocesses does not match that of the functional organization.* The macroprocess works its way through the domains of multiple major functions. There is no obvious answer to the question: Who is responsible for quality management of the macroprocess? This question is especially pertinent with respect to very critical macroprocesses,such as the process for launching new products. Such macroprocesses thread their way through virtually all major functional organizations (see the "Spiral of Progress in Quality," Figure 6–2, in Chapter 6).

Prior Neglect of Macroprocesses

Until the 1980s, most companies evidenced little concern over the fact that the anatomies of the macroprocesses were not compatible with that of the functional organization. The emphasis was on defining functional responsibilities, setting functional goals, and using the reward systems as an aid to meeting the goals. The functional goals often were met, but a heavy price was paid for neglect of the macroprocesses. Over the decades this neglect resulted in building up a huge accumulation of macroprocesses that were ineffective in meeting the needs of customers and were wasteful as well.

Some companies did show concern over the performance of the macroprocesses. However, at the time no effective means for dealing with the incompatibility problem had yet been evolved. Companies that tried to deal with it usually did so through committees or through a matrix structure, with mixed results.

Then, during the 1980s, the Big Q concept emerged, along with a realization that the business processes were profoundly influential in shaping the quality image of the companies. That realization stimulated many companies to look more closely at their major business processes, virtually all of which were macroprocesses. As attention was focused on that huge accumulation of ineffective, wasteful macroprocesses, it became evident that a solution would require the companies to:

Think out the goals: what are the criteria to be met by a macroprocess

Establish "ownership" for macroprocesses

Design a methodology for replanning existing macroprocesses

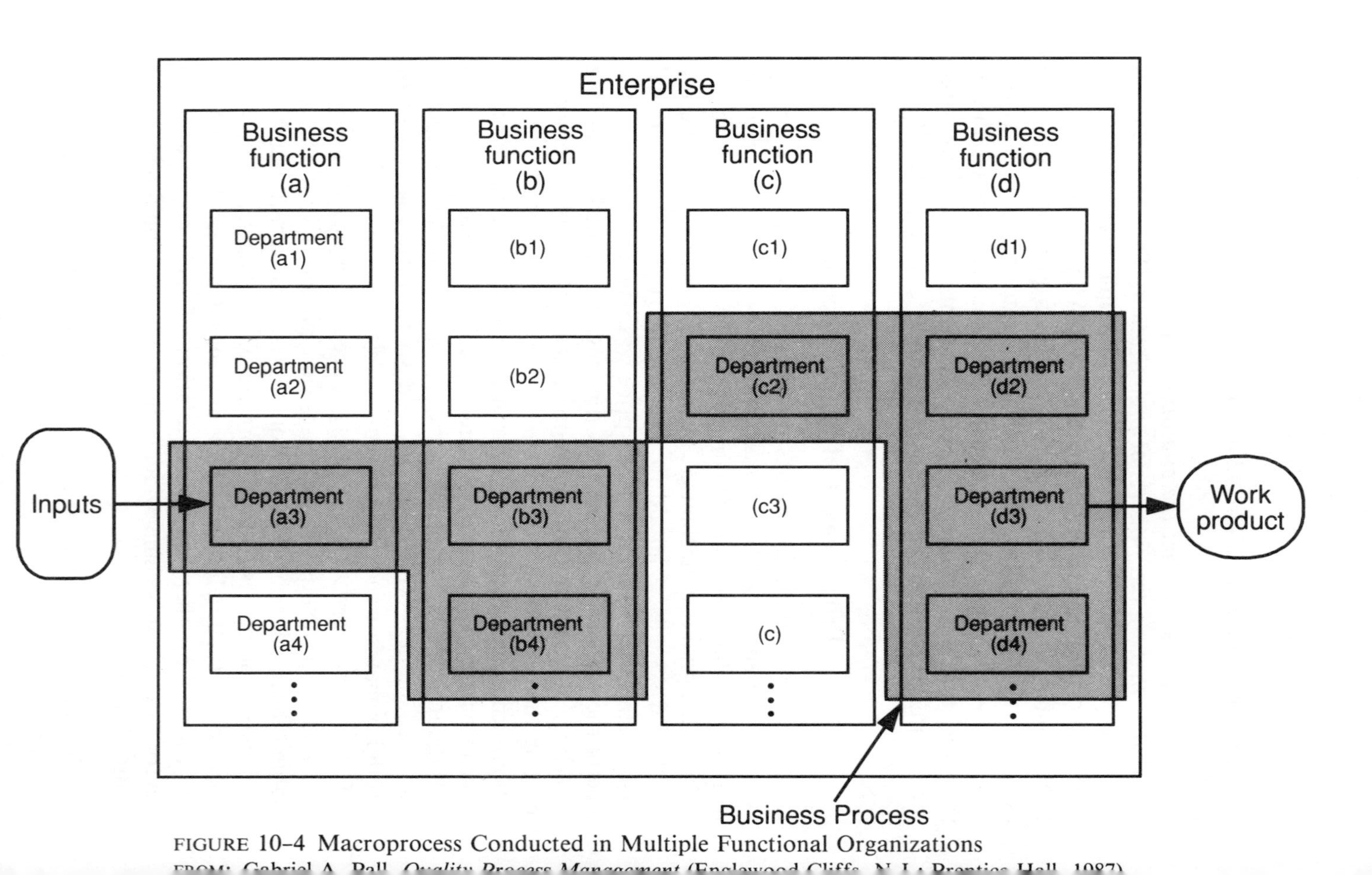

FIGURE 10–4 Macroprocess Conducted in Multiple Functional Organizations
FROM: Gabriel A. Pall, *Quality Process Management* (Englewood Cliffs, N.J.: Prentice Hall, 1987)

Design a methodology for planning new macroprocesses in ways that avoid creating new problems

During the 1980s some companies, especially IBM, made considerable progress in the above directions. The discussion that follows includes some of the thinking of these companies and makes reference to some of their publications on the subject.

Macroprocesses—The Criteria

Any macroprocess provides added value as a return on the work done. The ideal macroprocess also meets the following criteria—it is:

Effective. The product produced by the macroprocess meets the needs of the customers.

Adaptable. The microprocesses are designed in modular ways, which make the resulting macroprocess readily adaptable to changing customer needs.

Efficient. The various microprocesses (tasks, steps, etc.) are logically interrelated and coordinated. The macroprocess operates at minimum cost, at minimal time per cycle, and with minimal waste.

Measurable. Units of measure and sensors are established at key steps to provide the evaluations needed for control.

Controllable. The macroprocess is able to carry out repetitive cycles of work with minimal variability in the product.

Formalized. The macroprocess is described in formal documents approved by the cognizant authorities.

Beyond meeting the above criteria, there should be clear responsibility for overseeing the macroprocess. The failure to establish such clear responsibility has been widespread. When companies looked closely at their macroprocesses during the 1980s, it became evident that no one was in charge—there was no "owner" of the macroprocesses. It also became evident that for the key macroprocesses this situation should not go on and on. For such macroprocesses there should be a clear designation of ownership.

(In the case of the microprocesses, clear designation of ownership was less of a problem. The microprocess is by definition departmental in nature, and the departmental head is usually the natural owner.)

The Key Macroprocesses

Macroprocesses are numerous. In a large company the numbers run into many hundreds. To establish ownership for so many macroprocesses is a formidable job. Hence companies have at the outset elected to establish ownership only for the "key" macroprocesses.

Selection of the key macroprocesses is done by the Quality Council or by some subcouncil or committee specially designated for the purpose. The committee secures inputs from various sources: feedback from customers, opinion surveys, special studies, and so forth. The committee then makes its selection based on multiple criteria, which include:

Not effective. The macroprocess is not providing customer satisfaction.

Not competitive. Available information shows that the macroprocess is being outperformed by others.

Causes customer dissatisfaction. Customer complaints (external and internal) are traceable to deficiencies in the macroprocess.

Capital-intensive. Considerable company resources are tied up in the macroprocess.

Critical to the business. The criticality may be due to the impact of the macroprocess on employee relations, compliance with government regulations, meeting schedules, or other areas.

Big potential for improvement. Analyses may have shown that there are opportunities for significant improvements, such as in customer service or in cost reduction.

Responsibilities of Owners of Macroprocesses

A discussion of ownership of macroprocesses must begin by distinguishing clearly between:

Ownership relative to planning. If planning is to be done with participation by those impacted, then the need is for a *team effort.* This team effort is needed both for macroprocesses and microprocesses.

Ownership relative to operations. If a state of self-control can be established, then ownership can be *individual.* Historically, many microprocesses were planned to be in a state of self-control, so that individual ownership could be established. However, very few macroprocesses were planned to be in a state of self-control, resulting in lack of ownership.

In the discussions that follow, the emphasis is on ownership of *operations,* and especially on operation of macroprocesses.

How to define ownership of macroprocesses has been extensively studied, the most influential work again having been done by IBM. These studies have made clear that establishment of ownership must be preceded by agreement on what the responsibilities of an owner are. Those same studies have also made clear that in some companies, especially large companies, it may be necessary to establish multiple levels of owners (for elaboration, see below under "Ownership by Whom?").

In some companies, the gains from the "test sites" for improving macroprocesses have been extensive. Such companies have tended to establish a governing committee to scale up these improvements. (The committee may be identical with the Quality Council). This committee then oversees the management of macroprocesses generally. This same committee is regarded as having the highest level of ownership—ownership of macroprocesses collectively.

Figure 10–5 shows the responsibilities of such a committee in one major company.

A second level of ownership is the macroprocess level. Here a high-level manager is assigned to be the owner of a specific macroprocess. Such a manager may be designated as the "executive owner" in contrast to the "working owner" at the microprocess level. Figure 10–6 is an example of responsibilities of ownership at the macroprocess level.

A third level of ownership is at the microprocess level, where there is usually full compatibility between the functional responsibility and

Supply overall direction for managing the macroprocesses
Identify the key macroprocesses, and designate owners
Assure establishment of goals and measures
Provide resources
Review performance against goals and measures
Stimulate needed changes
Stimulate continuous improvement
Resolve conflicts

FIGURE 10–5 Responsibilities of Governing Committee

Responsibility of Macroprocess Owners
Determine the needs of the customers; secure concurrence
Define the boundaries of the macroprocess
Document the process flow
Establish quality goals and criteria to be met
Establish measurement; ensure integrity of information and measurement
Identify the critical success factors and key dependencies
Define the microprocesses
Assign ownership for the microprocesses; secure agreement
Define the responsibility and authority of the owners
Establish cross-functional relationships
Review performance against goals; report results
Identify deficiencies; secure changes to provide remedies
Establish goals for continuing improvement
Follow progress; stimulate improvement
Resolve cross-functional issues
Note: Some of these responsibilities require personal direction by the owner. Others involve delegation, followed by review and approval.

FIGURE 10–6 An Example of Responsibilities of Owners of Macroprocesses
Derived from Nickell and McNeil (1987). See also Kane (1986).

the responsibility relative to the microprocess. At this level the local departmental head is usually also the owner of the microprocess.

As of the end of the 1980s, the responsibilities of ownership were still undergoing field testing and experiment, as was the choice of owners (see below).

Ownership by Whom?

The choice of owner is a complex problem because of conflict between two realities:

The strong preference of companies in the United States for assigning responsibility for operations to individuals, especially to functional managers

The multifunctional nature of macroprocesses

Ownership of macroprocesses can be arbitrarily assigned to individual managers. The problem arises when the recipient managers try to carry out the assigned responsibilities. They can usually succeed as to (a) those microprocesses over which they have command, but not as to (b) those over which they lack command. As to (b) they lack "legitimacy" (see Figure 10–4). The priorities for microprocesses of category (b) will be set by their respective functional superiors, who do have command and legitimacy. Note that for the macroprocess depicted in Figure 10–4, the operating decisions and actions rest primarily with the hierarchical structure (the chain of command) and only secondarily with the owner of the macroprocess.

While the recipient managers lack legitimacy by reason of lack of command, it is feasible to create new forms of legitimacy. The tradition of favoring individual ownership has stimulated much experiment in design of organization forms that assign ownership of macroprocesses to individual managers despite the fact that their "command"—their functional responsibility—extends only to a part of the macroprocess. Most of these experiments have resulted in assignment to either of two categories:

1. An assumed owner
2. A designated owner

The Assumed Owner

It is often assumed that a manager from the dominant function owns the entire macroprocess. This assumption is not made blindly; it is known that multiple functions are involved. Nevertheless, the decision may be to act on the assumption. Such action can also take place by a sort of default. If there is no clear assignment,the ownership remains vague. It then becomes logical for the dominant function to be drawn into that vacuum.

In the judgment of the authors, much damage has been done by using the concept of the assumed owner. The reason is that the planning priorities are focused on the mission of the owner's functional organization rather than on the optimum for the company. To illustrate:

> The purchase of materials involves several costs, principally: the purchase price, the damage done internally due to poor quality, and the external service costs due to poor quality. In many companies this macroprocess is assumed to be "owned" by the purchasing director. Usually that director has good data as to purchase prices but not as to the costs traceable to poor quality of the purchased materials. As a

result, what is optimized is the performance of the purchasing function, not the performance of the company.

The situation of assuming that the dominant function owns the entire macroprocess is widespread. To illustrate, here are several macroprocesses along with the associated dominant function and a major focus of that function:

Macroprocess for Producing	*Dominant Function*	*A Major Focus*
Purchase orders	Purchasing	Purchase price
Sales contracts	Marketing	Sales volume
New products	Product development	Technology

What is really at issue here is whether ownership of macroprocesses can be left solely to individual owners. The judgment of the authors is a qualified no. Some kind of team is needed.

The Designated Owner

Under this concept someone is *designated* as owner despite lack of command over all steps of the macroprocess. The list set out in Figure 10–6 relates to just such a designated owner. That list consists of a mixture of both planning and operating responsibilities.

Companies that have made use of such designated owners have usually been careful to establish criteria to be met by the person so designated. One of these criteria is adequate managerial rank in the hierarchy. The following is the wording attributed to one company:

> An owner must be at a level high enough in the organization to identify the impact on the process of new business direction, to monitor effectiveness and efficiency, to influence change in practices/procedures affecting the process, and to make a commitment to a plan and implement change for process improvement [see Nickell and McNeil, 1987].

In this case one of the criteria for owner selection was "at a level high enough in the organization." It is a form of recognition of the realities faced in trying to achieve results in the absence of command.

A variation on the concept of designated owner is to establish two owners:

An "executive owner" who is assigned the responsibilities set out in Figure 10–6

A "working owner" who is at the microprocess level. This working owner is a direct subordinate of the executive owner. The working owner then has the responsibility of organizing a team consisting of the heads of the key microprocesses. That team then is available to help the executive owner to carry out the assigned responsibilities.

Staff Owners

Yet another form of "owner" is a staff manager who is designated to help prepare a cross-functional plan and who is then held "responsible" for operating results. Examples have included:

PRODUCT MANAGERS. They typically have the basic responsibility for preparing the budget (a financial plan) for a product line and securing commitments from the various operating managers. They are also responsible for measuring progress and for stimulating corrective action in the event of failure to meet goals. They are often held "responsible" for operating results, but they are not in a state of self-control.

RELIABILITY MANAGERS. They are also a form of designated owners. They have broad responsibility relative to planning product reliability, from concept to customer, and over the life cycle of the product. As with the product manager, they secure commitments from operating managers, evaluate performance, and sound the alarm in the event of failure to meet goals. They are similarly not in a state of self-control.

Individual or Team Ownership?

The concept of individual ownership of macroprocesses has some built-in limitations. Optimal conduct of operations requires participation by the microprocesses in such forms as data inputs, tradeoffs to arrive at the optimum, and agreements to take action. In practice the individual owner must provide for such participation. The result is an *informal team* structure but with built-in deficiencies:

An informal team lacks legitimacy in the organization hierarchy.

The owner's formal departmental responsibilities can bias the ownership role.

The major factors in securing results are the skills, training, and persuasiveness of the owner. Since these vary widely, the results will vary widely.

Impact on Career Patterns

The interplay between functional organizations and macroprocesses is strongly influenced by how the people involved perceive the impact on their careers. Many people consider their careers to be related to some trade or profession in which they have special training and experience, such as airline pilot, electrician, or software engineer. In such cases the concept of progress is strongly "horizontal." Progression in the career involves attainment of higher levels of skill, recognition as an expert in the field, and assignment to the most demanding tasks in the specialty. The rewards include self-respect and the respect of peers, as well as rewards in tangible form.

A further specialty is management—the art and science of securing results through other people. In this specialty the concept of progress is strongly "vertical." Progression in this career involves attainment of higher levels in the hierarchy, with associated command over more and more subordinates. The rewards are in the form of status and power as well as rewards in tangible form.

These two careers—horizontally in a specialty and vertically in management—may be pursued within a single company or by moving from company to company.

All this is pertinent to the performance of macroprocesses. The people involved will certainly look to see how the interplay of functional organization and macroprocess impacts their career progress. It follows that the designated owners should inform themselves as to the likely effects of their proposals on the career patterns of those impacted. This information should then become an input to their planning.

Organizations Built Around Macroprocesses

A further option for dealing with macroprocesses is to design the organization around macroprocesses rather than around broad functions.

> In the publications industry, one of the critical macroprocesses is "fulfillment." Fulfillment involves service to clients: getting them on the mailing list, sending out their journals and books, acting on their changes of address,

and so on. This macroprocess is customarily assigned to a "fulfillment manager," and matters are organized so that the associated microprocesses are all under the direct command of the fulfillment manager.

Such an organization design makes the scope of the function coextensive with command of the macroprocess. It also makes both of them compatible with a phase of the career concept. As organizations grow in size, however, there is no escape from organizing by function and incidentally creating the phenomenon illustrated by Figure 10–4. During the 1980s there were some exciting experiments in use of joint teams. Some of these were oriented mainly to planning; others were oriented to operations as well as to planning.

Quality Management of Macroprocesses

Quality management for macroprocesses is carried out by use of the Juran Trilogy: quality planning, quality control, quality improvement. Applied to macroprocesses, quality management has in the past handicapped by various deficiencies, chiefly:

Responsibility for ownership was vague, resulting in poor coordination and no mandate for improvement.

Planning was done by "amateurs," resulting in underutilization of modern quality-related methods.

Macroprocesses, though inherently important, received little attention from upper management.

To remedy these (and other) deficiencies, upper managers should establish the infrastructure needed to:

Determine who should own macroprocesses

Define the responsibilities of owners

Review performance regularly

In addition, it is necessary to take certain specific steps relative to the processes of the Trilogy, as discussed below.

Quality Planning for Macroprocesses

Quality planning for macroprocesses includes (1) defining the work to be done by the planners, (2) assigning this work to an appropriate team, and (3) making use of modern expertise.

The Two Missions

It is important at the outset to distinguish between (a) the mission of the planning team and (b) the mission of the macroprocess.

The mission of the planning team is set out in the basic definition of quality planning, repeated here for convenience:

> Quality planning is the activity of (a) establishing quality goals and (b) developing the products and processes required to meet those goals.

The mission of the macroprocess is to produce products that meet the planned goals, and to do so with minimal waste (effective and efficient).

Who Are the Planners?

The popular notion of a planner is a person who spends full time doing planning. Within most companies there are indeed persons who spend most of their time doing planning: budget officers, designers (hardware and software), systems analysts, process engineers, and so on. Some companies also have full-time quality planners: quality engineers, reliability engineers. However, most planning for quality has been done by managers and other personnel in the functional departments.

> As used here, the word "planner" applies to any person at the time he or she is engaged in planning, whether full time or as part of a broader list of responsibilities.

What emerges is that managers in the functional departments may be assigned three roles with respect to macroprocesses:

> Planners of the microprocesses within their functional departments
>
> Planners of the macroprocesses to which they are assigned as owners
>
> Designated owners of macroprocesses in the operational sense

The Work to be Done

The work list for quality planning for macroprocesses includes:

DEFINE THE MISSION OF THE MACROPROCESS. Each planning team is created for some specific planning purpose. One of the first steps is to clarify that purpose. In effect the team should finish the sentence: "This plan has been completed when______."

FOLLOW THE QUALITY PLANNING ROAD MAP. This road map is the step-by-step planning process set out in Chapter 1, under the heading "The Quality Planning Road Map," and elaborated in subsequent chapters.

DEFINE THE MICROPROCESSES. It is quite common to delegate planning for microprocesses to local departmental teams. Such an arrangement requires a clear definition of the mission of each such delegated microprocess along with criteria for the interfaces.

COORDINATE THE PLANNING. Planning for a macroprocess always includes some planning to be done by sources that are probably not members of the team. For example:

Planners of some of the microprocesses

External customers

Outside suppliers

Various forces of society

The planning team has the responsibility of coordinating all this so as to arrive at the optimum.

The Planning Team

Planning of macroprocesses is inherently a team effort. It is best done with the participation of those who will be impacted by the resulting plan. There are various ways of creating a team structure.

DESIGNATED OWNER PLUS INFORMAL PARTICIPATION. The nature of this approach is evident from the list of responsibilities of owners as set out in Figure 10-6.

FULL-TIME PLANNER PLUS FORMAL DESIGN REVIEW. Under this approach, formal design review committees are established to enable impacted departments to review the plans and to provide early warning to the planner, i.e., "If you plan it this way, here will be the effect in my area."

JOINT PLANNING. Under this approach one team of planners carries out all the planning, phase after phase. This approach has the potential to provide the most thorough planning. It is also the most demanding in terms of hours spent in planning and in terms of the calendar time.

MATRIX ORGANIZATION. This is a form of team structure superimposed on a functional hierarchy. In some companies it has been quite useful for coordinating the functions associated with specific products or markets. It has also been widely used for firefighting—dealing with sporadic problems that cut across functional lines. The use of matrix organizations as quality planning teams has not been widely documented. However, there is experience which indicates that even within a matrix organization, the best vehicles for successful planning are focused, joint planning teams.

Expertise for Quality Planning

A widespread deficiency of the past has been the phenomenon of quality planning by amateurs—quality planning without expertise in quality. The need is to provide the missing expertise. The major options for doing this have been:

1. Assign quality specialists to assist the planning teams, either as consultants or as team members. This option has been favored by companies in the United States.
2. Train the planners (line managers and line specialists) in the needed expertise, i.e., convert the amateurs into professionals. This option has been favored by major companies in Japan.

Each of these options has been widely tested. Based on extensive feedback from these tests, it is the opinion of the authors that option (2), training the planners in the needed expertise, has significantly outperformed option (1) and should therefore be adopted for the future.

For extensive additional discussion, see Chapter 12, under the heading "Training in Planning for Quality" and subsequent headings.

Replanning of Macroprocesses

The work done during the 1980s to designate owners for macroprocesses has led to replanning some of them. An example of such replanning relates to a process of bidding for contracts. As originally planned, the process required an average of fourteen weeks to prepare a bid. The yield in contracts was about 20 percent. Much of the reason for the low yield was the length of the bidding process.

A replanning of the process shortened the average bidding time to three and a half weeks and increased the yield to a range of 50–60 percent. Figure 10–7 shows the flow of the process before and after the replanning.

The changes that resulted in such a dramatic improvement included the introduction of an on-line contract management subsystem of the existing Marketing Information System, for the preparation of bids. The major benefits were:

1. A sequence of prompts, reflecting an up-to-date data base of rules, procedures, etc., greatly speeded preparation of the initial document and ensured conformance to contract guidelines, thereby reducing the frequent rework and resultant delays that had characterized the former system.
2. The electronic transfer of information among the geographically dispersed participants in this process eliminated the delays associated with transfer of paper copies by mail.
3. Deadlines for passoff at each step in the process and periodic review of performance against those deadlines were established.
4. A system of concurrent approvals was established to replace the previous system of consecutive approvals.
5. Provision was made for regional approval of certain low-revenue bids—about 20 percent of all bids.

Quality Control for Macroprocesses

Virtually all quality controls are built around the feedback loop. Figure 10–8 shows the graphic model (this is also Figure 5–7 reproduced here for convenience).

To apply quality control to macroprocesses requires establishment of the essential elements of control:

Goals for performance

Means for evaluation of actual performance

Review of performance against goals, and closing the feedback loop

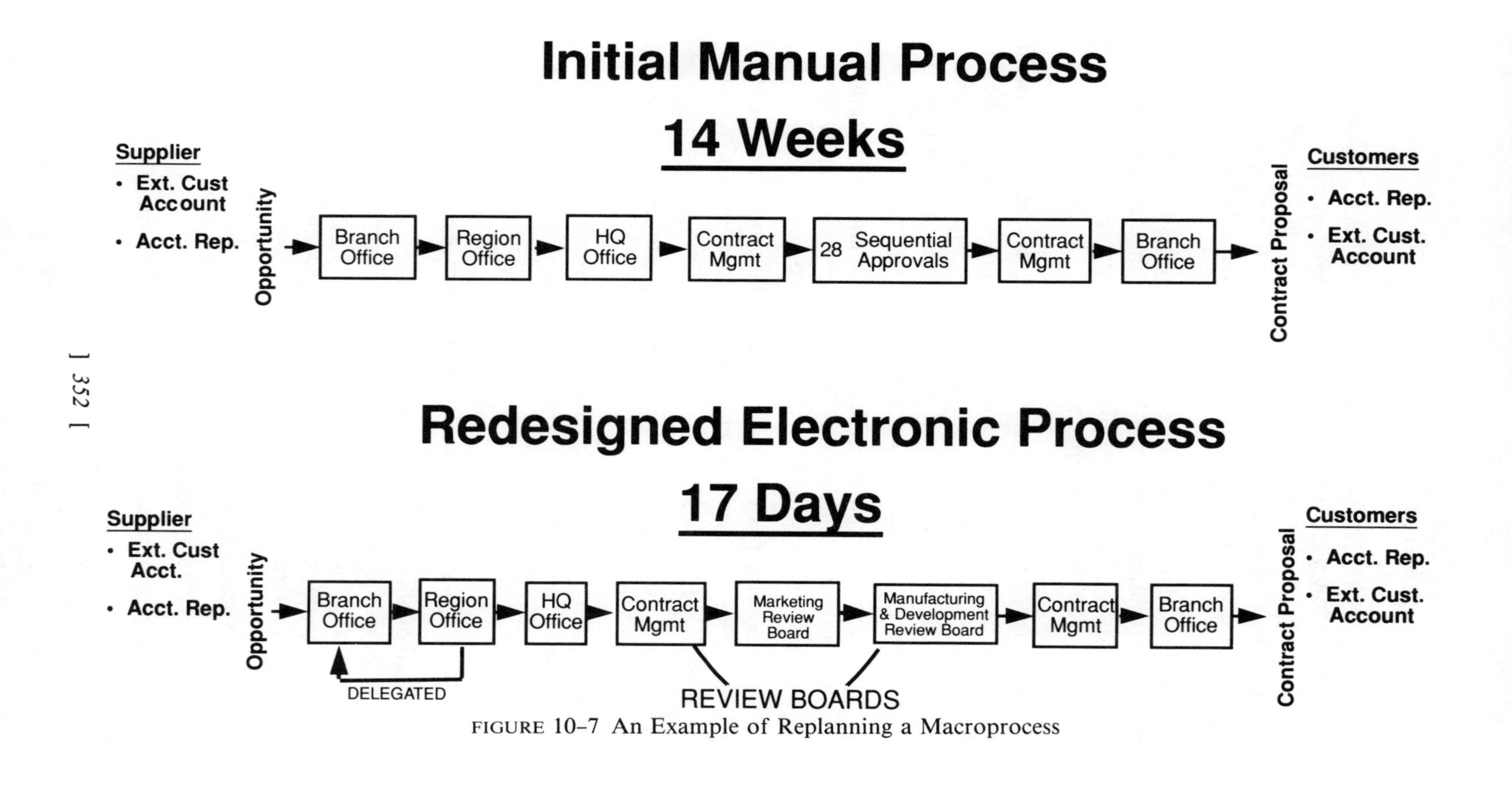

FIGURE 10–7 An Example of Replanning a Macroprocess

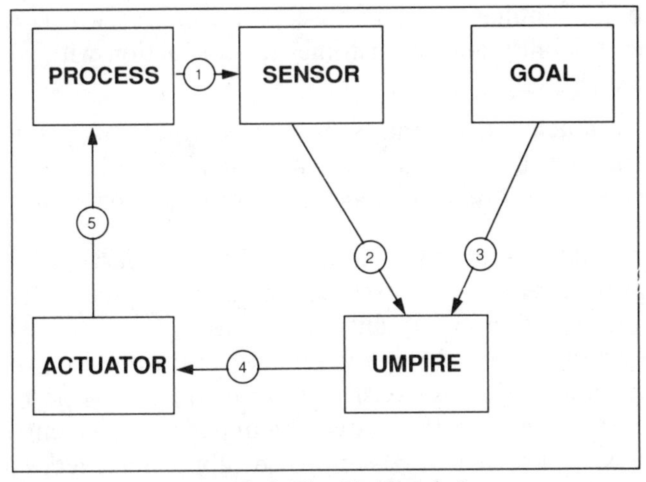

FIGURE 10–8 The Feedback Loop

Responsibility for Establishing the Elements of Control

For many macroprocesses, the responsibility for establishment of the elements of control has been vague. The original planning did not establish quality goals or make provision for evaluating performance. All too often it was assumed that if provision was made for quality control of the microprocesses, then the end result would be a well-controlled macroprocess. All too often the end result has been otherwise.

The optimal remedy for these deficiencies in quality control of macroprocesses is to establish the elements of the feedback loop during the original planning of the macroprocess. The responsibilities of each planning team should include establishment of these elements.

In those cases where the original planning has failed to provide these elements, it should become the responsibility of the "owner" of the macroprocess to provide them through replanning.

The Quality Instrument Panel

Most companies evolve a report package—an instrument panel—which summarizes for upper managers the performance for key parameters: sales, expenses, profit, schedule, productivity, and so on. In many companies this report system includes performance with respect to quality. In such companies there is a striking difference in emphasis as to control subjects:

The major emphasis is on those performances which relate to product salability and to customer dissatisfaction with respect to the products sold.

There is much less emphasis on performances of business processes despite the fact that these have significant impacts relative to the company's quality image and to the cost of poor quality.

This unbalance should not continue. Some researches have indicated that the business processes can be quite as influential, in terms of customer reaction and quality image, as the processes that produce the products for sale. In the opinion of the authors, the upper managers should take positive steps to bring the quality performance of macroprocesses into the system of upper management reports. The end result of such action is to provide upper managers with measures like those shown in the boxed table.

Control Subject	*Units of Measure*
Promptness of service	Average time elapsed; percent of promises met
Billing accuracy	Loss of revenue due to delay in payment; error rate; cost to correct errors
Success in bidding	Percent yield; cost per contract
Response to complaints	Response time; percent satisfied
Avoidable changes in engineering drawings, purchase orders, etc.	Percent of changes that were avoidable; cost of avoidable changes
Software quality	Errors per 1,000 lines of code; cost to correct errors

For elaboration on upper management control of quality generally, see Chapter 9, under the heading "The Infrastructure for Control." See also Chapter 5, under the heading "Measures for Operating Processes."

Quality Improvement for Macroprocesses

The project-by-project approach for quality improvement (outlined in Chapter 1, under the heading "The Juran Trilogy") is applicable to macroprocesses.

Nominations for Projects

Some potential improvement projects may be identified through feedback from customers, such as:

Customer needs are not being met

Service is not competitive

Upper managers are a major source of nominations because of their membership on the Quality Council and their exposure to inputs from customers, executive reports, audits, and the like.

A widespread opportunity for improving macroprocesses is reduction of cycle time in order to improve service to customers while reducing costs. We had an example in the bidding process (see above, under "Quality Planning for Macroprocesses: Replanning of Macroprocesses"). For an extensive discussion of methods of diagnosis and remedies for reducing cycle time, see Chapter 7, under the heading "Reduction of Cycle Time."

A further widespread opportunity for improving macroprocesses is through reduction of rework. One of the evidences of redoing work is the existence of rework "loops" in flow diagrams, as shown in Figure 3-5 of Chapter 3. Often the head of the associated microprocess has been unable to get rid of the loop because the problem is inherently multifunctional in nature. In such cases it takes an owner or a multifunctional team to provide a solution.

Leadership for Quality Improvement Projects

Quality improvement for macroprocesses may require diagnosis and remedy at two levels:

The multifunctional level. At this level the improvement project is directed by the owner of the macroprocess, if one has been designated. In the absence of a designated owner, the project is assigned to some multifunctional team. The designated team then becomes the owner so far as quality improvement is concerned.

The microprocess level. Here it may be feasible to delegate the diagnosis and remedy to the local supervision or to the nonsupervisory personnel. We shall examine such cases in Chapter 11.

Motivation for Quality Improvement of Macroprocesses

Our main discussion of motivation will be in Chapter 12, under the heading "Motivation for Quality." However, it is useful at this point to notice a special aspect of motivation for quality improvement as applied to macroprocesses and microprocesses.

A successful quality improvement within a *microprocess* often improves the departmental performance of the supervisor who carried out the project. This feature of personal benefit has stimulated many supervisors of microprocesses to undertake quality improvement on a voluntary basis, that is, even in the absence of an upper management mandate to improve quality.

In the case of macroprocesses, the motivational situation is quite different. Now the process is multifunctional in nature, so a multifunctional team is needed to carry out a quality improvement project. If the project is successful, there is a benefit to the company but not necessarily to the departmental performance of any team member.

This absence of personal benefit is a disincentive to voluntary quality improvement. As a result, it is necessary for the upper managers to establish the infrastructure needed for quality improvement and to put such improvement on a mandated basis.

The detailed process of project-by-project improvement is not discussed in this book. For a comprehensive treatment, see Juran (1989), Chapter Three, "Quality Improvement." See also the references at the end of the book.

Quality Audit of Macroprocesses and Functions

Macroprocesses can be difficult to revise, because they involve multiple major company functions. Yet many of these same macroprocesses do need revision, because they exhibit poor performance, involve costly wastes, and so on. The customers of the macroprocess are unhappy with the results, but there is no ready way to change things. So there is a deadlock. There is usually no owner of the macroprocess, and there is always cultural resistance by the functional owners of the components—the microprocesses. One way to break up such deadlocks is through the upper management audit.

The case of the macroprocess for producing credit cards involved twenty-two microprocesses progressing through the domains of five vice-presidents. Results were poor: the overall cycle time was lengthy; 15 percent of the applications failed to complete their journey through all those handoffs; some applicants received multiple credit cards. The resulting deadlock could be broken only by some form of upper management intervention such as a quality audit.

A Quality Audit Can Be a Lot of Work

To conduct a quality audit of a macroprocess is usually a lot of work, much of which consists of the following.

Identifying the questions to which answers are needed. Frequent key questions are:

Who are the key customers?

What are their needs?

How well are those needs being served?

How does this service compare with competition?

Securing the answers, some of which involve evaluation of performance of the macroprocess and that of its competitors. Other answers must come from understanding the way in which the process is carried out—the flow diagram, and so forth.

Conclusions, recommendations, and revisions are elements that vary from case to case. In some cases the need is to change the basic anatomy of the macroprocess. For example, in the credit card case the need may be to establish a separate organization entity to produce credit cards, and to reduce the number of "handoffs" as well. In other cases the remedy may require better definition of the microprocesses and the interfaces. In still other cases the need may be to improve the conformance of the microprocesses to their respective goals.

Much of the Work Can Be Delegated

Most of the work of quality audits consists of "securing the answers." This work can largely be delegated to subordinate levels. It consists in part of securing data on performance and deficiencies. The work also includes preparing flow diagrams, spreadsheets, exhibits, and the like to make it easy for upper managers to understand the macroprocess. In addition the work includes preparing summaries and recommendations as an aid to decision making by the upper managers.

The remaining elements consist of identifying the questions to which answers are needed, and making decisions based on the conclusions. These elements are normally not delegable.

Quality Audit of Macroprocesses: Some Key Questions

The subject matter of the quality audits will differ from company to company and also from time to time. (Quality is a moving target.) The subject matter will in any case include macroprocesses as well as functional performance.

The choice of which macroprocesses to audit is properly made by the Quality Council. Normally the list will be similar to the list of "key" macroprocesses discussed above, under the heading "The Key Macroprocesses," and based on the criteria listed there.

For macroprocesses, some basic questions dominate the quality audit:

Is the process effective—does it meet customer needs?

Is the process competitive with similar processes carried out by others?

Is the process efficient—does it operate with minimal waste?

To provide answers to such basic questions requires raising and answering many subsidiary questions. It can involve a good deal of work. Efforts to avoid such work can result in a superficial and misleading audit.

Quality Audit of Functions: Some Key Questions

Quality audits of functions have been carried out for decades, and a good deal has been published on the conduct of such audits. Most of this auditing has been done at the Little Q level, but some has extended to matters of a Big Q nature. What follows is a selection from some of the key questions that have been addressed during audits of functions.

FIELD INTELLIGENCE FUNCTION. Key questions have included:

What is the relative importance of our product features, as seen by the users?

As to those key features, what is the performance of our product relative to that of our competitors, as seen by the users?

What is the effect of these competitive differences on the users' economics and well-being?

What is the adequacy of our data base relative to the above questions?

How are we organized for securing credible field intelligence relative to quality?

PRODUCT DEVELOPMENT FUNCTION. Key questions have included:

What has been the track record of our product developments—the proportion of successes, failures, and near misses?

What is our cycle time from concept to customer, compared to that of competitors?

What measures are in use for judging the performance of the product development function?

What is the "cost of poor quality" generated by the product development function?

What is the adequacy of our system of early warning for detecting quality problems that the product development function creates for subsequent functions in the concept-to-customer sequence?

To what extent are failure-prone features of old products carried over into new products?

What training have our product developers had in modern quality methodology?

SUPPLIER RELATIONS FUNCTION. Key questions have included:

How well do we define our quality needs as perceived by us? As perceived by our suppliers?

How do we evaluate suppliers' quality performance?

To what extent are our field quality problems traceable to purchases from suppliers?

How much of our cost of poor quality is traceable to purchases from suppliers?

What criteria do we use for selecting new suppliers? For terminating suppliers?

What has been our turnover in suppliers?

PROCESS PLANNING FUNCTION. Key questions have included:

What are the measures in use for the process planning function?

To what extent do our process designs conform to customer demands for "Just in Time," Statistical Process Control, etc.?

How much of our cost of poor quality is traceable to process planning?

What is the adequacy of the process planning data base?

To what extent are process planners trained in modern quality methodology?

PRODUCING FUNCTION. Key questions have included:

What is the priority given to quality relative to other parameters?

To what extent are the employees in a state of self-control?

To what extent are the employees trained in use of the tools of quality control?

To what extent do employees have the opportunity to participate in quality planning and quality improvement?

QUALITY MANAGEMENT FUNCTION. Key questions have included?

What is the perception of the line managers relative to the role of the Quality Department?

What is the state of quality data feedback to the line functions?

What is the qualification of the Quality Department to help the company to bring quality goals into the strategic business plan?

MARKETING FUNCTION. Key questions have included:

What is known about the relation of the company's product quality to sales volume and to the price structure?

Where lies the responsibility to determine such relationships?

What is known about the effect of business process quality on sales volume and price structure?

CUSTOMER SERVICE FUNCTION. Key questions have included:

What are the measures of quality of customer service?

What are the customers' perceptions of the adequacy of our service?

Is the feedback of data from customer service a reliable basis for planning improvements in performance?

Training for Multifunctional Quality Planning

The stated purpose of this chapter was to explain "how to plan multifunctional processes in ways that will meet the needs of customers while minimizing the creation of chronic wastes during the subsequent operations." To achieve such results requires that the functional and other personnel undergo extensive training in modern quality planning.

Training for quality planning (and the associated tools) will be discussed in Chapter 12, under the heading "Training in Planning for Quality" and subsequent headings.

On to Departmental Quality Planning

The present chapter has dealt with quality planning for multifunctional processes. There is a collateral need for quality planning for the associated microprocesses, which are the building blocks of the multifunctional processes. Chapter 11, "Departmental Quality Planning," deals with that subject.

List of High Points

The anatomy of macroprocesses does not match that of the functional organization.

A macroprocess ideally exhibits features as follows:

Effective	Measurable
Adaptable	Controllable
Efficient	Formalized

During the 1980s it became evident that no one was in charge of macroprocesses—there was no "owner."

Companies have at the outset elected to establish ownership only for the key macroprocesses.

Discussion of ownership of macroprocesses must begin by distinguishing clearly between:

Ownership relative to planning

Ownership relative to operations

Establishment of ownership must be preceded by agreement on what the responsibilities of an owner are.

Much damage has been done by using the concept of the assumed owner.

Designated owners should inform themselves as to the likely effect of their proposals on the career patterns of those impacted, and should use this information as an input to their planning.

It is important to distinguish between (a) the mission of the macroprocess and (b) the mission of the planning team.

Most planning for quality has been done by managers and other personnel in the functional departments.

Planning of macroprocesses is inherently a team effort.

A widespread deficiency of the past has been the phenomenon of quality planning by amateurs.

Training the planners in the needed quality-related expertise has significantly outperformed providing the planners with consultants.

Where the original planning has failed to provide the elements of control, the "owner" of the macroprocess should provide them through replanning.

Improvement of a macroprocess through a team project provides a benefit to the company but not necessarily to the departmental performance of any team member.

The upper management audit is one way to identify macroprocesses that need revision but lack the ownership required to initiate change.

Tasks for Upper Managers

Establish the infrastructure needed to:

- Determine who should own macroprocesses
- Define the responsibilities of owners
- Review performance regularly

Train the planners in quality-related expertise. This approach has significantly outperformed that of providing the planners with consultants.

Take positive steps to bring the quality performance of macroprocesses into the system of upper management reports.

Establish the infrastructure needed for quality improvement of macroprocesses, and mandate their improvement.

Use the upper management audit to identify those macroprocesses which need revision but lack the ownership needed to initiate change.

] 11 [

Departmental Quality Planning

The Purpose of This Chapter

The mission of this chapter is to explain how to apply quality planning at the lower levels of the company hierarchy. These lower levels include the following organization units and processes:

The departments that are subordinate to the major functions

The microprocesses carried out by these departments

Teams of workers (nonsupervisory employees) organized to carry out the missions of the microprocesses

Tasks performed by individual workers

Note that the word "department" has not yet acquired a standardized meaning among our enterprises. As used here, the word "department" generally refers to an organization unit that:

Carries out operations (tasks, etc.) of a single functional nature

Consists of nonsupervisory workers supervised by a "first line" supervisor

The Legacy of the Taylor System

Quality planning at the lower levels remains profoundly influenced by the system of management stimulated in the late nineteenth century by Frederick W. Taylor. This system was widely adopted in the United States and became deeply rooted. A considerable residue is still in force. That residue is present in such forms as long-standing habit patterns and vested interests. That same residue is now a major obstacle to introducing modern processes for quality planning at lower levels.

To deal with this obstacle, it is helpful and even necessary to look back at the nature of the Taylor system, especially its impact on quality planning. The more managers understand that impact, the better will they be able to introduce modern processes for quality planning.

Separation of Planning from Execution

Taylor's basic concept was to manage factories through scientific methods rather than by use of the empirical "rule of thumb" so widely prevalent in those days. An important barrier to use of scientific management was the limited education of the lower levels of supervision and of the work force. Some factory workers were skilled craftsmen who had learned a trade through years of apprenticeship. Other workers were laborers who performed semiskilled or unskilled tasks, such as materials handling.

These laborers were a large part of the factory population. Most of them were recent immigrants, and they lacked literacy in the English language. Some were completely illiterate—education levels were comparatively low in those days. In Taylor's view, supervisors and workers with such low levels of education were not qualified to plan how work should be done. Taylor's solution was to separate planning from execution.

To apply this solution, Taylor created planning departments, staffed them with engineers, and gave them the responsibility to:

Develop scientific methods for doing work

Establish goals for productivity

Establish systems of rewards for meeting the goals

Train the personnel in how to use the methods and thereby meet the goals

Taylor's system was stunningly successful in raising productivity. It was widely adopted in the United States, and was probably the chief reason for the U.S. rise to the position of world leader in productivity.

Expansion into Other Areas

The Taylor system had its origin in the factory production departments. However, the concept of separating planning from execution was universal in nature and hence had potential application to other areas: production support services, offices operations, service industries. The gains in factory productivity were well publicized and aroused the interest of managers in those other areas. Further stimulus came from the change agents: industrial engineers, and systems analysts. So the concept did spread, and much of it was still in place at the end of the 1980s.

The Side Effects

The Taylor system also produced some unwelcome side effects:

> The line personnel resented the loss of the planning responsibility. The change took place over their bitter opposition, especially from the line supervisors and managers. Divisiveness set in and has smoldered ever since.
>
> The new emphasis on productivity had a negative effect on quality. The response of manufacturing companies was to create independent inspection departments (later "Quality Control" departments) in order to safeguard quality. In due course a widespread belief emerged that responsibility for quality rested with the Quality Department.
>
> The planning departments and their engineers built vested interests and careers around the planning responsibility. In due course those vested interests tended to grow into monopolies.

Obsolescence of the Premises

Nearly a century has passed since Taylor created his revolution. During that time much has happened to make obsolete the premises on which Taylor based his concepts:

> The concept of separating planning from execution rested on the premise that the supervisors and work force lacked the education needed to perform the planning activities. Meanwhile education levels have risen remarkably in most countries. Lack of education is by itself no longer reason enough to deny responsibility for planning to most supervisors and to many workers.
>
> In Taylor's time the balance of power between managers and the work force was heavily weighted against the workers. (Industrial unions were illegal restraints of trade.) Since then industrial unionism (or the threat of it) has profoundly changed that balance.
>
> There have also been changes in the climate of social thinking. Even in Taylor's time there were protests against the "dehumanizing" of work. Recent decades have seen strong trends toward

giving the work force a greater voice in broad decision making, even extending to the concept of having substantial ownership in the companies.

The Search for a New Approach

The Taylor system has become so obsolete that it should be replaced. We lack agreement on what should replace it, but many experiments have been tried. Others are in progress. From these experiments certain commonalities have emerged. Applied to the lower levels of the hierarchies, the trends are to:

Revise the anatomy of the processes so as to minimize the use of short-cycle, repetitive jobs and the associated "handoffs" from worker to worker

Enlarge the scope of jobs horizontally to include multiple tasks and skills

Enlarge the scope of jobs vertically to include multiple functions

Create self-supervising worker teams to perform the enlarged jobs

Restore much of the responsibility for process planning, including planning for quality, to the line personnel

Establish self-control (see Chapter 8, under "Self-control," for the criteria to be met)

Confer a higher sense of "ownership"

Enlarge job responsibilities to include responsibility for making improvements

Provide training in depth to enable the lower levels to carry out those added responsibilities

During this chapter we shall come back to the above trends in order to understand their impact on quality. Meanwhile, upper managers should face up to the question of whether to take positive steps to replace the Taylor System.

Quality Planning for Microprocesses

Compared to macroprocesses, microprocesses are much more numerous and much narrower in scope. There are also profound differences in organization form and in relationship to the hierarchy, as set out in Figure 11-1.

Note that as used here, the terms "department" and "micro-

Usual Scope	Macroprocess (Business Process) Multidepartmental: often Multifunctional	Microprocess (Subprocess) Tasks or Operations within a Single Department
Relation to hierarchical organization	Seldom closely related	Usually closely related
Ownership of macroprocess	No natural owner	Departmental supervisor is natural owner
Responsibility for quality planning	Requires multidepartmental team	Often can be delegated to local departmental personnel
Relationship of planners to operating personnel	Seldom identical	Often identical

FIGURE 11-1 Contrast: Quality Management for Macroprocesses Versus Microprocesses

process'' are generally coextensive. Our glossary definition of microprocess is as follows:

> An operational system involving few tasks, usually carried out within a single functional department.

Microprocesses are so numerous that the upper levels of companies cannot become involved with them individually. However, some companies have undertaken initiatives to deal with the microprocesses *collectively*. They design a broad methodology intended to help departmental supervisors replan their own microprocesses. The broad methodologies are launched under such names as Departmental Activity Analysis. They differ in content, all the way from vague exhortations to specific actions to be taken in accordance with a Departmental Analysis Manual. That manual sometimes provides forms and data sheets, along with instructions on how to fill them out.

An example of ''Department Activity Analysis'' forms is included at the end of this chapter (from Parker, 1984).

The subject matter addressed by the manuals varies considerably from company to company. Some of the topics relate to parameters other than quality. The more usual topics that do relate to quality are listed below, together with brief descriptions. (All manuals focus on some of the steps of the quality road map, but seldom on the entire sequence.)

Define the Departmental Mission

The supervisors are asked to address such questions as:

Why does this department exist?

What tasks does the department perform?

What purpose should the department be fulfilling?

The end result of this part of the analysis is a mission statement, which sets out what tasks the department should do and can do. In some cases the concept of self-control is brought in as a criterion of what the department can do.

The Triple Role Concept

This concept is readily depicted by a diagram, Figure 11-2, which we shall call the TRIPROL™ diagram.

The TRIPROL diagram is a basic model used to explain the roles played by any department as it carries out its assigned quality mission. There are three of these roles, namely:

Customer. The department acquires various kinds of inputs, which are used in carrying out its mission. The department is therefore a customer of those who provide the inputs.

Processor. The department processes those inputs in order to produce its products. The department is therefore a *processor.*

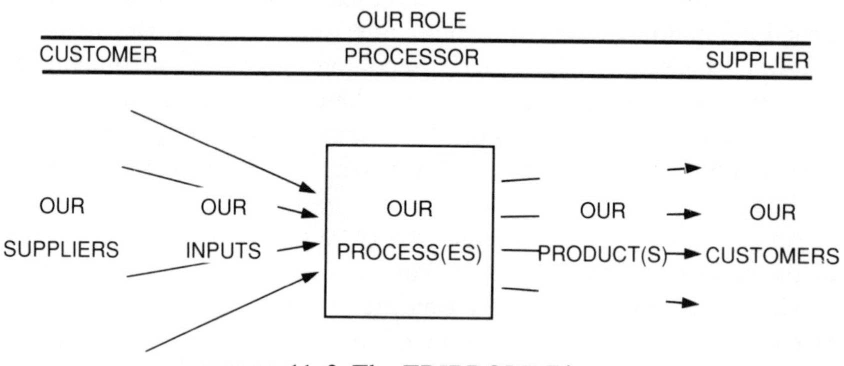

FIGURE 11-2 The TRIPROL™ Diagram

Supplier. The department supplies its products to its customers. The department is therefore a *supplier.*

Figure 11-3 exemplifies the triple role concept as applied to recruitment of employees and preparation of financial reports.

Some of the companies' training materials go to considerable lengths to explain this basic and useful concept. Note that the triple role concept is *applicable to any organization entity:* the company, a division, a function, a department, a project team, a nonsupervisory worker. For convenience we shall refer to any such organization entity as a *processor team.* Our glossary entry becomes:

A processor team is any organization unit (of one or more persons) that carries out a prescribed process.

Identify the Customers

All manuals stress the importance of identifying the customers. However, they seldom explain the Big Q concept of customers. They seldom explain what steps to take in order to identify customers.

Customer/User	*Processor*	*Supplier*
	Personnel (recruitment)	
Receive requisitions from interested customers Receive job descriptions Receive feedback from interviews	Review, critique job descriptions Publish information on job openings Interview, screen job applicants Conduct checks on references	Supply recruits to internal customers Provide associated documentation Provide induction to recruits when hired
	Finance (financial data) Function	
Receive basic data from various sources Receive feedbacks from published reports	Establish data processing system Process data into summaries Analyze data, prepare reports	Publish reports Disseminate to internal and external customers

FIGURE 11-3 Examples of Triple Roles of Customer/User, Processor, and Supplier
From *Juran's Quality Control Handbook,* Fourth Edition (New York: McGraw-Hill Book Co., 1988) p. 21.5

They seldom suggest the use of the flow diagram to help discover who is impacted (see Chapter 3 under "The Flow Diagram"). Some manuals fail to point out the presence of internal customers. Others adopt the simplistic concept of focusing on the next recipient as the customer. Still others focus on the users of the products but fail to point out that all who are impacted are customers.

> Some manuals reflect the special situations prevailing in their companies. One service company's manual stresses the importance of finding out the critical dates to be met and the consequences of failure to meet those dates.

Those who are given responsibility to prepare a manual on "Department Quality Analysis" should study Chapter 3, "Identify Customers," as an input to that section of the manual which deals with Identify the Customers.

Establish Customer Needs

The manuals put much emphasis on determining the needs of customers. Most go beyond the relatively simple concepts of meeting specifications and requirements, and pose searching questions such as:

> How is the product used by customers?
>
> How do customers view the relative importance of the various needs?
>
> How do the perceptions of customers differ from the perceptions of the supplying department?

Some of the manuals include forms to be used as questionnaires for securing the needed answers from customers. Other manuals propose that the supplying departments consult with customers in order to understand customer needs in depth.

All manuals stress the importance of closing any gap between customers and supplier as to the perceptions of customer needs. In some companies the manual stipulates that the analysis should be followed by *a written agreement* with customers, including internal customers.

Describe the Process

All manuals include instructions for describing the process. In some cases the manuals include forms for this purpose.

The manuals exhibit similarity in their views of what should be included in a description of the process. Typically the instructions ask for a description that includes:

A list of the tasks or elementary operations performed within the department

The time consumed in performing each of the tasks (hours, person-days, etc.)

The needs served by each of these tasks

The output from these tasks (This consists of products—goods or services in their various forms. In some manuals this output is described as "value added" or "contribution.")

For processes that involve numerous tasks, preparing such a description for each task, along with the subsequent analyses (see below), can be quite demanding of the time of the departmental supervisor.

Identify the Suppliers and the Needs from Suppliers

All manuals require identification of suppliers, both external and internal. This identification then leads to listing what is supplied by these suppliers and what the associated needs are.

Some manuals point out that the problem of determining needs from suppliers parallels that of determining customer needs. The difference is that in this case the supervisor is the customer rather than the supplier. As before, the manuals urge reaching an agreement with the suppliers on the needs of the process.

Establish Measures

All manuals mention the need for measures of quality. It is implied that these needs extend to each of the triple roles: supplier, processor, and customer. Occasionally a manual requires the supervisor to "evaluate process capability." However, the manuals do not spell out the methodology of arriving at measures. Here, as in the manuals generally, much is left to be filled in by training.

(For elaboration on measures of quality, see Chapter 5 generally, and especially under the heading "Measures for Operating Processes.")

Establish Feedback

The manuals point out the need to establish a feedback flow for the major paths within the Triprol diagram:

From the customers back to the supervisor's process

From the supervisor's process back to the suppliers

The paths of this feedback can be added to the Triprol diagram, as shown in Figure 11-4.

How to establish these feedbacks is seldom discussed in the manuals.

Review Performance, Take Corrective Action

The manuals usually stipulate that the supervisor should:

Collect feedback data on quality performances

Compare the performances with the quality needs (which were previously converted into specifications, standards, procedures, etc.)

Identify nonconformances, defects, etc.

Take corrective action.

Notice that these elements of the manual deal with quality control by use of the feedback loop, rather than with quality planning. Here again, the manuals are sketchy in the "how to do" for the prescribed actions, so much will depend on the supplemental training.

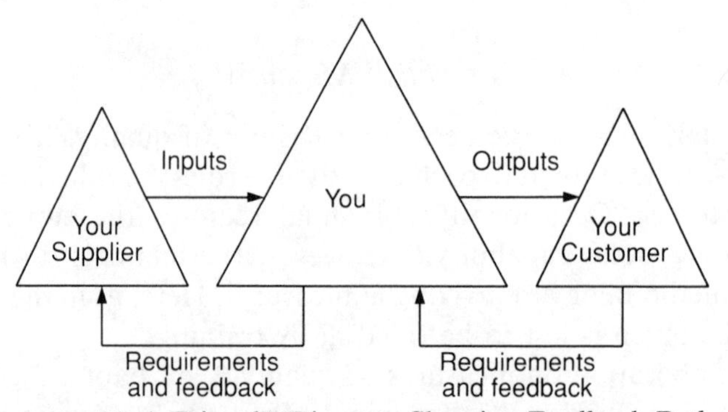

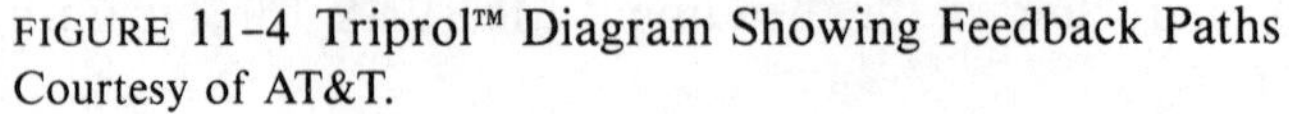

FIGURE 11-4 Triprol™ Diagram Showing Feedback Paths
Courtesy of AT&T.

Conduct Quality Improvements

The manuals are generally sketchy in their descriptions of the process for quality improvement. The segments that are covered differ from manual to manual.

Specifics in certain manuals include:

Analyze the cost of poor quality (The method of analysis follows the familiar categories of failure, appraisal, and prevention. Here and there a manual goes into great detail in setting up subcategories for various elements of these costs.)

Identify problems and opportunities for improvement

Select projects to be tackled

Implement the improvements

Lessons Learned from the Company Approaches

Companies that have initiated supervisory analysis of microprocesses have done so for reasons that are entirely constructive. The objectives have been to:

Improve the microprocesses through replanning

Utilize the experience and creativity of the supervisors (and of the nonsupervisory personnel)

Provide those same supervisors with greater participation and with a greater sense of ownership

Broaden the supervisors' understanding of their roles

Take some steps toward converting experienced amateurs into professional quality planners

The Methodologies

To meet these objectives, some companies have prepared a structured methodology, including forms to be filled out and training in how to go at the replanning. Collectively these methodologies have exhibited strengths and weaknesses.

The strengths have included:

A focus on supervisory ownership of the microprocesses

Adoption of much of the quality planning road map

Provision of a structured, understandable procedure, including forms to help in the data preparation (see, for example, the forms at the end of this chapter)

Extensive listing of the actions to be taken

Provision of training to supplement the manual

The weaknesses that have emerged during the field tests include:

Focus on microprocesses without provision for coordination with other elements of the macroprocess

Individual responsibility for a replanning activity that inherently requires extensive teamwork

Definition of what actions to take, but with inadequate explanations of the methodology to be used to take those actions

Training often focused on the manual instead of on carrying out an actual replanning project

Overly complex paperwork in some cases

Inadvertent emphasis on departmental performance at the expense of overall company performance

In the light of these lessons learned, upper managers should determine whether to take an initiative to provide supervisors with a structured approach for analyzing microprocesses.

A Common Illusion

All too often companies have gone into replanning of their microprocesses on the assumption that such replanning would solve the quality problems of their macroprocesses. Our experience has been otherwise. Replanning of the microprocesses seldom solves the major problems of the macroprocess. In the credit card example, the major need is to reexamine the macroplan, for example:

Should such a process involve the hierarchies of five different vice-presidents?

Can the number of steps be reduced drastically?

Several examples of successful reductions in the number of steps in macroprocesses were cited in Chapter 7, under the heading "The Anatomy of Processes." In those cases, no amount of refining of the microprocesses could have secured an equivalent improvement.

How to Improve the Company Approaches

The company initiatives have been few in number and of recent origin. Collectively, they must be regarded as experimental. The experience gained from these early experiments does suggest some ways to improve the approaches used to date:

Start with the macroprocesses. In general, the major problems of the macroprocesses are traceable to planning deficiencies at the macro-level. Hence the first efforts at replanning should be directed to the top of the process hierarchy. The methodology for doing so was explained in Chapter 10.

Include supervisors in the planning teams. Planning of macroprocesses requires multifunctional teams. There is opportunity to include supervisors of microprocesses on such teams. The associated training and experience will help those supervisors later when they tackle the replanning of their microprocesses.

With respect to quality management of microprocesses, there is definite value in the concept of preparing broad-spectrum manuals, which can help supervisors to plan, control, and improve their operations. Based on experience to date, these manuals could be strengthened and supplemented in the following ways:

Establish an infrastructure for creating project teams. For many microprocesses the responsible supervisor will need the help of a team to make the analysis and provide the remedies. It should not be left to the supervisors to create such teams by the methods of "beg, borrow, and steal." The upper managers should provide a channel through which the supervisors' proposals for setting up the needed teams can receive approval and legitimacy.

Include emphasis on projects relating to product salability. The manuals have generally emphasized projects for reducing the cost of poor quality. These are indeed important. However, making the products salable has even higher priority.

Explain the distinction between sporadic and chronic quality problems. (The former are handled by the control process; the latter require a very different approach—a structured approach to quality improvement.)

Focus on getting projects completed. The company manuals have focused on training—training related to actions to be taken. Such training is usually forgotten unless it is built around a project to be completed. The focus should instead be on completing a project, and the training should be considered an aid to that end.

Provide training in "how to do." The company manuals have generally limited themselves to defining what to do, but with little on how to do it. The manuals should contain (or be supplemented by) information on team building, the methodology and tools for analysis, the provision of remedies, the elements of self-control, etc.

Provide facilitators/trainers. The experience to date indicates that the needed training is seldom acquired through self-study. There is need for facilitators/trainers who themselves should first undergo intensive training in the subject matter and in how to train.

Include an example all worked out. Supervisors who have undergone training often suggest that the training materials provide a case example all worked out. The suggestion is entirely constructive.

Test out the extent of paperwork before issuing the manual. Some company initiatives have failed because of the amount and complexity of paperwork demanded from the supervisors.

Prognosis

A massive movement is under way to revise the system of separating planning from execution. The new concept is to delegate more and more of the planning to the supervisors and the nonsupervisory personnel. This new concept is inherently sound, and the movement is destined to spread throughout the economy.

We are still in the early stages of this massive movement. A number of substantial companies have tried to apply this concept to their operations, but their efforts during the 1980s did not result in establishing a widely accepted approach. This failure to secure wide acceptance seems to be traceable to the methods of application rather than to deficiencies in the basic concept. However, the methods of application can be improved. The feedbacks from the applications made to date have provided specific suggestions on what to do in order to make the improvements.

In the opinion of the authors, this massive movement is irreversible. The companies will continue their efforts to delegate more and more of the planning to the lower levels. As they do, they will improve their methods of application and will secure results that will stimulate more and more companies to do the same.

Analysis of the Microprocess: By Whom?

This analysis involves some time-consuming tasks: filling out questionnaires, contacting those who are impacted, preparing the flow diagrams and spreadsheets, collecting and summing up the available data, tracking down other needed data, and more.

Various options are available for getting this work done. We shall now look at several of these options.

Full-time Analysts

In this approach a full-time analyst (systems analyst, quality engineer, procedures analyst, industrial engineer, or other) is assigned to conduct the analysis. The analyst:

"Makes the rounds" to interview the cognizant people—managers, supervisors, workers

Prepares the flow diagrams and other aids to collecting and presenting information

Collects and summarizes the pertinent data

Prepares a report, including recommendations for revisions

For the line supervisor, use of a full-time analyst helps to solve the problem of finding the time to do the analysis. However, this approach has deficiencies, which some companies are no longer willing to accept:

The approach retains much of the concept of separating planning from execution. This concept is increasingly out of date at departmental levels.

The analysts exhibit the biases inherent in *their* culture. These biases then enter their recommendations.

Use of full-time analysts tend to assign "ownership" of the process to the analysts, rather than to the line personnel.

Lack of participation in the analysis reduces the line supervisors' willingness to support the resulting recommendations.

The Departmental Supervisor

In this approach the supervisor of the microprocess is given a "do-it-yourself" responsibility to get the analysis done. The supervisors are assisted by a manual such as "Departmental Quality Analysis."

The strengths and weaknesses of this approach have already been discussed.

Teams of Supervisors

Under this concept a team is organized, consisting of the supervisor of a microprocess plus other supervisors who are customers and suppliers. This team is assigned to do the analysis and replanning. This assignment is preceded by training in how to plan for quality.

Use of these supervisory teams has the potential to:

Arm the supervisors with the tools and skills of quality planning

Increase the supervisors' sense of participation in quality planning

Increase the supervisors' sense of "ownership" of the process

Minimize the effect of biases of full-time planners

Increase the willingness of customers and suppliers to support the recommendations of the analysis

The big disadvantage of using supervisory teams is the time it takes. Multiple people (teams) must do what could be done by one trained individual. In addition, this added work is often superimposed on the time of people who are already carrying a full-time load.

We do know that as the line supervisors acquire experience in use of the quality planning tools they become more proficient. But to reach a state of proficiency does require finding the time to participate in the work of the teams.

Teams That Include Nonsupervisors

The "massive movement" to revise the system of separating planning from execution includes a movement to enable workers to participate in decisions that impact on their jobs. A potential form of such participation is membership on teams set up to replan processes. The premises are that:

All workers have intimate knowledge of job conditions and are therefore able to make useful contributions to such teams.

These contributions can include identification of problems, theories of causes, and suggestions for remedy.

Many workers want to contribute.

Such contributions increase worker morale, provide a sense of ownership, and improve management–worker relations generally.

To date, organized methods to provide for worker participation have consisted largely of:

Provision for *individual* contribution through methods such as suggestion systems

Provision for *group* contribution by *teams of workers* through methods such as QC Circles (for elaboration, see below, under "Quality Planning by QC Circles")

Redesign of jobs (see below, under "Methodology for Participation in Quality Planning")

These methods have been widely tested, so that their strengths and weaknesses are well known. What has not been widely tested is "mixed" teams composed of both supervisors and workers. During the 1980s some companies did experiment with such teams. Those experiments were comparatively few in number, and the results did not lead to a clear consensus as to the effectiveness of this type of team structure. As of the early 1990s "the jury was still out."

The End Result of the Analysis

When done systematically, the end result of the analysis is an information package consisting of:

The conclusions reached by the analysis

Proposals (recommendations) relative to products, processes, inputs, etc.

Supporting information: flow diagram, spreadsheets, data, etc.

The proposals are generally presented in the standard formats used in the company.

Some of the proposals concern matters over which the microprocess itself has full jurisdiction. In such cases the departmental supervisor can adopt them forthwith. Other proposals require concurrence by or action from other departments. Such proposals then require follow-up until (a) the recommended action is taken, (b) the recommendation is modified, or (c) there is a decision by cognizant authorities not to adopt the proposals.

Workers and Quality Planning

The "massive movement" to revise the system of separating planning from execution is strongly supported by some powerful social forces. These forces have been urging and even demanding that workers participate fully in matters that affect them. Many companies have taken notice of these social forces. Some of these companies have published policies proclaiming their "partnership" with workers and emphasizing "people programs."

Who Are Workers?

As used here, "workers" includes all nonsupervisory employees except "knowledge workers" in the "professional" specialties. Under this definition "workers" includes administrative and support personnel as well as operating personnel. (The dividing line between workers and "management" is not precise, and there are borderline cases.)

(Note that as we abandon the Taylor System and adopt such forms as self-supervising teams, more and more "workers" are becoming "knowledge workers.")

The Roles of Workers

Workers are impacted by every one of the processes of the Juran Trilogy, though in varying degrees. Among these processes, the dominant quality-related responsibility of workers has been in *operation and control*—to run the processes according to the prescribed procedures, and to produce products that meet customer needs and/or quality goals. In view of this dominance, we shall start our examination of "Workers and Quality Planning" by looking at the role of workers in the quality *control* process. After that we shall look at other quality-related contributions of workers. Then, in the next chapter, we shall look at (a) the motivation to make the contributions, and (b) the training required to be able to make the contributions.

Workers and the Feedback Loop

In Chapter 8 we saw that control is carried out by use of the feedback loop, as depicted in Figure 8-2, which is reproduced here for convenience as Figure 11-5.

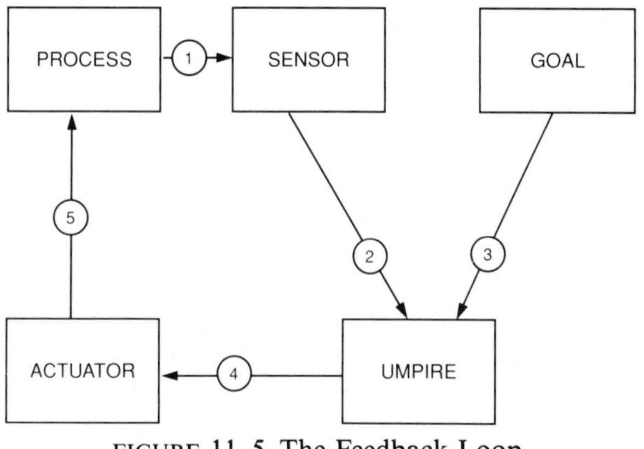

FIGURE 11-5 The Feedback Loop

As discussed in Chapter 8, most control is carried out by nonhuman means. There remain the human controls, most of which are delegated to workers. Such delegation is the ideal response to the prevailing social forces. Under this ideal arrangement, workers carry out all the repetitive roles within the feedback loop: sensor, umpire, actuator. Such delegation provides benefits for managers as well as workers:

A shorter feedback loop and therefore an earlier response to quality problems

A greater sense of participation and ownership by workers

Relief of managers from much delegable work

Before making such delegation it is essential to meet certain criteria—criteria for self-control and for self-inspection. These criteria are discussed below.

Workers and Self-control

The extent of delegation of control to a worker depends on the extent to which the worker is in a state of self-control. The criteria for self-control were set out in Chapter 8 under the heading "Self-control." Applied to the worker level, self-control requires that the worker be provided with:

The means for knowing what the quality goals are. This criterion is met by providing the worker with specifications, procedures, etc.

The means for knowing what the actual performance is. This criterion is met by providing the worker with a system of measurement.

The means for changing the performance in the event of nonconformance. This criterion is met by providing the worker with a process that is (a) inherently capable of meeting the quality goals and (b) provided with features that enable the worker to readjust the process as needed to bring it into conformance.

These criteria are directly related to the various elements of the feedback loop. The extent to which control can be assigned to workers is determined, in each case, by comparing (a) the activities performed within each element of the feedback loop with (b) the extent to which the criteria for self-control have been met for the respective elements.

For example, there are many cases in which the measuring instruments used to evaluate quality are not physically located in the producing department; the instruments are located in a separate laboratory. To evaluate quality the workers must send samples to the laboratory and wait for the results. During this waiting time self-control is incomplete, because the workers lack the means for knowing what the actual performance is.

Workers and Process Control

The generalized approach to process control is set out in Chapter 8 under the headings "Design for Process Control" and "Stages of Process Control." At the worker level, process control consists of a series of actions and decisions that exhibit a high degree of commonality despite wide differences in the technology. These decisions and actions are essentially as follows:

1. *Setup.* This action consists of assembling the information, materials, equipment, etc., needed to commence operations, and organizing them into a state of readiness to produce.
   In many cases the work of setup is assigned to the workers. If the workers lack the necessary training, the work of setup is done by setup specialists or by the supervisor.
2. *Verify setup.* This action is control-oriented. It consists of determining (evaluating) whether the process, if allowed to run, will produce good work. The evaluation may be done directly

on the process (checklist, countdown, etc). Alternatively, the evaluation may be done on the product, e.g., the printer's page proof (the product "tells on the process").
Assignment of responsibility for verifying the setup depends on the criticality of the operation, the training of the workers, the priority given to quality, etc. In many cases the workers verify their own setup. If not, the verification is usually done by the supervisor or by an inspector.

3. *Startup or not?* This decision is guided by the results of the evaluation made to verify the setup. The evaluation is largely factual: Is there conformance to the quality goals or not? The resulting decision is nevertheless influenced by other factors: the priority given to quality, the capability of the process, the pressure of the schedule, the effort and delay involved in revising the setup, etc. Whether to assign this decision to the workers depends in large part on the extent to which these factors are influential.
4. *Produce.* This is the familiar central action of conducting operations—running the process and producing the product. This action is almost always assigned to the workers.
5. *Reverify.* This control-oriented action is taken periodically to ensure that the process remains in a state of readiness to produce in accordance with the quality goals. This action is usually assigned to the workers.
6. *Continue to run, or stop?* This decision ("running control") is based on the results of reverification. Some of the criteria are identical with those of the "startup or not" decision. For mass production processes, this cycle (of reverify and decision making) is repeated over and over again. The assignment of this decision parallels the pattern followed above in "3. Startup or not?"

Workers and Product Control: Self-inspection

The above process control activities collectively result in producing the product. In a sense, the worker controls the process while the process produces the product. Once the product has been produced, several new questions arise:

1. Does the product conform to the product quality goals?

To answer this question requires determination of the facts: evaluate the product quality, compare the evaluation with the product quality goals, and judge whether there is conformance.

In many cases the workers can be trained to make this final determination. However, experience has shown that some workers exhibit biases due to the pressure of competing goals, conflicting signals from their superiors, and so forth. As a result, many companies in the United States do not assign this product conformance decision to be made by the workers. Instead, they assign the decision to be made by independent inspectors.

It *is* feasible to assign this decision to the workers, but only if the company first meets the essential criteria:

Quality really is the top priority goal.

There is an atmosphere of mutual confidence between the management and the workers.

There is a state of self-control.

Once these criteria have been met, it is usually feasible to train the workers to be able to make the conformance decision, subject to periodic audit.

2. What disposition should be made of conforming products? (As always, "products" includes services as well as goods.)

The universal rule is that products that have been judged (by an unbiased umpire) to conform to the quality goals should be sent on to the next destination. (It is assumed that the goals reflect customer needs). Note that this rule is not made by the inspectors; it is a policy established by management.

3. What disposition should be made of nonconforming products—products that do not conform to the product quality goals? This is the "fitness for use" decision, and is quite different from the "conformance" decision.

Some nonconforming products are clearly also unfit for use. So they are sent back to be redone, or they may be discarded.

Other nonconforming products may be usable despite their nonconformance: some applications are less demanding than others, the customer's need for prompt delivery may be acute, the economics may favor use as is, the goals may have been needlessly severe, and so on. It is evident that the fitness for use decision is of a multifunctional nature, requiring inputs and judgments from multiple functions. A common practice is to create a multifunctional team—a "Material Review Board"—to collect the data and to make the decision.

Who Is the Umpire?

While the situations discussed above all make use of the feedback loop, they differ with respect to who makes the decisions and takes the actions. The principal difference is in who the umpire is. In the above situations the umpire is commonly as follows:

Situation	*Umpire*
Setup control	Setup specialist Supervisor Worker
Running control	Worker
Conformance decision	Inspector
Fitness for use decision	Material Review Board

Tasks for Sensors and Umpires

During the operation of the feedback loop the roles of sensors and umpires include various tasks which provide inputs to decision making. These tasks include:

DATA COLLECTING AND PROCESSING. The starting point is the measurements and observations made by technological and human sensors. The resulting data undergo processing to provide information for decision making. At the lower levels this information is often on a real-time basis and is used for current control. At higher levels the information is summarized in various ways to provide broader measure, to detect trends, and to identify the vital few problems.

There is additional need to define who does what: who is to interpret the data; who is to determine what actions to take; who is to take the actions. In large organizations it is quite common to divide such responsibilities among different functions and levels.

INTERPRETATION OF "STATISTICAL SIGNIFICANCE." In some cases the data are conclusive on what action should be taken. In other cases there is need for interpretation. A frequent problem is to decide whether an observed difference is the result of:

a. a real change in the product or process
b. an apparent change—a false alarm, arising from chance variation

This problem was discussed in Chapter 8, under "Design for Evaluation of Performance," "Interpretation" and "Statistical Significance.'' That same discussion describes the use of the Shewhart Control Chart as a continuing test of statistical significance.

INTERPRETATION OF ECONOMIC SIGNIFICANCE. Ideally all real changes should stimulate prompt action to restore the status quo. In practice some real changes do not result in such action. The usual reason is that the indicated changes have appeared in such numbers that the available personnel cannot deal with all of them. Hence priorities are established based on economic significance or on other criteria of importance. Some changes at low levels of priority may wait a long time for corrective action.

INTERPRETATION OF TRENDS AND IDENTIFICATION OF THE VITAL FEW PROBLEMS. Discovery of trends is a useful aid to decision making. Trends are ''leading indicators'' that help to predict future events. Graphic methods such as cumulative sum charts are available to assist in detecting trends. The cumulative sum chart is more sensitive to trends than the control chart but is slower to detect sudden shifts.

Numerous other types of analysis are used to aid interpretation. One of the most common is the familiar Pareto analysis used to separate the vital few problems from the rest. Correlation analysis can be used to discover relationships among variables. And so on. We shall look at some of the principal tools of analysis in Chapter 12.

The above tasks may be assigned to workers, provided (a) the prerequisite criteria have been met and (b) the workers have been trained in the methodology.

The Shortest Feedback

The shortest feedback takes place when the worker is able to close both the process control loop and the product control loop. In such situations the worker is in a state of self-control and a state of self-inspection as well. Dr. A. Blanton Godfrey (the CEO of Juran Institute, Inc.) illustrates the opportunity for short feedback by a case example out of his experience.

Dr. Godfrey was observing a worker who produced reels of product, which were then sent on to an inspector. The inspector measured each reel and made the judgment on whether the reel conformed to the product specification. Conforming reels were sent on to store. Nonconforming reels were thrown into a reject bin. For each nonconforming reel the inspector made an entry in a data sheet. The following dialogue between Dr. Godfrey and the inspector ensued:

DR. G: What are you recording on that sheet?

I: I record the type of defect I found.

DR. G: What do you do with the data sheet?

I: At the end of the day, a quality engineer picks it up and takes it away.

Next, Dr. Godfrey hunted up the quality engineer (QE) and talked with him.

DR. G: What do you do with those data sheets?

QE: I prepare a weekly summary.

DR. G: What happens to the summary?

QE: I send it to the Assistant Quality Manager.

Next, Dr. Godfrey talked to the Assistant Quality Manager (AQM).

DR. G: What do you do with that engineer's report?

AQM: I bring it up at the biweekly staff meeting.

DR. G: What happens at that meeting?

AQM: The report is discussed, and if the situation is serious enough, someone will be assigned to do something about it.

In this case the worker was not in a state of self-inspection, since the product conformance decision was in the hands of the inspector. Neither was the worker in a state of self-control, since he lacked the means of measuring the product. The data feedback went through a lengthy series of "handoffs":

Inspector to quality engineer

Quality engineer to assistant quality manager

Assistant quality manager to staff meeting

Staff meeting (maybe) to production supervisor

Production supervisor to worker

During all this time the process continued to produce much nonconforming product.

A much shorter feedback loop would have resulted if the inspector were to inform the worker then and there of the types of defects being encountered. (The worker did have the means to revise the process and thereby to take corrective action). It might have been feasible to go still further and provide the worker with the means for measurement. That would have put the worker into a state of self-control.

In sand casting foundries it is necessary to maintain the density of the sand at a specified level to ensure the quality of the molds and the resulting castings. Sand testing was done by sending a sample to the laboratory to measure the density. The test results became available to the foundry about two hours later. Meanwhile the sand was being used to make molds. A team of workers then came up with a much simpler test, which could be made in a matter of seconds, right on the work floor. The results of the simple test correlated closely with the laboratory test results. The workers attained self-control by providing a "real-time" test on the work floor.

Building the Feedback Loop

To build the feedback loop at the worker level requires a structure to make the concept a reality. A great deal of experience is available to guide the planning of this structure.

Lessons from the Artisan/Craftsman

From the standpoint of achieving quality, the ideal arrangement is an autonomous process. This ideal is largely attained in the case of the artisan. The popular image of an artisan is someone who underwent an apprenticeship and thereby became qualified to practice a skilled trade as a village craftsman, e.g., cooper, shoemaker. Such craftsmen still abound. However, many artisans are now employed within organizations, as workers. Their occupations have such names as computer programmer, maintenance mechanic, field service representative, and toolmaker.

To build quality, the village craftsman was aided greatly by his intimate knowledge of customer needs. Not only did he sell his products directly to the market, but as he performed the numerous sequential tasks within his trade *he was his own customer, over and over again*.

One of the by-products of separating planning from execution is that workers become insulated from intimate knowledge of customer needs. Nevertheless, these workers need guidance as to what quality goals they are to reach. That guidance is supplied through a kind of substitute knowledge consisting of specifications, standards, procedures, and so on. Of course, the substitute is not as good as the real thing.

Work Stations, Control Stations, and Spreadsheets

At the worker level, work is organized by:

Work stations, which carry out the prescribed operations of running the processes and producing the products

Control stations, which are quality-oriented and carry out the remaining steps within the feedback loop

In the ideal situation the control station is identical with the work station, that is, the workers who conduct operations also carry out the quality controls. However, operation and control are different *functions*. The difference can be seen by comparing the respective spreadsheets. A generic spreadsheet for operations (sometimes called route sheet, etc.) is shown in Figure 11–6.

In Figure 11–6 the horizontal rows show the operation steps (tasks, etc.) to be performed and the sequence to be followed. The vertical columns contain information pertinent to performing the operations: specifications to be met; procedures to follow; equipment, tools, and instruments to use; and so forth.

A generic spreadsheet for quality control is shown in Figure 11–7.

In Figure 11–7 the horizontal rows are "control subjects"—various product and process features for which quality goals have been set. The vertical columns contain information relative to elements of the feedback loop: the quality goals, the units of measure, the means for sensing, the measurement plan (e.g., size of sample, frequency of sampling, data to be recorded and analyzed), and criteria for judging conformance (for a specific example, see Chapter 8, Figure 8–4).

SEQUENCE OF OPERATIONS	PRODUCT SPECIFICATIONS	PROCESS SPECIFICATION	PROCEDURES, CAUTIONS	EQUIPMENT, FACILITIES	TOOLS	INSTRUMENTS	DATA REQUIREMENTS	DECISION CRITERIA	
1.									
2.									
3.									
4.									
5.									
6.									

FIGURE 11–6 Generic Spreadsheet for Planning of Operations

CONTROL SUBJECTS	QUALITY GOALS	UNITS OF MEASURE	SENSORS	EQUIPMENT, FACILITIES	SAMPLE SIZE	FREQUENCY OF SAMPLE	DATA REQUIREMENTS	DECISION CRITERIA	
1.									
2.									
3.									
4.									
5.									
6.									

FIGURE 11-7 Generic Spreadsheet for Planning of Quality Controls

Workers and the Triple Role

At the worker level, the basic quality planning model is the TRIPROL diagram, Figure 1-12, reproduced earlier for convenience as Figure 11-2.

Each worker plays all the roles of the TRIPROL model: customer, processor, and supplier. However, in many job situations the workers have not thought of their jobs as consisting of those three roles.

> An internal survey conducted by one public utility found that only 25 percent of the workers recognized the fact that they had customers.

Such findings are to be expected in situations where planning has been cleanly separated from operations. It is common in such cases for workers to perceive their role as a matter of following procedures and meeting the goals. With that perception, it is understandable if workers conclude that:

> The inputs (procedures, goals, facilities, data, materials) are determined and fixed during the planning.
>
> The role of the worker is to conduct the process so as to conform to procedures and specified goals.
>
> The product is "conformance."

The customer is the supervisor/company.

If we redraw the TRIPROL diagram according to these perceptions, the result is something like Figure 11–8.

Figure 11–8 shows that the planners are perceived as the prime suppliers for the planning inputs, consisting of specifications, procedures, and quality goals. These same planning inputs are regarded as rigid and sacred—only the planners may change them. Other suppliers provide subsequent and continuing inputs: the data, materials, and so on, which become the grist for the processing mill. These inputs do vary, and the workers have a degree of responsibility to cope with these variations as well as with variations inherent in the processing facility.

Turning to the output side of Figure 11–8, the product is perceived as consisting of "conformance" to those specifications, procedures, and quality goals. The customer includes the supervisor and/or the company, but not subsequent users. These perceptions are reinforced if workers are kept out of the mainstream of feedback from customers to the process. The perceptions are further reinforced if the workers are kept out of the mainstream of feedback from the process to suppliers.

Some companies do provide workers with opportunities for direct feedback from customers. When customers come to visit the company, they are encouraged to talk with the workers who make the products. In other cases workers are sent to visit customer facilities and to talk there with the users of the products (Peters, 1987, p. 166).

Suppliers	*Inputs*	*Process*	*Outputs*	*Customers Visible* / *Other*
Planners	Goals Procedures Specs		Conformance to: goals, procedures, specs	Supervisor
		Worker		Company
Other suppliers	Facilities Materials Etc.			

FIGURE 11–8 TRIPROL Diagram as Perceived by Some Workers

Methodology for Participation in Planning

For workers to participate in quality planning requires creating a methodology as well as providing the opportunity. Such has been the pattern in the other processes of the Trilogy:

> In the case of quality control, the Statistical Process Control (SPC) movement has trained many workers in how to apply basic statistical tools to strengthen quality controls.
>
> In the case of quality improvement, the QC Circle concept has enabled many teams of workers to make improvements on job-related matters.

Job Redesign as an Option

Another approach to worker participation in quality planning is to redesign jobs in ways that bring the worker closer to the status of artisan. The artisan is solidly involved in quality planning through (a) direct exposure to the needs of various customers and (b) being his own customer, over and over again. The opportunity for such redesign of jobs is largely traceable to the rise in education levels since the days of Frederick W. Taylor.

In most cases it is not feasible to go to a full artisan concept; the damage to such parameters as cost and productivity is too great. So there is much groping and some experimentation. The job designs undergoing test have included:

JOB ENLARGEMENT—HORIZONTAL. Under this concept jobs of a repetitive short-cycle content are converted into jobs of broader scope. A factory assembly line is redesigned to enable each worker to perform multiple tasks—even to assemble units of product completely. Similar job enlargements have been carried out in the office.

> In the telephone directory case, the work had been done as a procession of twenty-one different short-cycle tasks. After redesign, each worker performed all twenty-one tasks to produce a complete directory. In such job redesigns the workers become their own customers, over and over again, leading to easier identification of deficiencies in quality planning.

JOB ENLARGEMENT—VERTICAL. In this approach the worker is assigned multiple *functions*. For example, a production worker may be made responsible for material supply, tool maintenance, judgment of product conformance, and so on. Such job designs bring the worker into quality planning of a multifunctional nature.

In one company (Peters, 1987, p. 291), the assigned responsibilities of production workers include many functions, with associated planning:

Quality control	Safety
Budget preparation	Planning for staffing
Timekeeping	Recruitment
Housekeeping	Layoffs
Maintenance	Work team leadership
Proposals for equipment	Problem solving

SELF-SUPERVISING TEAMS. This is a form of job enlargement both horizontal and vertical. An added significant feature is that the teams are largely self-supervising. The team decides which workers are to perform which operations. The team also takes on multiple functions. The need for quality planning is extensive, and the team participates actively in such planning.

> Two examples of such self-supervising teams were set out in Chapter 7 under the heading "The Anatomy of Processes: Revisions in Process Anatomy."
>
> In each case the process for preparing insurance policies was redesigned to be run by self-supervising teams of workers. In each case there were dramatic improvements in productivity and in the time required to issue policies (see Bowen, 1986; and Hoerr, 1988).

"New Work Systems"

The term "new work systems" is used in some companies to describe a planning approach that focuses on creating self-regulating work systems involving little or no management and very few specialists. Under this concept workers are paid according to skills attained rather than according to job classification or seniority. Workers within these systems schedule their own work times, shift assignments, job assignments, and vacations.

Within these systems are ongoing teams, which review the social structure as well as the technology.

For example, in one chemicals company a "design team" of sixteen workers from a 180-person department met weekly to design new or improved production systems. Their technical review covered ten key unit processes (microprocesses). They identified seventy-two possible variances in these areas. They then built an impact matrix to determine the effect of these variances downstream. They developed flow diagrams and decision trees for control of the key variances. All this resulted in twelve recommendations for changes in manufacturing technology.

Their social review involved questionnaires and interviews for each of the 180 employees. These resulted in five recommendations for changes in job design or organization design.

Obstacles to Worker Participation in Quality Planning

The obstacles to bringing workers actively into the quality planning process are similar to those set out below under the heading "Quality Planning and Improvement by QC Circles: Vested Interests." Overcoming these obstacles is not done simply by logical reasoning. What is decisive is the results achieved during field tests of the concept of worker participation in quality planning.

Quality Planning and Improvement by QC Circles

A QC Circle is a volunteer group of workers who have undergone training for the purpose of solving work-related problems.

Quality planning by workers has been largely done through use of QC Circles. Many of these circles have tackled projects to replan departmental processes. These projects have demonstrated that most workers have the education, job knowledge, and creativity to be able to contribute to quality planning if the opportunity is provided.

To solve work-related problems, the QC Circles employ the same project-by-project approach as is used by managerial project teams. However, there are important differences, and these are summarized in Figure 11-9.

The Contrast: Japan and the United States

The growth patterns of QC Circles in Japan and the United States exhibit striking differences, and much can be learned from the rea-

Feature	*QC Circles*	*Quality Improvement Teams*
Primary result	To improve human relations	To improve quality
Secondary result	To improve quality	To improve participation
Scope of project	Within a single department	Multidepartmental
Size of project	One of the useful many	One of the vital few
Membership	From a single department	From multiple departments
Basis of membership	Voluntary	Mandatory
Hierarchical status of members	Typically in the work force	Typically managerial or professional
Continuity	Circle remains intact, project after project	Team is *ad hoc*, disbands after project is completed

FIGURE 11–9 Contrast: QC Circles and Project Teams

sons behind these differences. Figures 11–10a and 11–10b show these contrasting patterns.

In Japan the QC Circles started in 1962. The numbers have been growing ever since: circles, workers, and projects completed. In the

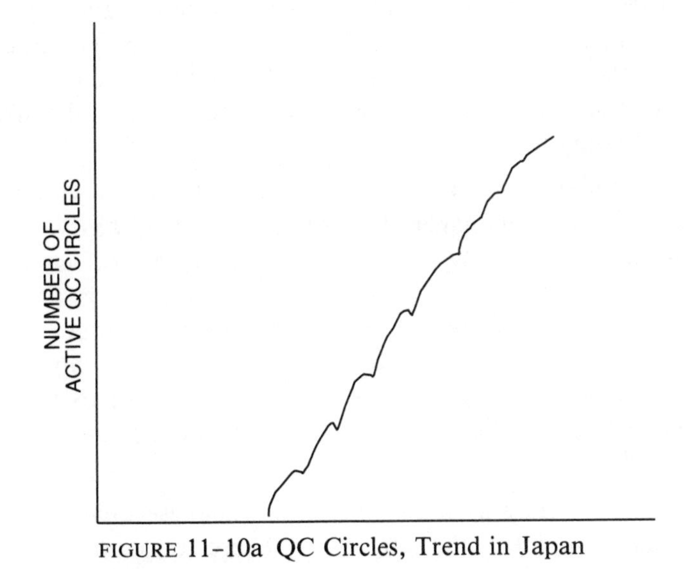

FIGURE 11–10a QC Circles, Trend in Japan

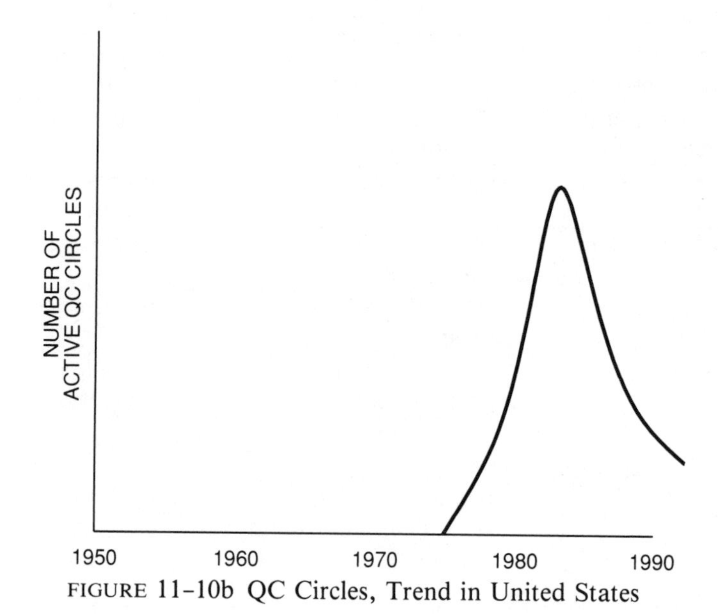

FIGURE 11-10b QC Circles, Trend in United States

United States QC Circles started in the late 1970s, underwent an explosive growth, and then declined just as precipitously. The difference in these growth patterns appear to be traceable to three major factors (Juran 1987):

1. *The conceptual approach.* In Japan the QC Circle concept was viewed as an extension of the efforts made during the 1950s to improve quality by managerial means. By 1962 it seemed logical to extend QC training to workers and to use teams of workers to achieve further improvements, as well as to broaden the extent of worker participation in the affairs of the company.

In the United States the QC Circle concept was not viewed as an extension of prior managerial activity. Instead, it was viewed as a separate entity with its own purposes: (a) to improve human relations by providing a new form of worker participation and (b) to solve the companies' quality problems. (In those days many upper managers believed that the prime cause of poor quality was the workers.)

The participation feature proved to be attractive to the media. They gave much publicity to the QC Circle concept, and this publicity then stimulated a rapid growth rate.

2. *Prior training of managers.* The Japanese quality crisis became evident in the late 1940s. There followed more than a

decade of massive training of the Japanese management hierarchy in how to manage for quality. By 1962, when the QC Circle movement was launched, the Japanese managers and supervisors were qualified to direct the QC Circles into productive channels. They did not delegate this direction to "facilitators" or outsiders.

In contrast, most U.S. companies were not faced with a quality crisis until the middle 1970s. At that time U.S. managers had not yet undergone extensive training in managing for quality. The QC Circle concept was attractive to them, but they lacked the training needed to guide the QC Circle movement. They chose to delegate the direction to facilitators and consultants. This delegation bypassed the supervisory structure, leading to much confusion and resentment.

3. *Coordination and guidance.* In Japan the QC Circle movement was from the outset coordinated by the Japanese Union of Scientists and Engineers (JUSE). JUSE prepared the training materials, provided the seed training courses, provided consulting assistance, organized conferences, published the leading papers, set up the award system, and so forth.

In the United States there was little such central coordination and guidance during the formative years. The absence of such coordination and guidance probably was a factor in the subsequent decline of the movement.

QC Circle Methodology

A good deal of experience has been accumulated with respect to the operation of QC Circles:

Worker participation in QC Circles is on a voluntary basis.

Facilitators/trainers are provided to assist the teams.

Training is provided for the supervisors and facilitators as well as for team members.

Nominations for projects may come from either workers or managers.

Choice of projects is a matter of agreement between the QC Circle and management.

Projects are selected so as to be closely related to the regular jobs of the QC Circle members (workers are regarded as experts on their jobs).

Training and project work are carried out on company time.

Recommendations of the team must be acceptable to management before they are made effective.

QC Circles and Errorproofing

QC Circles have been very effective in eliminating low-incidence defects by replanning the process to make it errorproof. Projects to eliminate such low-incidence defects seldom receive the priority required for assignment to a team of managers and engineers. However, many such projects have been successfully undertaken by QC Circles.

> In a task requiring the tightening of eighteen bolts, the workers occasionally missed one or more of the bolts. A QC Circle came up with a concept of enabling the process to count the number of bolts tightened, and to sound the alarm if any had been missed.

Some of these errorproofing projects require revision of the facilities (as in the case of tightening the bolts). In such cases the QC Circle needs assistance from the managers. The communication linkage may be through the departmental supervisor or the facilitator.

> Low-incidence defects also take place in the office. An obvious example is misspelling of words. The overall error rate is usually low, and it is spread over many different words. Nevertheless, human minds have found a solution: a computer memory that can be used to check the spelling of words within sizable manuscripts.

(For additional discussion on errorproofing, see Chapter 7, under the heading "Design to Reduce Human Error." See also Nakajo and Kume, 1985.)

Vested Interests

Much has also been learned about the major vested interests that underlie the cultural resistance to use of QC Circles:

Managers remain concerned about losing "prerogatives" and about the relative value of employee time spent on projects versus time spent producing the product.

Staff specialists face competition in planning and analysis—a threat to the near-monopoly they have enjoyed under the Taylor system.

Workers are concerned with threats to their job security and with extra rewards for project work.

Unions are wary of shifting employee loyalty from the union to the company.

Prognosis

The present trend is clearly to train all managers in how to manage for quality. It will take at least a decade for the majority of managers in the company hierarchies to acquire this training and then to acquire experience in its use. That same trend will, as a by-product, qualify the managers to guide the application of QC Circles in their companies. As all this proceeds, it is quite likely that a revival of interest in QC Circles will emerge.

Workers and Quality Improvement

As used here, "improvement" is defined as organized creation of beneficial change or attainment of unprecedented levels of performance. The general approach to quality improvement is described in the references listed for this chapter.

Quality improvement is closely linked to quality planning. (See Chapter 1, under "The Juran Trilogy" and "Quality Planning Distinguished from Quality Improvement.") The tools of analysis have much in common. For many quality improvement projects, the remedy consists of replanning the product/process. Essentially:

> Quality improvement is concerned with solving existing chronic quality problems, while quality planning is concerned with shutting down the hatchery that creates those problems in the first place.

Forms of Worker Participation

Under the Taylor system, workers had no responsibility for contributing to improving quality or improving anything else. Volunteered improvements would benefit the company but not necessarily the workers. Sometimes they would be detrimental to the workers. Over the decades this lack of responsibility hardened into a tradition.

For example, a foundry worker had the job of filing off a bump that was present on each casting—the same bump, in the same place, on every casting. The worker's job was one of control. The piece part drawing showed no bump, so the bump had to be removed.

In due course someone raised the question: Why is the bump there in the first place? Why not change the casting pattern so that there is no bump to be removed? Those questions led to changes in the pattern, to elimination of the bump on the castings, and elimination of the filing operation.

Note that from the perception of the worker, an initiative to question the reason for the presence of the bump might well lead to results as follows:

A cost reduction for the company

A threat to the worker's job security

During this century companies have tested out various ways to secure quality improvement from workers. These have included:

REWARDS AND PENALTIES. Under this approach the worker's pay is directly affected, up or down, by the quality of the work produced. Early in the century this method was used in some factories as an adjunct to piecework pay systems. The method aroused criticism on the ground that many defects were outside the control of the workers. Following passage of the National Labor Relations Act (Wagner), such methods of rewards and penalties were essentially abolished and have not been reinstated.

DRIVES, EXHORTATIONS, PLEDGE CARDS. These approaches were widely used in recent decades in an effort to induce workers to produce higher quality. A major underlying premise was that the workers were in a state of self-control. Where this premise was invalid (as it usually was), the drive could lead to an atmosphere of unwarranted blame. The recent trend has been toward approaches based on factual analysis.

JOB ENLARGEMENT. (See above, under the heading "Methodology for Participation in Planning: Job Redesign as an Option".)

SUGGESTION SYSTEMS. In this well-known approach, workers are urged to propose improvements of all sorts, including quality improvements. The systems always provide for recognition and rewards.

It takes a good deal of work to administer a suggestion system. Most suggestions are of limited significance, yet they must be investigated and answered. As a result many suggestion systems have been abandoned as not cost-effective. However, in some companies these systems continue to thrive. Proponents contend that suggestion systems have intrinsic merit because they provide workers with an opportunity to participate in creative activity. Proponents also contend that the systems are cost-effective if well managed.

PROJECT-BY-PROJECT IMPROVEMENT. At the worker level, project-by-project improvement has been carried out largely through QC Circles. (See above, under "Quality Planning and Improvement by QC Circles".) For information on how to introduce project-by-project improvement into a going company, and on the methodology and tools, see the references for this chapter.

Potential Roles

Workers have considerable potential to assist in the various tasks of the quality improvement process. The extent of this assistance varies from task to task. It also varies depending on whether the scope of the project is within a single department or is multidepartmental. Figure 11-11 lists some of the steps of the quality improvement process, along with the usual potential contribution by the work force.

Extent of Contribution to Quality Improvement Projects:		
Nature of Contribution	*Departmental*	*Interdepartmental*
Identify problems	+	+
Describe symptoms	+	+
Theorize as to causes	+	+
Test theories by data collection and analysis	+	
Identify cause	+	
Propose remedy	+	+
Design remedy	+	
Install remedy	+	
Test remedy	+	+
Establish controls	+	+
Legend: Strong + + Moderate +		

FIGURE 11-11 Work Force Contribution to Quality Improvement Projects

On to Chapter 12

Chapter 12 takes up several topics that are critical to all planning: the data base, motivation, and training.

List of High Points

In Frederick W. Taylor's view, the supervisors and workers of his era lacked the education needed to plan how work should be done. Taylor's solution was: Separate planning from execution.

The Taylor system was probably the chief reason for the U.S. rise to the position of world leader in productivity.

Creation of independent inspection departments (later Quality Control departments) stimulated a widespread belief that responsibility for quality rested with the Quality Department.

The Taylor System has become so obsolete that it should be replaced, but there is a lack of agreement on what should replace it.

Microprocesses are so numerous that the upper managers cannot become involved with them individually.

The triple role concept is applicable to any organization entity.

Replanning of the microprocesses seldom solves the major problems of the macroprocess.

A massive movement is under way to revise the system of separating planning from execution.

This massive movement is irreversible.

Lack of participation in the analysis of microprocesses reduces the line supervisors' willingness to support the resulting recommendations.

The dominant quality-related responsibility of workers has been in operation and control.

The extent of delegation of control to a worker depends on the extent to which the worker is fully in a state of self-control.

The shortest feedback takes place when the worker is able to close both the process control loop and the product control loop.

From the standpoint of achieving quality, the ideal arrangement is an autonomous process.

In the ideal situation the control station is identical with the work station.

Tasks for Upper Managers

Upper managers should face up to the question of whether to take positive steps to replace the Taylor System.

Upper managers should determine whether to take an initiative to provide supervisors with a structured approach for analyzing microprocesses.

DEPARTMENT ACTIVITY ANALYSIS

page

Function Name	Production Control	
Department Name	Receiving, Administration, Back orders	Dept. No.

GENERAL DESCRIPTION OF WORK PERFORMED WITHIN THIS DEPARTMENT (LISTING MAJOR OR ALL ACTIVITIES):		
Keypunch		
Transaction screening		
Receiving buy / pay parts		
Credit req. activity		
Daily activities report		
Fill back orders		
Type letters		
Drop shipping		
R.O.M. control		
Receiving / Distribution		
Z / A Relations		
Plus and minus transfers		
Manager's Signature	Date	Extension

DEPARTMENT ACTIVITY ANALYSIS

page 2

Function Name	Production Control	
Department Name	Receiving, Administration, Back orders	Dept. No.

Activity: Keypunch	Date:	Prepared by:

INPUT

What:	Unassigned inventory: bulk fill reqs., (+) (-) delta adj. scrap tensions, new vendor P/N's & bal. changes, credit reqs., planned reqs. R.O.M., non-consumptive, header and program
	cards, count cards, loc. changes, grey stripes, + & - transfers, stock receipts
From:	Knitting, sequence area, coordinators, receiving, finished cards, zones

VALUE ADD—WORK ACCOMPLISHED IN DEPT

Why do:	System is updated by the input of keypunched cards. It updates our inventory and vendor inventories
Value added:	The proper punches in the proper fields of each card - necessary to update system
Impact if not done:	Loss of control: physical inventory, unassigned inventories

OUTPUT

What:	Decks of transactions sorted by the header and loader cards submitted daily through screening
To:	Receiving, knitting

DEPARTMENT ACTIVITY ANALYSIS page

Function Name	Production Control	
Department Name	Receiving, Administration, Back orders	Dept. No.

Activity: Keypunch	Date:	Prepared by:

What are the input requirements that you and your supplier have agreed to?:
Correct cards used for various types of activities
All input fields correctly filled out (zero defects)
No missing information
All schedules for data input strictly adhered to

What are the output requirements that you and your customer have agreed to?:
All transactions punched with zero errors
All schedule for data output strictly adhered to
All transactions have proper TX codes

What are the quality measurements that will show if your output meets requirements?:
Tracking of.............Schedules
Defective Keyboards
Transaction errors
Turnaround time

How many hours/week are spent on this activity?____________________hours/week
COQ can be further classified into prevention, appraisal, and failure. What are they?

Prevention:______________________hours/week
Appraisal:______________________hours/week
Failure:________________________hours/week
Total COQ ______________________hours/week

] *12* [

The Data Base, Motivation, Training

Purpose of This Chapter

The purpose of this chapter is to explain several matters that are essential to putting quality planning on a structured, participative basis:

Building the *data base* for planners

Motivating the personnel to adopt modern ways of planning for quality

Training the personnel in how to plan for quality

These critical matters are common to all steps of the quality planning road map, to all functions and to all levels of the hierarchy.

The Data Base

A data base is a body of information derived from prior cycles of activity, and organized to aid in the conduct of future cycles.

A good data base is a major resource for planners. The need for this resource is so great that planners in all walks of life devote some of their time to building their data base. The accompanying table shows some examples of data bases.

Planner	*Database*
Housewife	File of recipes
Motorist	Maps
Preparer of bids	File of standard costs for work modules

Planner	*Database*
Scheduler	Timetables; data on past performance
Purchasing manager	Data bank on supplier performance
Product designer	Tables of properties of materials
Process designer	Tables of process capabilities

Data bases are the result of *lessons learned from human experience*. These lessons learned are then stored in memories to be used as needed.

Lessons Learned, and Retrospective Analysis

Lessons learned is a catchall phrase describing what has been learned from experience. In varying degrees, all animal species store their experiences in their memory. Human beings go much further. They extend their memories through records and libraries. Some *analyze the experiences collectively* to discover hidden patterns of meaning. They make the resulting knowledge readily available to future generations through writings and teachings as well as through systems of beliefs, rituals, and taboos. This extensive human use of the concept of lessons learned has been decisive in human dominance over all other animal species. That is an awesome result. It is also a preview of the potential role that lessons learned can play during competition in the marketplace.

The basis of lessons learned is experience, which in turn is made up of prior historical events. Historical events become lessons learned only after they have undergone *retrospective analysis*. It is this analysis that converts those scattered events into useful knowledge. For managers, a major use of such knowledge is to improve decision making.

Sources of Data Bases

All data bases are built up out of knowledge derived from prior events. However, the approaches used to acquire this knowledge and convert it into useable form differ widely, depending on whether:

a. the data base is a by-product of operations, or

b. the data base is a goal in its own right

Alternative (a) is widespread. Any person who performs multiple cycles of repetitive activities runs into obstacles now and then. Some of them are overcome; others are not. Experience accumulates as to what works and what does not. *That experience is a by-product*, which then becomes a part of that person's data base.

Alternative (b) is quite different. It involves activities in which *the purpose is to create a data base.*

Figure 12–1 sets out the critical aspects of construction and use of data bases and the associated consequences under these two alternatives.

The Santayana Review

We need a short name for the process of studying history to derive lessons learned as a basis for decision making. The authors propose

Aspects of Data Base	*Data Base Is a By-product*	*Data Base Is a Goal*
Acquire information on prior cycles of activity	Acquisition is incidental to other purposes	Acquisition is for the purpose of building a data base
Analysis to discover commonalities and other usable relationships	Reliance is on fallible memories and empirical methods	Analysis is structured and methodical; done with scientific tools
Validity of conclusions	Limited for lack of participation and challenges	Likely to be valid owing to scientific approach, participation, and challenges
Conversion into usable guides for decision making	Limited for lack of plan for dissemination	Likely to be converted into usable forms in order to meet the goals of dissemination
Dissemination	Limited; not a goal	Dissemination through publication, training, etc., is part of the original goal
Extent of use	Limited for lack of dissemination and to doubts as to validity	Likely to be used because of prior consensus as to needs, methods, etc.

FIGURE 12–1 Data Base: By-product or Goal?

to call this process *"the Santayana Review."* The philosopher George Santayana once observed:

> Those who cannot remember the past are condemned to repeat it.

That is a terse and accurate expression of the concept of lessons learned through retrospective analysis. Our definition becomes:

> The Santayana Review is the process of deriving lessons learned from analysis of historical events, in order to improve decision making.

The Influence of Cycle Time and Frequency

The extent of use of the Santayana Review has depended largely on:

- The cycle time of the historical events
- The frequency of these same events, which is closely correlated with their cycle time

The influence of these two factors, cycle time and frequency, is best understood by looking at a few examples.

Application to High-Frequency Cycles

High-frequency events abound in companies of all kinds. The associated processes are of a mass production nature, and they process various products:

Industry	*Mass Processing of:*
Banks	Checks
Utilities	Invoices
Factories	Goods
All	Employee payroll checks

The numbers of the resulting cycles can run to millions and even billions annually. Nevertheless, many companies manage to run those processes at low levels of errors. To do so they *study samples* from the processes to learn about the causes of errors, about inherent process capability, and so forth. We saw some examples earlier in this book:

Errors in invoices. An electric power utility produced millions of invoices annually. Each year 60,000 were in error. By tracking a sample of the errors, the company identified the major causes. Remedial action (chiefly replanning) then reduced the errors to about 5,000 per year.

Mass manufacture. Some manufacturing companies produce goods in millions of units per year. By measuring relatively few samples, they are able to evaluate process capability. They then use this evaluation as an input to quality planning.

It is fairly easy to apply the Santayana Review in such mass production cases. The data are available in large numbers—sampling is a necessity to avoid drowning in data. The data analysis is often simple enough to be done locally by personnel trained in basic statistics. The effort involved is modest, so there is seldom any need to secure prior approval from higher levels. As a result the Santayana Review is widely applied. Of course, those who make such applications seldom consider that they are engaged in a study of prior historical events. Yet that is precisely what they are doing.

Application to Intermediate-frequency Cycles

As used here, "intermediate frequency" is an order of magnitude of tens or hundreds of cycles per year—a few per month or week. Case examples within this range of frequency include:

RECRUITMENT OF EMPLOYEES. Many companies would like to reduce the time required to recruit new employees. Some have succeeded. They have done so by replanning the recruitment process through analysis of prior cycles of recruitment.

BIDS FOR BUSINESS. Many companies must secure their sales through competitive bidding. In some industries the proportion of successful bids is below 10 percent. It is feasible to analyze prior cycles of bidding (successful as well as unsuccessful) in order to raise the proportion of successful bids.

PURCHASES FROM SUPPLIERS. Many companies maintain data systems on the quality of products received during prior cycles of purchase from outside suppliers. The resulting summaries then become a part of the data base for future purchasing decisions.

Applications of the Santayana Review to intermediate-frequency cycles have been comparatively few in number. Yet the opportunities abound. This limited extent of application is traceable to some realities of the Santayana Review as it relates to intermediate frequency cycles:

The application is to a multifunctional process, usually requiring a team effort.

It can require a lot of work now, for benefits to come later, and with no known way of computing return on investment.

There is rarely a clear responsibility for doing the work.

The urge to volunteer to do the work is minimal, since the improvement will benefit the organization generally but not necessarily the volunteer's department.

The above realities do not preclude application of the Santayana Review to high-frequency cycles, since usually the application is to microprocesses, the amount of work is small, and the urge to volunteer is present, since the results will benefit the volunteer's department.

Application to Low-Frequency Cycles

As used here, "low frequency" refers to a range of several cycles per year down to one cycle in several years. Examples on an annual schedule include the sales forecast, and the budget. Examples on an irregular schedule include new product launches, major construction projects, and acquisitions.

Application of the Santayana Review to low-frequency cycles has been rare. Each such cycle is a sizable event; some are massive. A review of multiple cycles becomes a correspondingly sizable undertaking.

> A case example is the historical reviews conducted by a team of historians in British Petroleum Company. This team conducts reviews of large business undertakings: joint ventures, acquisitions, major construction projects. The reviews are concerned with matters of business strategy rather than with conformance to functional goals. Each review consumes months of time and requires about forty interviews to supply what is not in the documented history. The summarized conclusions and recommendations are presented to managers at the highest levels (Gulliver, 1987).

A widespread low-frequency process that desperately needs application of the Santayana Review is the launching of new products.

Such launchings are carried out through a macroprocess. Each product launched has a degree of uniqueness, but the macroprocess is quite similar from one cycle to another. Such being the case, it is entirely feasible to apply the Santayana Review.

Much of the time required during the launch cycle is spent redoing what was done previously. Extra work is imposed on internal and external customers. The extent and cost of these delays can be estimated from a study of prior cycles. Retrospective analysis can shed light on what worked and what did not, and can thereby improve decision making.

Note that the bulk of this delay and cost does *not* take place within the product development department. An example is seen in the launch of product X, which incurred expenses as follows (in $millions):

Market research	0.5
Product development	6.0
Manufacturing processes	22.0
Marketing planning	2.0
Total	30.5

All this was lost because a competitor captured the market by introducing a similar product two years before the launch of product X. The bulk of the loss—80 percent—took place *outside* of the product development department.

Creation of New Conceptual Approaches

The optimum macroprocess can never be attained solely by refining the component microprocesses; the basic concept of the macroprocess itself must be sound. The most memorable contributions to quality planning have been through new or revised macroprocesses. It is useful to look at some examples of memorable contributions and then to derive lessons learned from them.

The Ancient Sky Watchers and Their Calendars

One of the astounding achievements of ancient civilizations was the development of precise calendars. These calendars were derived from numerous observations of the motions of celestial bodies, cycle after cycle. Some of those cycles were many years in length. The resulting lessons learned were vital to the survival of those societies, e.g., when to plant crops.

Prince Henry's Think Tank

During the voyages of discovery in the fifteenth and sixteenth centuries, Portuguese navigators established themselves as leaders in guiding ships to their destinations and bringing them back safely. As a result, Portuguese navigators were preferred and demanded by shipowners, governments, and insurers. The source of this superiority was an initiative undertaken by a Portuguese prince—Prince Henry the Navigator (1394–1460).

In the early fifteenth century, Prince Henry established (at Sagres, Portugal) a center for marine navigation—a unique, unprecedented think tank. The facilities included an astronomical observatory, a fortress, a school for navigators, living quarters, a hospital, and a chapel. To this center Prince Henry brought cartographers, instrument makers, astronomers, mathematicians, shipwrights, and draftsmen. He also established a data bank—a depository of logs of marine voyages describing prevailing winds, ocean currents, landmarks, and so on. Lessons learned from these logs were taught to Portuguese navigators. Those same lessons learned contributed to Portuguese successes during the voyages of discovery around the coast of Africa, through the Indian Ocean, and across the Atlantic.

Mathew Maury's Navigation Charts

Mathew Maury was a U.S. Navy Lieutenant who in 1842 was assigned to the Depot of Charts and Instruments. One of the functions of the depot was custody of the logs of naval voyages—thousands of them. Each log recorded the conditions encountered by the vessel during its voyage: current speeds and depths, water depths and temperatures, wind directions and strengths. These logs had been gathering dust in the depot's archives. Maury took the initiative to organize the information and analyze it. He then entered the results into navigation charts using standardized graphics and terminology. For example, wind direction was shown by an arrow pointing downwind; the length of the arrow designated wind strength.

> One of the first ships to use Maury's charts was the famous Flying Cloud. In 1851 it sailed from New York to San Francisco. The previous record was 119 days. The Flying

Cloud made it in 89 days (Whipple, 1984). That record then endured for 138 years!

Research of Recurring Disasters

Some individual disasters are so notorious that the resulting glare of publicity forces the creation of a formal board of inquiry. However, the most damage is done by repetitive disasters that, though less than notorious individually, are notorious collectively. Every year many people sicken and die of disease. Many others die in accidents. Every year many buildings burn down. Each such incident attracts a modicum of local attention: first aid, the fire brigade, the ambulance, the hospital, the morgue.

Some of society's institutions exist to study these disasters *collectively.* At their best these institutions have contributed mightily to the wars against diseases, to reduction of accidents, and to making buildings fireproof. A fascinating example is a multinational study to shed light on the relation of diet to cancer. The resulting correlation is shown in Figure 12-2 (Cohen, 1987).

Creditworthiness Based on the Track Record

Business organizations are ever extending credit. In centuries past, prediction of creditworthiness was done empirically. The new concept was to create a formal data bank, e.g., Dun & Bradstreet (see Chapter 7, under "Process Capability—the Concept"; "Target Achievement").

Note that such data banks are not the result of incidental experience. They result from an initiative—a purposive, structured process of collecting and compiling data from multiple sources.

Dr. Paul Dudley White and The Long Follow-up

Dr. Paul Dudley White was a leading cardiologist—a heart specialist. (He came to public attention as the physician chosen to treat President Eisenhower following the latter's heart attack.) An important contribution to his leadership was the data logging system he created early in his career. See Chapter 5, under "Human Sensors: Lack of Technique." See also, White (1971).

Gunfire at Sea

Until the late 1890s, naval gunfire was extremely inaccurate. During the Spanish-American War, 9,500 shots were fired at various close ranges, resulting in 121 hits, just over 1 percent.

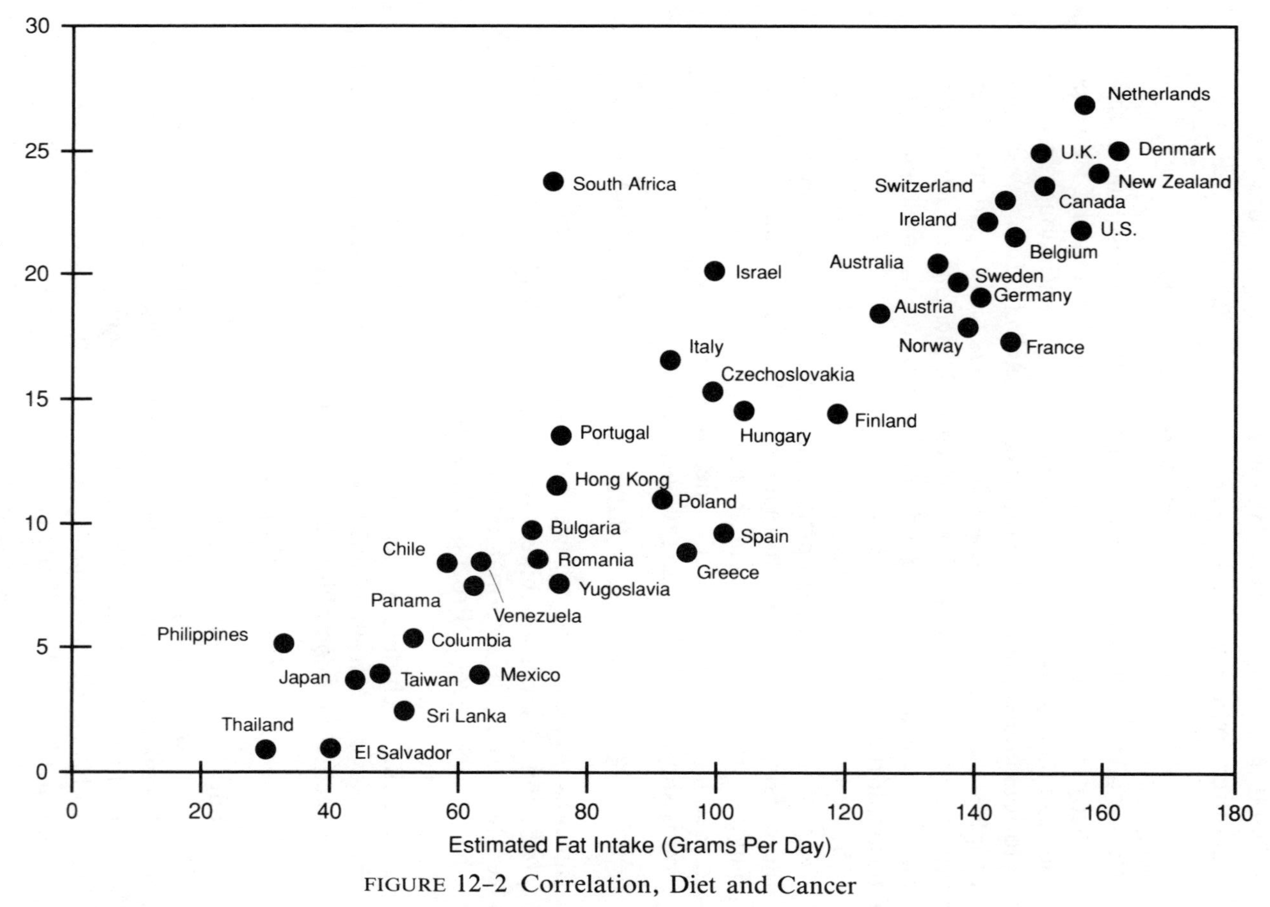

FIGURE 12–2 Correlation, Diet and Cancer

A breakthrough in precision evolved in 1898. A British officer, Admiral Sir Percy Scott, had become preoccupied with efforts to improve gunnery. One day while his ship was at target practice, he observed numerous rounds being fired by various gunners. He noted that one gunner was significantly more accurate than the rest. Sir Percy also discovered why. This gunner was manipulating the elevating gear of the gun to compensate for the anticipated roll of the ship.

Sir Percy then undertook to bring all gunners up to the level of the best. He also added some essential changes in technology. None of these were Sir Percy's inventions, but he was the first to assemble them in combination. Collectively his changes made possible a so-called continuous-aim firing. It revolutionized accuracy, as shown in the following comparison of firing at a range of 1,500 meters:

	1898	*1905*
Target	A lightship hulk	An area of 75 × 25 feet
Firing done by	Five ships	One gunner
Duration of firing	15 minutes	One minute
Hits	2	15

The increase in accuracy was about 3,000 percent (Morison, 1966).

Commonalities

The above cases, despite their diversity, exhibit certain commonalities. Foremost is the Santayana Review itself—the concept of analyzing history to derive lessons learned as a basis for decision making.

The Concept

In every case *there was a purposive analysis* of prior cycles of activity in order to discover lessons learned. Figure 12–3 tabulates who the analysts were and what prior cycles of activity they analyzed.

Positive Initiatives

In each of the above examples, *human beings took the initiative* to acquire the lessons learned. Lieut. Maury, Dr. White, and Sir Percy were all driven by the urge to improve performances in which they had a keen interest. Others wanted to put decision making on a more objective basis. Still others had the responsibility to avoid recurrence

The Analysts	*The Prior Cycles of Activity*
Ancient sky watchers	Movements of celestial bodies
Prince Henry's navigators	Prior naval voyages
Mathew Maury	Prior naval voyages
Various researchers	Recurring disasters
Publishers of credit ratings	Prior repayment record of prospective debtors
Dr. Paul Dudley White	Clinical history of patients
Sir Percy Scott	Rounds fired by naval gunners

FIGURE 12–3 The Analysts and the Activities Under Study

of disasters. What none of them did was to wait for lessons learned to turn up conveniently.

Key Roles

In each of those examples, we can identify two key roles that were played:

the sponsor for the Santayana Review

the historian

Figure 12–4 shows those who are known (or surmised) to have played the key roles. Figure 12–4 discloses two organization commonalities. In each case:

Example	*Sponsor(s)*	*Historian(s)*
Study of the heavens	The high priest; self-appointed astronomers	Sky watcher(s)
Prince Henry's think tank	Prince Henry	Subordinates
Review of logs of naval voyages	Mathew Maury	Subordinates
Research on disasters	Various agencies	Various researchers
Reports on creditworthiness	An entrepreneurial company	Financial investigators
The long follow-up	Dr. Paul Dudley White	Dr. Paul Dudley White
Gunfire at sea	Sir Percy Scott	Sir Percy Scott

FIGURE 12–4 Key Roles During Santayana Review

The sponsor took the initiative in response to some perceived opportunity or threat.

In contrast, the historian(s) acted as a result of direction from the sponsors.

Data Acquisition

In each case it was necessary to acquire the data, which then could be processed into lessons learned. In Mathew Maury's case the data were already in existence in those naval logs. In other cases it was necessary to create data afresh by persistent observations of the heavens, night after night; entries into Dr. White's ruled spreadsheets; and so on.

Data Analysis

In each of those examples, it was necessary to carry out some degree of data analysis: to summarize, to identify major variables, and to establish cause–effect relationships. All this required appropriate methodology. The sponsors were faced with somehow providing the essential methodology.

The End Result

The end result of the Santayana Review is lessons learned. Those lessons learned must then be converted into forms that can aid decision making. Figure 12–5 shows, for our case examples, the end results of such conversion.

Transfer to Operations

In each example *the end result was transferred to the operating forces* and became a part of the process of conducting operations.

Subject Matter	*End Result*
Movements of celestial bodies	A calendar
Improvement of marine navigation	Trained Portugese navigators
Optimal routes for sailing ships	Revised navigation charts
Disasters	Recommendations for new legislation, procedures, etc.
Creditworthiness	A formal data bank
Practice of medicine	A convenient data array
Gunfire at sea	Revised equipment, procedures

FIGURE 12–5 The End Result of the Santayana Review

The transfer also required the operating forces to be trained in use of the new ways.

Transfer to operations is helped out if the sponsor is also in command of operations, as in the case of Dr. White. Otherwise, the transfer can be impeded and even blocked by cultural resistance.

> In Gunfire at Sea, an American naval officer, Lieut. William S. Sims, learned in 1900 all about Sir Percy's findings, from Sir Percy himself. Lieut. Sims then undertook to transfer those new methods to the U.S. Navy. He met an astonishing amount of cultural resistance. However, eight turbulent years later he was universally acclaimed as "the man who taught us how to shoot" (Morison, 1966).

The Flow Diagram for the Santayana Review

Figure 12-6 shows the flow diagram for the Santayana Review.

Conducting the Santayana Review

While the flow diagram is universal, the details of carrying out a project will vary, a major variable being the cycle frequency.

Project Selection

For high-frequency cycles, recognition of the need is typically at departmental levels. Project selection is usually local. The subsequent work is often done on a voluntary basis.

For low-frequency cycles, recognition of the need takes place at high levels. Project selection is by the upper managers, e.g., the

Recognition of the need; project selection
Definition of the mission
Assignment of responsibility:
- For the sponsor(s)
- For the historian(s)

Review of prior cycles of activity
Analysis and summary
Conversion into usable form
Transfer to operations

FIGURE 12-6 Flow Diagram for the Santayana Review

Quality Council. The selection process is quite similar to that followed in choosing major quality improvement projects. The projects are highly multifunctional and are quite demanding as to time and resources. The subsequent work is mandated under a formal organization structure.

In departmental projects the organization is highly informal. The sponsor and historian are often the same person. In multifunctional projects it is necessary to be more formal. The sponsor is often a multifunctional team, and this team prepares a mission statement to ensure that there has been a meeting of the minds.

Role of the Sponsor

The sponsor has responsibilities that can be generalized as follows:

Define the boundaries of the project

Identify the questions to which answers are needed

Appoint the historian(s)

Provide the needed resources

Monitor progress

Apply the findings

Role of the Historian

The functions of the historian(s) can also be generalized. They include the following:

Search out pertinent data already in existence

Prepare a plan for collection of the supplemental data needed

Collect and analyze the data, existing and supplemental

Report conclusions in digestible form

As yet the job classification of Historian is a rare species in industry. Nevertheless, many employees spend some or much of their time analyzing history, mainly in the form of high-frequency cycles of activity. They include market research analysts, quality control engineers, industrial engineers, and productivity analysts. They have not been trained as historians, but their training in data analysis is a decided asset. The main pitfall is usually the written record. This record is incomplete. It also contains biases of all sorts, even maddening contradictions. (The guilt or innocence of Sacco and Vanzetti is still being debated.)

The Final Product

The findings of the historians are presented in digestible forms, such as:

IDENTIFICATION OF THE CRITICAL VARIABLES. In the British Petroleum case, one of the reviews involved two refineries built to convert natural gas into a component of gasoline. One of the refineries was built in Australia. It came in on schedule and under budget. The other, built in the Netherlands, was late and over budget. Nevertheless the results from the Dutch refinery were superior. The reason was that the market forecast for its products proved to be valid. Hence the refinery could run at a high percent of capacity. In the case of the Australian refinery, the market forecast did not prove to be valid. Hence the refinery ran at a low precent of capacity. The principal lesson learned was that in such projects the most critical variable was the market forecast.

ESTABLISHMENT OF CAUSE-EFFECT RELATIONSHIPS. An example was set out in Figure 6–15 of Chapter 6 under "Interaction: Product Development and Marketing." There the Santayana Review, applied to forty-one different food products, established some new and useful relationships of consumer preference to share of market (Juran, 1959).

A second example is a study made to test out various theories of why new products were experiencing an uneven success rate in the market. Nine prior product launch cycles were studied, leading to a consensus as to causes and to associated remedial action (Gust, 1985).

A third example is a study of twenty cycles of unsuccessful bids for business. (See Figure 6–13 in Chapter 6, and the associated discussion under "Customer Behavior.")

An example on a multinational scale is the correlation between diet and cancer, as depicted in Figure 12–2.

THE DATA BANK. The data bank is a collection of numerous inputs specially organized to facilitate information retrieval and decision making. Examples are the lists prepared to classify inputs for the use of decision makers:

Lists	*Decision Makers Who Use Such Lists*
Accident-prone drivers	Transportation companies, insurance companies
Approved sources of supply	Purchasing managers
Approved components	Design engineers
Creditworthy clients	Credit managers

THE CHECKLIST. An aid to human memory, the checklist is a reminder of what to do and what not to do. It is widely used for training new employees.

THE COUNTDOWN. The countdown is a list of deeds to be done, in a predetermined manner. One of the most widely publicized has been the elaborate countdown used for launching a space vehicle.

Some Common Features

Once available, the above (and other) forms of lessons learned exhibit some useful built-in features:

They make available to any user the collective experience and memories of numerous individuals, organized in ways that permit ready retrieval.

They are of a repetitive nature. They can be used over and over again for an indefinite number of planning cycles.

They are impersonal. They avoid the problems created when one person gives orders to another person.

In some projects the findings may include a generic action plan, which can greatly reduce the work of decision making.

A company that issues huge numbers of credit cards analyzed the credit histories of a sample of customers. For this sample they correlated the presence (or absence) of certain customer attributes with the customers' track records of paying up. This correlation enabled them to create a model that uses a point scoring system and a computer to make a prompt screening of each application for a credit card. If the application is rejected by the point score, that is the end of it—no credit card. If the application survives the point scoring, then a credit check is made, using any of various local services.

The Santayana Review and the Quality Planning Road Map

The output of the Santayana Review is lessons learned. These lessons learned have application to all the processes of the Juran Trilogy. For the quality planning process, the lessons learned are converted into a quality planning data base. This data base becomes one of the principal means for improving quality planning.

The relation of this data base to the quality planning road map is shown graphically in Figure 12–7.

In Figure 12–7 the data base is shown to apply to all the steps of the quality planning road map. This is similar to the situation with respect to measurement, which also applies to all the steps of the quality planning road map.

A Concluding Comment on the Santayana Review

The potentialities of the Santayana Review have been amply demonstrated in the case of short-cycle, highly frequent activities. As a result, the Santayana Review is widely applied to such cases, and with good effect.

The opportunities for application to long-cycle, low-frequency

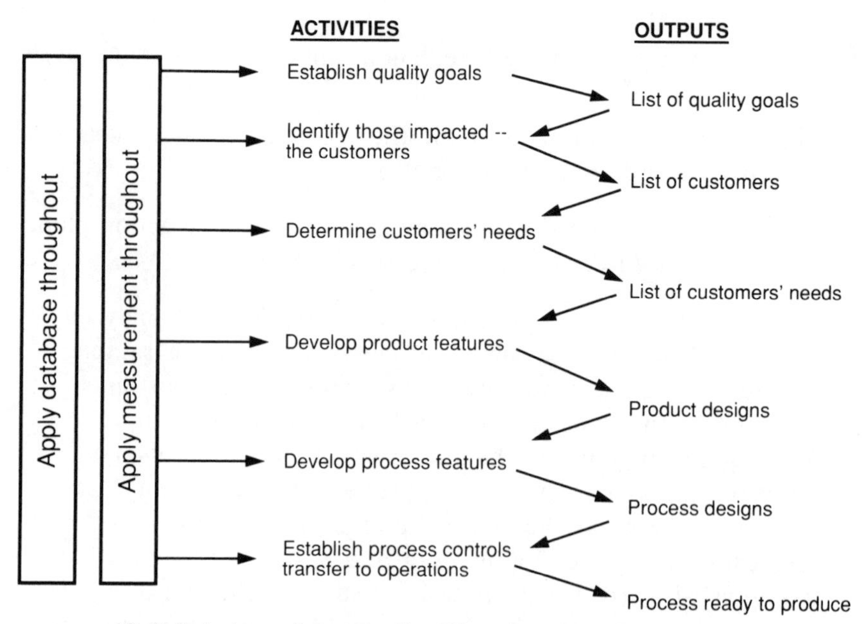

FIGURE 12–7 Relation of the Quality Planning Data Base to the Quality Planning Road Map

activities are extensive. However, the actual applications have been comparatively few because of some severe realities:

Sponsorship requires a consensus among multiple managers rather than an initiative by one manager.

The associated work (of the historian) is usually extensive and intrudes on the time of others.

The resulting lessons learned do not benefit current operations. The benefits apply to future operations.

The results do not necessarily benefit the departmental performance of the participating managers.

There is no known way of computing return on investment.

It is understandable that projects which face such realities have trouble in securing priorities. As matters stand, an initiative by upper managers is needed to apply the Santayana Review to long-cycle, low-frequency activities. To date, such initiatives have been few. Published papers have been rare. Gulliver's paper relative to the experience at British Petroleum is decidedly an exception.

Will the pace of application accelerate? The authors doubt it. Our prognosis is that the pace will remain evolutionary until some spectacular result is achieved and widely publicized. It is a discouraging forecast, the more so if we reread the words of the philosopher whose name we have chosen to apply to the process:

> Those who cannot remember the past are condemned to repeat it.

For additional discussion and references, see Juran (1988), pages 6.28 to 6.30; 16.47 and 16.48; and 31.19 and 31.20.

Motivation in Quality Planning

Motivation is an essential element in attaining quality, and especially in attaining quality leadership. The subject is broad, since it involves all the processes of the Juran Trilogy, multiple levels in the hierarchy, and still other variables. In this book the treatment is limited to those aspects of motivation which relate to quality planning. For treatment relative to other aspects of managing for quality, see:

Juran, J. M., *Making Quality Happen* (1988)

Juran, J. M., *Juran on Leadership for Quality* (1989)

The Necessary Actions

The decade of the 1990s will require extensive changes relative to quality planning. The driving force is the need to remain competitive and to respond to the demands of society for failure-free performance. The basic change is to give top priority to quality. To bring about such a change requires taking some very specific actions. These actions and the reasons behind them should be fully understood before trying to formulate the approach to motivation. *There should first be an answer to the question: Motivation to do what?*

The necessary actions and the reasons behind them have already been discussed earlier in this book. For convenience, here is a brief summary:

The Necessary Actions	*The Reasons*
Bring planning for quality into the strategic business plan	Anything that has top priority belongs in the strategic business plan
Train the planners in quality-related methodology	Most quality planning has been done by amateurs
Provide participation to all who are impacted	Lack of participation has resulted in plans that fail to meet the needs of customers
Provide a structured approach to quality planning	The empirical approach is no longer competitive
Enlarge the planners' data base	The data base has been inadequate

Those actions (and others) add up to a profound change in company culture. Any discussion of motivation should focus on the impact of those actions on the managerial processes and on the personnel.

The Obstacles Are Highly Predictable

During the 1980s many companies tried to carry out the above list of actions. In all cases the companies encountered various obstacles, some of which could have been avoided through motivation. It is useful to look back at the more frequent of those obstacles. They include:

Unawareness. People are not aware that they are creating quality problems.

To some degree, awareness can be supplied by exhibits, propaganda, exhortation, and so on. What is far more effective is participation in the planning process in order to understand how one's work impacts the various customers, internal and external. *Doing the deeds creates the awareness, not the other way around.*

Competition in priorities. People are unable to give top priority to quality because other goals actually have higher priority, and hence get in the way.

As perceived by the middle and lower levels in many companies, the prevailing managerial practices do *not* add up to giving top priority to quality. Moreover, a managerial edict that henceforth quality is to have top priority has little effect unless certain other actions are taken, notably a change in the reward system.

Suboptimization. Achievement of quality locally gets in the way of overall quality.

The remedy is again to provide participation to the impacted customers, external and internal. In some situations joint planning is better yet.

Some practitioners feel that many reward systems are inherently designed for suboptimization because they emphasize departmental performance rather than overall goals. There is merit in this contention. It follows that those who design reward systems should understand clearly how emphasis on departmental performances affects overall performance (see below, under "Motivation Through the Reward System").

"Here comes another one." Prior unsuccessful drives will result in a cynical reaction to any new initiative, including an effort to give top priority to quality.

Most companies periodically undertake efforts (programs, drives, etc.) to make improvements in various directions: productivity, safety, human relations, and the like. Each such effort goes through a cycle of launch, scale up, maturity, decay, and phase out. Often these efforts are directed at all personnel—the workers as well as the managerial. (Those not directly involved are in any case interested spectators.) From their perceptions, all draw conclusions as to the merits and deficiencies of the prior cycles. Those conclusions will obviously influence the reception the personnel will give to a quality planning initiative.

Managerial Myths as Obstacles

Some managers hold certain quality-related opinions that have little basis in fact. These "myths" are obstacles to constructive efforts to achieve quality leadership. The most frequent of these opinions include:

1. *The work force is mainly responsible* for the company's quality problems. In fact, objective researchers have regularly shown that about 80 to 90 percent of the damage done by poor quality is traceable to managerial actions.
2. Workers could do good quality work but they *lack the motivation* to do so. The realities are that many workers are not in a state of self-control, so they cannot always produce good work; they can avoid making bad work only by shutting down the process and calling for help.
3. *Quality will get top priority if the upper managers so decree.* The reality is that quality gets top priority only if the upper managers follow through with an action plan: establish goals, determine the deeds required to meet those goals, provide resources, measure performance, review progress, revise the reward system, and so forth.
4. *To change people's behavior, it is first necessary to change their attitudes.* There is some validity to this, but *mostly it is the other way around*—if we first change people's behavior, that will change their attitudes. For example, managers who have been required to serve on quality improvement teams (a mandated change in behavior) exhibit much greater receptivity to participation in quality improvement than managers who have merely been urged to change their attitude.

(Workers also hold certain beliefs that have little basis in fact. See below, under "Impact on Cultural Values of the Workers: Workers' Myths.")

Use of Internal Surveys

Identification of the obstacles can be helped by conducting an internal survey to discover the nature and extent of the prevailing beliefs. Such a survey should extend to all categories of personnel: upper managers, middle managers, supervisors, specialists, nonsupervisory workers. The questions to be addressed by such a survey should be tailored to the special needs of each company. Typical questions have been:

> What is your perception of the company's quality compared to that of competitors: Superior? The same? Inferior? Don't know?
>
> Whom do you regard as your customer: The company's clients? The next department? The boss? Someone else? The specifications? The procedures? No customer? Don't know?
>
> How do you rate the quality of the product you are turning out: High? Adequate? Low? Don't know?
>
> If you rate the quality of your product as low, what do you feel are the obstacles that stand between you and producing high quality product? List up to three obstacles.
>
> When your supervisor judges your performance, which element of performance receives the greatest weight: Meeting the budget? Meeting the cost standard? Productivity? Quality? Safety? Meeting Schedules? Other?

In a survey conducted by one large company, one of the questions was: What are the prime inhibitors to making quality happen in your area? The overwhelming number one response was "lack of measurement, recognition, and reward for quality improvement."

Human Behavior and Cultural Values

Motivation is concerned with human behavior. A major force in human behavior is the so-called *cultural pattern*. The cultural pattern is a body of beliefs, habits, practices, and so on that a human society evolves to deal with its perceived problems. Each cultural pattern, being a logical response to those perceived problems, is highly valued by the society of origin. In consequence the patterns are perpetuated—new members who enter a society are required to adapt to the pattern. In addition, any perceived threat to those cultural values is resisted by the members of the society: they exhibit "cultural resistance."

Every company is also a human society. In large companies there are multiple societies: the various functions, the levels in the hierarchy, the professional disciplines, and so on. These societies differ in their perceptions and therefore evolve cultural patterns that differ one from another. However, each exhibits cultural resistance to threats to its cultural values.

Social Consequences of Intended Changes

The actions required to give top priority to quality involve changes that impact every one of the societies in the company. On the face of it, these changes are merely revisions in managerial or technological processes. However, any intended change actually consists of two changes:

1. *The intended change*
2. *The social consequence of the intended change* (This is a sort of uninvited guest that rides in on the back of the intended change.)

The social consequence is the troublemaker. The trouble arises from a clash of two cultures: (1) that of the advocates of the change and (2) that of the recipient society. The recipient society always examines the proposed change from the standpoint: What threats does this change pose to the cultural values of this society? To the recipient society, this question is of critical importance. Often enough, the cultural values take precedence over company rules.

Threats to cultural values can be identified for every society in the company. For example:

> Upper managers face additional work loads if the company adds planning for quality to the strategic business plan. Many upper managers would prefer to delegate this work to the lower levels.
>
> Some line managers exhibit cultural resistance to the change in priorities. Through experience they have acquired mastery over the previous top priority, e.g., meeting the schedules. A change to give top priority to quality is also a change in the game being played. The champions at playing the old game cannot be sure that they will also be champions at playing the new game. It would be safer to continue playing the old game.
>
> Functional heads also exhibit cultural resistance. They usually have monopolies or near-monopolies in decision making on functional matters. Giving top priority to quality may invade these monopolies. Also significant is the loss of status—being pushed off center stage.

Two additional societies are specially impacted by the trends in planning for quality. They are (a) the planners and (b) the workers. The effect on their cultural values warrants a more detailed look.

The Planners and Structured Quality Planning

Experienced planners tend to exhibit cultural resistance to a structured approach. A structured approach *reduces the status* of experienced planners. Such planners have acquired useful knowledge from their work on previous planning cycles. This knowledge confers a status that is not possessed by inexperienced planners. The experienced planners can of course become trained in the new ways and thereby maintain an advantage over their younger colleagues. However, new negative reactions are created. Younger personnel seem to learn the structured methodology more readily. There is also an unstated resentment about the unfairness of any situation in which younger people are able to take a shortcut to a status previously requiring long years of experience.

Experienced planners also exhibit cultural resistance to increased participation, again for stated and unstated reasons:

Participation delays the planning process. The facts support this reaction. The review meetings consume time. It also takes time to respond to the comments that emerge from the review meetings.

Participation infringes on prior monopolies. These monopolies are a source of status, and they may for that reason be fiercely defended.

Experienced planners also resist mandated training in quality planning. They contend it is not essential for them. An unstated reason is the implication of prior illiteracy. Mandated training also carries an implication of mandated use thereafter, which conflicts with the long-standing concept: "Tell me what result you want but don't tell me how to produce it."

Impact on Cultural Values of the Workers

Work force involvement in quality planning has been discussed in Chapter 11 under various headings:

"Analysis of the Microprocess: By Whom?"

"Workers and Quality Planning"

"Workers and the Feedback Loop"

"Workers and the Triple Role"

Our present topic is the impact of modern quality planning on the cultural values of the workers. The nature of that impact depends largely on the extent to which the company intends to make use of that major underemployed asset—the education, experience, and creativity of the workers.

Effect of Giving Top Priority to Quality

At the worker level, the effect of giving top priority to quality can be extensive. Here are some of the changes that may be needed:

Policy on job design, e.g., making jobs inherently interesting and establishing a state of self-control (strict separation of planning from execution, i.e., the Taylor system, is inherently a poor motivator for quality)

Recruitment criteria— giving consideration to the ability and willingness to meet quality standards

Induction procedure—giving adequate emphasis to quality

Training—explaining the why as well as the how of doing quality work

Supervision—setting a good example through decisions and actions relative to quality

Special provisions—certifying workers (for critical tasks) or offering opportunities for participation in project work

To enable workers to give top priority to quality also requires increasing the communication of information on quality. The higher priority requires managers to:

Provide positive means for workers to communicate their views and ideas

Evaluate worker performance on quality, and provide feedback in ways comparable to that provided on other parameters

Provide communication to workers to explain those management actions which, on their face, are antagonistic to quality (If communication is incomplete, it is easy for managers and the work force to draw different conclusions from the same basic facts.)

A further need is to improve the climate in those cases where the prevailing atmosphere is one of blame. The new emphasis must be on analysis for causes rather than on looking for someone to blame; on providing answers to the question: What should I do that is different from what I have been doing?

Workers' Myths

Workers (in common with everyone else) hold certain beliefs that have little basis in fact. One such belief has been especially troublesome to managers: the belief that job security can be achieved by establishing monopolistic rights to certain tasks—in effect, job ownership. This belief was enforced by certain events in the United States where many labor unions, for decades, were able to establish such monopolies, along with associated restrictive work rules. (Ever since the 1930s, the labor unions have been exempt from the antitrust laws.)

Management efforts to avoid the resulting high costs then contributed to an adversary relationship. Many of these accumulated monopolies have since been broken by a flood of imported goods. What had seemed to be a well-founded belief turned out to be a myth.

To discover and deal with work force apprehensions and myths it is helpful to conduct a survey of the type discussed above under the heading "Motivation in Quality Planning: Managerial Myths as Obstacles."

Dealing with Cultural Resistance

Managerial styles vary, resulting in various ways of dealing with cultural resistance. One of those ways is to mandate the needed changes without being concerned about cultural resistance. Such a mandate creates a clash between the two cultures, in its most adversarial form. If the damage to cultural values is substantial, the members of the culture will find ways to retaliate. They withhold their cooperation, resort to foot-dragging, and use other subtle ways to make the changes not worth having. The resulting lowered morale is one of the prices paid by managers who choose to ignore the social consequences of the intended changes.

More usually, the managers do try to anticipate the nature of the cultural resistance and to take responsive action. Such managers are well advised to study the "*rules of the road*" for dealing with cultural resistance. Those rules, evolved by behavioral scientists and practicing managers, have been shown to be applicable to a wide variety of human societies. These rules of the road are set out below.

Rules of the Road

Provide participation to the recipient society, during both the planning and the execution of the changes. Such participation establishes a communication link between the cultures and facilitates creating a sense of ownership by the recipient society.

No surprises. A major benefit of the cultural pattern is predictability. A surprise is a disturber of the peace. (Providing participation is one way to minimize surprises.)

Provide enough time for the recipient society to:

Evaluate the merits of the change versus the threat to their cultural values

Find an accommodation with the advocates

Start small and keep it fluid. A proposal for an experiment arouses fewer apprehensions. Use of a test site reduces the risks for the advocates as well as for the recipient society, and implies provision for midcourse correction.

Create a favorable social climate. If upper managers set an example by serving on quality councils and on project teams, that sends a signal to the rest of the hierarchy. Revisions in the system of recognition and rewards similarly can help create a favorable climate.

Weave the change into an existing, acceptable part of the cultural pattern. An example is bringing planning for quality into the strategic business plan.

Provide a quid pro quo (something for something). A proposal to mandate certain training for professionals may include a provision to make the training optional for persons with extensive experience.

Respond positively. Positive responses to problems raised by the recipient society contribute to a constructive atmosphere.

Work with the recognized leadership of the culture. The culture is best understood by its members. They have their own leadership, and this is often informal. Convincing the leadership is a significant step in getting the change accepted.

Treat the people with dignity. The classic example is that of the relay assemblers in the "Hawthorne experiments." Their productivity kept rising, under good illumination or poor, because in the "laboratory" they were being treated with dignity.

Keep it constructive. Proposals for change should emphasize benefits and solutions, not prior deficiencies or blame. An atmosphere of blame is fatal to essential communications.

For elaboration on the subject of dealing with cultural resistance, see Juran (1964). The major, seminal work is Mead (1951).

Motivation Through Recognition

The approach to motivation as evolved by practicing managers has (in the United States) focused on "recognition" and on reward systems.

"Recognition" is used here in the sense of public acknowledgment of work well done. Applied to quality planning, this work relates to such matters as:

Adapting to a structured approach to quality planning

Taking training in modern quality planning methodology

Providing for participation by those impacted

Adopting the concept of Big Q

Working on team quality planning projects

Forms of Recognition

When companies address the problem of recognition, they usually enlist the collective ingenuity of those who have special skills in communication (Human Relations, Marketing, Advertising) as well as the line managers. The numerous forms of recognition reflect this ingenuity:

Certificates, plaques, and the like are awarded for completing training courses, serving as facilitator, and serving on project teams.

Project teams present their final report in the office of the ranking local manager.

Summaries of reports on completed projects are published in the company news media, along with pictures of the teams. Some companies have created special news supplements or special newsletters devoted to quality.

Dinners are held to honor project teams.

Prizes are awarded to teams judged to have completed the "best" projects during some designated time period.

Published accounts of successful projects serve not only to provide recognition; they also serve as case materials for training purposes and as powerful stimulators to all.

Communication

The communication associated with recognition can add greatly to the clarity and credibility of management's message. Human interest stories deal with the individuals behind the projects, their families, and their work environment. Well-related accounts of successful projects supply a ring of reality to the earlier management advocacy and to the promises made in the training materials.

Motivation Through the Reward System

As used here, the term "reward system" refers to those salary increases, bonuses, promotions, and so on which are more or less keyed to job performance. In most companies there are annual performance reviews and associated annual rewards. Our present focus is on those rewards which are keyed to performance relative to quality planning.

At the outset it is necessary to distinguish between mandated work and voluntary work. Mandated work is the scope of the "regular" job. To a high degree, companies reward mandated work through the reward system, and at the time of the periodic performance reviews. Voluntary work (such as in QC Circles or within the Suggestion System) is often rewarded then and there, on an *ad hoc* basis, and is usually keyed to the results achieved.

"Performance" actually consists of performance on numerous parameters: productivity, on-time delivery, costs, and so forth, as well as quality. In view of this, *upper managers have generally concluded that quality-oriented rewards should be woven into the overall reward system.* Job descriptions almost invariably include responsibility for meeting quality goals. Performance rating systems almost invariably include rating of performance against quality goals.

Raising the priority given to quality has required some revision of the reward system. Some companies have made this revision simply by changing the weight given to the quality parameter in the overall performance evaluation.

> Automobile manufacturers have for years evaluated the performance of their dealers with respect to various parameters, including quality of service to automobile buyers. During the 1980s the manufacturers demanded better quality of service. A strategy employed by one of the manufacturers was to increase the weight given to quality of service to a total of 50 percent, i.e., quality of service received as much weight as all other parameters combined.

A different problem is presented when people are given added responsibilities (such as serving on planning teams) or are asked to make radical revisions in practice (such as use of structured planning methodology). The newness requires new "metrics" for evaluating performance relative to the new or changed responsibilities. A further area requiring new metrics is the planning and operation of macroprocesses. In this connection, see Chapter 5 under the heading "Measures for Operating Processes."

Evaluation of performance relative to new parameters always requires a period of experimentation and awkwardness in order to acquire experience. During this period the usual practice is to leave it to supervisory judgment to evaluate performance against the goals.

> For example, many projects require *team* efforts for completion. However, the reward systems require evaluation of the efforts of *individuals*. As a result, supervisory judgment must be used to evaluate the performance of the individuals during the team projects.

Efforts to aid supervisors in making their judgments have included preparation of a graduated series of statements ranging from total lack of performance to complete performance. The supervisor then judges which of the statements comes closest to expressing the actual performance under consideration. For a case example, see McGrath (1986).

A special form of motivation is emerging with respect to training in planning for quality. Some companies feel that certain quality-related training has become essential for specific planning jobs. Yet the company is reluctant to mandate the training, since there is much cultural resistance from some of the personnel. One solution has been to make the training voluntary rather than mandatory. However, it is also made clear that the *training is a prerequisite to advancement*.

Note that in some cases rewards are inherent in voluntary efforts to replan processes. A successful replanning within a microprocess often improves the departmental performance of the supervisor who carried out the project. This feature of personal benefit has stimulated many supervisors of microprocesses to undertake quality improvement on a voluntary basis, in the absence of an upper management mandate.

In the case of microprocesses, the motivational situation is quite different. Now the process is multidepartmental in nature, so a multidepartmental team is needed to carry out a replanning project. If the project is successful, there is a benefit to the company but not necessarily to the departmental performance of any team member.

Training in Planning for Quality

The preceding chapters have made clear that adoption of modern ways of planning for quality requires some sharp breaks with tradition—virtually a change of culture. A change of such magnitude requires some corresponding changes in the area of training—training in how to plan for quality.

In the United States the tradition has been to concentrate training in quality planning within the Quality Department. The new need is to extend such training throughout the organization—all functions and all levels. Such extension is necessary if the amateurs are to be trained to become professionals.

The Training Curriculum

The subject matter of planning for quality is multidimensional. One dimension is concerned with fundamental *concepts*: the definition of quality, the role of quality in the business mission, and so on. A second dimension is the *hierarchical level* of the trainees. A third dimension is the various organization *functions*: finance, marketing, product development, and so on. A further dimension is the numerous *tools and techniques*.

In the face of this multidimensional content, the company must establish a training *curriculum*. This curriculum is a list of training courses (modules, packages), which collectively can meet the training needs for all those dimensions. Design of such a curriculum is done keeping in mind the training needs of the categories of company personnel. The end result of planning the curriculum should be a matrix that shows the list of courses along with which categories of personnel are to take which courses. An example of such a matrix is shown in Figure 12–8.

The content of the curriculum always reflects the experience and biases of those who are assigned the job of designing that curriculum. As a result, that content has varied considerably from one company to another. In view of this variation, the choice of who is to determine the curriculum becomes critical. There are various options, and they have been widely field-tested.

Use of a Broad-based Task Force

One of the more successful options has been to use a broad-based task force for the purpose of designing the curriculum. Under this

Courses		Program Managers of Quality	Executive Management	Middle and First-line Management	Non-management Employees
Quality Management System II	(1)	X	X		
• Concepts of Quality Management					
• Concepts of Cost of Quality					
• Managerial Breakthrough					
• Elementary Statistics					
Upper Management & Training	(2)	X	X		
Quality Awareness Training	(3)		X	X	X
Quality Implementation Training	(3)		X	X	Selected
• Concepts of Quality Management					
• Department/ Task Analysis Workshop					
• Problem Analysis Workshop					
• Elementary Statistics					
• Vital Issue Selection					
Data Handling Statistics	(1)	X			
Basic Statistics	(3)			Planned	Planned

FIGURE 12–8 Example of a Matrix for Training in Quality (*continued on p. 440*)
From Nickell (1985).

Courses		*Program Managers of Quality*	*Executive Management*	*Middle and First-line Management*	*Non-management Employees*
Juran on Quality Improvement	(2)	X			
• Video Program					
Note: Classes/ Sessions Taught By:					
(1) IBM Quality Institute					
(2) Juran Institute, Inc.					
(3) IBM/NMD Program Managers of Quality					

FIGURE 12–8 *Continued*

concept the Quality Council creates a task force (project team, etc.) whose mission is to develop a plan for training in planning for quality.

The task force membership consists of high-level managers, including the quality manager and the training manager, along with representatives from the major operating and staff departments.

More specifically, the task force mission is to:

Identify the company's needs for training in planning for quality

Propose a curriculum of courses that can meet those needs

Identify which categories of personnel should take which courses

Identify the sources of needed training materials, whether to be self-developed or acquired from suppliers

Identify the needs for leaders: trainers, facilitators, etc.

Propose a timetable

Estimate the budget

In the experience of the authors, the training plans developed by such task forces have been decidedly superior to those developed through other options. It usually took longer to evolve the training plan, but the result was more responsive to the company's needs. This experience suggests that:

Upper managers should establish a broad-based task force to plan the company's approach to training in planning for quality.

Mandatory or Voluntary?

Opportunities for managers and specialists to acquire training in planning for quality became widely available during the 1980s. As the decade progressed, companies increasingly began to urge their personnel to undergo such training. In some cases this urging grew into mandates. Where these mandates encountered strong cultural resistance, the companies adopted alternative strategies. For example, possession of certain training was made a prerequisite to job progress (e.g., assignment to higher-grade work), much like a license to practice.

In the judgment of the authors, once it is determined that universal training in planning for quality is essential to meeting the company's quality goals, then such training should *not* be put on a voluntary basis. Instead, the upper managers should mandate training in planning for quality.

At the worker level, training in planning for quality has generally been on a voluntary basis. However, various inducements are offered in such forms as opportunity for participation in projects or qualification for higher grades.

In What Sequence?

Companies have tested out various sequences in their approach to training at all levels of the hierarchy. Feedbacks from their experiences point to a "lesson learned": upper managers should be the first to acquire the new training. The reasons are quite persuasive:

By being first, upper managers become better qualified to review proposals made for training the rest of the organization.

By setting an example, the upper managers change an element of the corporate culture, i.e., they create a perception that to take the new training is to do what has been done in respected circles.

For some purposes the upper managers themselves should serve as trainers. To do so requires prerequisite training.

To illustrate, during the 1980s numerous companies tried to carry out accelerated quality improvement with the aid of the videocassette series *Juran on Quality Improvement* (Juran Institute, Inc. 1981.)

One of the more successful of these companies was Texas Instruments, Inc. Under Texas Instruments' approach each division general manager became the trainer for his subordinates. Those subordinates in turn became the trainers for their subordinates. This top-down approach continued throughout.

Policy Guidelines

Some questions relative to training are broad enough to deserve policy guidelines from upper management. These questions include:

CORPORATE DESIGN OR NOT? The practice varies. Some very large companies have left it to each division to work up its own plan of approach, with only limited coordination from corporate headquarters. Smaller companies tend to do the planning on a corporate basis, with participation by the divisions (or regions, plants, etc.)

Where broad corporate planning is used, it tends to concentrate on broad matters:

Coordination with other active programs (e.g., productivity improvement, participative management)

Development of training materials that are applicable to multiple divisions

Development of leaders/facilitators for the seed courses

SELF-SUFFICIENCY OR NOT? Large companies tend to become self-sufficient with respect to training. Employee turnover creates a continuing need for training. So does growth. So does creation of new products, new processes, and so forth. An internal resource can conduct training with knowledge of the company culture while being cost effective as well. Such a training resource extends to trainers as well as to training materials. (Even when training materials are purchased, they undergo revision to adapt them to the culture.)

The policy question posed is whether to extend the concept of self-sufficiency to training for quality.

TAILOR-MADE OR OFF-THE-SHELF? A related question is the extent to which the training materials should be tailored to the specific culture of the company. Some companies buy training materials from suppliers but then adapt them to the company's dialects and culture. They revise certain parts of the language. They introduce local case examples. Such adaptation simplifies the job of the trainers. It also makes it easier for the participants to relate to the training.

EDUCATION OR DOING? It has been a widespread practice to carry out training in quality purely as an educational process. For example, many managers have been trained in the quality improvement process but without carrying out a quality improvement project. Similarly, many supervisors and work force members have undergone training in basic statistical tools but have not applied the tools to actual job situations.

In the opinion of the authors, such a practice misplaces the emphasis. *The basic purpose of the training should be to secure a change in behavior*: to replan some existing plan; to carry out an improvement project. The purpose of the training should be to assist the participants to make the change in behavior. It is usually feasible to design the training in ways that provide the participants with means of applying the training to actual job situations. In the judgment of the authors:

> Upper managers should mandate that training in planning for quality be designed so as to require trainees to make applications of the new knowledge to their own jobs.

THE NEEDED EXPERTISE. There is a subtle yet critical distinction to be made relative to expertise possessed by trainers. This expertise is actually a combination of expertise in:

The subject matter

The skills of how to train

The relative importance of these two kinds of expertise varies depending on (a) what is the subject matter and (b) who are the trainees.

To illustrate, in teaching simple subjects (reading, writing, arithmetic) to children, the prime qualification for the teacher is possession of the skills of how to teach. In contrast, for teaching advanced subjects at the postgraduate level, the prime qualification of the teacher is mastery of the subject matter—to be able to answer the questions. This same principle is applicable to training in various quality-related subjects:

> To train workers in basic statistical tools, the prime qualification of trainers is knowledge of how to teach. They acquire this knowledge by being specially trained in how to teach the subject and by being supplied with trainers' guides designed by experts in the teaching process.

To train engineers in use of advanced statistical methodology, the prime qualification of trainers is expertise in the subject matter. The crises arise when the trainees raise questions that the trainer is unable to answer. (If the trainer is also a good teacher, so much the better.)

To train managers in how to enlarge strategic business planning so as to include planning for quality, the prime qualification of the trainer is expertise in the subject matter. The trainer should be able to answer the questions of the managers.

These requirements for expertise suggest that those who are planning the approach to training should specify that trainers possess the needed expertise in the subject matter as well as possessing the teaching skills.

TRAINING FOR NONEMPLOYEES. Some companies have concluded that quality-oriented training should be extended to nonemployees. The most common of these extensions has been to suppliers. For example, early in the 1980s various major original equipment manufacturers (OEMs) undertook large-scale training of their supervisors and workers in basic statistical tools, or statistical process control (SPC). Some of these OEMs then extended this training to their suppliers. In part this was done by offering training courses that suppliers could attend without charge. In part it was done by imposing new criteria to be met by suppliers—a mandated use of SQC during conduct of their operations.

A company should first test out among its own employees any training it proposes to extend to nonemployees. Once it finds that such training has merit, a policy question arises: Should the company take steps to extend the training to nonemployees? Whether to do so by persuasion or by mandate is a separate question.

Training for Upper Managers

Training in making quality happen should include the entire company hierarchy, *starting at the top*. Until the 1980s such a proposal was seldom welcomed by upper managers in the United States. Their instinctive belief was that upper managers already knew what needed to be done, and that training was for others—the middle managers, the engineers, the workers. The events of the 1980s then forced a reexamination of that belief.

Events in Japan followed a different scenario. The Japanese quality crisis emerged soon after World War II and was more severe than the subsequent crisis in the West. That crisis stimulated the Japanese managers to go into training in managing for quality, starting at the top. The seed courses took place in 1954, and were given by one of the present authors (Juran).

The Subject Matter

Experience in conducting numerous training courses for upper managers, on the subject of planning for quality, has evolved a body of subject matter somewhat as follows:

Some basics: the key definitions; Big Q and Little Q; the Juran Trilogy

Strategic quality management: developing a quality strategy; the quality council; quality policies; goal setting; deployment of goals; provision of resources; establishment of measures; revision of the reward system

Quality planning. Use of the quality planning road map in planning/replanning some product/process; planning for macroprocesses

Quality audits as a means of reviewing the company's status with respect to quality planning

Some Realities

Upper managers have exhibited some distinct preferences relative to training in managing for quality:

They regard themselves as business managers. Hence, the training should establish a clear linkage to business goals.

They are results-oriented—they are measured by business results. Hence, the training should be oriented to results, not techniques or tools.

They are usually aware that they themselves may be a part of the problem. Hence, they look for answers to the question: What should I be doing that is different from what I am doing now?

They strongly prefer to be in training meetings with other upper managers. They feel that no one else understands the problems faced by upper managers.

They prefer a training site away from the office, e.g., a "meeting in the woods."

As a consequence of the foregoing, upper managers are reluctant to accept insiders or subordinates as trainers. Instead, their preference is to listen to outsiders, especially upper managers from well-managed companies. They are willing to visit companies that have earned recognition through their quality. They are also willing to listen to consultants who have a public status and who appear to be

Knowledgeable in quality-oriented matters

Able to convey this knowledge in ways that relate squarely to the business realities faced by upper managers

Able to provide answers to the question: What should I do that differs from what I am doing now?

This behavior pattern of upper managers offers guidelines to those who have the responsibility to plan meetings in which upper managers will be the trainees.

Specific Design of Training Course Contents

It is possible to design the training courses based on any combination of dimensions of the subject matter: hierarchical level, organization function, tools and techniques, and still others. The actual practice has varied widely.

The lists that follow set out some specific designs of training courses as conducted in various companies, but with some editing done by the authors. Generally, the upper managers do not become involved with the details of these designs.

Course Contents for Quality Planning

The present book, *Juran on Quality by Design,* is itself a course on quality planning. The topics and subtopics are so numerous that only the key topics can appear in a list of "course contents." The actual contents will vary with the special needs of the companies. Figure 12–9 is an example of contents for a course in quality planning.

The course contents shown in Figure 12–9 are widely applicable. However, we can expect an evolution of specialized courses in quality planning. Some of these will be oriented to specific industries. Others

Definitions of key terms
Basic concepts: Little Q and Big Q; the Juran Trilogy; the TRIPROL concept
Strategic quality management—putting quality into the business plan
Quality policies
Quality goals; deployment of goals
The quality planning road map
Customers: external and internal
Identifying customers; the flow diagram
Discovering customer needs
Measures of quality
Planning of macroprocesses
Planning of microprocesses
Product design; the product design spreadsheet
Process design; process capability; process design spreadsheet
Planning for process control; the feedback loop; the process control spreadsheet
Transfer to operations
Lessons learned; the Santayana Review; the quality planning data base
Tools for planners

FIGURE 12-9 Course Contents for Quality Planning

will focus on specific functions, such as product development (see below). Still others will relate to specific processes, such as macroprocesses.

> The first course conducted in Japan under the sponsorship of the Japanese Union of Scientists and Engineers was in 1949. By the 1980s JUSE was offering more than forty types of courses. However, five of these types accounted for over 70 percent of the registrations.

Course Contents for Product Development

An example of a function-oriented course is product development. Competition in new product development has become intense, both for providing new product features and for shortening the cycle time. This competition has stimulated a growth in quality-oriented training courses for those managers, engineers, and others who are active in the product development process. The subject matter usually includes a selection from the list shown in Figure 12-10.

Definitions of quality; customer, customer needs; etc.
The quality planning road map
Product development—the phases
Measures of quality
Models and data systems for evaluating and predicting product reliability and maintainability
Models and data systems for analysis relating to criticality, salability, failure-proneness, carryover of prior designs, etc.
Process capability studies for evaluating and predicting producibility
Design of experiments for discovering the optimum result attainable from multiple converging variables
Spreadsheets for assembling numerous interrelated data into condensed, easy-to-grasp forms
Flow diagrams, decision trees, and still other aids to quality analysis and decision making
Methods for guarding against human error

FIGURE 12–10 Course Contents for Product Development

Courses on product development usually look at "product" and "process" in the "Little Q" sense—physical goods and manufacturing processes. Some of these courses focus on the "research and development" portion of the new product cycle, so the orientation is to technology: product design, reliability engineering, process engineering, and so on. Other courses focus on the detailed use of spreadsheets and on optimizing the effect of multiple variables (Sullivan, 1986).

Course Contents—Other

Training has long been available for such specialists as quality engineers and reliability engineers. The most widely used text has been Juran and Gryna (1980).

During the 1980s, there was a dramatic growth of training in basic statistical methodology for first-line supervisors and for workers. The principal text materials have consisted of derivations from the popular Japanese training manual (Ishikawa, 1972).

Trainers

The diversities in subject matter and audiences have required a corresponding diversity of trainers. Numerous approaches were tested in the 1980s. The feedbacks from these tests are reflected in the comments that follow.

Upper Managers as Trainers

Upper managers should participate in training of subordinate levels. In this role of trainer, the upper managers should concentrate on those areas in which they have the widest experience and are the most authoritative sources. With respect to such areas, upper managers can bring to the trainees:

An explanation of what the company is trying to accomplish, and why

Information on policies, goals, results, competitive status, and prognosis of what lies ahead

Answers to troublesome questions

It is clearly desirable for the trainees to receive such information at first hand from the most authoritative source.

Upper managers who become trainers should keep in mind that to subordinates this trainer is also the boss. It is all too easy for the two roles to become confused, by the trainer as well as by the trainees.

Trainers for Middle Managers

Like upper managers, middle managers are oriented to results. However, middle managers have functional and departmental responsibilities. In large companies these departmental responsibilities can dominate the attention of middle managers, that is, they are judged based on measures of departmental performance. This same dominance influences their response to broad-spectrum training programs. In such programs these middle managers show a clear preference for case examples in their functional specialty.

Middle managers have not resisted training by insiders or even by subordinates, provided the trainers possess expertise in the subject matter and have the needed teaching skills.

Trainers for First-line Supervisors

In large companies the numbers of first-line supervisors are also large. Such numbers require the development of in-house trainers and "facilitators" (see below, under "Use of Facilitators"). The seed courses may be provided from the outside, along with training of those who are to be the in-house trainers. Thereafter, the in-house trainers take over.

At this level, some of the training will relate to the company's organization, markets, technology, systems, procedures, human relations, and so forth. In many companies the Training Department's specialists are qualified to conduct in-house training in such matters. Similarly, when the subject matter requires interplay among trainees (as in project teams for quality planning) there may be a need to provide training in group dynamics. Such training is commonly provided on an in-house basis through the use of facilitators.

A substantial area of training is in tools and techniques. The most widely used tools are quite simple. Trainers in the use of such tools can be developed on an in-house basis, either from the Quality Department or from the Training Department.

Use of Facilitators

In cases where training is built around carrying out projects, most companies make use of "facilitators" to assist the project teams, especially teams that are working on their first project. Facilitators are usually supervisors or specialists who have undergone special training for this purpose. In most cases their role as facilitator is a part-time assignment, over and above their "regular" job.

The usual roles of facilitators consist of a selection from the following:

EXPLAIN THE COMPANY'S INTENTIONS. The facilitator has usually attended briefing sessions at which there has been explanation of what the company is trying to accomplish. Much of this briefing is of interest to the project teams.

ASSIST IN TEAM BUILDING. In this role the facilitator helps the trainees to learn to act as team members: to intercommunicate, contribute theories, challenge theories of others, share experiences, and propose lines of investigation.

ASSIST IN TRAINING. The facilitator has usually gone through the training course, and has probably guided other teams through their first project. Such experiences enable the facilitator to play a teaching role: provide previews of what will be coming up, and lead the discussion relative to the content of the training materials.

RELATE EXPERIENCES FROM OTHER PROJECTS. The facilitator has multiple sources from which to provide such experiences:

Project teams previously served

Meetings of facilitators at which they share the experiences of their respective project teams

Final reports of project teams, as published in-house

Projects reported in the literature

ASSIST IN REDIRECTING THE PROJECT. The facilitator usually has a detached view, which can help to sense when the team is getting bogged down and can help guide them to a redirection of the project.

ASSIST THE PROJECT TEAM CHAIRPERSON. The facilitator can be helpful to the team chairperson in such ways as stimulating attendance at team meetings or improving human relations among team members.

REPORT PROGRESS TO THE COUNCILS. In this role the facilitator is a part of the process of reporting on progress of the projects collectively. Each project team issues minutes of its meetings. In due course each project team also issues its final report. However, reports on the projects collectively must be worked up in other ways. The facilitators are often a part of this reporting process.

Note that the above roles of facilitators are needed especially during startup. As project teams and team members acquire training and experience, the need for facilitator support declines.

Trainers for Specialists

The term "specialists" here refers to such professional categories as systems analysts, product designers, and process engineers. Training courses for these categories are built around general use tools plus methodology specifically applicable to the specialty, e.g., reliability modeling and quantification for product designers.

In some large companies, qualified trainers are available in the form of internal consultants from corporate service departments such as Corporate Quality Assurance. Such departments have been an important source of training materials and training expertise for in-house use.

Where in-house sources are not available, it is necessary to use outside sources at the outset. Potential trainers can be chosen and sent to outside courses. Alternatively, outside trainers are brought in to conduct the seed courses. (Some training materials are specially designed to simplify use by in-house trainers.)

In small companies it is seldom economic to develop in-house training at this level. Hence, outside sources are used, e.g., training at outside courses or use of consultants.

Trainers for the Workers

The chief form of training for workers has been for QC Circles. The training consists of study of tools for problem solving, followed by application of those tools to solution of quality-oriented problems.

One widely used approach has been to bring in consultants who specialize in such QC Circle training. These consultants conduct the seed courses for leaders, facilitators, and even the pioneering QC Circle members.

Training for Trainers

The approach to training of trainers has included:

1. Use of consultants
2. Use of outside training courses
3. *"Leader train leader."* During each course the leader identifies those trainees who might be good candidates to become leaders for future courses.
4. *Learn from the trainees.* The trainees have extensive experience in the realities of the subject matter. They bring up cases for discussion. They raise pertinent questions. They challenge the course materials and the assertions of the trainer. All these constitute inputs for improving the content of the training materials and the know-how of the leader. In this way, a training course may be launched with the awareness that it will be "debugged" with the aid of the trainees.

Examinations, Certification

To date companies have avoided the use of examinations and certification with respect to courses for upper and middle managers. It is in fact difficult to write examination questions on managerial subject matter, that is, to secure objectivity in questions or answers. In addition, managers have exhibited considerable cultural resistance to being examined. They prefer to be judged by results on the job.

At lower levels (specialists, first-line supervisors, workers), much of the course content consists of techniques and tools. These do permit objectivity in questions and answers. In addition, there is less cultural resistance. Hence, some companies do conduct examinations with such purposes in mind as:

To evaluate the effectiveness of the trainers

To evaluate the trainees' grasp of the subject matter

To provide a basis for recognition and/or certification

Why Training Fails

Training in planning for quality can fail for a variety of rather conventional reasons: inadequacies in facilities, training materials, instructors, budgets. Such inadequacies are usually obvious enough to generate alarm signals to those directing the training.

The more subtle reasons for failure are also the most serious since they may generate only subtle alarm signals or no signals at all.

Lack of Prior Participation by Line Managers

The line managers should participate in the planning of the training. Failing this there is a real risk that the training will become technique-oriented rather than results-oriented, that is, the emphasis will be on the tools rather than on operating results. Such emphasis then carries over into the evaluation of progress, so that progress is measured by how many persons have been trained, how many control charts are in use, how many pledge cards have been signed, and so on.

Too Narrow a Base

The decades that followed World War II have generated a series of waves of interest and publicity relative to various quality-oriented tools: statistical methods, quality awareness, quality cost analysis, QC Circles, and so on. Each of these tools has potential merit for companies. However, none is broad enough to serve as the basis for taking a company into quality leadership.

The principal safeguard against "too narrow a base" is again to include the line managers on the team that plans the training curricula. The planning should not be left solely to tool-oriented specialists. All too often their proposals are centered on their speciality.

Failure to Change Behavior

Training in planning for quality should be centered on creating a change in behavior. The focus should be on actually planning/replanning some product/process by using the quality planning road map, providing for participation by customers, and so on. The purpose of the training should be to assist the participants to make that change in behavior.

If there is no provision for change of behavior, the likelihood is that the training will not "take." It will not be put to use, and it will soon be forgotten.

A Role for Upper Managers

Upper managers have a role to play in heading off failures of training programs. That role consists of laying down the guidelines discussed earlier under the heading "Policy Guidelines." Relative to heading off failures in training, those guidelines included:

> Upper managers should establish a broad-based task force to plan the company's approach to training for quality.
>
> Quality-related training should require trainees to make applications of the new knowledge of their own jobs.

The Quality Disciplines: Tools and Methodology

"Quality disciplines" is one name given to the array of tools and methodology that collectively constitute our quality-related know-how. These tools are managerial as well as technological. During the 1980s there was an imbalance in training relative to tools and methodology. There was great emphasis on the tools of statistics, and an underemphasis on the managerial tools. This imbalance should be addressed during the 1990s. Both types of tools are necessary. Neither is sufficient.

The following lists of tools and methodologies are extensively used for quality planning. There are additional lists relating to quality improvement, quality control, specific functions, and more. (See more generally, *Juran on Leadership for Quality*, under "Tools and Methodology," pages 343–49. See also *Juran's Quality Control Handbook*, pages 9.3, 11.3, and 11.4. See also Juran Institute's course on Quality Improvement Tools.)

Managerial Tools That Are Widely Applicable

Basic definitions: quality, customer, product, process; Big Q, etc.

The Juran Trilogy: quality planning, quality control, quality improvement

The spreadsheet, a universal aid to orderly arrangement of masses of detail

The responsibility matrix, a table that lists the needed decisions and actions, and identifies who does what

The Spiral of Progress in Quality, which sets out the sequence of "concept to customer" for new product activities

The feedback loop, basic to all quality control

The breakthrough sequence, basic to all quality improvement

Early warning—the concept of discovering, before the fact, the likely effects of intended actions

The factual approach—use of facts (rather than opinions) as a basis for decision making

Questionnaire design; interviewing technique

Participation—the process of securing inputs from those who will be impacted by an intended action

Rules of the road for dealing with cultural resistance

Brainstorming, a technique for securing ideas during a meeting of multiple participants

Nominal group technique, a process for reaching a consensus among multiple participants

Force field analysis, a process for identifying driving forces and restraining forces as an aid to problem solving

Story boarding, a method of problem analysis featuring incremental accumulation of input information

Standardization

Glossaries

Tools for training

Tools for motivation

Managerial Tools that Are Planning-oriented

The quality planning road map, which generalizes the approach to meeting customers' needs

The flow diagram, a graphic means for depicting the steps in a process; also a universal aid to identifying who the customers are

The spreadsheet (applied to quality planning), an orderly arrangement of planning information consisting (usually) of (a) horizontal rows to set out the elements undergoing planning, and (b) vertical columns to set out the resulting product/process responses

Standard symbols for flow diagrams

The triple role concept of supplier, processor and customer, which applies to every person and organization entity

Quality planning spreadsheets; standard symbols

Market research

Simulation of use

The product development phase system; Concept to Customer

Concurrent planning

Design review

The participation concept; joint planning

Process capability

Study of cost of poor quality

Life cycle costing

Santayana Review; lessons learned

Data banks, checklists

Analysis for criticality, competitiveness, salability, value

Failure mode and effect analysis; fault tree analysis

Reliability analysis: modeling, quantification, prediction, apportionment, demonstration, Weibull analysis

Quality warranties

The Japanese "Seven Management Tools for QC"

In 1972 a committee of the Japanese Union of Scientists and Engineers (JUSE) was established for "developing QC tools." The committee made its recommendations in 1977. Their proposals then underwent field tests and further discussion. A special report (Nayatani, 1986) describes the resulting "Seven Management Tools for QC." They consist of the following:

1. *Affinity Diagram.* It is a method of converting vague concepts into specifics through use of language and diagrams. It

is essentially a generalization of the "black box" design concept to make it applicable to any broad concept.

2. *Relations Diagram.* It is a graphic method of depicting the numerous cause/effect relationships within a complex problem. It maps out the various cause/effect linkages. It also identifies the interrelationships, i.e., an effect within one linkage becomes a cause within another linkage. In addition, it identifies which are the major causes.
3. *Tree Diagram.* This generalizes a well-known tool widely used in such forms as fault tree analysis. It starts with an end result to be attained or avoided. It then identifies the potential contributors to that result. Each contributor may itself be a subresult, which has subcontributors. The diagram may extend to multiple levels of analysis.
4. *Matrix Diagram.* This generalizes the widely used matrix featuring horizontal rows, vertical columns, and their intersections. The quality planning spreadsheets are familiar examples.
5. *Matrix Data Analysis.* This method generalizes the data arrays (horizontal and vertical) so widely used to facilitate evaluating composite relationships.
6. *PDPC (Process Decision Program Chart).* This is similar to the familiar flow diagram but modified to include *unpredictable* outcomes and thereby to assist in anticipating future events. (The conventional flow diagram deals only with predictable events.)
7. *Arrow Diagram.* This tool is quite similar to the Gantt chart so extensively used for scheduling, along with the critical path technique or PERT (Program Evaluation and Review Technique).

Statistical Tools

The modern origins of quality-oriented statistical tools are traceable to work carried out within the Bell System during the 1920s. At that time the principal focus was on:

Sampling inspection tables

The Shewhart control chart

Evaluation of quality of manufactured product

Industrial interest grew during the 1940s and 1950s under the stimulus of numerous courses sponsored by the War Production Board during World War II. The emerging quality specialists then evolved new tools as well as variations of earlier methodology.

A parallel development occurred in Japan, resulting in widespread training of supervisors and QC Circle members in the "Seven QC Tools." The publicity given to the Japanese QC Circles then led to wide use of these same tools as the basis for training courses for QC Circles in the United States. These seven tools are:

Check sheet. This is any blank form used to tally up quality data.

Histogram. This is a frequency distribution in unsmoothed form.

Cause and effect diagram. This is Prof. Ishikawa's "fish bone diagram" for listing theories of causes.

Pareto principle. This is the phenomenon that in any population which contributes to a common effect, a relative few of the contributors account for the bulk of the effect.

Control chart. This is W. A. Shewhart's chart for continuing test of statistical significance (see Chapter 8, Figure 8-3, and association explanation).

Scatter diagram. This is a graphic representation of the interrelation between variables. Figure 12-2 is an example.

Graphs. These are pictorial representations in various forms: bar charts, pie charts, time series graphs, etc.

In addition to these "classic" statistical tools, there are numerous others that have come into use. Figure 12-11 lists some of the more widely used tools and indicates the principal areas of use.

Lists of tools can never be complete. Most tools exist in multiple forms and variations. New variations are constantly being invented. Most of the terminology has yet to be standardized.

What Shall I Do on My Return?

This question is on the mind of every participant in every training course. We shall address this question in the Epilogue of this book, under the same heading: "What Shall I Do on My Return?"

	Quality Evaluation, Estimation	Quality Prediction	Diagnosis	Quality Planning	Quality Control	Quality Improvement
Sampling tables	X				X	
Lot Plot	X		X	X	X	
Box Plots	X				X	
Probability paper	X		X			
Process Capability Analysis		X	X	X	X	X
Tests of Hypothesis	X		X			
Confidence Limits	X	X	X			
Statistical Significance	X		X			
PRE-Control				X		X
Statistical Tolerancing				X		X
Design of Experiments			X	X		X
Analysis of Variance			X	X		X
Orthogonal arrays			X	X		X
Regression Analysis			X	X		X
Evolutionary Operations			X	X		X
Response Surface Methodology			X	X		X
Reliability Quantification		X	X	X		
Reliability Prediction		X		X		
Reliability Apportionment				X		
Weibull Analysis		X	X	X		
Maintainability Analysis		X	X	X		
Process Dissection			X			X
Stratification Analysis			X			X
Stream-To-Stream analysis			X			X
Time-To-Time analysis			X			X
Actuarial Analysis		X	X			X
Concentration Analysis			X			X

FIGURE 12–11 Statistical Tools and Areas of Application

List of High Points

Data bases are the result of lessons learned from human experience.

Historical events become lessons learned only after they have undergone retrospective analysis.

It is fairly easy to apply the Santayana Review to high-frequency cycles.

A widespread low-frequency process that desperately needs application of the Santayana Review is the launching of new products.

The end result of the Santayana Review is lessons learned.

For high-frequency cycles, recognition of the need is typically at departmental levels.

For low-frequency cycles, recognition of the need takes place at high levels.

To secure motivation there should first be an answer to the question: Motivation to do what?

Doing the deeds creates the awareness, not the other way around.

A major force in human behavior is the cultural pattern.

Any intended change actually consists of two changes:

1. The intended change
2. The social consequence

In communication with workers the new emphasis should be on analysis for causes rather than looking for blame.

When dealing with cultural resistance, managers are well advised to study the "rules of the road."

To motivate through the reward system, it is necessary at the outset to distinguish between mandated work and voluntary work.

Quality-oriented rewards should be woven into the overall reward system.

The newness of rewards for quality requires new "metrics" for evaluating performance.

It is necessary to extend training in managing for quality throughout the organization if the amateurs are to become professionals.

The end result of planning the training curriculum should be a matrix that shows the list of courses along with which categories of personnel are to take what courses.

Upper managers should be the first to acquire the new training.

The basic purpose of the training should be to secure a change in behavior.

Those who are planning the approach to training should specify that trainers possess the needed expertise in the subject matter as well as possessing the teaching skills.

Most companies make use of "facilitators" to assist the project teams.

The line managers should participate in the planning of the training.

The planning of the training should not be left solely to tool-oriented specialists.

During the 1980s there was an imbalance in training relative to tools and methodology. There was great emphasis on the tools of statistics, and an underemphasis on the managerial tools. This imbalance should be addressed during the 1990s.

Tasks for Upper Managers

Upper managers must take the initiative if the Santayana Review is to be applied to long-cycle, low-frequency activities.

Upper managers must create an action plan as a prerequisite to giving top priority to quality.

Upper managers should establish a broad-based task force to plan the company's approach to training in planning for quality.

Upper managers should mandate training in planning for quality.

Upper managers should mandate that training in planning for quality be designed to require trainees to make applications of the new knowledge to their own jobs.

Upper managers should participate in training of subordinate levels.

] 13 [

Quality Planning for the Taurus

Case Example

Ford Motor Company's planning for the Taurus model of automobile is a good example of following the quality planning road map (Veraldi, 1985).

The Primary Goal: Best in Class

During the early 1980s the company began planning a new Ford model—a front-wheel-drive, midsize car to be produced during the late 1980s. The company's future required that this model be successful. The company had been losing market share to foreign competition. The North American operations had incurred heavy financial losses for several years. The model was named Taurus. (A similar model, to be planned for the Mercury line, was named Sable.)

With respect to quality, the upper managers concluded that Taurus should be "Best in Class": the quality should be equal or superior to that of any competing model in the "class," domestic or foreign. That mandate became the strategic quality goal.

Organization Structure

Traditionally Ford had used the conventional functional organization structure to plan new models. The planning was done sequentially. Each function (market research, product design, etc.) carried out its function and then "handed off" the result to the next function. For the Taurus, Ford adopted a new approach, a project-oriented form called Team Taurus. Figure 13–1 shows the conventional organization form. Figure 13–2 shows the Team Taurus form.

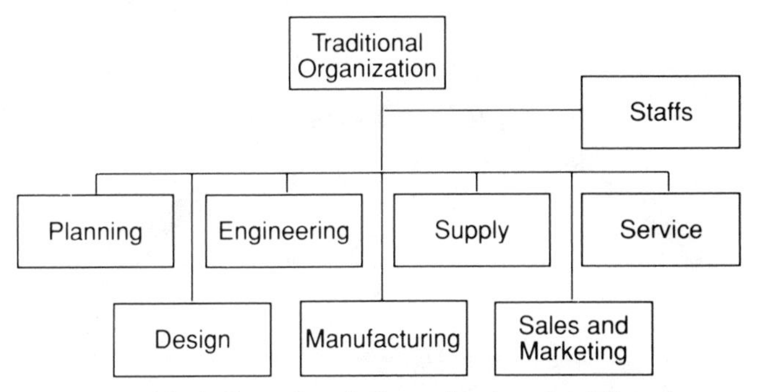

FIGURE 13–1 Functional Organization for Planning

All the functions associated with launching the new model were brought into Team Taurus. The purpose was to carry out all those planning functions concurrently rather than consecutively, and at the same time to broaden greatly the participation of all who were impacted by the project.

Who Are the Customers?

Ford took a close look at who the customers were—those who would be impacted by the project. This close look stimulated Ford to identify and meet customer needs with greater precision than ever before.

> For example, the insurance companies are impacted by any new model. They pay for the repair of cars damaged in accidents, and they look for ways to reduce the repair costs. Those costs depend in part on how the car is designed. Team Taurus was able to help this impacted customer—the insurance companies—by providing the Taurus with features that facilitated body alignment during repair of damaged cars.
>
> In like manner, the Department of Transportation is impacted; it administers the laws governing highway safety. Ford learned that the agency was contemplating mandating "high mount" brake lights on future new models. Ford planned for this contingency even though it had not yet been mandated. Thereby Ford minimized the future cost of compliance. (The high mount brake light was in fact mandated subsequently.)

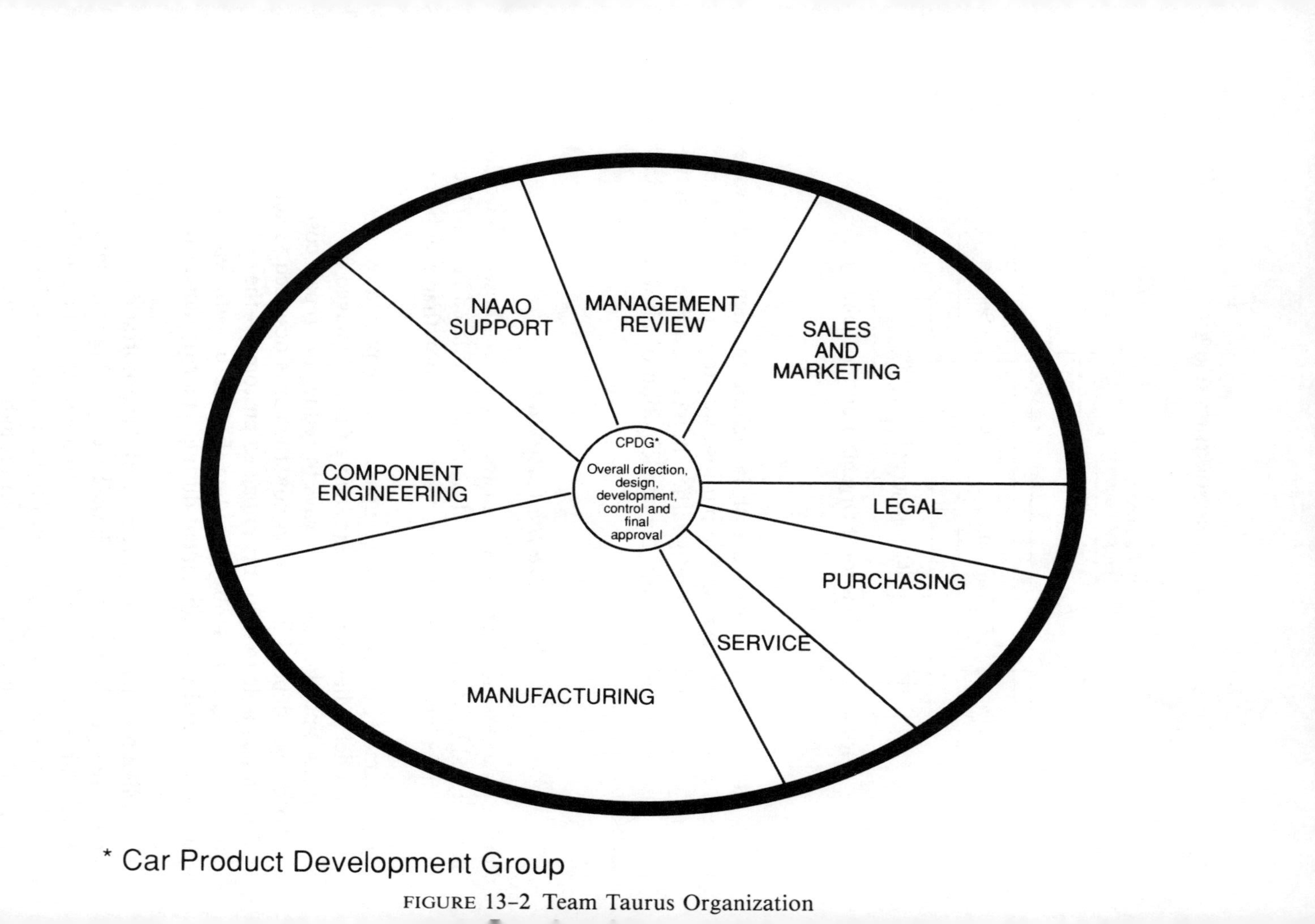

FIGURE 13–2 Team Taurus Organization

Why Buy Taurus? Customer Needs: Product Features

Of course, the major customer is the buyer of the cars. Ford went deeply into the question: Why buy Taurus? Specifically which product features are decisive in a customer's decision on which car to buy? There are literally tens of thousands of quality features that enter into the design, manufacture, sale, and service of automobiles. Which of those features are the vital few—those which can be sensed by the customers and are therefore influential in the buying decision? Ford supplemented its market research by securing experts' opinions, plus input from customers and from many company functions. From the resulting numerous nominations, Ford selected those vital few features which directly impacted the senses of these major customers. The vital few turned out to be more than four hundred features! Examples were such features as:

Effort required to raise the hood from "pop up"

Trunk storage height

Braking distance

"Feel" of the steering wheel

Wind noise

Effect of Best in Class Concept

In response to the "Best in Class" mandate, Team Taurus acquired samples of the competing models to discover which was best in class for each of those 400+ features. Then came the job of equaling or exceeding best in class (or securing a license). This job consisted of more than four hundred projects, each requiring:

A quality goal

An organization with responsibility to meet the goal

A budget

A schedule

The needed investment was enormous. Ford's subsequent disclosures indicate that the goal of best in class was met for the large majority of those 400+ features. For many of the rest, there were conscious tradeoffs to avoid suboptimization.

Translation and Measurement

At the outset those 400+ features were expressed in customers' language, which is usually in qualitative terms. The engineers needed to translate everything into technological, measurable terms: temperature in degrees, distance in meters, time in minutes, noise in decibels. This translation had always been a part of the quality planning process but became acute because of the many sensory qualities in the list.

Process Development

Within Ford much was done to secure factory ideas on process development. Employees from all manufacturing and assembly areas were asked for their suggestions. More than 1,400 "wants" were identified and evaluated for potential incorporation into the design of the Taurus. As to outside suppliers, Team Taurus took some significant steps toward implementing the company's new thrust toward "partnership with suppliers." Prototype test parts were sourced to the same company that would get the production business, providing earlier quality parts and increased opportunity to use suppliers' expertise in refining manufacturing processes. Ford cites the example of Masland Carpet Company, which cut the various pieces of carpet on the floor of the station wagon model so that the nap would lie in one direction, giving a better color match.

A number of factors helped ensure that processes would be capable of meeting the engineering design goals. First, as with the manufacture of any established product, many processes with long history and well-understood capability were carried over from the past. Joint planning provided early warning of potential capability problems and enabled action to avoid them. Earlier availability of full automobile prototypes allowed last-minute design and process refinements. Ford's existing systems of statistical process control and supplier qualification also contributed to ensuring process capability.

Transfer to Operations

The Team Taurus concept resulted in an improved transfer thanks to all that joint planning, team coordination, and full-cycle involvement of the engineers and managers.

The Overall Results

The Taurus became a stunning success in the market. Ford's profitability became the highest of all the domestic producers, and Taurus was a major contributor to this result. Ford's image as a domestic quality leader was correspondingly raised. In addition, Ford's use of innovative planning provided lessons learned that will be valuable during launch of future models. These lessons learned include some concepts of a grand strategy nature:

Upper management leadership
Customer focus
The best-in-class concept
Cross-functional teams
The project approach
Concurrent instead of sequential planning

] *14* [

Decisions for the Consumer Price Index

Case Example

Background

The Consumer Price Index (CPI) is prepared by the United States Bureau of Labor Statistics (BLS) as the measure of changes in prices paid by consumers. In addition to its extensive use as an economic indicator and decision variable, it is widely applied as an escalator to adjust wages, salaries, transfer payments, and taxes. Federal government payments for Social Security, Federal Retirement, school lunches, and many other programs are adjusted by changes in the CPI. These applications are so extensive that in 1986 every 1.0 percent increase in the CPI generated an additional $2.8 billion in Federal outlays. What is more, because federal personal income tax brackets were also escalated by the CPI, each 1.0 percent increase in the CPI reduced tax receipts by $1.8 billion.

One of the important characteristics of the CPI is that it should price *exactly* the same set of goods and services from one month to the next. The set of priced items is updated periodically, but the price *change* should always be between sets of identical items.

Of course, in practice, goods and services do undergo changes, and exactly the same item cannot always be priced. Items disappear for many reasons. Automobile manufacturers issue new models that differ from the previous model year. Clothing styles change. Federal law eliminates leaded gasoline. The conditions for purchasing a discounted airline ticket change. A bus company changes the times of day during which a senior-citizen discount applies, or a state institutes a mandatory bottle deposit, thereby eliminating all "no deposit" bottles.

Process Background

The CPI is prepared every month from about 100,000 prices that are collected each month by more than 350 field representatives located throughout the nation. These representatives enter prices and other information on paper collection forms, which are sent to headquarters in Washington, D.C. There the forms are reviewed and keyed into a data base. The data are then subjected to extensive computer edits and clerical verification.

Among the specialized groups performing CPI work are about sixty economists, each of whom specializes in a specific set of closely related goods or services. Among their many duties is the review of the collected price data. In addition to a general review of their specific market assignments, they must normally analyze about 10 percent of the individual prices collected. It is this analysis of collected price data that was the process to be replanned.

The Process

Figure 14–1 gives a highly simplified overview of the analysis. The first step is to verify that the data are correct and fix any that are not. At least 90 percent of all prices are successfully validated through

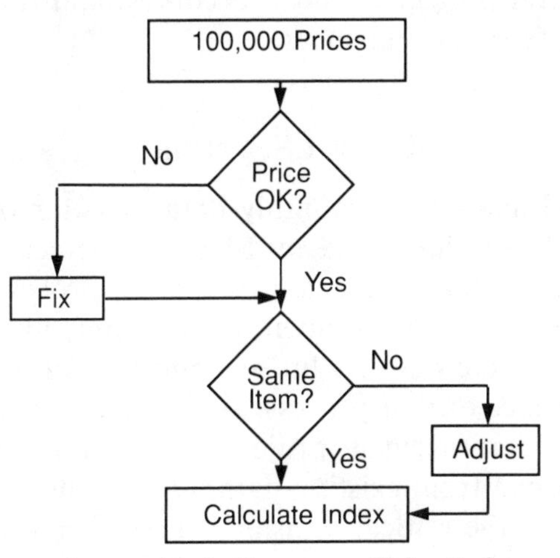

FIGURE 14–1 Consumer Price Index

computer edits and clerical review. Some highly unusual cases and those cases about which the field representative has raised a question must still be reviewed and validated by the appropriate economist.

Even more significant, however, is the second decision point that identifies those cases in which it has been impossible to price exactly the same item as was priced in the previous month. Any time exactly the same good or service cannot be priced from the same outlet, the field representative selects the most similar available item as a "substitute." This substitute is fully described and priced. The responsible economist must then evaluate the differences between the original item and the substitute. The general model for this evaluation is as follows:

$$\text{Pure Price Change} = \text{Observed Price Change} - \text{Quality Change}$$

The pure price change is the change to be used in the index. The observed price change is the difference in reported prices for the original and substitute items. The quality change is the market value of the differences in characteristics between the two items. Sometimes this quality change value is zero. Other times a positive or negative value can be estimated. And at still other times the value cannot be estimated with sufficient precision for use in the CPI. In those latter cases, the comparison simply cannot be made, and the particular item is not used in the index for that month.

As one might imagine, this evaluation of a quality change is a complex technical task requiring training, skill, and professional experience. Like many such professional processes, documentation was limited to general principles and procedures, and there was heavy reliance on professional judgment.

Project Selection

The review and analysis of monthly data by commodity-specialist economists had been identified by BLS management as a possible process for quality improvement. It was a key process that had not yet been the target of improvement efforts. But, like most professional processes, there was very little summary information available on the performance of that process. As a prelude to mapping out a series of quality improvement projects, some preliminary information was developed from existing data. One of the key preliminary studies looked at the critical decision on whether the original and substitute items were economically comparable to each other. Charts similar to Figure 14–2 were constructed for each product classification in the CPI. These charts showed the proportion of substitution items that were determined to be noncomparable for each month during a thirty-month period. There can be no standard for this proportion, because it is determined in large measure by market forces. But one would expect that for a given product area there would not normally be sudden, sustained shifts in the proportion like the one that occurred after April 1984 in Figure 14–2. In this case, the shifts in the process outcomes were directly related to the change in assignment of the economist responsible for the product. For about half of the products, similar process shifts were identified that could be associated with specific internal operational changes such as staff assignments. This finding suggested that there was not a single process at work. Rather, there were a number of individual processes that were not replicable. The breadth and degree of this variation coupled with the limited amount of process documentation indicated that a full replanning of the process would be worth the effort.

The Team

The team assigned to this quality planning project consisted of one senior economist from each of the four major product groups in the CPI, a member of the Quality Assurance staff, a representative from CPI data processing, and a representative from field operations. The

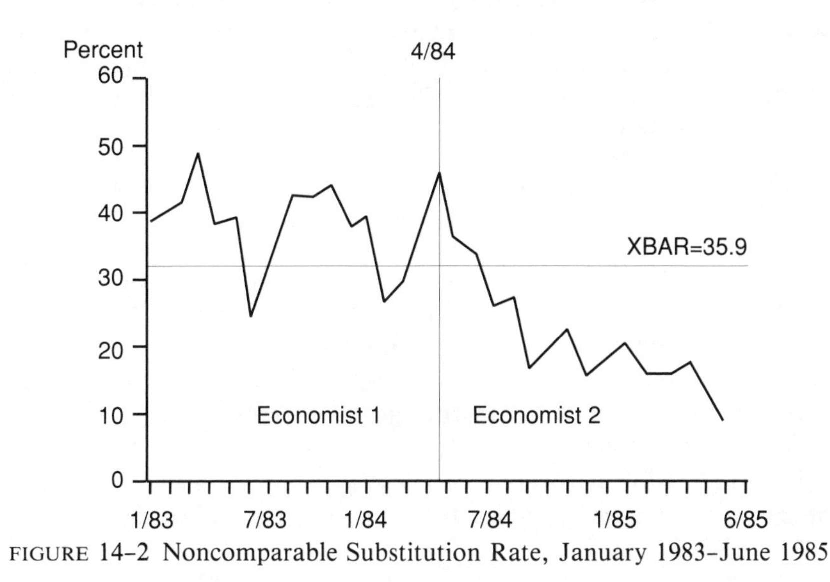

FIGURE 14–2 Noncomparable Substitution Rate, January 1983–June 1985

latter two are principal customers of the process. While most were not supervisors or managers, all were experienced professionals who fully understood the process objectives. In addition, the team always had direct, immediate access to top management and reported on their progress frequently. The Quality Assurance Manager served as facilitator. The following paragraphs highlight some of the results of each of the steps from the Quality Planning Roadmap. Because of the great complexity of the process, only a few examples are given. To some degree the description is also idealized, because progress was not always quite as linear as the presentation might imply. The team would sometimes become bogged down at one step and decide to move ahead to the next step, in order to prevent paralysis. For example, because a technical service was the "product" being designed, it was difficult to keep the process that creates the service differentiated from the service itself. In the end, the team eventually sorted it all out, but it was helpful to remain flexible and be prepared both to press ahead and to return to previous steps once omissions became apparent.

Identify the Customer

The team identified two principal internal customers outside the immediate office: the data processing operations staff and the field operation staff. Within the immediate office, customers included the economist supervisors and the product economists themselves, who used the results of this micro-analytical process in other aspects of their own work. And finally, of course, there were the many users of the CPI—those who used it for economic analysis, for process reporting, for indexation, for public policy, and so on.

Discover Customers' Needs

All major internal customers of the process were either represented on the team or contacted directly for their needs from the process. No new information collection was undertaken for the external customers. Instead, the team used summary guidance that had already been developed from advisory committees and technical conferences sponsored by BLS.

It is not possible in this space to describe all or even a large portion of the results for this complex project. But, some *examples* of these needs follow.

Customer: CPI User		
Needs		
Primary	*Secondary*	*Tertiary*
Conform to theoretical structure	Fixed market basket	—
	Pure price change	Eliminate all quality change Capture all pure price change
Minimum error* within budget	Minimize cumulative errors* Systematic errors* Minimize random errors*	
*The term "error" here relates to statistical characteristics of the estimates, *not* to *mistakes*.		

Customer: Data Processing Staff		
Needs		
Primary	*Secondary*	
Timeliness	All review completed by deadline Work submitted on a flow basis	
Customer: Supervisor		
Needs		
Primary	*Secondary*	*Tertiary*
Coverage for absences	Know status	Work complete Step in process for incomplete Work not started
	Know unique procedures for index item	What are they? What do they mean? How do you use them?

Translate Customer Needs

Most internal customer needs required little translation, partly because the presence of internal customers on the team created almost unconscious translations during the prior step. But the check for needed translation was an important verification and did produce a number of needed classifications. Two examples follow.

Need	*Translation*
Work submitted on a flow basis	All changes entered for a price quote or outlet within an established time of its availability on the data base
Minimize systematic error	Minimize bias

Establish Units of Measure and Sensor

The following are the units of measure and the associated sensors set for the above translated needs.

Translated Need	*Unit of Measure*	*Sensor*
All change entered for a price quote or outlet within an established time of its availability	Work days % complete	Data base tabulation
Minimize bias error in substitution tabulation	% substitutes compared; % substitutes quality adjusted	Data base
Know unique procedures for index item		
What are they?	Existence of information	Supervisor checklist
Where are they?	Designated storage of information	Supervisor checklist
How do you use them?	Does supervisor understand (Y/N)	Supervisor

Product Features and Goals

Because the team was redesigning the delivery of a service rather than a physical good, there was some difficulty in separating the planning step for *product* features from the planning step for process features. In retrospect, however, it is possible to see the distinction, so the following is a more orderly reconstruction of what happened so that the results will be more helpful for others.

If the product that a team is designing is a service, that service still has *features* that are analytically distinct from the process that delivers the service.

Using a simplified example, if one is designing an overnight delivery service, the time of delivery is a feature of the *product* with an associated goal of, say, 10:00 A.M. The process for making that delivery will consist of a sequence of package sorting and delivery steps, which constitute the *process*.

One way to distinguish between the features of the service product on the one hand and the features of the process that produces that service is to think of the *product* features as the *what*. What does the service accomplish? The *process* features are the *how*. These are the methods used to achieve the *what*.

The following are examples of product features and their goals that are strongly associated with the above translated needs.

Translated Need:	All changes entered for a price quote or outlet within an established time of its availability
Product Feature:	Percent of quotes and outlets completed within specified time
Product Goal:	99.99%
Translated Need:	Minimize bias in substitution
Product Feature:	Comparability choice
Goal:	Expected value of implicit quality adjustment is zero
Translated Need:	Know what are procedures for index item
Product Feature:	Standardized formal substitution adjustment procedures
Goal:	Exists for every CPI entry-level item

A summary of information and decisions that link customer needs to product features and feature goals is seen in the product design spreadsheet, Figure 14–3.

Process Features and Goals

Multiple process features are required for some product features, and a single process feature may affect more than one product fea-

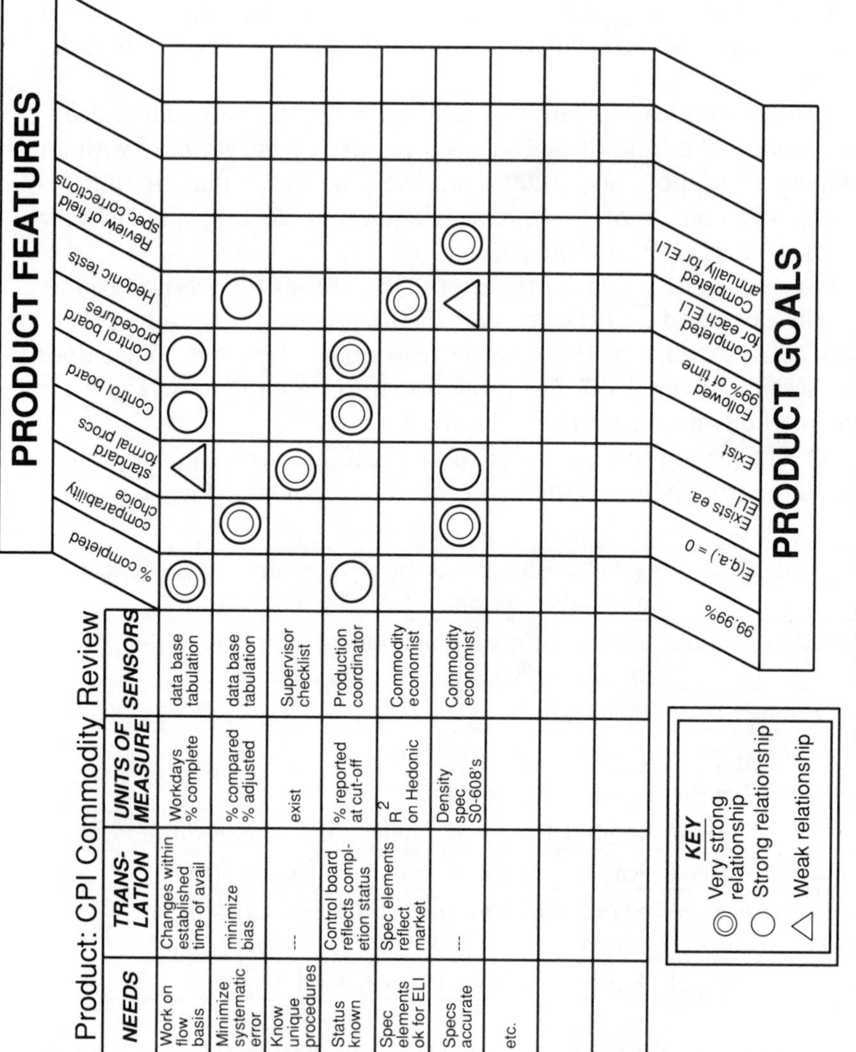

FIGURE 14–3 Product Design Spreadsheet

ture. Listed below are three process features and their goals that relate significantly to the above product features.

Process Feature:	Automated status and action-required report issued to each economist
Goals:	Always accurate. Displayed at each log-in
Process Feature:	Adherence to a formal hedonic regression-based set of estimates to guide decisions on comparability
Goal:	Complete for each entry-level item by December 1989. (This sub-process was the object of another quality planning effort)
Process Feature:	Standardized document on each item's procedures
Goal:	Present for all items by December 1987

It should be noted that some process features on this spreadsheet call for the development of some of subprocesses. These subprocesses, in turn, were designed by other teams.

A summary of information and decisions that link product features and product goals to process features and process goals is seen in the process design spreadsheet, Figure 14–4.

Design Quality Control

Because of the technical complexity and the newness of standardized procedures, many of the control mechanisms continued to rely on human sensing. But some important improvements were made in control, like the following example.

Process Feature:	Adherence to a formal hedonic regression-based set of estimates to guide decisions on comparability
Sensor:	Routine frequency tabulations from data base
Criterion:	Shift outside historical or research-set limits
Assigned to:	Section Chief over a set of items

A summary of information and decisions that link process features and process goals to process controls is seen in the process control spreadsheet, Figure 14–5.

Product: CPI Commodity Review

PROCESS FEATURES

PRODUCT FEATURES	***PRODUCT GOALS***	Automated status report	Adherence to hedonic-based decisions	Standard document by ELI procedure	Maintain control board	Write board procedure	Train in board procedure	Train in Hedonics	Establish Hedonic process	Design review process	
% quotes & outlets completed within specified time avail	99.99% of time	○		○							
Comparability choice	E(q.a.) = 0		◎	○				◎	○		
Standardized formal substitution adjustment process	Exists for every ELI			◎				○	◎		
Control board	Exist				◎	◎					
Control board procedures	Followed 99% of time				◎	◎	◎				
Hedonic tests	Completed each ELI							◎	◎		
Review of field spec corrections	Completed annually per ELI									◎	
etc.											
	PROCESS GOALS	always accurate displayed @ login	for each ELI by 12/89	present each ELI 12/89	board always accurate layout w/ supplies	written & understood	100% trained	100% trained	designed & written	designed & written	

KEY

◎ Very strong relationship

○ Strong relationship

△ Weak relationship

FIGURE 14–4 Process Design Spreadsheet

Process Features	*Process Goals*	*Sensors*	*Criteria*	*Assigned to:*
Adhere to hedonic decisions	for each ELI by 12/89	Frequency tabs from data base	Shift from history or research limits	Section Chief
Standard procedure documentation	for each ELI by 12/89	checklist of ELI	complete checklist	Section Chief
Maintain control board	always accurate layout & supplier	checklist	supplies ready & complete	Board Coordinator
Control board procedures	written & understood	Section Chiefs' reviews	do they accept	Production Control Coordinator
Trained in board procedures	100% trained	C/A roster	all checked off	Section Chiefs
Trained in hedonics	100% trained	C/A roster	all checked off	Branch Chief
Establish hedonic procedure	designed & written	Team report	follow quality planning	Quality Council
etc.				

FIGURE 14–5 Process Control Spreadsheet

Prove Process Capability

The study of this process with formal process capability methods did not appear feasible at the time, but the replanned process was implemented for a few items at a time and the results were evaluated. A plan was also put in place to schedule specific research and analysis projects to optimize some of the less well understood features of the process.

Results

There was considerable evidence of the effectiveness of the new processes, although a number of quality improvement projects completed during the same period also undoubtedly contributed to the overall results. From time to time an operational error has been found in the CPI. In the early 1980s it was necessary to publish a correction to previously released data about ten times a year. Those corrections were usually quite small and never affected a major national index. Most were corrections to local area data. As the result of this and other projects, even those errors were eliminated. For the two years ended December 1988, there were no such corrections.

Also, the new procedures reduced by about 10 percent the amount of time economists needed to spend reviewing current data. This relief gave them more time to conduct longer-term research projects focused on improving the quality of the CPI.

] 15 [

Replanning the Product Development Process

Case Example

Background

Perkin-Elmer is the world's largest manufacturer of analytical instruments. These instruments, which include spectrophotometers, chromatographs, and thermal and elemental analyzers, are used in a wide variety of applications in industry, government, and education to analyze solids, liquids, and gases for their constituent parts. The Instrument Division is responsible for the design, development, and manufacture of these instruments in the United States.

In 1984, as part of Perkin-Elmer's effort to improve the quality of its products and services, the Instrument Group developed its Quality Business Plan. One of the elements of this plan called for the early involvement of all departments in the product development process. Fortuitously, as replanning of the product development process began, the first draft of *Juran on Quality Planning* became available for field testing. Juran Institute asked Perkin-Elmer to be a test site. This case presents the Instrument Group's experiences using Juran's quality planning steps to replan the product development process in its organization.

As in many U.S. organizations, product development at the Instrument Division suffered to some degree from the "over-the-wall" syndrome. The Product Department (marketing) handed the specifications to Engineering. Engineering designed the product and threw it "over the wall" to Manufacturing. Manufacturing produced the product, then threw it "over the wall" to Quality Assurance for testing after the first units were produced (and *after* the product had become a part of the financial plan and had been announced for sale). This approach to product development was very inefficient and had great potential for producing costly, low-quality products. To remain competitive against emerging Japanese competition, the Division felt it was imperative to improve in three respects: meeting the needs of customers, both internal and external; achieving competitive quality levels; and responding quickly to market requirements. Replanning the product development process was the key to this improvement.

A unique opportunity presented itself, which encouraged replanning the development process. Before 1985 there were separate divisions, each responsible for the development and manufacture of one line of analytical instrument. In 1985 the instrument divisions in North America were reorganized into one large Instrument Division, responsible for the development of all instrument types. Now under one management, the Division could effect a change that would have been difficult before.

Project Selection

The project mission was to develop a new product development process that would involve all departments early in product design in order to discover and correct quality problems before the product was released for manufacture. The first step was to examine the existing process.

Process Background

To keep the task at hand manageable, the replanning focused on activities within the Division. The team defined the process to be replanned thus:

Process name: Product Development Process

Input: Market research information

Output: A first production lot, delivered and installed

First step: Establish the product concept in the product department (where marketing responsibility resides)

Last steps: Deliver and install the first routine production lot

The process included such traditional activities as: product specification; determination of feasibility through construction of a breadboard model; construction and testing of prototype instruments; release of class A drawings; fabrication of preproduction instruments; quality testing; and delivery and installation of instruments to customers.

In setting these boundaries, the team chose not to examine the market research process or the process by which the resulting newly designed instrument would be marketed and sold. These marketing-oriented processes provide additional opportunities for replanning.

The Project Team

The team included the representatives of all the departments involved in product development: Vice President, Director of R&D; two R&D managers from different product lines; Director of Manufacturing; Director, Manufacturing Engineering; Manager, Reliability Engineering; Manager, Service Support; and Director, Quality Assurance. The Manager, Quality Planning, played the role of facilitator and trainer. The Vice President of R&D was the team leader.

Identify Customers

The team began to identify customers of the process by reviewing existing product development processes in use for the product lines and then identifying the steps that were essential to developing a product (Figure 15-1). Each of the blocks within the figure is thought of as a process unit. Within each process unit, each department is viewed as a customer of input by other units, a processor of that input into a product, and a supplier of products to its customers.

In developing the flow diagram, each block was completed by defining it and answering the questions:

Who are its customers?

What are their quality needs?

What must be done to meet these needs?

What does the unit require as input?

For most of the process steps analyzed, the customers were departments within the organization.

The next task was to provide a detailed description of the activities

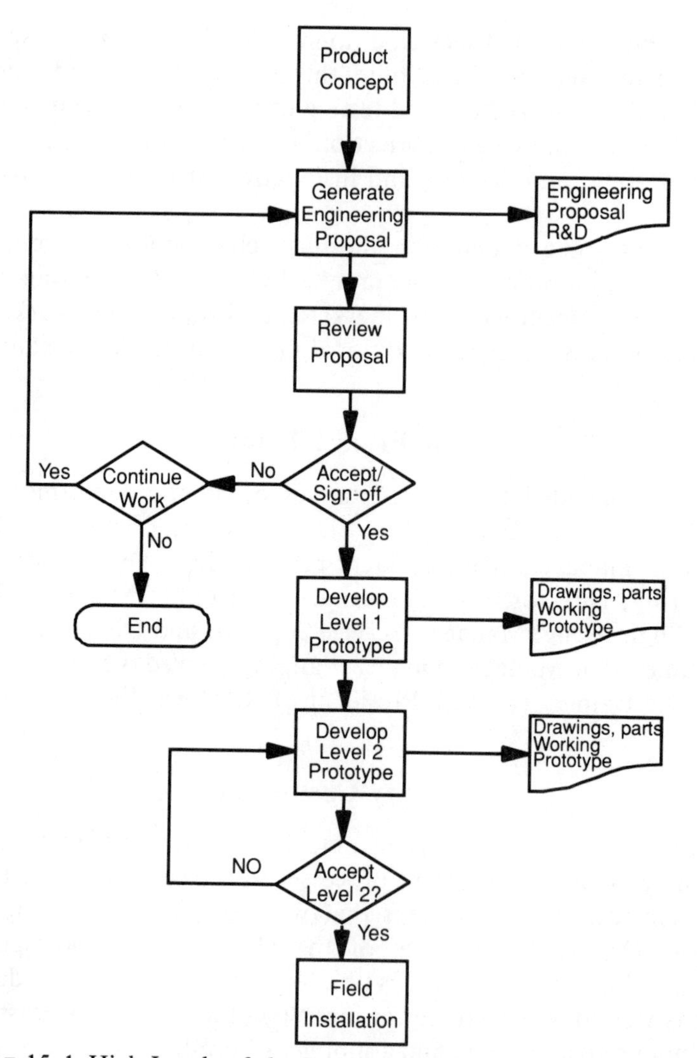

FIGURE 15-1 High Levels of the Product Development Process Flow Diagram

for each block of the flow diagram. This is where the team stumbled. Although the Division had recently reorganized, most of the people on the team had worked together in one capacity or another for a considerable period of time. Yet it was discovered that different departments had different meanings for the same words describing the development stages. This was a very valuable insight, as it was realized that these terms had to be precisely defined if the finished product, the replanned product development process, was going to be used by those outside of the team.

Discover Customer Needs

Having carefully defined each block on the flow diagram, the team set about identifying the needs of each department involved in each block. This activity turned up aspects of each block that caused them to change the description of it. It was a surprise to see how many needs existed of which other departments were not aware. Once these surfaced, it was easy to see how needs could be met. Statements of needs were complete to the point of being slightly redundant.

Translate Customer Needs

In this project a need generally related to information required by one department from another in order to carry out its assigned tasks. After the team had worked through each block of the flow diagram, they began the task of translating the needs into quality characteristics. Quality characteristics were specific aspects of that information as stated in the language that the supplier department understood and could indeed deliver. An example of the results is shown in the simplified quality planning spreadsheet in Figure 15-2.

Establish Units of Measure and Sensors

Two concepts that were initially difficult to grasp were the "unit of measure" and the "sensor" when dealing with quality characteristics that were not goods. Figure 15-2 shows several examples of these; cost estimates and tooling requirements are two. The team overcame this difficulty by describing in broad terms the kinds of units available. The sensors were the reports, data bases, and the like, where measurement information was to be found. They felt that the discussions were helpful in later stages of the project, when they would be forced to be more specific about measurement as applied to specific pieces of the process. Treating measurement in this way at this stage of the project enabled them to obtain reasonable and useful results.

Partway through completing the quality spreadsheet, the team recognized the need to provide additional information. In particular it was felt to be important to identify who was going to supply the material to meet each of the needs. It was also important to them to

Team Project: Develop Level 1 Prototype				
Needs	Information from different functions to enable R&D to create an acceptable Level 1 prototype			
Quality Character-istics	Product structure	Cost Estimate	Tooling requirements	Assessment of selected components
Unit of Measure	Any Family Tree information for EDB from MFG	Any information on costs	Information on tooling, and tooling cost estimates	Any information on defective components
Sensor	EDB	Reports, EDB	Reports, meetings	Quality Assurance report
Goal	Understanding levels of assembly	Verification that design approaches are consistent with cost goals	Understanding of special tooling	Elimination of defective components and/or those which do not meet applicable codes
Supplier	Manufacturing	Manufacturing vendor	Manufacturing vendors	QA
Output	Level 1 Prototype	Level 1 Prototype	Level 1 Prototype	Level 1 Prototype

FIGURE 15–2 Quality Planning Spreadsheet

identify the product that was the output of each subprocess. These two pieces of information are contained in "Supplier" and "Output" columns of the spreadsheet and are an addition to the spreadsheet as described by the Juran planning process.

Product Features and Goals

This detailed analysis of customer needs indicated that a new approach was needed to develop high-quality analytical instruments and to manage the entire project from product concept through first shipments. As a result, a feature of the new product development process was the creation of Early Involvement Teams. The composition of each team depends on the nature of the specific project, but generally includes five or six representatives from Manufacturing, Quality, Service, Product Marketing, and R&D. This team manages the project, ensures that the needs of their respective departments are met, and secures the necessary resources from their departments to accomplish the tasks at hand.

Another feature developed was the creation of four broad phases of product development, as seen in Figure 15–3. The first phase is defining the product, determining feasibility, and planning the remaining development. The second phase involves designing and making a series of prototypes. The third phase centers on manufacturing process development and culminates in a pilot run. The last phase concerns market introduction, first shipments, and field feedback on product quality and acceptance. Although one functional area can dominate the activities in a particular phase (e.g., R&D in the prototype development, and Manufacturing in manufacturing process development), all departments play an important role in each of the four phases. Also, some of the activities that were traditionally done in the later stages of the product development process were moved into the earlier phases, such as reliability, manufacturability, and serviceability.

An analysis of each department's needs in the product development process showed that there were advantages to doing more work

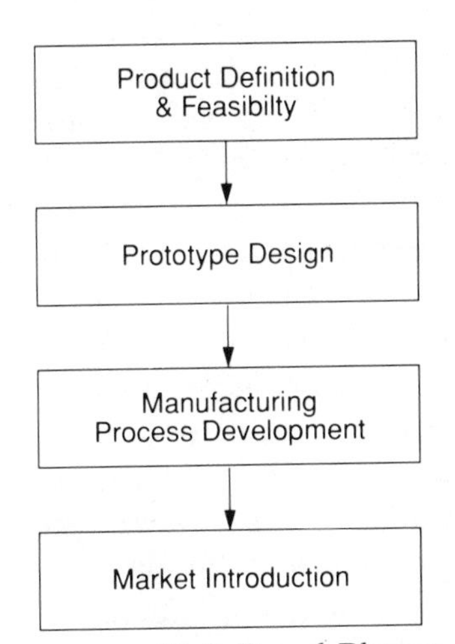

FIGURE 15–3 Broad Phases

prior to the development of a prototype. Although the first phase takes longer than before, feedback is less difficult and less costly to implement. Also, this early activity gives a clear description of the product being developed.

These Early Involvement product development activities begin when the product marketing department, with input from the field, generates a product-concept document. A product definition is then drafted by R&D; in it the product's hardware and software are described. At this point feasibility studies are begun. These studies go beyond traditional design feasibility:

- The Quality Department determines if reliability goals can be met.
- Manufacturing examines the design concept to determine if new processes and manufacturing technology are required.
- The Service Department explores approaches for installing and maintaining the new instrument.

When these activities are complete, the project team prepares a product development proposal, which includes complete specifications, a development schedule, and a resource plan. A presentation of these plans is made to management for approval.

Process Features and Goals

Some activities in the "early involvement" approach were new. These activities focus on the new features of the product development process that involve other departments working with R&D in design-related activities to achieve high-quality products. Historic reviews, the software test plan, the design for manufacturability analysis, and the reliability studies are examples of such features that have been added to the earlier stages of product development.

During feasibility studies, the Quality Department and R&D conduct joint reviews of past instrument designs relevant to the new product to expose all major problems associated with these designs. Service records are searched to identify field problems. Warranty replacements and customer complaint files are examined to determine problems associated with customer acceptance and improper marketing of a product, that is, selling a product for an application for which it was not intended. Manufacturing records are reviewed to determine where difficulties were experienced in producing the earlier products. Having exposed the problems associated with the previous product designs, the project team examines the new product design to ensure that these same problems are not built into it. One of the most frustrating experiences general management can have is for a new product to exhibit an older product's shortcomings because some of the designs were carried forward inadvertently without a critical examination. These historic reviews are designed to prevent that from occurring.

In generating a software test plan, there is the need for a top-level software design early in the design process to determine feasibility and to estimate the required software development resources. In the past, an *ad hoc* testing plan was developed after the software coding phase was complete, which occurred much later in the process. With each new release of software, questions arose as to how much retesting was necessary. With a software design available early, R&D and the product department can agree on the logical points for new releases and which modules require testing (or retesting) at each release. By optimizing the testing process, sufficient time can be allocated to correcting software bugs, which can greatly improve the quality of the finished product. Also, the overall development time can be shortened.

Historical reviews and software test plans begin and end at definite points in the development cycle. They involve a series of reviews in the first instance and the generation of a test plan in the second. The new design for manufacturability analysis, however, pervades the entire design process. Manufacturing personnel, during the feasibility stage, review the proposed approach for potential difficulties that may arise in production. The design is reviewed until a satisfactory solution is found. When the prototypes are being designed, several formal reviews are held at which the results of a design for assembly analysis are presented. This analysis is made using the Boothroyd and Dewhurst methodology and software, and is done by R&D with help from manufacturing engineers who are familiar with production processes.

Using this software system, a design may require several iterations to be acceptable. Designers soon recognize which approaches yield better results. Continually trying to reduce parts and make assembly easier throughout the design process, both when new designs are initiated and when existing designs are changed, helps improve assembly times and product quality.

Reliability studies also pervade the entire development process and are done jointly by the Quality Department and R&D. Previously, all of Perkin-Elmer's new instrument products were subjected to rigorous stress life tests prior to market introduction and customer shipment. However, any problems uncovered at that stage were costly to fix, because this phase occurred just before shipment. Designs had to be modified under the stress of time pressures; often the most cost-effective solution could not be implemented. Retesting caused additional delays. New parts and new software needed to implement the solution had to be expedited at some risk to quality. In the new development procedure, reliability studies are done throughout the design cycle. During the development of the prototypes, the Quality Department and R&D work together to identify critical components and assemblies. Test are devised to determine the reliability of these critical parts and their effect on instrument performance. Designs are modified appropriately. While there is no intention of eliminating the pre-introduction testing, that testing is now a better predictor of subsequent field reliability.

Prove Process Capability

An important part of replanning any process is testing the process capability. For the first trial of the new product development process, two project teams were chosen to test the approach. One team developed a software product; the other developed a hardware product. The problems the teams experienced in implementing the new approach were as important as the results they achieved in their product development efforts. As a result of the two projects, the methodology has been fine-tuned and the process capability determined.

All new projects that have been initiated since the first pilot program are using the new methodology. Input from these projects to the Product Development Process Team is encouraged. Many of the projects that were in progress when the new methodology was introduced adopted the relevant portions of it.

It was clear from the feedback of the teams involved in the initial testing and those teams that joined them along the way that the quality spreadsheets plus some supplemental documentation were inadequate to describe the new process. There were a large number of questions and some confusion. It quickly became obvious that there was a need for a comprehensive guide to our new product development process. The finished document took the form of a product development guide.

Proving process capability did not stop with the issuance of the first edition of this guide. The original replanning team met regularly to consider recommendations for changes made by the users. For example, a complete set of appendices is now being written. They describe, with illustrations, the many documents called out in the guide. Another example of the type of change being incorporated is the expansion of the introduction to better communicate the philosophy behind the new process to give managers the background to make the right decisions on a day-to-day basis. The document is under formal change control, so these revisions are handled in a manner similar to engineering change notices.

Transfer to Operations

A major event during 1986 was the presentation of the new process to the organization. Top-level management within the division and operating group had been informed on an informal basis of our progress since the inception of the project. There was little need to make a presentation to them. They felt it was important, however, to make a formal presentation to all managers in the departments affected by the new process. These included Manufacturing, Quality, Service, Marketing, Accounting, and R&D. This formal presentation was scheduled prior to the completion of the publication of the Product Development Guide, which was the document explaining the new process.

Upper management thought it was vital that they hear the concerns of this group before issuing a finished procedure.

At a meeting of approximately one hundred people, the new process was presented. The presentation focused on the philosophy behind the revised process and how the team accomplished it, rather than the details of the steps in the new process. It was designed to solicit input and support from the managers who had to make the new system work. The reception was overwhelmingly positive.

Following the successful presentation to management, a series of presentations were conducted for the working-level engineers, supervisors, and other technical and manufacturing functions from all departments, which are part of the product development process. The managers who were present at the first meeting were asked to be present at this second-level presentation to lend support for the adoption of the new process. The Product Development Guide was sent well in advance of the presentation to all participants. They were asked to read it carefully and to bring their questions to the presentation. The presentation was more elaborate than the first one and involved graphics to catch the attention of those present. It was considered important that this presentation be made by one speaker from each of the departments represented at the meeting. This helped make clear to the audience that their management already supported the new product development process. There were many questions. All were answered by the presenter with support from top management present at that meeting.

Results

An obvious question is how well the change has been accepted. While there was some initial skepticism among design engineers about projects taking longer, reactions have been generally positive. Those exposed to the change are enthusiastic, because the methodology provides answers to recent product development dilemmas:

It addresses how quality can be designed into a product from the beginning rather than fixing it late in the cycle.

It shows engineers and designers how to address the needs of manufacturing, quality, service, and marketing without slowing down the development process.

It fosters communication among different groups and hence improves the overall working environment.

The best way to assess the gain quantitatively is to compare process performance for development projects conducted with the new process against projects under the old process. What follows is a comparison of three projects of approximately the same level of technical complexity and the same development duration. Each benefited to some degree from the new early-involvement process. Projects A, B, and C were initiated in that order. Only Project C began after the formal establishment of the new process; B and A were less affected by early involvement activities.

One important measure of success is the number of engineering change notices (ECNs) that are generated during product development and early production. Figure 15–4 shows the cumulative number of ECNs against time for the three projects. The graphs have been aligned so that the start of the prototyping phase for each project lies at the origin of the graph, time = 0. Project C, the one with

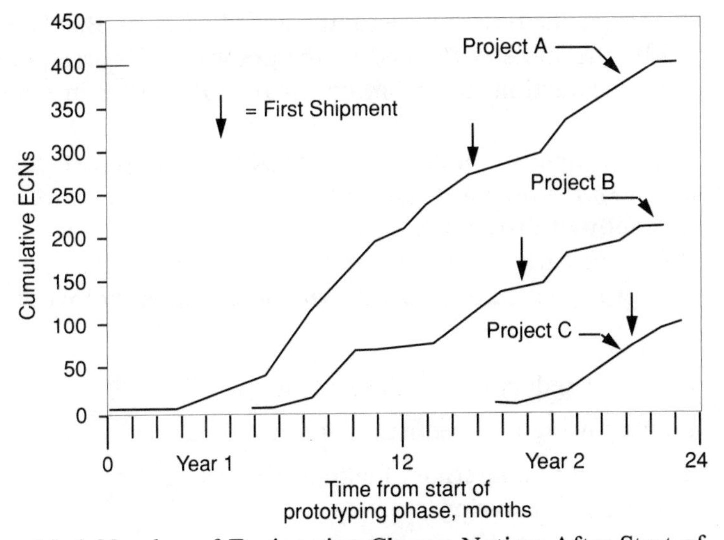

FIGURE 15-4 Number of Engineering Change Notices After Start of Prototyping Phase

full early involvement, has 75 percent fewer ECNs than A, 50 percent fewer ECNs than B.

Another measure of success is the time it takes to ramp up to a full production rate. Figure 15-5 compares production rates for the three projects. The date of first shipment is the origin. Project C

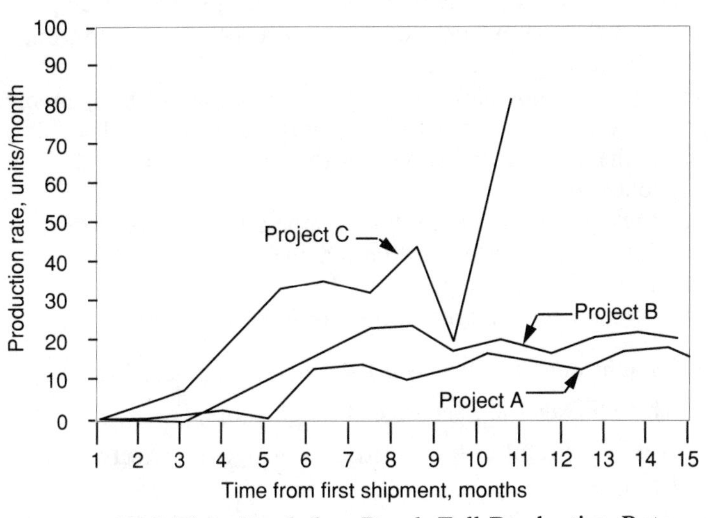

FIGURE 15-5 Time Needed to Reach Full Production Rate

reached full production some months ahead of A or B. (The drop followed by the spike at the end of the graph for C corresponds to moving its production line from one plant to another in Connecticut.)

Yet another measure of success is the percent of systems installed without a major problem. C gave the best results; B gave acceptable results; A showed difficulties.

Finally, as of early 1989, there are encouraging results from projects under way that have had full benefit of the early-involvement process:

- Part count reductions of 50 percent
- Manufacturing cost reductions of 25–55 percent
- Simpler bill of materials, making it easier to incorporate just-in-time manufacturing

A Final Note

In an address to the Conference Board, Dr. Daniel Pisano, who led the replanning of the Product Development Process, made these observations:

> It was not easy getting to where we are. As you saw earlier, it has taken us over four years. When we started, our manufacturing engineers, as well as those from other departments, did not have role models to follow for early involvement. Our product development guide gave them some ideas of what was expected of them, but they had to make it work in real life.
>
> One of the major barriers was that the concept of early involvement represented a threat to the R&D organization's power. They now had to share the design responsibility with others. This was difficult for many to accept.
>
> As a result of this, we think it is imperative to have strong leadership in both R&D and Manufacturing when a cultural change as broad as this is attempted.
>
> In summary [of remarks to the Conference Board]:
>
> - Establishing links between R&D and Manufacturing takes time.
> - These linkages are achieved through people.
> - It is very useful to have metrics to gauge the effectiveness of the linkages.
> - And for us at least, we found these linkages resulted in better prod-

ucts and smoother projects. This last point is a big factor in improving the quality of work life for both R&D and Manufacturing.

Further Reading

Huizenga, T. P.; K. Liepins; and D. J. Pisano, Jr. "Early Involvement." Reprint from *IMPRO 87, Juran Institute's annual conference on quality improvement.*

Pisano, D. J., Jr. "Replanning the Product Development Process." Reprint from *IMPRO 86, Juran Institute's annual conference on quality improvement.*

———. "Quality Planning—One Year Later." Reprint from *IMPRO 87, Juran Institute's annual conference on quality improvement.*

———. "Better Quality Through Stronger R&D/Manufacturing Links." Speech at the Conference Board's conference, "Key Issues for Management 1989: R&D Technology," March 1989.

What Should I Do Next?

Upper Managers and the Action Plan

The ideal answer to "What should I do next?" is "*Create an action plan.*" In the opinion of the authors, the upper managers should here heed the advice of a famous political leader: "Make no small plans."

The action plan should be oriented to the goals inherent in quality planning: *saleable products and minimal waste.* The means for reaching those goals have been set out in the various chapters of this book. They are mainly:

Provide personal leadership, through membership on the Quality Council.

Adopt the Big Q concept.

Train the managers and specialists, at all levels, in how to plan for quality. The goal here is to train the amateurs to become professionals.

Put quality goals into the strategic business plan. To create a revolution in quality requires setting of "stretch goals," which cannot be met by ordinary means and hence require extraordinary means.

Replan selected existing processes and products.

Mandate participation in quality planning by those impacted.

Mandate the use of structured quality planning to replace empiricism.

The ingredients of the action plan will be unique to each company. A major factor will be the company's current status with respect to the above list. For example, one company was in the very early stages of moving into a structured approach to managing for quality. They held an in-house seminar on the subject "Making Quality Happen." At the conclusion of the seminar, the CEO took the following actions, then and there:

He announced the creation of a Quality Council. He named the members, and appointed himself as chairman.

He established the date for the first meeting of the Council, two weeks from then.

He designated the quality manager as secretary of the Quality Council.

He asked each person present to nominate two quality goals to enter the business plan, and to turn these nominations over to the quality manager within a week.

He asked the quality manager to consolidate the nominations into an agenda for the first meeting of the Quality Council.

Through these actions his company took a leap forward, probably gaining several months over the more conventional approaches.

Implementing the Action Plan

The nature of "implementing" will vary from company to company, again depending on what steps have already been taken.

"Implementing" involves many specifics, which have been dealt with at length in the earlier chapters. The more critical specifics include:

Deploy the strategic quality goals to lower levels in the hierarchy so as to identify clearly the projects to be carried out, and the resources needed.

Provide the resources.

Assign clear responsibility for carrying out those projects. (Such assignments are usually made to teams).

Train the teams in the quality disciplines and in how to work as teams.

Establish measures of progress, and then review progress regularly.

Revise the reward system to reflect the new priorities given to quality and to include the new responsibilities of helping the teams to complete their projects.

The major case examples set out in the preceding chapters also include discussion of how implementing was carried out. Those same case examples reflect the realities faced by practicing managers, and therefore deserve careful study. However, since each company is "different," implementing will usually require a degree of adaptation and innovation.

Additional details of implementing include specifics such as:

Deploying goals and arriving at the projects to be carried out

Team selection and organization

Provision of training materials

Training of facilitators/trainers

Training of teams

Measuring and reporting progress

Providing recognition

Revising the reward system

Some of the details of implementing have been discussed in earlier chapters of this book. More extensive detail is available in training materials such as are referenced below, under "Training Directors and Inputs for Training Programs."

Quality Managers and Inputs for Proposals

Some companies look to quality managers (and other functional specialists) to prepare proposals for action plans, or minimally to provide essential inputs to needed action plans. Participants who are in this category should likewise think in terms of "make no small plans." Such an approach requires at the outset a wholehearted acceptance of the concept of Big Q, which is itself a major break with tradition.

In preparing proposals for the approval of upper managers, it is important to provide for participation by organization units that will be affected. Such participation broadens the input base and also depersonalizes the resulting proposal.

A useful strategy for acquiring inputs is to request nominations from the organization units in interest. These nominations can be stimulated by raising pertinent questions with the managers, such as:

What are the company's three most important unsolved quality problems as you see them?

What kind of action plan is needed to solve these problems?

What are some major obstacles in the way of improving our quality?

Such questions can be raised in specially organized brainstorming sessions. Alternatively the quality manager "makes the rounds," that is, sits down with each key manager, one at a time, to secure the inputs. Such inputs help to shape the action plan in ways that respond to the realities faced by the impacted managers. The very fact of securing inputs from those who will be affected confers a share of ownership and simplifies the ultimate job of selling the action plan. Those same inputs can help to identify the most likely test sites and to anticipate the nature of the cultural resistance.

Ideally, the action plan should:

Establish a linkage between the proposals and the mission of the enterprise. In the case of commercial enterprises, the proposal should make clear what the effect will be on product salability, service to customers, reduction of waste, and so on. For noncommercial enterprises, the mission is different: national defense, protection of the environment, etc. The proposal must in each case relate clearly to the mission.

Show the relation of the proposals to problems and results. Avoid placing the priority on methods and tools.

Define the roles of the upper managers—what they should do that is different from what they have been doing.

Adopt the language most widely used by the upper managers. In commercial enterprises, the prime language is money. This is not necessarily the prime language in other enterprises.

Make sure that the proposals are compatible with the personal responsibilities and aspirations of the upper managers. (Most upper managers regard themselves as business managers rather than functional managers.)

Any proposal for an action plan should also try to anticipate the questions that will be raised by the upper managers. Questions frequently raised have been:

What resources are needed up front in order to carry out the action plan?

What will be the return on those resources?

How long will it take?

What are the needed organizational steps?

How do I get started?

What should I personally do that is different from what I have been doing?

The proposal for an action plan should provide for answering such questions.

Training Directors and Inputs for Training Programs

The extent of training needed will be keyed to the breadth of the action plan. In addition, the training will be done in phases that are keyed to the timetable of the action plan.

Many companies are faced with doing a substantial amount of training. Such companies are also faced with establishing a broad training plan: determining who is to be trained in what, designing the curriculum, and so on. There are numerous options for preparing such a broad plan. One of the more successful options was set out in Chapter 12 and is repeated here for convenience:

Use of a Broad-based Task Force

One of the more successful options has been to use a broad-based task force for the purpose of designing the curriculum. Under this concept the Quality Council creates a task force (project team, etc.) whose mission is to develop a plan for training in planning for quality. The task force membership consists of high-level managers, including the quality manager and the training manager, as well as representatives from the major operating and staff departments.

More specifically, the task force mission is to:

Identify the company's needs for training in planning for quality

Propose a curriculum of courses that can meet those needs

Identify which categories of personnel should take which courses

Identify the sources of needed training materials, whether to be self-developed or acquired from suppliers

Identify the needs for leaders: trainers, facilitators, etc.

Propose a timetable

Estimate the budget

In the experience of the authors, the training plans developed by such task forces have been decidedly superior to those developed through other options. It usually took longer to evolve the training plan, but the result was more responsive to the company's needs. This experience suggests that:

Upper managers should establish a broad-based task force to plan the company's approach to training in planning for quality. (End of quotation from Chapter 12.)

While the approach quoted suggests that the upper managers establish the task force, it is usually possible for the Training Department to develop a proposal, making use of an informal task force if necessary.

If the company opts for extensive self-sufficiency, it will need to:

Prepare training materials, including manuals for training facilitators/trainers

Develop qualified facilitators/trainers

Prepare local case materials as supplements

Assign projects that relate to company operations

Establish the infrastructure needed to administer the training activities.

Sources of Training Materials and Trainers

Most companies, including large companies, make use of outside suppliers as one of the resources for training materials and trainers. Resources available from Juran Institute include:

The videocassette series *Juran on Quality Improvement®*

The videocassette series *Juran on Quality Planning®*

The facilitator training courses (a) *Facilitating Juran on Quality Planning©* and (b) *Facilitating Juran on Quality Improvement.™* These are used to develop and certify facilitators for training in quality planning, and in quality improvement, respectively.

The videocassette *Juran on Quality Leadership.©*

Glossary of Terms

Accuracy (of a sensor) The degree to which the sensor tells the truth; the extent to which its evaluation of some phenomenon agrees with the "true" value as judged by an accepted standard

Anatomy of processes The structural linkage of the multiple operations (tasks, steps, unit processes, etc.) that collectively produce the product

Assembly tree A form of process anatomy in which inputs from numerous suppliers converge into subassemblies and assemblies, whether in manufacturing processes or in business processes

Assumed owner The manager of the dominant function within a macroprocess

Autonomous department A form of process anatomy that receives various inputs and converts them into finished goods and services, all within a single self-contained department

Autopsy Analysis of products to determine the causes of deficiencies (literally, to see with one's own eyes)

Benchmarking The concept of setting goals based on knowing what has been achieved by others

Bias A tendency or inclination of outlook that is a source of error in human sensing

Big Q A term used to designate a broad concept of quality in which "customers" includes all who are impacted; "product" includes goods and services; "processes" includes business and support processes (For contrast, see Little Q.)

Biological process A form of process anatomy in which a cell divides into multiple cells, all coordinated by a nervous system (An enterprise created by a single founder and then "franchised" follows a similar process of growth.)

Brainstorming A process for securing ideas during a meeting of multiple participants

Breakthrough See Quality improvement

Business process In general, an office process, as distinguished from a factory process (There is substantial overlap.)

Capability index See Process capability index

Carryover The use of existing product (or process) design features as elements of new products (or processes)

Cause A proven reason for a quality deficiency

Cause and effect diagram Prof. Ishikawa's "fishbone" diagram for listing theories of causes

Champion See Sponsor

Checklist An aid to human memory; a reminder of what to do and what not to do

Check sheet Any blank form used to tally up quality data

Chronic waste The loss due to continuing quality deficiencies that are inherent in the system

Coloration A deliberate distortion of data sensed by a human, for a variety of (usually) self-serving human purposes

Company Any organized entity that produces products (goods or services), whether for sale or not, whether for profit or not

Companywide Quality Management See Strategic Quality Management

Competitive analysis Analysis of product and process features and performance against those of competing products and processes

Compromise A means for resolving differences in which each party meets some desired goals at the price of taking some unwanted actions

Concept to customer A term used by Ford Motor Company to designate the progression of events for creating a new model and putting it on the market

Conformance A state of agreement between actual quality and the quality goal

Conscious errors Nonconformance to quality goals resulting from actions taken knowingly

Constructive conflict Follett's term for a teamwork approach to discover the optimum

Consumer A buyer for personal use

Control The regulatory process through which we measure actual performance, compare it with standards, and act on the difference

Control chart W. A. Shewhart's chart for continuing test of statistical significance

Control station A quality-oriented activity center for carrying out one or more steps of the feedback loop

Control subject Any product or process feature that is to be regulated through use of the feedback loop

Controllability The extent to which the criteria for self-control have been met

Coonley-Agnew process A process for resolving differences in which the parties to the difference must (1) identify their areas of agreement and their areas of disagreement, (2) agree on why they disagree, and (3) decide what they are going to do about it

COPQ See Cost of poor quality

Corrective action Consists of diagnosis of the cause of a sporadic problem, and provision of a remedy

Cost of poor quality Those costs which would disappear if our products and processes were perfect. (COPQ)

Countdown A list of deeds to be done, in a predetermined order

Craftsman A category of worker qualified by training and experience to carry out a recognized work specialty

Critical process A process that presents serious dangers to human life, health, and the environment, or risks the loss of very large sums of money

Criticality analysis The process of identifying product features that may be critical for various reasons, e.g., essential to human safety, legislated mandates, essential to salability

Cultural needs Needs for job security, self-respect, respect of others, continuity of habit patterns, and still other elements of what are broadly called cultural values

Cultural pattern A body of beliefs, habits, practices, etc., which a human society evolves to deal with its perceived problems

Cultural resistance A form of resistance to change based on opposition to the possible social consequences

Customer Anyone who is impacted by the product or process; may be external or internal

Customer dissatisfaction A result achieved when deficiencies adversely affect customers

Customer needs Those desires of customers which can be met by the product features of goods and services

Customer opinions Customers' assertions based mainly on judgment

Customer perceptions Customers' conclusions derived mainly from use of the product

Customer satisfaction A result achieved when product features respond to customer needs

Data bank A compilation of numerous inputs specially organized to facilitate information retrieval and decision making; a form of lessons learned

Data base A body of information derived from prior cycles of activity, specially organized to aid in the conduct of future cycles

Deficiency See Product deficiency

Department An organization unit that carries out operations (tasks, etc.) of a single functional nature, and consists of nonsupervisory workers supervised by a "first line" supervisor

Deployment (of goals) The process of subdividing goals and allocating the subgoals to lower levels

Design review A participative process for securing early warning of the impact of a proposed design on subsequent functions

Designated owner A person or team specifically assigned as the owner of a macroprocess despite lack of command over all the component microprocesses

Detection A concept of managing for quality based on inspection and test to detect and remove defects prior to shipment to customers

Diagnosis The activity of discovering the cause(s) of quality deficiencies

Diagnostic journey Those activities of the quality improvement process which start with the outward symptoms of a quality problem and end with determination of the cause(s)

Dominance A method of resolving differences in which one party imposes its terms on the other

Dominant variable The most important of the variables requiring process control

Dry run A test of a process, conducted under operating conditions

Early warning The concept of discovering, before the fact, the likely effects of intended actions ("If you plan it this way, here are the problems I will face.")

Errorproofing Building safeguards into the technology of a process to reduce inadvertent human error

External customers Those who are not a part of our company but who are impacted by our activities

Facilitator A person specially trained to assist project teams in carrying out their projects

Facilities control A form of process control that provides for maintenance of the physical facilities—equipment, tools, instruments

Factual approach Use of facts (rather than opinions) as a basis for decision making

Feedback An input of information on performance to permit comparison to goals

Feedback loop A systematic series of steps for maintaining conformance to quality goals by feeding performance data back to corrective actuators

Field intelligence Any information that relates to product performance and to its impact on customers

Firefighting The activity of getting rid of sporatic quality troubles and restoring the status quo

Fishbone diagram See Cause and effect diagram

Fitness for use A short definition of quality, intended to include product features as well as freedom from deficiencies

Flow diagram A graphic method for depicting the steps in a process and identifying who is impacted

Foolproofing See Errorproofing

Force field analysis A process for identifying driving forces and restraining forces as an aid to problem solving

Frequency distribution The mathematical relationship between the value of a variable and the relative frequency with which that value occurs; also, the graphic representation of the relationship

Glossary A list of terms and their definitions

Goal An aimed-at target; an achievement toward which effort is expended

Graphs Pictorial presentations of data

Histogram A frequency distribution in unsmoothed form

Immune system A characteristic of organizations that, like biological immune systems, tends to reject the introduction of new concepts

IMPRO® Juran Institute's annual conference on quality improvement

Improvement The organized creation of beneficial change; the attainment of unprecedented levels of performance

Inadvertent errors Human errors that have their origin in unintentional inattention

Input All the means employed by a process to produce its product

Internal customers Those who are a part of our company and are also impacted by our activities

Internal failures Failures that occur before product is delivered to external customers

Joint planning A concept under which quality planning is done by a team made up of customers and suppliers

Juran Trilogy® The three managerial processes used in managing for quality: quality planning, quality control, and quality improvement

Lessons learned A catchall phrase describing what has been learned from experience

Life behind the quality dikes A phrase used to describe how life in industrial societies requires high quality to maintain continuity of services and to protect against disasters

Little Q A term used to designate a narrow scope of quality, limited to clients, factory goods, and factory processes (For contrast, see Big Q.)

Macroprocess Any multifunctional system through which some major activity of the company is conducted (usually a business process)

Management-controllable A state in which the criteria for self-control have not been met at the worker level (see Self-control)

Market research Research to discover the quality needs of customers

Matrix diagram See Spreadsheet

Microprocess An operational system involving few tasks, usually carried out within a single functional department

Misinterpretation A form of human error due mainly to imprecise communication

Operation A task of limited scope

Operations (1) The general activity of carrying out planned processes; (2) organizations that carry out planned processes

Optimum A planned result that meets the needs of customer and supplier alike and minimizes their combined costs

Pareto principle The phenomenon that in any population which contributes to a common effect, a relative few of the contributors account for the bulk of the effect

Participation The process of securing inputs from all who will be impacted by an intended action

Perceived needs Customers' needs based on their perceptions

Phase system A division of the progression from concept to customer into definable segments or phases, with provision for business decisions at logical intervals

Pilot test A test of process capability, conducted under conditions short of full-scale operation

Plan See Quality plan

Planner See Quality planner

Policy A guide to managerial action

Precision (of a sensor) A measure of the ability of a sensor to reproduce its results on repeat test

President's quality audit A form of quality audit conducted by a team of upper managers under the chairmanship of the president

Process A systematic series of actions directed to the achievement of a goal

Process capability (1) The inherent ability of a process to reproduce its results consistently during multiple cycles of operation; (2) the results a process could achieve if we removed the significant causes of poor performance; (3) six standard deviations

Process capability index The ratio of product tolerance width to process capability

Process control The systematic evaluation of performance of a process, and the taking of corrective action in the event of nonconformance

Process design The activity of defining the specific means to be used by the operating forces for meeting the product quality goals

Process development A comprehensive term that includes the activities of product design review, choice of process, process design, provision of facilities, and provision of software (methods, procedures, cautions)

Process features Those properties or attributes which collectively define the process

Process performance The results achieved by a process; what the process actually does; the variability of the products that emerge from a process

Process redesign Work done to provide the means to meet unchanged product quality goals

Process validation A documented analysis intended to provide a high degree of assurance that a specific process will consistently produce conforming products

Processing The activity of conducting operations; running the process and producing the product

Procession A form of process anatomy in which the product progresses sequentially through multiple departments, each performing some operation that contributes to the final result

Processor team Any person or organization unit that carries out a process and produces a product

Processors Those who run the process; also, customers who employ our product in their processes

Product The output of any process; consists of goods and services

Product control The activity of deciding whether the product conforms to the product quality goals

Product deficiency A nonconformance to the product quality goals

Product design The activity of defining the product features required to meet customer needs

Product development The experimental process of choosing the product features that respond to customer needs

Product dissatisfaction See Customer dissatisfaction

Product feature A property possessed by a product and intended to meet specific customer needs

Product satisfaction See Customer satisfaction

Product subdivision A hierarchical separation of a product from the system level into subsystems, components, parts, etc.

Project A problem scheduled for solution; a specific mission to be carried out

Project mission The intended end result of a project

Project team A group of persons assigned to carry out a project

Project team charter The list of activities to be carried out by project teams

Public The members of society collectively, as an external customer

QC Circle A volunteer group of workers who have undergone training for the purpose of solving work-related problems

Quality (1) Product features that respond to customer needs; (2) freedom from deficiencies

Quality audit An independent review of quality performance

Quality control See Control

Quality costs See Cost of poor quality

Quality council A committee of upper managers having the responsibility to establish, coordinate, and oversee managing for quality

Quality disciplines The body of methodology, skills, and tools required to manage for quality

Quality engineering An engineering specialty focused largely on quality planning and analysis

Quality goal An aimed-at quality target

Quality improvement The organized creation of beneficial change; (also Breakthrough) improving performance to unprecedented levels

Quality management The totality of ways for achieving quality (Quality management includes all three processes of the Juran Trilogy: quality planning, quality control; quality improvement.)

Quality plan The end result of establishing quality goals and developing the products and processes required to meet those goals

Quality planner Any person at the time he or she is engaged in quality planning

Quality planning The activity of (a) establishing quality goals and (b) developing the products and processes required to meet those goals

Quality planning road map A universal series of input–output steps that collectively constitute quality planning

Real needs The fundamental desires that motivate customer behavior

Rehearsal A method of providing the operating forces with experience before operations commence

Recognition Public acknowledgement of work well done

Reliability The probability that a product will carry out its intended function under specified conditions and for a specified length of time

Reliability engineering An engineering speciality focused largely on minimizing field failures through reliability modeling and quantification, data banks, etc.

Remedial journey Those activities of the quality improvement process which start with the known cause(s) and end with an effective remedy in place

Responsibility matrix A table that lists the needed decisions and actions, and identifies who does what

Retrospective analysis Analysis of data from prior cycles of operation

Rewards Those salary increases, bonuses, promotions, etc., that are more or less keyed to job performance

Running control A form of process control that takes place periodically during the operation of the process, the purpose being to make the decision "run or stop"

Salability The extent to which the product features stimulate customers to "buy" the product; applies to internal as well as external customers

Santayana Review The process of deriving lessons learned from analysis of historical events, in order to improve decision making

Scatter diagram A graphic representation of the interrelation between variables

Self-control A state in which people are provided with the means of knowing what their quality goal is, knowing what their actual performance is, and changing their performance in the event that performance does not conform to goals

Sensor A specialized detecting device, designed to recognize the presence and intensity of certain phenomena and to convert this sensed knowledge into "information"

Service Work performed for someone else

Setup (startup) control A form of process control, the end result of which is the decision of whether or not to "push the start button"

Simulation A form of planning that makes use of mathematical models or small-scale models; also, a means of providing operating personnel with experience prior to conduct of operations

SPC See Statistical process control

Spiral of Progress in Quality A graph that shows the sequence of activities for putting a product on the market

Sponsor A manager who is assigned to maintain broad surveillance over specific quality improvement projects and to help the project teams in the event of an impasse

Spreadsheet An orderly arrangement of planning information consisting (usually) of (a) horizontal rows to set out the elements undergoing planning, and (b) vertical columns to set out the resulting product/process responses

Standard deviation A widely used statistical measure of variability

Stated needs Needs as expressed by customers

Statistical process control A term used during the 1980s to describe the concept of using the tools of statistics to assist in controlling the quality of operating processes

Strategic Quality Management (SQM) A structured process for establishing long-range quality goals, at the highest levels of organization, and defining the means to be used to reach those goals

Suboptimization Pursuit of local goals at the expense of company goals

Symptom The outward evidence of a quality deficiency

Target achievement The ability of a process to meet the product quality goals

Taylor system A system of management based on separating planning from execution

Technique error A species of human error traceable to lack of knowledge of some essential ''knack''

Theory An unproven assertion of the cause of a deficiency

Total Quality Management (TQM) See Strategic Quality Management

Transfer to operations The shift of responsibility from planners to the operating forces

Trilogy See Juran Trilogy

Triple role The three roles carried out by every processor team: processor, supplier, and customer

TRIPROL Diagram™ An input-output diagram that depicts the triple role of processor, supplier, and customer

Troubleshooting See Firefighting

Umpire The agency (human or technological) in the feedback loop that judges conformance to goals

Unit of measure A defined amount of some quality feature that permits evaluation of that feature in numbers

Upper managers The managers who constitute the upper layer of a company, including the corporate officers and staff, and, in a divisionalized structure, the division general managers and staff

Useful many Under the Pareto principle, a large majority of the population that nevertheless accounts for only a small part of the total effect

User (of a product) A customer who carries out further processing or ultimate use of a product

Value analysis A process for evaluating the interrelationships among (a) the functions performed by product features and (b) the associated costs

Variability The dispersion or scatter exhibited by evaluations of successive events resulting from a common process, e.g., measurement of successive units of product emerging from a process

Vital few Under the Pareto principle, a small minority of the population that nevertheless accounts for most of the total effect

Work force See Workers

Work station An activity center for carrying out the prescribed operations of running the processes and producing the product features

Worker-controllable A state in which the criteria for self-control have been met at the worker level

Workers Nonsupervisory employees in nonprofessional work categories

Zero defects (1) A term meaning defect-free product; (2) a slogan used during "drives" to exhort workers to improve quality

References

1. How to Think About Quality Planning

Juran, J. M. "Product Quality: A Prescription for the West." *The Management Review,* June and July 1981; first presented at the 25th Conference of the European Organization for Quality Control, Paris, June 1981.

———. "A Prescription for the West: Four Years Later." European Organization for Quality Control, 29th Annual Conference, 1985. Reprinted in *The Juran Report* No. 5, Summer 1985, Juran Institute, Inc.

———. "The Quality Trilogy: A Universal Approach to Managing for Quality." *Quality Progress,* August 1986, pp. 19–24.

2. Establish Quality Goals

Branco, George J., and Robert S. Willoughby. "Extending Quality Improvement to Suppliers." *Proceedings* of Fourth Annual Conference on Quality Improvement (IMPRO 86), Juran Institute, Inc., Wilton, Conn., 1987.

Brunetti, Wayne. "Policy Deployment: A Corporate Roadmap." *Proceedings* of Fourth Annual Conference on Quality Improvement (IMPRO 86), pp. 20–29. Juran Institute, Inc., Wilton, Conn., 1987.

Camp, Robert C. "Benchmarking: The Search for Best Practices that Lead to Superior Performance." *Quality Progress,* January through May 1989.

Kegarise, Ronald J., and George D. Miller. "An Alcoa-Kodak Joint Team." *Proceedings* of Third Annual Conference on Quality Improvement (IMPRO 85), pp. 29–34. Juran Institute Inc., Wilton, Conn., 1986.

Pisano, Daniel J., Jr. "Replanning the Product Development Process." *Proceedings* of Fourth Annual Conference on Quality Improvement (IMPRO 86), pp. 260–64. Juran Institute, Inc., Wilton, Conn., 1987.

Veraldi, L. C. "The Team Taurus Story." MIT Conference paper, Chicago,

August 22, 1985. Center for Advanced Engineering Study, MIT, Cambridge, Mass., 1985.

Wolf, John D. "Quality Improvement: The Continuing Operational Phase." *Second Annual Conference on Quality Improvement* (IMPRO 84), Juran Institute, Inc., Wilton, Conn., 1985.

3. Identify the Customer

Business Week. "Campbell's Taste of the Japanese Market is MM-Good," March 28, 1988.

Engle, David, and David Ball. "Improving Customer Service for Special Orders," *Proceedings* of Annual Conference on Quality Improvement (IMPRO 85). Juran Institute, Inc., Wilton, Conn., 1986.

Juran, J. M. *Managerial Breakthrough.* New York: McGraw-Hill Book Co., 1964. Chapter Four, "The Pareto Principle."

Olsson, John Ryding, and Per Rommer. "The Market-Leader Method: User-Oriented Development." *30th EOQC Conference,* Stockholm, 1986, pp. 59–68.

Tomkins, Calvin. "Colored Muds in a Sticky Substance." *The New Yorker,* March 16, 1987.

4. Determine Customer Needs

Ackoff, Russell L. *The Art of Problem Solving Accompanied by Ackoff's Fables.* New York: John Wiley & Sons, 1978.

Becker, Franklin D., and Amy Hoogesteger. "Employee Adjustment to an Office Relocation." *Human Ecology Forum.* New York State College of Human Ecology, Cornell University, Fall 1986.

Bennett, Amanda. "Once a Tool of Retail Marketers, Focus Groups Gain Wider Usage." *Wall Street Journal,* June 3, 1986.

Bluestone, Mimi. "A Premature Taste of Old Age." *Wall Street Journal,* December 2, 1984.

Business Week, "How Ford Hit the Bull's-Eye with Taurus." June 30, 1986, pp. 69–70.

Center for Policy Alternatives of Massachusetts Institute of Technology, and Charles Stark Draper Laboratory, Inc. "The Productivity of Servicing Consumer Durable Products." Report 74-4, Cambridge, Mass., 1974.

Consumer Report Books. *I'll Buy That.* 1986.

Galante, Steven P. "Bookshop 'Superstore' Reflects the Latest Word in Retailing." *Wall Street Journal,* February 23, 1987.

Holusha, John. "Helping Driver Feel at Home." *Wall Street Journal,* February 28, 1985.

——. "Chrysler Odometer Compensation." *New York Times,* July 2, 1987.

Hughes, Kathleen, "Zowie! Newspapers Poll Readers on Comic Strips." *Wall Street Journal,* June 15, 1988.

Juran, J. M. *Managerial Breakthrough.* New York: McGraw Hill Book Co., 1964.

——. *Juran's Quality Control Handbook.* Fourth Edition. New York: McGraw-Hill Book Co., 1988.

Kahn, Herbert L. "Looking Forward to the Casino Society." *New York Times,* July 12, 1987.

Kegarise, Ronald J., and George D. Miller. "An Alcoa-Kodak Joint Team." *Proceedings* of Third Annual Conference on Quality Improvement (IMPRO 85), pp. 29–34. Wilton, Conn.: Juran Institute, Inc.

Levine, Richard. "Breaking Routine: Voice of the Subway." *New York Times,* January 15, 1987.

Levitt, Theodore. "Marketing Myopia." *Harvard Business Review,* September–October 1975.

Reibstein, Larry. "A Finger on the Pulse: Companies Expand Use of Employee Surveys." *Wall Street Journal,* October 27, 1986.

Sellers, Patricia. "The ABC's of Marketing to Kids." *Fortune,* May 8, 1989, pp. 114–20

United States Office of Consumer Affairs. *Update: Consumer Complaint Handling in America—An Update Study.* Washington, D.C., 1985–86.

Veraldi, L. C. "The Team Taurus Story." MIT Conference Paper, Chicago, August 22, 1985. Also published in *EOQC Conference Proceedings,* 1986, pp. 62–63.

5. Provide Mesurement

Aubrey, Charles A. *Quality Management in Financial Services.* Hitchcock, 1985.

Becker, Richard A., *et al.* "Analysis of Data from the *Places Rated Almanac.*" *The American Statistician,* August 1987, pp. 169–86.

Brainard, Edgar H. "Just How Good Are Vendor Surveys?" *Quality Assurance,* August 1974, pp. 22–25.

Brunetti, Wayne. "Policy Deployment: A Corporate Roadmap." *Proceedings* of Fourth Annual Conference on Quality Improvement (IMPRO 86), pp. 20–29. Wilton, Conn.: Juran Institute, Inc., 1987.

Carlzon, Jan. *Moments of Truth.* Cambridge, Mass.: Ballinger, 1987.

Dahl, Jonathan. "Danger Aloft: Evidence Suggests Many Near Misses Go Unreported." *Wall Street Journal,* July 21, 1987.

Dumaine, Brian. "Corporate Spies Snoop to Conquer." *Fortune,* November 7, 1988.

Hicks, Richard D. "American Express Practices." In Shetty and Buehler, eds., *Quality and Productivity Improvements: US and Foreign Company Experiences.* Chicago: IIT Manufacturing Productivity Center, 1983, pp. 209–14.

Hoggart, Simon. "Around Disney World in 80 Queues." *Punch,* September 16, 1988, pp. 42, 44.

Juran, J. M. *Managerial Breakthrough.* New York: McGraw-Hill Book Co., 1964.

——, ed. *Juran's Quality Control Handbook.* Fourth Edition. New York: McGraw Hill Book Co., 1988.

Kearns, David T. "Payment in Kind" (interview). *Quality Progress,* April 1988, pp. 16–20.

Louis Arthur M. "The Worst American City." *Harper's Magazine,* January 1975, pp. 67–71.

McGrath, James H. "Successful Institutionalized Improvement in Manufacturing Areas." *Proceedings* of Third Annual Conference on Quality Improvement (IMPRO 85). Wilton, Conn.: Juran Institute, Inc., 1986.

Molotsky, Irvin. "Detection Test Shows Airlines Didn't Find 20% of Weapons." *New York Times,* June 18, 1987.

Nakajo, Takeshi, and Hitoshi Kume. "The Principles of Foolproofing and Their Application in Manufacturing." *Reports of Statistical Application Research,* Japanese Union of Scientists and Engineers, 32, no. 2 (June 1985): 10–29. Also presented (in abbreviated form) at the EOQC Annual Conference, Stockholm, June 1986, *Proceedings,* pp. 221–28.

Onnias, Arturo, "The Quality Blue Book." *Proceedings* of Third Annual Conference on Quality Improvement (IMPRO 85), pp. 127–31. Wilton, Conn.: Juran Institute, Inc., 1986.

Sandberg-Diment, Erik, "'Barcodes' Come into Their Own." *New York Times,* March 24, 1985.

Talley, D. J. "The Quest for Sustaining Quality Improvement." *Proceedings* of Third Annual Conference on Quality Improvement (IMPRO 85), pp. 188–92. Wilton, Conn.: Juran Institute, Inc., 1986.

Utzig, Lawrence. "Quality Reputation: A Precious Asset." ASQC Technical Conference *Transactions,* Milwaukee, 1980, pp. 145–54.

White, Paul Dudley. *My Life and Medicine.* Boston: Gambit, Inc., 1971, pp. 195–96.

6. Develop Product Features

Ackoff, Russell L. *The Art of Problem Solving Accompanied by Ackoff's Fables*. New York: John Wiley & Sons, 1978.

Argyris, Chris. *Strategy, Change, and Defensive Routines*. Boston: Pitman, 1985.

Boothroyd, Geoffrey, and Peter Dewhurst. *Product Design for Assembly Handbook*. Wakefield, R.I.: Boothroyd Dewhurst, Inc., 1987.

Coonley, Howard, and P. G. Agnew. *The Role of Standards in the System of Free Enterprise*. Washington, D.C.: American National Standards Institute, 1941, pp. 8–26.

Cushman, John H., Jr. "Making Arms Fighting Men Can Use." *New York Times,* June 21, 1987.

Dodge, H. F.; B. J. Kinsburg; and M. K. Kruger. "The L3 Coaxial System: Quality Control Requirements." *Bell System Technical Journal,* 32 (July 1953), pp. 943–1005.

Engle, David S., and David L. Ball. "Improving Customer Service for Special Orders." *Proceedings* of Third Annual Conference on Quality Improvement (IMPRO 85), pp. 106–10. Wilton, Conn.: Juran Institute, Inc., 1986.

Fialka, John J. "Weapon of Choice." *Wall Street Journal,* February 15, 1985.

Ford Motor Company. *Continuous Improvement: Batavia Transmission Plant*. 1981.

Fosse, Chris J. "Quality Assurance Through Strategic Product Development." *Proceedings* of Fifth Annual Conference on Quality Improvement (IMPRO 87), pp. 4B-5–12. Wilton, Conn.: Juran Institute, Inc., 1988.

Gryna, Frank. "How Engineering Can Improve Product Quality." *Machine Design,* May 8, 1986, pp. 81–85.

Hays, Laurie. "DuPont's Difficulties in Selling Kevlar Show Hurdles of Innovation." *Wall Street Journal,* September 29, 1987.

Hauser, John R., and Don Clausing. "The House of Quality." *Harvard Business Review,* May–June 1988.

Iwahashi, Masaru. "Research Program on the New Product X Through Seven Management Tools for QC." *Reports of Statistical Application Research,* 33, no. 2, (Japanese Union of Scientists and Engineers, Tokyo, June 1986), pp. 43–52.

Josephson, Matthew. *Edison*. New York: McGraw-Hill Book Co., 1959.

Juran, J. M. *Juran's Quality Control Handbook*. Fourth Edition. New York: McGraw-Hill Book Co., 1988.

Juran, J. M. *Managerial Breakthrough*. New York: McGraw-Hill Book Co., 1964. Chapter 9, "Resistance to Change: Cultural Patterns."

Kanter, R. M. *The Change Masters.* New York: Simon & Schuster, 1983.

Kegarise, Ronald J., and George D. Miller. "An Alcoa-Kodak Joint Team." *Proceedings* of Third Annual Conference on Quality Improvement (IMPRO 85), pp. 29–34. Wilton, Conn.: Juran Institute Inc., 1986.

Kotter, J. P. *Power and Influence.* New York: Free Press, 1985.

Kupfer, Andrew. "How to Be a Global Manager." *Fortune,* March 14, 1988, pp. 52–54, 58.

Maczka, Walter J. "GE Has 'Designs' on Assembly." *Assembly Engineering,* June 1984, pp. 16–18.

Mead, Margaret, ed. *Cultural Patterns and Technical Change.* Paris: UNESCO, 1951. Also published by Mentor Books, New American Library, New York, 1955.

Metcalf, H. C., and L. Urwick, eds. *Dynamic Administration.* New York: Harper & Row, 1941. Citing Mary Parker Follett.

Morrell, Norman E. "Quality Function Deployment." SAE International Congress, Detroit, February 1987.

Morris, Betsy. "In This Taste Test, the Loser Is the Taste Test." *Wall Street Journal,* June 3, 1987.

Ross, Philip E. "Auto Industry Is Now Using Bar Codes." *New York Times,* August 19, 1987.

——. "2 U.S. Agencies Act to Impose Curbs on All-Terrain Vehicles." *New York Times,* December 22, 1987.

Sanger, David E. "Chip Designers Seek Haste Without Waste." *New York Times,* January 6, 1988.

Schmidek, Don. New Product Introduction Quality Process. N.p.:n.d.

Schoeffler, Sidney; Robert D. Buzzell; and Donald F. Heany, "Impact of Strategic Planning on Profit Performance." *Harvard Business Review,* March–April, 1974, pp. 137–45.

Schuon, Marshall. "Putting Consumers in the Driver's Seat." *New York Times,* May 25, 1989, p. C13.

Sterling, Michael. "Linking Manufacturing to Design." *Manufacturing Engineering,* October 1984, pp. 67–69.

Stevenson, Richard W. "Shared Cash Machines Boom." *New York Times,* March 11, 1986.

Sullivan, L. P. "Quality Function Deployment." *Quality Progress,* June 1986, pp. 39–50.

Thomas, Paulette. "Texas Air's Rapid Growth Spurs Surge in Complaints About Service." *Wall Street Journal,* February 26, 1987.

Veraldi, L. C. "Ford Motor Company." MIT conference paper, Chicago, August 22, 1985. EOQC Conference, 1986, pp. 62, 63.

Withers, Sonia. *Functional Cost Analysis: An Interdisciplinary Analytical*

Language. Loughborough, Leicestershire: Centre for Extension Studies, University of Technology, LE11 3TU. Paper presented at Royal Aeronautical Society's Spring Convention, May 1983.

7. Develop Process Features

Anderson, Dave. "When '3' Meant 6." *New York Times,* December 27, 1982, pp. C-1 and C-5.

Bemesderfer, John L. "Approving a Process for Production." *Journal of Quality Technology,* 11, no. 1 (January 1979).

Bowen, William. "The Puny Payoff from Office Computers." *Fortune,* May 26, 1986.

Copley, Frank B. *Frederick W. Taylor, Father of Scientific Management.* New York: Harper & Row, 1923.

Dumaine, Brian. "How Managers Succeed Through Speed." *Fortune,* February 13, 1989, pp. 54–59.

Hoerr, John. "Work Teams Can Rev Up Paper-pushers, Too." *Business Week,* November 28, 1988.

Holusha, John. "New Presses Spur Detroit Productivity." *New York Times,* February 25, 1987.

Juran, J. M. "The Taylor System and Quality Control." A series of articles in *Quality Progress,* May through December 1973, listed under "Management Interface."

Juran, J. M., *Juran's Quality Control Handbook,* Fourth Edition. New York: McGraw-Hill Book Co., 1988.

Kane, Victor E. "Process Capability Indices." *Journal of Quality Technology,* 18, no. 1, Jan. 1986, pp. 44–52.

Main, Jeremy. "The Winning Organization." *Fortune,* September 26, 1988, p. 56.

Markoff, John. "American Express Goes High-Tech." *New York Times,* July 31, 1988.

Nakajo, Takeshi, and Hitoshi Kume. "The Principles of Foolproofing and Their Application in Manufacturing." *Reports on Statistical Application Research,* 32, no. 2 (Japanese Union of Scientists and Engineers, June 1985):10–29. Also presented (in abbreviated form) at the EOQC Annual Conference, Stockholm, June 1986, *Proceedings,* pp. 221–28).

Stewart, James B., and Daniel Hertzberg. "How the Stock Market Almost Disintegrated a Day After the Crash." *Wall Street Journal,* November 20, 1987.

Wessel, David. "Computer Finds a Role In Buying and Selling, Reshaping Businesses." *Wall Street Journal,* March 18, 1987.

8. Develop Process Controls: Transfer to Operations

Bemesderfer, John L., "Approving a Process for Production." *Journal of Quality Technology,* 11, No. 1, January 1979.

Burgam, Patrick M. "Application: Reducing Foundry Waste." *Manufacturing Engineering,* March 1985, p. 44.

Fisher, Lawrence, M. "A New Tool to Track That Noise." *New York Times,* February 10, 1988.

Juran, J. M. *Juran's Quality Control Handbook.* Fourth Edition, New York: McGraw-Hill Book Co., 1988.

White, Joseph B. "Auto Mechanics Struggle to Cope with Technology in Today's Cars." *Wall Street Journal,* July 26, 1988, p. 37.

9. Strategic Quality Planning

Brunetti, Wayne. "Policy Deployment: A Corporate Roadmap." *Proceedings* of Fourth Annual Conference on Quality Improvement (IMPRO 86), pp. 20–29. Wilton, Conn.: Juran Institute, Inc., 1987.

Ishikawa, Kaoru. "The Quality Control Audit." *Quality Progress,* January 1987, pp. 39–41.

Juran, J. M., ed. *Juran's Quality Control Handbook.* Fourth Edition. New York: McGraw-Hill Book Co., 1988.

Kegarise, Ronald J., and George D. Miller. "An Alcoa-Kodak Joint Team." *Proceedings* of Annual Conference on Quality Improvement (IMPRO 85), pp. 29–34. Wilton, Conn.: Juran Institute Inc., 1986.

Kondo, Yoshio. "Quality in Japan." Ch. 35F in Juran (1988). Kondo provides a detailed discussion of quality audits by Japanese top managements, including the president's audit. See under "Internal QC Audit by Top Management."

Shimoyamada, Kaoru. "The President's Audit: QC Audits at Komatsu." *Quality Progress,* January 1987, pp. 44–49.

10. Multifunctional Quality Planning

Juran J. M. *Juran on Leadership for Quality: An Executive Handbook.* New York: Free Press, 1989.

Kane, Edward J. "IBM's Quality Focus on the Business Process." *Quality Progress,* April 1986, pp. 24–32.

Nickell, Warren L., and J. Sylvia McNeil. "Process Management in a Marketing Environment." *Proceedings* of Fourth Annual Conference on Quality Improvement (IMPRO 86). Wilton, Conn.: Juran Institute, Inc., 1987, pp. 71–78.

Pall, Gabriel A. *Quality Process Management*. Englewood Cliffs, N.J.: Prentice-Hall, 1987.

11. Departmental Quality Planning

Bowen, William. "The Puny Payoff from Office Computers." *Fortune*, May 26, 1986.

Hoerr, John. "Work Teams Can Rev Up Paper-pushers, Too." *Business Week*, November 28, 1988.

Juran, J. M. "QC Circles in the West." *Quality Progress*, September 1987, pp. 60, 61.

Nakajo, Takeshi, and Hitoshi Kume. "The Principles of Foolproofing and their Application in Manufacturing." *Reports on Statistical Application Research*. Japanese Union of Scientists and Engineers, 32, no. 2 (June 1985): 10–29. Also presented (in abbreviated form) at the EOQC Annual Conference, Stockholm, June 1986 (*Proceedings*, pp. 221–28).

Parker, Kenneth T. "Departmental Activity Analysis: Management and Employees Working Together." *Proceedings*, 1984 Annual Conference, International Association of Quality Circles, pp. 202–7.

Peters, Thomas J. *Thriving on Chaos*. New York: Knopf, 1987.

12. The Data Base, Motivation, Training

Cohen, Leonard A. "Diet and Cancer." *Scientific American*, November 1987, pp. 42–48.

Gulliver, Frank R. "Post-project Appraisals Pay." *Harvard Business Review*, March–April 1987, pp. 128–32.

Gust, Lawrence J. "Nonmanufacturing Quality Improvement." *Proceedings* of Second Annual Conference on Quality Improvement (IMPRO 84). Wilton, Conn.: Juran Institute, Inc., 1985, pages 116–20.

Ishikawa, Kaoru. *Guide to Quality Control*. Asian Productivity Organization, 1972. Details of the tools taught to Japanese foremen on QC Circles, by the leading Japanese authority. Also available from UNIPUB.

Juran, J. M. "A Note on Economics of Quality." *Industrial Quality Control*, February 1959, pp. 20–23.

———. *Managerial Breakthrough*. New York: McGraw-Hill Inc., 1964. The seminal book on creating beneficial change (breakthrough) and preventing adverse change (control).

———. *Making Quality Happen: Upper Management's Role*. Wilton, Conn.: Juran Institute, Inc., 1988. The fifth edition of training course notes on what upper managers should do in order to manage for quality.

——. *Juran on Leadership for Quality.* New York: Free Press, 1989. The book version of the training course notes for *Making Quality Happen.*

——, ed. *Juran's Quality Control Handbook.* Fourth Edition. New York: McGraw-Hill Book Company, 1988. The international standard reference work in the field.

——. *Juran on Quality Improvement.* Wilton, Conn.: Juran Institute, Inc., 1981. A sixteen videocassette series on quality improvement, with associated training materials.

Juran, J. M., and F. M. Gryna. *Quality Planning and Analysis.* 2nd Edition. New York: McGraw-Hill Book Co., 1980.

McGrath, James H. "Successful Institutionalized Improvement in Manufacturing Areas." *Proceedings* of Conference on Quality Improvement (IMPRO 85). Wilton, Conn.: Juran Institute Inc., 1986.

Mead, Margaret, ed. *Cultural Patterns and Technical Change.* Paris: UNESCO, 1951. Also published by Mentor Books, New American Library of World Literature, Inc., New York, 1955.

Morison, Elting E. *Men, Machines and Modern Times.* Cambridge, Mass: MIT Press, 1966. Chapter Two, "Gunfire at Sea."

Nickell, Warren L. "Quality Inprovement in Marketing." *Proceedings* of Conference on Quality Improvement (IMPRO 85). Wilton, Conn.: Juran Institute, Inc., 1985.

Nayatani, Yoshinobu. "Seven Management Tools for QC." *Reports of Statistical Application Research,* Japanese Union of Scientists and Engineers, 33, no. 2, (Tokyo, June 1986).

Sullivan, L. P. "Quality Function Deployment." *Quality Progress*, June 1986, pp. 39–50.

Whipple, A. B. C. "Stranded Navy Man Who Charted the World's Seas." *Smithsonian*, March 1984, pp. 171–86.

White, Paul Dudley. *My Life and Medicine.* Boston: Gambit, 1971, pp. 195–96.

13. Quality Planning for the Taurus

Veraldi, L. C. "Ford Motor Company." MIT conference paper, Chicago, August 22, 1985. EOQC Conference, 1986, pp. 62, 63.

Publications and Training Courses Relative to Quality Improvement, from Juran Institute, Inc.

Juran on Quality Improvement.® A series of sixteen videocassettes (plus related written materials), designed to assist companies to go into project-by-project quality improvement on a continuing basis.

Facilitating Juran on Quality Improvement.© A week-long course designed to prepare facilitators and team leaders to train and guide project teams.

Management of Quality—Manufacturing.™ The course manual used for training at middle management levels. A significant part of this course is devoted to quality improvement.

Quality Improvement for Manufacturing.™ A course manual oriented specifically to quality improvement in manufacturing industries.

Quality Improvement for Services.© A course manual oriented specifically to quality improvement in service industries.

IMPRO Conference Proceedings. Contain the papers presented at Juran Institute's annual conference on quality improvement.

Additional Pertinent Publications, also Authored by Juran Institute's Professional Staff

Juran, J. M., editor-in-chief. *Juran's Quality Control Handbook.* Fourth Edition. New York: McGraw-Hill Book Co., 1988. The International standard reference book on the subject.

Juran, J. M. *Managerial Breakthrough.* New York: McGraw-Hill, 1964. The seminal book on creating beneficial change (breakthrough) and preventing adverse change (control). In this book the processes of improvement and control are expounded as they relate to managing in general rather than being limited to managing for quality.

Index